OUT OF THE WILD

OF
THE

ALSO BY MARK RASHID

A Journey to Softness
Considering the Horse
A Good Horse Is Never a Bad Color
Horses Never Lie
Life Lessons from a Ranch Horse
Horsemanship through Life
Big Horses, Good Dogs, and Straight Fences
A Life with Horses
Whole Heart, Whole Horse

OUT ᴼᶠ WILD
ᵀᴴᴱ

Mark Rashid

T$

TRAFALGAR SQUARE
North Pomfret, Vermont

First published in 2016 by
Trafalgar Square Books
North Pomfret, Vermont 05053

Library of Congress Cataloging-in-Publication Data

Names: Rashid, Mark, author.

Title: Out of the wild : a novel / Mark Rashid.

Description: North Pomfret, Vermont : Trafalgar Square Books, 2016.

Identifiers: LCCN 2016010720 | ISBN 9781570767685 (softcover)

Subjects: LCSH: Ranchers--Fiction. | Life change events--Fiction. | Man-woman relationships--Fiction. | Human-animal relationships--Fiction. | Horses--Fiction. | BISAC: SPORTS & RECREATION / Equestrian. | PETS / Horses / General.

Classification: LCC PS3618.A763 O88 2016 | DDC 813/.6--dc23 LC record available at https://lccn.loc.gov/2016010720

Cover photographs by Paul Krizan
Book design by DOQ
Cover design by RM Didier
Typefaces: Chaparral Pro, Bembo Std

Printed in the United States of America

10 9 8 7 6 5 4 3 2 1

For Crissi

CHAPTER 1

It seemed as though he would no sooner finish helping one of his first time momma cows deliver a calf in the muck of late winter when he'd see another cow down and struggling. This happened repeatedly, no less than one hundred and thirteen times by his count, once he started to keep count. He still felt lucky. He only had to call the vet out to help with nine of the births. Of those nine, eight calves lived and one didn't. The one that died did so during the birthing process, having presented to the birth canal backwards, upside down and much too big for the cow, who was one of his smallest. He had found the cow, red ear tag #67, many hours into her labor, down in draw a mile or so from the main herd. The vet guessed the baby had already been dead for a while; it was the vet who ended up having to dismember the calf while still inside #67 to get him out and save the cow.

Spring had always been a very busy time of year for struggling cattle rancher Henry McBride and his family, and that year had been no exception. It started in late January with the beginning of calving season, the time of year most cattlemen look forward to and dread at the same time. Calving season, by its very nature, brings new life to a working cattle ranch, and new life always offers new beginnings. No matter how good or bad the previous year was, once the babies start arriving the opportunities for improvement in the New Year always look just a little better.

Many ranchers also dread calving season for one of the reasons Henry was dreading it this year. Any other year Henry's herd would have consisted mostly of older cows, all with many years of calving behind them. In those years he wouldn't have needed to be so watchful and diligent about helping the cows calve. However, the summer before, a large number of those older, trustworthy cows died during a freak lightning strike in the high meadow. Many of the older cows that survived the initial strike would ultimately need to be destroyed later due to their internal injuries. Because of that one unfortunate mishap, the majority of Henry's herd this year was made up of first time mothers who almost always needed more looking after than the older, more experienced cows would.

Luckily, by mid March calving was over, just in time for the six mares to start having their foals. About that time a series of spring storms started pushing up the valley, accompanied by bone-chilling winds and dumping freezing rain and snow on everything in sight. Knowing the mares were close to foaling, Henry brought them all up to the old wooden barn, a sort of landmark in the area, which had been built in the late 1800's by the original owners of the place. There he put the mares all in separate box stalls he had constructed over the years and spent many more a sleepless night slogging his way from the house, through the rain and muck, to check on them.

By April, all but one of the mares had foaled and had been turned out into the lower pasture where the new spring grass was starting to come up. The last mare to have her baby was, again, a first-time mother and seemed to be holding on to her foal like it was gold. The good news was by now the weather had started settling down a bit, and although he probably would have been fine turning the mare out with the others, Henry chose to keep her in the barn at night so he could check on her.

Henry was a lifelong stockman and took great pride in the health and well being of his animals, particularly during calving and foaling season. This, even at the constant ribbing of a number of his neighbors who were more of a mind that animals should be prepared to take care of themselves during such times, not be pampered and coddled. Of course, for the most part, Henry agreed. Animals should be able to take care of themselves. And he was more than willing to let them, once they were on the ground and healthy. It was just that he didn't want to lose any stock for want of paying attention.

It was also in April that irrigating began on the five hundred acres of bottomland Henry had acquired only five years before, to add to the seven hundred acres he and his wife Annie already owned. The seven hundred acres that came with the ranch, when they bought the place five years before that, was mostly rocky scrub with some good grass, but not much. It was also criss-crossed a number of times by a mostly dry, shallow ravine that hardly had enough water in it for the stock to drink out of, unless there was rain and plenty of it. As a result, the seven hundred acres were fine for grazing stock, but not at all useful for growing hay, which was what the five hundred acres of bottomland was for.

Like everything else on the ranch that spring, irrigating was a time-consuming process for Henry. The entire bottomland sloped gently to the south, and Henry would lay dams made out of blue plastic tarp in the irrigation ditches so water would back up behind them and eventually start to flood the acreage below the ditch. After a few days, when the area was sufficiently saturated, he would then set up another dam farther down the ditch, remove the previous dam, and then begin to saturate that area as well. This process would continue until the entire five hundred acres had been irrigated sufficiently. There was a total of twenty ditches, which meandered their way for miles, and changing water—or moving the dams—in and of itself was nearly a full time job.

Of course then there was the branding, doctoring, ear tagging, castrating of bull calves, de-lousing of the entire herd, sorting then moving the herd to their respective summer pastures, and hauling steers to market. On top of that there was the fencing that needed to be done, along with the repairs on tack and equipment, all of which was never-ending.

Because Henry and Annie's place had always been more of a subsistence ranch than a real money maker, the vast majority of the work was always done by either Henry, Annie, or both, along with their twelve-year-old son Josh. Hiring help, even just day help, was simply out of the question. In fact, things had been so tight recently that a couple years before, Annie took a job in town, working part time at the local market as a checker. It was terribly difficult for Henry to swallow at the time—the fact that the ranch wasn't making enough money to support his family. But then, times were tough for nearly everybody, and more than one ranch wife found a town job to help supplement income.

Annie, on the other hand, while understanding how difficult it was for Henry to see her take the job, actually enjoyed her time at the market. Ever since she was a little girl she had always been very social and outgoing and while she loved the ranch and the life it provided, she found the market a welcome distraction from its solitude.

It was that outgoing personality that attracted Henry to her in the first place, when the two of them were kids in the fourth grade—that, and her green eyes. At the time, Henry fancied himself a pretty good roper, which he was, and had been out on the playground at recess showing off to some of his friends. Before long, Henry had attracted quite an audience, while throwing one fancy loop after another. First he caught one, then two and even three of his friends with one loop. Then he caught their feet as they ran past him, simulating the act of "heeling," or catching an animal by the hind legs.

He then moved on to a couple of more technically challenging loops, one of which is known as a houlihan. The loops he had been throwing up to this point were pretty standard, all of which had been tossed sort of like one would a baseball and slightly off to the side of his body. The houlihan is thrown in a backhand fashion, with the release of the rope being nearly directly overhead. It is a tough loop for some experienced ropers to throw, but even as a child, Henry made it look easy.

This loop is generally known as a horse loop, as it is often used to catch loose horses out of a remuda. Unlike a standard loop, which would come directly at the horse due to the way it is thrown, often causing him to shy from the loop and avoid being caught, the houlihan, because of the way it is thrown, floats gently over the head and allows the person doing the throwing to catch the horse around the neck.

Henry had thrown several of these loops, effortlessly catching several of his friends, before one of the loops missed. Almost immediately, out of the small crowd of onlookers came a voice.

"I have a better houlihan than that," the voice said unapologetically. Henry looked at the group while coiling his rope.

"Who said that?" he asked with a self-assured chuckle. There was no answer. "That's what I thought," he finished coiling his rope, and then started to build another loop. "Ain't nobody here better than me."

"I am," the voice said. Then, from the back of the crowd stepped a small girl with long blond hair hanging down the middle of her back in a ponytail. She wore a yellow, flowered cotton dress and scuffed saddle shoes and white socks. Her eyes were the greenest Henry had ever seen, and he had to stop for a minute just to take them in. "I can do better than that."

"You?" Henry snapped out of his stare and was indignant, or at least as indignant as a ten-year-old boy can be. "A girl! No way!"

The group, made up mostly of ranch boys and girls, all laughed. All except another little girl standing next to the blond.

"She is better," the little girl said matter-of-factly. "She could out-rope you any day of the week and twice on Sunday."

"Oh yeah," Henry grunted. "Then prove it."

With that, the little blond-headed girl with the green eyes stepped up. "Let's have a contest," she said. "We throw as many houlihans as we can before the bell rings. First one to miss, loses."

"Fine with me," Henry chuckled. "Targets got to be moving, though."

"Fine with me," the little girl said.

"Good," Henry said. "I pick Leon to be my target."

"No way," the girl protested. "I pick your target—you pick mine. That way we both know a friend ain't gonna cheat for either one of us."

"Whatever," Henry grinned. "Ain't gonna matter anyhow."

With that, targets were picked, rules were established (such as no ducking out from under a loop or running too fast), and the contest began. Each contestant would throw five loops, then give the rope to the opponent for five loops, and so on until someone missed or until recess was over, whichever came first. At that time, whoever had the most catches would be declared the winner.

Henry hit his first five with ease, and much to everyone's surprise, so did the little girl. Then both hit the second five, then the third. On Henry's sixteenth throw, however, he released a just little too late and the loop landed harmlessly on his target's head and slid down the boy's back.

The little girl stepped up and made another five in a row, then for good measure, made another three. About that time, the bell signaling the end of recess rang, and that was that. As the kids all made their way back into school, the girl coiled Henry's rope and graciously handed it back to him.

"Thanks for letting me use your rope," she said.

At first, Henry couldn't think of anything to say. He was embarrassed and impressed all at the same time. Embarrassed because he had been beaten by a girl, and impressed, also because he had been beaten by a girl. He gently took the rope. "You got a nice houlihan," he said, with all the humility he could muster.

"You, too." She smiled. "I'm Annie Ford. We're new here. Just moved from Idaho. This is my second day."

"I'm Henry." They started for the school. "I've lived here all my life."

Like Henry, Annie had grown up in a ranching family. Her father had been working as ranch foreman on the Box L Ranch in Northern Idaho before recently taking a job as ranch manager on the Nine-Bar-Nine just up the road from where Henry and his family's little ranch was. The Nines, as folks in the area referred to it, was one of the biggest cow/calf operations in the state, and it was considered quite a coup for Len Ford to have snagged the manager position there. Nearly every cowboy in a three-state area applied for the job, which was vacated when Tink Weber, the previous manager, died of pneumonia the winter before.

Annie had learned much of her roping skills from her father, along with the ranch hands on the Box L when her family was still there, and she had spent countless hours practicing both on and off her horse in hopes that one day she'd get to help out on the ranch and do some real roping, helping out at branding time, for instance, instead of just roping stationary targets like hay bales and fence posts. As of yet, she hadn't gotten her chance. It was those roping skills she had developed, however, along with her natural beauty, outgoing nature and those green eyes that caught Henry's attention, and gradually Henry found himself spending more and more time with her.

The two found they had a lot in common. Even at their early age, both were excellent with and knowledgeable about stock and land management, as well as excellent riders and even leather workers. Over time, the two of them became best friends, seldom one being somewhere without the other. In high school they both became heavily involved with their high school rodeo team, where Henry team roped and rode saddle broncs, and Annie ran barrels on her big bay gelding named Blister. Once out of school, the two of them took up rodeoing full time, with both of them having the goal of getting their PRCA cards, which they both eventually did.

They rodeoed hard for three years, during which time they decided to get married while on a stop in Las Vegas. They actually got married on a sort of bet that came from one of their traveling buddies, Les Fowler, a wiry little bull rider with big ears and a smashed nose he acquired when a bull he was riding threw his head up at the same time Les's went down. The collision also knocked out two of Les's front teeth, which he hadn't bothered getting replaced. Sitting behind the chutes with a bunch of friends after the rodeo one night, Les had said that while there was no question Henry and Annie were good friends, it was pretty clear to everybody that knew them that they'd never get married because neither one of them was the marrying kind.

Even though marriage had never been discussed between the two of them, Henry and Annie both disagreed, saying that they were, indeed the marrying kind. In fact, Henry had said indignantly, he wanted to get married one day and have a mess of kids to boot! Annie stopped him, and in her way that completely disarmed him, said quietly that one or two would probably be plenty. After all, it wasn't Henry that would have to carry them for nine months. Everyone laughed.

Later that night, however, after their friends had gone off to their respective hotel rooms, or climbed in their horse trailers to bed down, as Henry and Annie did, the two of them started discussing marriage for real. It was a foreign subject for both of them, neither one having given it much thought, but the more they talked about it, the better the idea sounded. Before long, one thing led to another, and the next thing they both knew, they were in a little chapel off the Vegas strip.

Later that year at a rodeo in Granby, Colorado, Henry drew a bronc by the name of Coffee's Western Twister, a horse that had bucked every one of his riders off in the past one hundred outings. Henry had been happy to get the draw, not only because if he stayed on for the allotted eight seconds he was likely to get a great score, and possibly take home the first place prize money, but also because the rodeo promoter had put a five thousand dollar bounty on the horse's head. Meaning, if anyone rode the horse for the eight seconds without getting bucked off, he would win the five thousand, on top of any prize money.

Henry eased down into the chute and onto his saddle, which was already strapped to the big bay horse's back. He carefully adjusted the length of his thick rope rein, making sure the horse would have plenty of room to get his head down while bucking. This one adjustment could make or break his ride. If the rein was too short, Henry would get jerked out of the saddle, too loose and Henry wouldn't be able to use it to help with his balance. When he had what he thought was an appropriate length in his rein, he shoved his feet deep into his oxbow stirrups and nodded to the cowboy on the ground to open the chute.

Twister reared straight up on his hind legs as soon as the chute opened, slamming Henry's right shoulder hard against the metal piping. Most riders would have lost their concentration right then and there and more than likely would have fallen off at the horse's first jump. But not Henry. Hitting his shoulder only made him mad and more determined. The horse, still on his hind legs, turned and burst into the arena in a spectacular display of athleticism most folks had never seen. The horse's hind legs snapped twenty feet high in the air, then he twisted his body so much that his belly was exposed to the sun, at the same time he flung his head one way then the other, then he launched himself this way then that, and repeating the pattern over and over.

Henry rode him like he was a carousel horse on a merry-go-round and made it look easy. The buzzer that signaled eight seconds went off and a huge roar went up from the crowd, although Henry couldn't hear it. The pick-up man galloped over to Henry and Twister to help Henry get off, but before he got to them the big bay jammed his front legs so hard into the ground that his nose hit the dirt and he flipped himself head over heels with Henry still in the saddle. Henry landed hard on the same right shoulder that was injured in the chute, severely dislocating it, and fracturing six ribs when he was pinned between the saddle and the ground.

Henry had ridden the horse to a score of ninety-seven, good enough to take home the first place prize of three hundred dollars. That, coupled with the five thousand dollars bounty money he made for making the buzzer, gave him a nice chunk of money for the day's work. Even though his hospital bill was fifteen hundred dollars, that still left him with thirty-eight hundred, which was more than he'd ever won before. The injuries he suffered that day sidelined Henry for a good long while, and while he was recuperating he was also trying to decide whether he would go back to a life in rodeo after he healed up, or go back to a more stable life in ranching. About that time Annie's barrel horse came up lame and out of commission when he stepped on a nail left over from the sloppy habits of a maintenance worker at the Cedar City, Utah, rodeo. Just like that his decision was made, and Annie happily followed suit. Both were out of rodeo and back to ranching.

Not long after, the two of them went home and were able to secure a job managing a ranch not far from where they grew up, and about that same time, Josh was born. Three years later, with some of the money they had saved from their rodeo days, along with some of the savings from their ranch job, a little more from their families, and a loan from the bank, they had enough money to buy the ranch they currently owned.

As much work as things had been that spring for Henry and Annie, for the most part everything had actually been going along smoothly. That was, until the morning of branding. It was mid April and as was his habit, Henry got up before dawn on branding day, always a Saturday, and headed out about daybreak to gather the cow-calf pairs that he had moved to the nearest pasture a couple days before. He had a number of neighbors coming around 7:00 a.m. to help with branding of the new calves, and he wanted to have the cattle ready and in the large catch pen before the neighbors got there, so as not to waste anybody's time unnecessarily.

Normally, the men would do the majority of the roping and dragging the calves to the fire, mounted on experienced ranch horses who weren't bothered by swinging ropes or burning hide, while other men and some of the younger boys (the ones around Josh's age) would hold the calves down once they got to the fire. The women would take care of vaccinating the calves, while at the same time someone would bring an iron from the fire and brand the calf with the McBride's quarter circle MC brand on the calf's left hip. Then the calf would be untied and turned loose to run bawling back to its mother that was standing nearby.

While Henry was out gathering the pairs, Annie and Josh would be back in the catch pen, digging a fire pit, getting the fire started, and getting some fresh coffee brewed for the folks who would be showing up. While Annie always took charge of the ground crew—keeping the vaccinations in order, checking ear tags, keeping notes on which calves had gotten what—she also enjoyed doing a little roping herself. Normally she waited until about half the calves had been branded before trying her hand. Henry always saddled her horse when he saddled his so all she had to do was grab her rope, slip the bridle on her horse and join in.

He would also tie her rope to her saddle so she wouldn't have to go hunting it up before she rode. But on this day, because he had slept a little later than he should have, he ran out of time that morning and left her rope in its bag hanging on the tack room wall. So later that morning, before Annie could join in on the roping, she needed to make the trip to the tack room to retrieve it.

Since Henry was so busy, one of the projects that had to take a back seat that spring was replacing the second step in a set of three that led up to the tack room door. The tack room was actually an old chicken coop, which sat on low stilts just a few yards from the front door of the barn. Because Henry and Annie had more tack then they had chickens, it only made sense to turn the little, nearly one-hundred-year-old building into something they could use. Turning the coop into a tack room was one of the first things they did after they moved in, and it remained pretty much the way they'd built it ever since.

The downside to having the tack room where it was, was that in the wintertime what little snow they got would blow between the barn and the tack room and drift up against the tack room door. It would build up on the steps leading up to the door, and more specifically, on the second step. Because of the mildness of the winters in the area, the snow would quickly melt, with much of the water that was then created by the melting snow pooling primarily in the middle of the second step. Over time, the step had become rotted and weak, and Annie had been after Henry to replace it for going on three years. The step was on Henry's list, just not very high on it.

Besides, the step was never really a problem for Henry because he seldom used the steps anyway. They weren't very tall steps, measuring less than about three inches between the top of one and the bottom of the next, so he'd simply step from the ground to the top step, skipping the first and middle steps all together. Annie, on the other hand, not being very tall, always used the three steps. On that day, because she was in a hurry, she jogged toward the tack room, skipped the first step and put her full weight on the second.

The step, which had been slowly disintegrating for years, finally gave way under the impact of her foot. There was a loud CRACK as Annie's right foot crashed through the board. Instinctively, she turned to her right so she wouldn't fall face first into the tack room door, but the spur on her boot hung up under the first step, putting the weight of her entire body on her right ankle. Her shin hit the top step as she fell hard into the door on her right shoulder. Simultaneously, there was another CRACK as her tibia splintered just above the ankle.

Oddly, there was no pain at first. In fact, there was more pain in her shoulder than in her ankle. She shifted herself slightly, turning her body away from the door and coming to a sitting position on the top step. Doing so freed the spur from under the step and allowed her to lift her foot out of the hole she just made. It was about then the pain in her ankle shot through her body and she let out an anguished moan that quickly turned into a long, loud shriek.

The branding pen was over one hundred yards away on the other side of the barn, and with that distance, coupled by all the noise that is inherent to a branding, nobody heard her. She grabbed her leg just behind the knee and lifted it ever so slightly in the air. Her foot hung off the end of her leg at an unnatural angle, confirming her worst fears.

She knew what broken bones looked like. She had doctored plenty of them for Henry over the years. His ribs, wrist, femur, several fingers and toes and a collarbone had all been fractured at one time or another. But this was her first broken bone—and it hurt like hell! As she sat there in unbearable pain, she couldn't understand how it was Henry was able to be so stoic all those times when he had broken something. In fact, other than when he fractured his femur, and after the wreck he'd had on Coffee's Western Twister, he had never even gone to the doctor. Well, not her. It was pretty clear to her already that she'd be going to the local medical clinic just as soon as she could. Annie sat on the step for what seemed like an eternity before Evelyn Trucks, her neighbor from down the road, came around the barn on her way up to the house to use the bathroom.

"Annie," she cried, seeing Annie's crumpled form near the tack room door. "Are you all right?" She ran over to where Annie was sitting. By now, Annie's perpetually tanned face had turned an ashen white, and her mouth was so dry she could hardly speak.

"I broke my leg," she said hoarsely. "Could you go get Henry for me?"

For years to come Henry would curse himself for not fixing that damn step when he had the chance. He couldn't stand to see Annie in any kind of pain, and pain that he felt he caused her was almost too much for him to bear. But there would be more to it. The way he would come to see it, if he had fixed the step, Annie wouldn't have fallen through it. Had she not fallen through, she wouldn't have broken her leg, and if she hadn't broken her leg, there's a good chance that with her having had more rest than he over the past several months, it would have been her driving on that moonless night two weeks later—not him.

CHAPTER 2

Chronologically, it had been seventeen years since the accident. But for Henry, it was always just the day after. After seventeen years, the sights, sounds and smells of what happened that night were just as fresh, just as vivid and just as terrifying as they had been the night they occurred. While many of the details were still fuzzy, what he did know was he and Annie had taken Josh to the finals of the regional talent show, in which Josh was a finalist for his age group. Josh had gotten to the finals by playing an impressive rendition of "Ghost Riders in the Sky" on his guitar in the semi-finals that were held at the local high school a week before.

Neither Annie nor Henry could ever figure out where Josh had gotten his talent for the guitar, and for singing for that matter, as nobody in either of their families was particularly musical. Yet, when Josh was six, out of the blue he started begging for a guitar. It took some convincing, mostly because Henry really couldn't afford to buy a guitar, much less the guitar lessons that were sure to follow, only to have Josh lose interest a month or so later—as kids often do with such obsessions.

Their little boy had been so persistent that Henry and Annie broke down and got him a small, inexpensive, three-quarter size guitar for Christmas the following year. Much to both of their surprise, Josh not only stuck with it, he took lessons twice a week, practiced every day, and became very proficient. Within two years he was playing and singing along with songs he heard on the radio. When he was eleven, he had obviously outgrown his inexpensive guitar and Annie found what turned out to be a 1930's era Gibson L-00 acoustic guitar with a hard case and strap at a garage sale.

She was able to buy all three items for fifty dollars, only to find out later the guitar alone was actually worth well over a thousand dollars. It was also when Josh was eleven that he was asked to sit in with a local band that was playing at the annual fall festival down at the VFW hall in town. Josh had been a big hit that night, playing and singing songs by Johnny Cash, Merle Haggard and Willy Nelson. Now, at twelve, Josh had entered the local talent show and had moved confidently through the various stages of competition until he made it to the finals.

The finals were held over in Blanchard, some fifty miles away and over Cambridge pass, which reached an elevation of nearly eight thousand feet. The road was good, although not at all straight, and relatively desolate particularly at night.

Henry never could remember much, if anything of the two-and-a-half-hour show itself. He had been so exhausted from the months of hard work and sporadic rest he fell asleep almost as soon as the lights went dim in the auditorium. Annie woke him just as Josh went on, and Henry fought to stay awake. But even as hard as he tried, he still ended up nodding off about half way through Josh's performance. Josh took home the first place prize that night for his age group. In his hands he held a big blue ribbon and a check for one hundred and fifty dollars. The plaque with his name on it he would get later after it had been engraved. But it was in the smile on his son's face that Henry found the biggest reward.

Henry remembered bringing the truck up to the entrance so Annie, who was still on crutches, wouldn't have to walk all the way out to where the truck was parked. He remembered helping Annie into the truck, putting Josh's guitar and her crutches in the bed and Josh climbing in next to his mother. He remembered leaving the parking lot and getting on the road that took them over the pass. He could recall Annie and Josh talking, but couldn't remember what they were talking about. The next thing he always heard was both Annie and Josh screaming in the distance and the sound of breaking glass and twisting metal.

The highway patrol accident report noted there weren't any skid marks where the truck left the road. It was as if Henry had simply missed the turn and drove right off the edge and down the five hundred foot embankment. The lack of skid marks was because Henry had never touched the brakes. He had fallen into a deep sleep behind the wheel and had been ejected from the truck almost immediately after it left the road. He woke only after he hit the ground and thudded to a stop against a tree. The truck, with Annie and Josh still trapped inside, continued flipping and rolling down the side of the mountain. He couldn't see the truck, nor was he fully aware of what had happened, until the truck came to a stop near the bottom of the draw, then burst into flames. It was only then the gravity of what had just happened came crashing down on top of him.

He had broken his arm and two ribs in the fall, and had a six-inch long gash that ran from his left eyebrow, up and over the top of his head, through his scalp and exposing his skull. Still, as soon as he had his wits about him, he jumped to his feet and scrambled down the hill calling frantically for his wife and son as blood poured down his face and stung his eyes.

Because the terrain down to the bottom of the draw was so rough, it took Henry what seemed like an eternity to get to where the truck had come to its fiery rest. By the time he got there, some of the nearby bushes and trees were either smoldering or burning, with more looking as if they would explode into flames at any minute. Still, Henry ran through the fires and over to the truck. He was quickly forced back because of the intense heat the truck was putting off, and no matter how hard he tried, he was only able to get within fifty feet of the wreck. By the time the fire and ambulance crews arrived, they found an unresponsive and bloodied Henry standing near the wreckage, staring blankly at the twisted heap. The fire had subsided, but the truck and its occupants were unrecognizable.

Annie and Josh's funeral was held a week later and was attended by over fifteen hundred people. Henry stayed by the gravesite for two full days and nights, not eating, sleeping or drinking, until Leon Geyser, one of Henry's childhood friends, came to take him home. In his grief, Henry quickly found he was unwilling and unable to stay in the house where he, Annie and Josh had spent the last ten years. Within days he was sleeping either in the barn, or in a tent he pitched down in the lower pasture. He spent as little time in the house as possible, and even less time taking care of the ranch.

In his effort to stay away from the house, Henry took to driving the old, barely road-legal ranch truck into town, and doing nothing more than driving up and down Main Street over and over. Eventually, he might stop in one of the three diners, order a cup of coffee and sit for hours staring out the window. As night fell, he began stopping in the Wheel Bar, and even though he never was much of a drinker—not even in his rodeo days—he would order a beer and sit in the corner until closing time.

At first, he would show up at the bar around nine or so and stay until the bright lights came on, always drinking only one beer. Then one day a package arrived in the mail. It was the plaque with Josh's name on it, the one he won the night of the accident. Shortly after that, Henry began stopping in the bar earlier and earlier until finally he started showing up at three, then two, and one o'clock in the afternoon. One beer would turn into ten and before long he was drunk, staggering out the door at closing time and collapsing unconscious onto the seat, and sometimes even in the bed of his truck. He would often wake up in the morning having vomited on himself sometime during the night. He'd unfold himself from wherever he was, drive home, be there long enough to clean himself up, and then head back into town.

Henry's decline was as swift as it was complete. In less than six months, not only was he drinking heavily, having switched from beer to whiskey, but he also allowed his hay crop, one of the best he'd ever had, go to seed and rot in the field. He also started selling off his livestock to pay the mortgage on the ranch. Each month he'd sell off just enough to pay the mortgage and have enough left over for drinking money, until he ran out of livestock to sell. At that point, he simply stopped paying the mortgage.

Not surprisingly, the ranch went into foreclosure that winter, and the following spring, almost a year to the day from the accident, Henry sat on the steps of the tack room and watched as everything he owned was auctioned off to the highest bidder. A couple of his long-time friends, Leon, George Meyer, Abe Custus and a few others, all got together and bought his old ranch truck, his rifle and pistol, his bridle and saddle, saddle bags, saddle pad and blanket, and then turned around and gave them all back to him. Henry was truly thankful at the gesture, although none of the items really meant all that much to him—with the exception of his saddle.

The saddle had been his father's, and his father's before him and his father's before him. Now that Annie and Josh were gone, it was really the only possession he had that meant anything to him at all, and even though he had been prepared to see it go, he found he was happy to be able to keep it. Henry left the ranch that day, his life now strewn about the seat of the old truck, and never went back.

He began a life of drifting and picking up day work and odd jobs throughout the West. Almost immediately, however, his drinking intensified. He'd go to bed drunk, then get up in the morning and start drinking again. It was his only defense against the nightmares he experienced at night, and the flashbacks during the day. In fact, the drinking never did get rid of the nightmares and flashbacks. It only dulled them. Most of the time he was able to hide his day drinking from those he worked with, usually only taking enough to keep the edge off. But there was nothing he could do to hide his night drinking, and more than one job slipped through his hands because of it.

Now, seventeen years later, and after a long dry spell without work (as his reputation for being a hard drinker had started to precede him) Henry found himself working a good job as a cowboy on the Rafter Seven Ranch in northern Arizona. He was still drinking but had found ways to regulate himself. He had almost stopped the day drinking all together, and for the most part was staying out of the bars, although there was never a bottle far away from wherever he was.

To make sure he could sleep through the night, he'd sneak out of the bunkhouse after everyone else was snoring in their beds, uncork a bottle and drink enough to sleep clear through till morning without a nightmare waking him, and everyone around him. Henry figured no one knew what he was up to. In reality, everyone did. Even with that, however, so far his drinking didn't seem to hinder his work. There were the odd times he'd come to breakfast late and then stagger around for an hour or two until the previous night's buzz wore off. But those times were rare, and besides, if old man Hill, the owner of the ranch, fired every cowboy who staggered around in the morning from drinking too much the night before, he'd be working the ranch by himself.

But then about three months into his time at the Rafter Seven, Henry was sent to town with the ranch truck to pick up a load of lumber. Town was nearly forty miles away, with fifteen of those miles—the ones closest to the ranch—gravel road. His trip to town was uneventful, as was his stop at the lumberyard. Within about a half hour of his arrival, the boys there had the lumber, mostly eight-foot two-by-fours and two-by-sixes, loaded on the flatbed of the pickup and strapped down.

Henry signed for the lumber, climbed into the truck and as he was pulling out of the parking lot, he heard the screeching of tires and the loud crash of metal impacting metal. He looked to his left in time to see a woman in a blue Chevy Impala run the stoplight on the corner and slam into the side of a school bus that had just entered the intersection. Both vehicles came to a stop in the intersection, and almost immediately muffled screams from children began emanating from inside the bus. The now crushed radiator from the Impala began hissing and sending steam high into the air.

Henry sat, fixated on the scene and unable to move. The high-pitched screaming, the hissing, the steam, the sound of metal on metal and breaking glass transformed itself into the night Annie and Josh died. It was dark, he could hear Annie and Josh screaming, he could smell the tires on the truck burning, the paint as it melted off its metal body, burning trees and bushes…and flesh. He could feel the heat on his face, and the hopelessness of not being able to do anything. Time stood still.

Then, through the din, there was the long honking of a horn. *Beeeeeeeeeep, honk, honk, beeeeeeeeep.* It was distant at first, as if it were a long way off. *Beeeeeeeeep, honk, beeeeeep.* It was closer now. *Honk, honk, honk.* Henry snapped back. Someone behind him in the lumberyard parking lot was trying to get out, and Henry was blocking the way. In his rearview mirror, Henry could see a heavyset man with the stub of a cigar between his teeth in the truck behind him. He was yelling something, but Henry couldn't hear what it was.

Henry's heart was racing, his breath was short and his hands were sweating so much it was hard for him to hold on to the steering wheel. *Beeeeeeeeep.* Henry shook his head, and then shook it again. He was back, but still couldn't move. Sweat dripped off the end of his nose, and he shook his head again. The fat man was climbing out of his truck.

Hands shaking, Henry instinctively reached down and grabbed the floor shift, jammed the transmission in gear and hit the gas. The truck came to life, lurching forward into the street. Henry wrenched the wheel to the right and the truck responded with a quick jerk in that direction. He floored it and sped away from the scene as fast as the truck could carry him.

CHAPTER 3

"All right folks," the man behind the bar said as he switched on the lights, illuminating the inside of the place. "That's it—closing time. Drink up." He walked over and unplugged the jukebox. Lynyrd Skynyrd's "Gimme Three Steps" ground to an unceremonious halt. Henry sat on the stool that had been his home for the past ten hours and stared at his reflection in the mirror behind the bar—a reflection he could see clearly now that the lights were on. He looked old, and thin, and drunk. He hated his life, the drinking, the nightmares, and the guilt. What would Annie think of him and who he had become? What would Josh think of his dad being drunk for days on end? Henry's chin fell to his chest.

"Come on, man," the bartender slapped Henry on the back as he walked past. "You don't have to go home, but you can't stay here." It wasn't the first time Henry heard the quip. He groggily raised his head and wondered if bartenders went to school to learn clever closing time sayings. That one and, "It's no-tell motel time," were the two he'd heard most bartenders say.

The bartender went back around behind the bar and picked up Henry's now empty glass. Henry was staring at his reflection again. "Gotta go," the bartender repeated.

He lightly slapped his hand on the bar twice in front of Henry. "Come on pard," he said "I know you put in a full shift, but you ain't getting anything extra for overtime." Henry had never heard that one before.

Henry tried to talk, but nothing came out. He just nodded, waved his hand in front of his face, as if brushing a fly away, slid off the stool and staggered to the door. There were other people in the bar, but Henry didn't notice them, and they didn't notice him. He had become invisible, and that was just the way he liked it. He pushed the door open and stepped out into the night. It was cool and raining, and apparently had been for quite some time. It had been warm and sunny when Henry almost unconsciously slid the truck loaded with lumber into the parking lot of the bar only minutes after seeing the accident. He didn't even know the name of the bar. But then, there were very few bars he had been in that he *did* know the names of. The name of the place was never important. Just that they had liquor, and plenty of it—and this one had.

He stumbled his way to the truck that was parked at an angle near the tall, flashing neon sign that said "Mike's Tavern" in bright orange. He stood by the truck door digging in his pockets for the keys and getting soaked by the rain. His motor skills had been sufficiently dulled by the gallons of alcohol he had poured into himself in an effort to once again erase the nightmare that this day had been. As a result his hands slowly and clumsily went from one jeans pocket to the next. He then he checked his shirt pockets, and then all his jeans pockets again.

The rain intensified the smell of cigarette smoke that permeated his clothes, and as he checked all of his pockets again, to no avail, he simply opened the door and slid in behind the wheel. The familiar buzzing sound when he opened the door told him the keys he had been searching for were still in the ignition, and after several seconds of trying to get himself situated in the driver's seat, he slammed the door shut and started the engine. Water poured off his hat and onto his lap. He fumbled for the switch to turn on the headlights, and after finding it and pulling it out, he jammed the transmission into gear and jerked the truck forward into the road. About the same time, the flashing neon sign behind him went dark.

Miraculously, Henry found Route 6, the road that headed in the direction of the ranch, and even more miraculously, thirty miles later he found the gravel road off Route 6 that took him to the ranch. He hit the shoulder and crossed the centerline more times than he could count—if he were to try to count—which he wouldn't, and now on the gravel road with no shoulder he was doing everything he could just to keep the truck out of the ditch. Henry wasn't driving fast. He rarely did, even when he was sober. It was still no easy task keeping the truck on the road, and it took all the concentration he could muster, concentration that kept being interrupted with three words circulating through his whiskey-soaked mind, words he could swear Annie was saying to him: "Time to change," she said in her smiling voice. Henry blinked hard and rubbed his eyes trying to focus on the road. "Time to change, Henry," the voice repeated.

The voice was interrupted when in the distance and through the rain and dark, the main gate of the ranch slowly came into range of his headlights. It was a big thing, with two heavy, round wooden uprights twenty feet tall on either side of the entrance to the mile-long driveway that led to the main grounds of the ranch. Between the uprights hung a large, heavy wooden sign. In the middle of the sign was a two-foot tall, wood-carved Rafter Seven brand. On the left side of the brand were the words: "Established in 1889," and on the right side of the brand read: "James T. Hill and Sons Cattle Company."

About three hundred feet from the gate entrance was a dip in the road, two-and-a-half feet deep and twenty feet wide. It was part of a dry creek bed that ran just outside the Rafter Seven's boundary line. As is the custom in many arid parts of the country, creek beds like this are simply left as dips in the road, as opposed to placing a bridge over them, as might be the case in a wetter part of the country. In this case, when the weather was dry, it was simply a dip in the road. But when it rained, the dip in the road would become a two-foot deep, twenty-foot wide, swift running creek, which it now was. A half hour or so after it would stop raining, the water in the ditch would dissipate to a point where you never even knew there was water in it.

Henry brought the truck to a stop about ten feet from the edge of the creek. He stepped out into the pouring rain and staggered to the front of the truck. The headlights shone over the rushing water, and had Henry been sober, or even a little more sober than he was, he more than likely would have just turned the truck off and slept there for the night. By then the rain would certainly have stopped and the creek would have gone down.

Ironically, had he done that, nobody would have been the wiser. The creek started flooding about an hour after it started raining. The ranch was on the southern most edge of a gigantic storm that would dump eight inches of rain over nearly the entire western half of the United States. Here, however, it would have blown out by morning. Had Henry just slept in the truck, folks on the ranch would have figured he got back after the creek started flooding and would have understood he couldn't get across. They would have figured he'd been sitting there in the truck all night, instead of sitting in a bar.

But Henry slid back in the truck and slowly backed up for over a quarter mile, repeatedly almost sliding off the slick and muddy road. Once he'd traveled what he considered a sufficient distance from the creek, he threw the truck in gear and floored it. At first, the tires spun wildly in the mud and gravel. Then, after several seconds, they picked up traction and the truck started for the creek. Henry went through the gears quickly and even though he was fishtailing wildly, he was also traveling nearly fifty miles per hour by the time he hit the creek. The truck hydroplaned over the creek, throwing gallons of water on the windshield and making it impossible for Henry to see.

By the time it reached the other side, the truck was turned slightly to the right, and it rolled up on the right side tires for just a second. Henry couldn't see what was going on, but he could feel it and he instinctively threw the wheel to the left, bringing the truck back down on all fours. The truck lurched back to the left, shot across the road and into the rain-soaked desert on the other side. Henry floored it once again and cranked the wheel to the right, trying to get back on the road, but the truck simply slid farther to the left.

Eventually, the front of the truck turned to the right and it started traveling forward, fishtailing as it went. Henry cranked the wheel to the left, and it began fishtailing to the left. The engine whined wildly as the truck skidded first one way, then the other. He could see out the windshield now, and was trying to get the truck back towards the gate, which passed briefly into his view every time the truck fishtailed one direction or the other. Just as he had convinced himself he was going to make it, suddenly, and without warning, the truck lurched to a dead stop, the headlights shining on the gate only twenty yards away. Henry's head hit the steering wheel, cutting him just above his left eye, something he wouldn't even be aware of until he looked in a mirror twelve hours later.

The truck's motor was no longer running, and as he sat motionless, the only sound he could hear was the rain on the roof and the windshield wipers beating back and forth.

Had he been sober, or more sober than he was, he more than likely would have gotten out of the truck and looked to see why he had come to a halt so abruptly. Had he done that, he would have seen the truck had become high centered on a large rock he had driven over. The rock was now just behind the right front tire, wedged in the wheel well. It was also big enough that it reached clear back to the center of the truck, just behind the transfer case for the four-wheel drive.

But Henry didn't look. Instead, he climbed out of the truck, saw only that it was stuck in the mud, and decided to pull the vehicle out of the slop using the winch bolted to the frame on the front of the truck. He dug around behind the truck seat and found the operating system for the winch, which consisted of a twenty foot cable that plugged into the winch itself and a box with two buttons—one to let the cable out, and the other to bring the cable back in.

He stumbled to the front of the truck, eventually found the outlet to plug the cable in, and pushed the button to let the cable out. Or so he thought. He had actually pushed the button to bring the cable in, which it already was. The winch did nothing but hum and chatter. After several seconds Henry finally realized his mistake, let his thumb off that button and pressed the other. This time the winch reversed itself and the cable began to let itself out. Henry let out what he figured would be enough cable to get it around the nearest upright on the gate entrance, took a hold of the heavy metal hook on the end of the cable and slipped and slid his way over to the upright. He had figured the length too short and had to go back and let out a little more cable. The second time he had let out enough to get the cable around the upright and secure the hook back to the cable. He went back to the truck, picked up the box with the buttons and began winching the cable back on the spool. At first, the winch hummed smoothly as it took the slack out of the cable. Then, as the cable tightened, the winch began to slow, chatter, and eventually smoke.

The truck tried to move, but being wedged tight on the rock made it simply impossible. Undaunted, Henry kept his finger on the button and watched carefully for any movement. After a minute or two, the winch stopped straining, which told Henry something was starting to move. The chattering went away and the normal hum came back. Through the rain, Henry thought he heard a crack, like a twig or a stick being stepped on. Then a bigger, much louder crack, and finally there was a cracking like that of a big tree being felled.

Henry, still nowhere close to sober, thought it strange that a winch would make such a noise and looked at the side of it to try and get a better idea why it was cracking like that. Behind him, the wooden upright he had attached the cable to was breaking off at the ground and falling unceremoniously to the water-soaked road, taking the heavy wooden ranch sign and the other upright along with it. Henry wearily glanced up just in time to see the splash the whole thing made when it landed. He took his thumb off the button.

"Time to change," he muttered.

CHAPTER 4

Henry was warm and dry and sober, reading the paper in his favorite chair in the living room back home at the ranch. There came a knock at the door.

Henry wondered who it was, but wasn't interested in getting up. He was comfortable sitting in the chair. In that chair there was no pain in his joints or in his stomach and no perpetual headache, the one he'd had for years from being just this side of hungover. From his chair there was just Josh in the other room playing his guitar and Annie in the kitchen cooking dinner—Henry's favorite, by the smell of it. Barbequed beef brisket with mashed potatoes and gravy, corn on the cob, a salad with the greens from the garden, and for desert, a strawberry and rhubarb crumble.

Knock, knock, knock. "Henry," Annie's voice came from the kitchen. "Could you see who that is?" *Knock, knock, knock.*

Henry looked at the door, and through the glass he could see the dark silhouette of a man in a cowboy hat. He tried to get up to see who it was but couldn't move.

Knock, knock, knock. "Henry," came Annie's voice again. "Are you all right?"

"What?" Henry asked.

"Are you all right?" Annie's voice was a little deeper now. "Henry…You okay?" *Knock, knock, knock.* "Henry?" Annie's voice was different — deeper, more masculine. "Henry, you okay?"

Henry looked toward the kitchen, but it was starting to disappear in a bright yellow light that slowly turned into yellow, then orange flames.

Knock, knock, knock. "Henry," came the voice again. "Can you hear me? Are you all right?" *Knock, knock, knock.*

"No," Henry said, as he sat in his chair. Unable to move, he reached for the kitchen door that was still visible through the flames, but just barely. "NO!" he yelled.

"Henry!" The voice shouted. "It's Judd. Are you all right?"

Henry opened his eyes and sat up quickly. "NO!" he yelled again.

"Henry! HENRY!" it was the voice of Judd Thompson, one of the younger hands at the Rafter Seven. "Are you okay?" Henry shook off the cobwebs and looked around. He had passed out across the seat of the truck the night before. His head began to ache, partly because of the hangover that was quickly beginning to set in, and partly because of the bump over his eye from hitting the steering wheel.

"Are you all right," Judd had been outside the truck, banging on the passenger side window. Somehow during the night, Henry had managed to lock both the truck doors.

Henry put the heel of his left hand over his left eye and rubbed hard. His head was pounding now. "Hell no, I ain't all right," he said, opening the door and pushing himself out. "Do I look like I'm all right?" His mouth was dry and he felt sick to his stomach, although he knew he wouldn't get sick. He hadn't thrown up from drinking in years. A sign, he suspected, that his body was actually getting used to being poisoned. This morning, as with many mornings, he didn't much care.

Henry squinted at the bright, early morning sun, and for the first time was able to take a good, if blurry, look around. Being out on the passenger side, he could now see that the truck was perched on the big rock, something he couldn't see, nor did he look for, the night before. He looked at the winch cable still attached to the gate upright now lying in the road. Three more ranch trucks were parked in the area and men were scattered around with chain saws, cutting the uprights into smaller pieces so they could be removed. He looked back at the path he had taken with the truck the night before, could see the ruts the truck made in the desert after it had left the road, as well as lumber scattered everywhere. Wherever there were tire ruts, there were two by fours and two by sixes. Not only had he wrecked the truck and pulled the gate down, but he had also lost and ruined the entire load of lumber.

"The boss wants to see you, Henry," Judd said sheepishly.

"I'll bet," Henry grunted.

It didn't take Henry long to pack his things after he was fired. By now he didn't have much to pack anyway. A couple pairs of jeans, three shirts (all of them dirty), a coat and his chaps, which he kept in an old satchel, a bedroll, saddle and saddle bags, saddle blanket, slicker, bridles, ropes, and his pistol that he kept in its holster and pushed down in the bottom of the saddle bags. That was all he had left. He had pawned his rifle several years back when he ran out of money. The old Winchester didn't bring near what it was worth, but by then the gun wasn't worth much to Henry either, just like anything else in his life. In place of the rifle, he had picked up a cast iron fry pan, tin plate, coffee pot and tin cup somewhere along the way. As much time as he spent sleeping under the stars, it made much more sense to have those items than the rifle.

For the next couple weeks, Henry took what little money he had from his last paycheck from the Rafter Seven and drove aimlessly through Arizona and Nevada, up through western Idaho and eastern Oregon, then back down to Nevada. During the trip he stopped at nineteen different cattle ranches and even four sheep ranches looking for work. Nobody was interested. Of course it probably didn't help that he was always dirty, unshaven and smelled of liquor when he stopped. His reputation always preceded him and nobody seemed all that interested in hiring a broke-down old drunk cowboy to tend to their place or their stock, not even sheepherders.

Then, just as he was running out of money, somewhere in the back of his mind Henry recalled having been offered a job a few years back by Sam Mitchell down near Elko. Mitchell owned one of the biggest cow/calf operations in Nevada, and by all accounts was a good man to work for, providing you could get hired on, which wasn't always easy. Henry knew Sam only hired the best hands he could find. Once you worked for Sam Mitchell, you were considered to have made the "big time," and the cowboys who worked for him usually did so for a very long time. Henry recalled the reason he didn't take the job when it was offered was because he was riding for another outfit at the time, and by the time he lost that job, he'd forgotten about Mitchell's offer all together.

Henry had hoped to get to Elko in one day from Mountain Home, Idaho, but ended up stopping out in the middle of nowhere. As dusk set in, he pulled off the main road, over a cattle guard and into a pasture. The road on the other side of the cattle guard was little more than a seldom-used two-wheel path. He followed the path off the main road into miles of fenceless pasture and brown, treeless rolling hills. He could have stopped anywhere, but he was looking for something very specific. He knew by experience when there was a pasture that size in an area that was that dry, there had to be a water source for the livestock somewhere. He figured this path was more than likely a maintenance road for that water source and he was hoping to find it before he stopped for the night.

Sure enough, as he rounded a gentle bend to the left and past a lone tree on the side of a hill, there it was: a thousand-gallon water tank with a decades-old, but still functional windmill spinning gently next to it. Henry drove the truck in a large circle about a quarter mile in diameter around the windmill, and with the headlights illuminating the darkening pasture, stopped and picked up old, dried piles of cow manure, and put them in the bed of the truck. When he had what he figured would be enough to last the night, Henry drove back to the windmill and dug a small fire pit. Breaking a few of the pies into smaller pieces and placing them over several pieces of tightly rolled up newspaper in the pit, he lit the paper and immediately started the old manure on fire. Eventually he placed some of the bigger pies on the fire and just as it turned dark, he had a fire big enough to not only keep him warm for the night, but one he could cook over, as well.

Henry fried up and then ate what was left of a three-day-old can of Spam and made himself a weak pot of coffee, of which he only drank about half before setting the rest aside for the morning. He then broke out the bottle of cheap whiskey he opened that morning and had been nursing most of the day as he drove down the road. It was one of only two he had left. After slipping into the numb oblivion that kept the nightmares at bay, he lay down in his bedroll and got ready for one more of a thousand sleepless nights spent tossing and turning, and wishing things were different.

Henry woke early, just as it began to get light, but before the sun would peek up over the hill that was home to the lone tree. He stirred the fire, bringing the dying embers back to life, chucked another cow pie on the flames, and stirred it again. Once he had a decent fire going, he heated the coffee pot and drank what he hadn't finished the night before. The substance in the pot was even worse that morning, and Henry could barely get it down his throat without wincing.

When he had choked down about as much of the rancid concoction as he thought was prudent, he grabbed his last bottle of whiskey that he had opened after finishing the one he had been nursing the day before, along with a bar of lye soap, and went to the water tank. He stripped himself naked, and taking the bottle and the soap, he carefully climbed into the tank. The water in the tank was relatively warm for that early in the morning, around sixty degrees, but still plenty cold for someone with so little fat on his body. Henry had always weighed between one hundred seventy-five and one hundred eighty pounds when he worked his own ranch—about right for his leggy six-foot frame and the amount of work he did. But since Annie and Josh died, he was down to one hundred sixty pounds. When he climbed into the tank, he was actually closer to one fifty-five, and his ribs and shoulders showed it.

He took a long drink from the bottle, put the cap back on and sent it adrift in the tank. Then, as quick as he could, he went to washing himself. He spent as little time in the tank as possible and still tried to get all the important parts as clean as he could before taking his bottle and his soap and getting out. He used his dirty shirt to dry off, then went to his satchel and got out the cleanest clothes he could find. The shirt he chose, a faded denim button down, was wrinkled and dirty, but the cleanest of the bunch. That was more than he could say for any of his jeans.

He then placed a small, round mirror on the windmill and shaved the week's worth of stubble off his face. When he finished, he put on his shirt, reached into the satchel and pulled out a light wool vest and wrinkled neckerchief and put them both on. He took a swig from the bottle and looked in the mirror at his weathered and tired image. He shook his head in disgust, as if not believing what he was seeing, took the mirror down and placed it back in the satchel. After carefully cleaning up his campsite, and taking two more long pulls from the bottle, Henry climbed in the truck and headed back down the little path to the main road.

Henry got to the Mitchell ranch mid morning and quickly found the office, which was attached to a very large and very well kept red barn. The sign on the door said, "Please come in," and so Henry did. He entered into a small, but comfortable outer office where Sally Mitchell, Sam's daughter, sat behind an orderly desk.

"Good morning," she smiled, almost as soon as Henry came through the door.

"Mornin'," Henry said clearing his throat. "I was won-derin' if Mr. Mitchell might be around."

"Yes, he is," Sally said, still smiling. "He's in with his fore-man right now, though. Can I tell him who's calling?"

"Henry McBride," Henry winced, as if saying his own name out loud hurt him in some way.

"Well, Mr. McBride," Sally got up from her desk. "I'll tell him, but it may still be a little while before he can see you."

"That'd be all right," Henry forced a smile. "I'm not all that busy today."

Sally disappeared behind a large wooden door for only a few seconds, before returning.

"He said you could go right in," Sally held the door open for Henry.

"He did?" Henry asked, a bit surprised.

"He did," she smiled.

Henry walked to the door and just before entering, removed his hat. Once inside, the heavy door closed behind him with muffled thud. In front of him, behind a large wooden desk sat Sam Mitchell, a heavyset, balding but obvi-ously well-off rancher with a large graying walrus moustache and matching eyebrows. Every time Henry had seen him in the past, he always had a small patch of stubble somewhere on his face that he missed that morning when shaving. On this day, the stubble was on the cleft of his chin.

To Henry's right, sitting in a chair near the wall, was Willy Pratt, a life-long cowboy and foreman of the Mitchell operation. Willy was dressed in faded light brown trousers that buttoned up the front, high-top cowboy boots in which the bottom of his trousers were tucked, red suspenders over a chambray shirt and a wide-brimmed felt hat. Willy had round, wire-rim spectacles and a large black handlebar moustache.

"Damn, Henry," Sam said from behind his desk. "You look like hell. You okay?"

"Fine sir," Henry replied. "Thank you."

"To what do we owe this visit, Henry," Sam smiled.

"Well sir," Henry started. "A little while back you offered me a job here but I couldn't take it because I was still at the Circle R. I just wanted to let you know I'm available now."

"Henry," Sam's smile faded slightly. "That was twelve years ago that I offered you that job."

Henry sat quietly for a second, taking in what Sam had just said. "Twelve years," he said under his breath.

"I understand you've been hitting the bottle pretty hard since the accident." Sam said matter-of-factly.

"No sir," Henry looked down at the hat in his hands. "Not really."

"Sorry Henry," Sam said, looking at the disheveled Henry and shaking his head. "Even as good a hand as you are, you're of no use to me or anyone else in the condition you're in."

"Hell, Mister Mitchell," Henry protested quietly. "I'm okay, I just didn't get much sleep last night. That's all."

"I can smell the whiskey on you clear over here." Sam was blunt now. "Who do you think you're kidding?"

Henry wanted to say something. Maybe that all he needed was one more chance. That it was time to change, as the voice had told him. That he was ready to try and turn his life around—that he was willing to do what it took to clean himself up and put the past behind him. But in the end, all he could do was stare blankly into space. He suddenly felt very old and all the words racing through his head stayed there. Henry turned and walked to the door a beaten man.

"Henry," Sam said

Henry stopped and slowly turned toward Sam. Sam hesitated for a second, then got up from behind his desk and walked over to Henry. "Have you got any money?"

"I've got some," Henry said.

Sam pulled a wad of cash out of his pocket and peeled off a number of one hundred dollar bills.

"No sir," Henry put up his hand. "I can't…"

"I know what you're thinking, Henry," Sam said. "And this ain't no charity."

Sam stuffed the money in Henry's shirt pocket.

"This is six months' pay," Sam told him. "When you get yourself sober you come here and work this off. But don't come back till you're off the bottle. You hear?"

Henry was torn between accepting the money and refusing it. In the end, it was more money than he'd seen at one time in the last ten years, and he talked himself into thinking it would be the incentive he needed to do something different with his life. Perhaps he actually could put the past behind him. Maybe he could sober up. Maybe he could come back and get a good job again and get back on his feet. In the end, Henry simply nodded his thanks, took the money and shook Sam's hand, then slowly turned and walked out the door.

"Hell, Mr. Mitchell," Willy said after the door closed behind Henry. "That's money you'll never see again."

Sam walked back to his desk, putting the wad of cash back in his pocket. "You don't know ol' Henry very well, do you, Will."

"I seen him around some. Mostly when he's been plumb full of whiskey and makin' a fool of himself."

"Well," Sam took his seat behind the desk. "He wasn't always that way. In fact, some time back Henry came on a bunch of our strays while he was out working a gather for another outfit. He didn't have a pot to piss in at the time and could have just gathered the strays up, sold them at auction and kept the money for himself." Sam pulled a cigar from the top drawer of his desk. "But he didn't. He brought them down off the mountain on his own and left them in the back pen, there. Didn't tell anyone he did it, and didn't ask for anything in return. The only way I knew about it was a couple of the boys saw him bring 'em down. That's not something I'm likely to forget anytime soon." Sam lit his cigar. "Henry's a good man in a bad way. He'll be back to work off that money."

CHAPTER 5

The small band of seventeen wild horses was in its third day of what would ultimately be a five-day journey to better grazing. The horse leading the way was a sixteen-year-old bay mare with a star on her forehead with her foal, a dark gray, almost black, stud colt running and playing by her side. Not far away was the mare's baby from the previous year, a bay filly now old enough to fend for herself, and the one from the year before that, a dun filly, was also nearby.

On the outskirts of the herd was her baby from three years ago, a gray stud colt like his father. This colt, already fifteen hands tall and nearly one thousand pounds, was normally of a playful and curious nature. However, recently he had begun to develop a slightly more aggressive attitude toward others and had been trying to establish his dominance over several members of the herd, including his mother. His efforts had been quickly and severely reprimanded by the herd's patriarch (the gray colt's sire), a big graying, almost white, stallion with a thick neck, broad chest and powerful hindquarters. The stallion's mane was white at the crest of his neck, and turned darker toward the ends. The end of his mane, which hung nearly a foot below his neck, was still black. The hairs of his tail looked very similar…white at the head of his tail, black on the end.

As the patriarch, the stallion was not only responsible for maintaining structure in the herd, but was also responsible for fending off the numerous advances from other stallions. Among the gray stallion's many battle wounds suffered while defending his band was a deep scar on his upper lip from the kick of a young rival stallion suffered three years before. The gray was in his prime then, and the young stallion had been no match for his power, speed and experience. Within minutes of making their initial contact, the young stallion had already taken an unrelenting beating and had turned tail to run when the gray reached out to give him one final bite. Instinctively, the young stallion kicked out and caught the gray square on the mouth. The gash was severe enough to make it near impossible for the gray to eat for days on end, but even though he lost weight and strength during that time, very few challengers would come his way.

The old gray stallion came by his speed, stamina and tenacity honestly, a product of generations of breeding which began in the year 1532. It was the year another gray stallion was being ridden by a Spanish soldier by the name of Raul Gomez Mendoza through the southwest of the new world while under the command of the famous conquistador, Hernando Cortés. Cortés, who was back in Mexico at the time and in a battle with a fierce rival, Nuño Beltrán de Guzmán, for the rule and exploration of the area, had secretly sent a small party north in search of gold and other riches.

Over time, the party of mostly young and inexperienced soldiers, including Mendoza, had gotten lost and ended up in the desert of what is now modern-day Arizona. Short on water and supplies, the main focus of the party soon became finding a source to replenish its water casks. However, it was during this search that the entire party was caught up in a massive and violent sandstorm that lasted several days. When the storm finally subsided, all of the men and several horses had perished, having been buried alive under sand that drifted like snow. Mendoza's gray stallion, with a strikingly long mane and tail—white on the top, black on the bottom—along with a smaller black stallion and five mares, all of Andalusion or Barb descent, swam out of the sand and began wandering in search of food and water.

The small group eventually ended up in the area that is now Flagstaff, Arizona, and although the soil in the area consisted mainly of cinder from the final explosion of an ancient volcano, the band began to thrive on the relative abundance of good grass and water it found there. Over the years, descendants of that band branched out all over the west and southwest, some being captured and domesticated by the indigenous people that lived in the area, others escaping into remote areas and surviving on meager forage and water.

This band of seventeen in the middle of Nevada, three days into a five-day journey in search of better grazing, was one of those bands directly descended from Mendoza's gray stallion and one of those Spanish mares from all those years ago. Many of the herd still carried the traits of their early ancestors—hard, black feet, thick-boned legs, thick manes that split evenly down the middle of the neck, wide foreheads, intelligent and deep eyes, unmatched stamina, and lightning quick reflexes.

The herd had been on the move since before dawn that morning, and it was mid afternoon before the bay mare brought the band to a halt on the top of a mesa where there was enough dry, brown grass for the horses to eat before they moved on. A thunderstorm rumbled in the distance, but it wouldn't be bringing any moisture that day. No sooner had the herd stopped than all of the horses, including the nine youngsters of various ages, dropped their heads and began grazing, except the big gray stallion that had been walking along behind the rest of the herd. The stallion had been on alert for the last two hours, hearing and smelling something out of the ordinary, but unable to see anything. He stood at the rim of the mesa, head high and muscles tight, looking out across the high desert from which they had just come but still unable to identify anything that would bring his herd into danger.

The old bay mare had taken on the role of herd leader two years earlier when her mother, the previous herd leader, simply disappeared one night during a freak blizzard. The herd wandered with little or no direction for nearly two months before the bay mare with the star on her forehead stepped in and—with the band on the verge of perishing from thirst—led them to water. From that point forward, the herd willingly followed her wherever she went.

It was mid July during one of the driest years on record, and with forage and water running out on their usual grazing lands, the bay mare with the star on her forehead took the herd on a trek she had been on only one time before. That time had also been during a year of severe drought, back when she was six months old and running beside her mother, another bay with a narrow blaze down her fine-boned face. With pasture and water running out, the bay mare's mother led the herd along this very route for five days and nights, eventually ending up in a large open, green meadow with a wide, shallow river running through it. There had been cattle there, and humans on horseback eventually showed up and chased the herd off, but not before they had eaten and drank their fill over the course of the moon's cycle from sliver to full.

The bay mare's memory of the route had been accurate so far, right down to the good grazing areas along the route, like this one. The herd would graze for the rest of the day and into the night before resting and moving again just before dawn. There was a narrow game trail not far from where they currently were that led from the top of the mesa to the canyon floor, nine hundred feet below. The path was steep, rocky and dangerous, but once at the bottom, the traveling would be easy for the herd for the remaining two days and they would certainly make good time.

The stallion let out a loud warning snort that brought all the horses to attention. He snorted again, and then bolted back in the direction from where the herd had just been. Within seconds he had disappeared over a little ridge. The gray colt had been hanging on the outskirts of the herd. He followed briefly, getting to the ridge from where the gray stallion had last been seen. He could see the stallion running in the distance, away from the herd and toward nothing the colt could see.

He watched until the stallion was little more than a small dot in the distance, then turned and made his way back to the herd that by now had gone back to grazing quietly. He was cautious at first, looking back over his shoulder for the stallion from time to time. But the closer to the herd he approached, the bolder he got until he was closing in on the mares. He trotted up, dropping his head and snaking it, pinning his ears and flicking his tail. He circled around menacingly, driving the mares into a small circle, then chasing babies and scattering the youngsters. He then turned back to the mares that were splitting up and calling for their babies, forcing them back into a circle, then going back at the babies and youngsters.

Over and over he circled the mares and chased the youngsters, until his behavior was all consuming. He never sensed the stallion return, and he certainly never saw or heard him charging up from behind. The stallion, neck bowed, ears pinned and mouth open, came at top speed and bit the colt hard in the flank, easily tearing the hide and opening up a ten-inch-long gash. The colt was taken by surprise at this flash of pain, and instinctively jumped and kicked in the direction of the bite. The stallion, undaunted, came forward with ferocity like the colt had never seen before. He bit the colt hard on the hindquarters and opened up another gash, the searing pain of which drove the inexperienced stud colt away from the herd. The colt tried to kick again, but was driven to the ground by the stallion. The stallion pawed at him unmercifully, opening up a gash on his right shoulder and another over his right eye. The stallion reared high in the air and pawed wildly, giving the colt enough time to scramble to his feet and bolt with his tail tucked tightly between his bloody hindquarters. The stallion came down and went after him. He drove the colt past the herd, pawing at his hocks and biting at his hindquarters, squealing and bawling so loudly the sound echoed off the walls of the distant canyon wall over a mile away. The colt dodged and spun, making every attempt to get away from the enraged stallion, but at every move, the stallion was on top of him, biting and pawing.

The colt ran for all he was worth, kicking out only occasionally, concentrating more on escape than defense. The stallion was unrelenting and kept pushing the colt farther and farther from the herd. The pair had traveled nearly a quarter mile with the colt being so focused on getting away from the stallion that he never saw the edge of the mesa approaching. By the time the pair got to the mesa's edge, the colt had been trying so hard to evade yet another vicious bite he simply ran right off the edge. The stallion knew this area and how the shape of the ground felt under his hooves. He turned at the last second and was able to pull up short. As the colt disappeared, the big gray stallion let out another loud snort, shaking his head under a cascade of white-to-black mane.

The colt tumbled helplessly several hundred feet down the steep embankment, finally coming to an unceremonious rest against a large rock outcropping on a ledge just before a seven hundred foot drop straight to the bottom of the canyon floor. Disoriented and in shock from his numerous and severe injuries, the gray colt could do nothing more than lay motionless against the rock, and it was there he stayed for the rest of the afternoon, through the night and into the early morning.

Just as the sky began to lighten in the east, the colt heard the band start down the narrow game trail on the way to the bottom of the canyon. He was in nearly unbearable pain, and for the most part had been lying on his side in a puddle of his own blood throughout the night. But as he heard the band leaving him, he forced himself upright until his legs were folded underneath his body. Even though his fall had been horrendous, the colt had no broken bones. He tried to push himself to a standing position, but was still in too much pain and too disoriented to get up, and after two meager attempts, he sunk back down. He let out a soft nicker, which was all he could muster, but the game trail and the herd were too far away for any of the other horses to hear him, not that any of them were looking for him or would have even called back in the first place. The colt had been banished from the herd, and in the horse world, that rule was never broken.

Even though the herd moved efficiently down the game trail that morning, it would still take the horses over an hour to reach the canyon floor. They could have fanned out once at the bottom but they seemed content to stay in single file. The bay mare with the star on her forehead out in front, the other mares, babies and youngsters in an orderly row behind her, and the stallion, still extremely cautious and weary, bringing up the rear. The sun was up now and the air was starting to warm. From time to time the colt could even feel cool air from the canyon floor briefly floating up past him before it dissipated completely somewhere over his head.

The colt was starting to get thirsty and hungry—a sign that his body was already trying to heal itself and was going to need nourishment to do it. He tried to get up twice more, but instinctively understood it would be a little longer before he would be able to complete that task. So he laid quiet, legs tucked underneath and his head resting on the ground out in front of him.

As he lay there, he thought he could hear a noise in the distance. It was an unusual sound, and one he had never heard before. *Thump, thump, thump, thump....* Faint at first, then louder as if it were getting closer. *Thump, thump, thump, thump....* It was enough to get the colt to raise his head and look up in time to see a large machine—a helicopter—flying up the canyon toward the herd, now two miles farther up the canyon floor. The machine was about eye level to where the colt was lying, and the noise and strange sight was enough to send a shot of adrenaline through the colt's body, and frightened, he finally scrambled to his feet. His movement caught the eye of the helicopter pilot, who radioed back to crews on the ground.

"We've got one on a ledge up here," he said into the microphone on his headset. "On the north rim of Castle Mesa, about three hundred feet from the top. Looks like he went over the edge. He's in pretty bad shape. Might want to send someone up to shoot the poor bastard—Over."

"Nah," a voice came back. "We got bigger fish to fry today. If he's stuck up there, he'll be dead soon enough."

"Roger that."

The helicopter made the turn up the canyon and quickly came up on the gray stallion's band. Frightened, the horses began galloping up the canyon. They ran for all they were worth for three miles. Hooves were pounding the ground, air was being forced in and out of burning lungs, babies were calling for mothers, and mothers were calling for babies as a mass of tails, manes and legs mingled together in the red and brown dust the herd kicked up. The stallion wanted to defend the herd, but there was no defending them from this. The helicopter, flying low to the ground now, pushed the herd and kept them moving until the canyon narrowed and the helicopter was no longer able to follow. It slowly lifted, banked to the right and flew off.

Just as the herd felt it safe to slow down, humans on horses, swinging ropes and making hooting and whistling noises, burst from the bushes and from behind rocks and took up the chase. After five miles of running non-stop, the babies were falling hopelessly behind the adults, and while still running as best as their young legs would carry them, were running out of air. The canyon narrowed even more, until there was only enough room for the now sweat-soaked horses to travel two or three abreast. They rounded a blind turn and found themselves in a catch pen one hundred yards square where horses from other bands were already caught inside and milling around frantically. The horses from the gray stallion's band shot into the pen, adding to the already confused and frenzied scene, when two large camouflaged gates swung shut behind them.

CHAPTER 6

As the helicopter flew past the mesa, the panicked colt began scrambling up the bank he had tumbled down the afternoon before. He lunged straight up the side of the canyon wall four times, sliding back down to the ledge each time. The helicopter disappeared as quickly as it had shown up and the colt, tired, hungry, thirsty and in pain from his injuries, stopped and stood, his legs quivering under him, breathing hard and looking up at the steep slope. He was a mountain horse, born and bred, and while the slope may have looked insurmountable to the casual observer, the truth of the matter was, even at his young age this colt had already traveled on much worse.

Once the colt's initial panic and trembling had subsided and he again had his wits about him, he slowly and cautiously began his ascent back up the slope. This time, instead of trying to go straight up the steep bank, he traversed it upward in a large zigzag pattern, walking first ten or twelve steps to the left, then doubling back on himself and walking ten or twelve steps to the right. The ground was composed mostly of loose red dirt and grapefruit-sized rocks, both of which would scatter down to the ledge and beyond with every step he took. The colt slipped several times, nearly causing him to tumble back down to the ledge himself, but in each case he had caught himself by digging in with his front feet and pushing hard with his hind until he found relatively solid footing. The deep cuts he had received from the old stallion were filled with the red, sand-like dirt. He had bruises on both front legs, and his hips and shoulders gave out excruciating pain that would shoot through his entire body with every step. To catch himself after slipping was almost more than he could physically take and he would need to rest and let the pain subside before continuing upward.

As the sun made its way through the sky, the colt virtually willed his way back up the slope, often taking one step forward and two steps back. Still, each time he felt he couldn't go on, something deep inside him would instinctively take over and he would push himself that next step, or two steps or three. By the time he finally scrambled the last few steps and lunged himself over the edge and back on top of the mesa he had fallen from the day before, many of his wounds, the ones that had begun to lightly scab over during the night, were once again bleeding freely.

The exhausted colt limped away slowly from the mesa's edge, dropped his head into the first patch of dried brown grass he found, and began eating. The sun was closer to the western skyline by the time the colt had eaten his fill. He found himself in one of the small groves of cedar trees that dotted the middle of the mesa. He was still hungry, but as he stood in the shade of the low-branched, sweet-smelling trees, his eyes began to get very heavy. His tail lazily swished back and forth, sending the flies that were trying to get to his open wounds back into the air. The dislodged flies would buzz around for a second or two before once again landing on or near a wound, taking a quick meal and eventually laying their eggs in the cuts.

The colt stayed in the shade of the little grove of trees and dozed off and on until the blazing sun slowly dropped down behind a distant mountain range to the west. The sky turned a brilliant yellow, then it changed into different shades of bright red and purple before finally giving way to dark blues and black. It was only then the air started to cool and the colt felt like moving again. He wanted to eat and he did lower his head and nibble a bit, but he was actually much more thirsty than he was hungry.

It had been nearly two full days since he had drunk any-thing, and his body, wracked with pain, was also dehydrating. He didn't know where the herd had gone, but he knew where they had been and he also knew there was water about a half day's walk to the north, toward the herd's traditional grazing lands. The mesa he was on sloped very gradually downward to the northwest and dropped nearly six hundred feet in ele-vation over a seventeen-mile stretch to a large dry valley with a river flowing through the middle of it. Normally, the river would be nearly twenty feet wide with gently sloping banks, knee deep with cool, clear water and an abundance of green grass all along the banks on both sides. But in this year of drought the river had shriveled into nothing more than a seven-inch-wide sliver of mud with hardly enough water in it for the herd to quench its thirst from a long days journey. Still, water was water and he knew it wasn't going to come to him, so he would have to go to it.

Instinctively the colt slowly left the comfort of the cedar grove and started moving down the mesa toward the valley with the little river. It wasn't the best time of day for a horse to be on the move. Especially a horse injured as badly as he was. It was early evening, when the predators became active. Normally not many predators would be interested in an animal his size, especially if he were in or near the protection of the herd. As big as he was he'd be too hard for a cougar to bring down by itself if he were healthy. But he wasn't healthy, nor was he in the protection of the herd. He was alone and injured and would be an easy target for a predator, should he come across one. There was no question moving to water was a risk. But it was one he had to take. After all, while there was a chance he could get killed by making the journey, if he stayed on the mesa without water, he was certain he would die.

The colt immediately picked up the lingering scent of the herd through the hoof marks each horse left in the dirt and the piles of manure and urine spots they left behind. As the colt walked he would often briefly stop to smell the manure or urine spots he found along the way and easily identified the member of the herd who had left it. The colt was comforted by the familiarity of the odors, particularly the ones of his mother, but he didn't give it much thought. There was something in the recesses of his mind that told him that chapter of his life was over. He had been banished from the herd, as most young horses are at one time or another, and he knew there would be no going back to the life he had.

While it was the piles of manure that marked the way to the river for the colt, it was actually the strength of scent from the hoof marks in the dirt that told him when he was getting closer. The scent of any herd was always stronger where the herd had last been, so the farther he was from the river, the stronger the physical scent of the herd. The closer he got to the river, the fainter the scent. Within another day or so, the scent would be gone completely along the entire path the herd took to the mesa. But for now, it could still be used as a beacon.

The trip to the valley with the river was relatively uneventful, although very time-consuming and arduous. Normally a horse walking could easily make fifteen miles in about five hours. But because of the severity of the colt's injuries, it took him nearly twice that long, and by the time he reached the river the eastern sky was already getting light.

The once lush green grass along the river's bank was now brown and dry, and it crunched under his hooves with every step he took. He had expected to pick up the scent of water long before he reached the river, but as he slid down the bank and into the riverbed he quickly realized why he hadn't. The river was completely dry. Even the small muddy sliver the herd drank from two days earlier was gone, and all that was left were dark spots in the cracked and dry river bottom.

The colt pawed at the dark spots in hopes of perhaps bringing up some moisture that was trapped underground, but all that he raised was mud. He turned and limped a mile or so upstream, and then downstream, in search of something to drink, but it seemed the entire river had simply disappeared. He stood in the middle of the dry riverbed as the sun began to climb higher in the sky, and the cool morning air quickly heated up to over ninety degrees. The colt's energy reserves were gone now. His injuries, along with the fifteen-mile trudge to get him to the river had used up everything he had. He slowly glanced to the north, back toward the land he had been born and raised in, and knew the next closest water was over two days away, too far for him to travel in the condition he was in. He didn't know it, but that river was dry too, and the ground around it was just as bare. It was why the herd left in search of water and food. He looked to an old cottonwood tree near the bank of the river. There was shade under its branches, but even at only fifty feet away it was still too far for him to walk. He lowered his head and closed his eyes.

By mid afternoon the temperature in the riverbed had reached one hundred ten degrees, and the colt's only defense from the stifling heat was to instinctively try to make as small a shadow as possible. Every thirty minutes or so, almost without even knowing he was doing it, he would pivot his body slightly so the sun was always on his tail. This kept his head, which by now was nearly down between his knees, in the shadow of his own body and allowed the sun to heat the least amount of surface area along his back, instead of the area on his side.

In between pivoting, he would lock the stifle joints in both rear legs, which allowed him to remain standing as he fell into an almost trancelike sleep. In the weakened state he was in, had he lain down there was a very good chance he would have never gotten up again. So there he stood, hour after hour in the scorching sun, pivoting every thirty minutes. By the time darkness fell, the colt was facing the opposite direction from where he started that morning, even though his front feet had barely moved at all. He didn't move from that position through the night.

As morning eased its way into the valley, the colt began to dream of his days as a foal, sleeping in the spring grass, playing with the other foals, rearing, bucking, spinning, and racing as fast as his feet could carry him over logs, around boulders and splashing through creeks with cool, fresh water in them. He raced around in the trees, then out into the meadow, then back across the creek and over to the other foals for more rearing and bucking.

In his dream the air was cool and he could hear thunder off in the distance. Long, rolling thunder that echoed through the meadow. It started quietly, came to a loud crescendo, and then quieted again. The meadow would go silent for a second or two, then the thunder would come, almost nonstop, for what seemed like a long time before coming to another loud crescendo. The colt could smell rain, the kind that almost always accompanied thunder like this, and could see flashes of lightning in the distance. In his dream the colt ran headlong across the meadow, jumped a log, then splashed into a creek where he stood for a long time. The water in the creek was shallow, barely making it over the top of his hooves, but it felt cool on his feet and, thirsty from all the running he'd done, he reached down to get a drink.

There suddenly came a tremendous roll of thunder and a massive flash of lightning so bright it woke the colt from his sleep. Startled, the colt quickly jerked his head up and opened his eyes to see the early morning sky dark with real storm clouds. In the distance there was lightning and thunder, but no rain...at least there wasn't any rain where he was. There was, however, rain somewhere, as he could not only smell it in the air, but he was now standing in a widening, one-inch-deep stream of water running in the riverbed. He pawed the water tentatively to see if it were real, and then pawed it again more vigorously once he realized it was, splashing the cold wet stuff on his legs and belly and up over his head and back. A dark gray wall of water soon poured out of the sky and headed toward him from up the valley. With his body still aching and in pain, the colt turned his tail to the mild wind the leading edge of the storm was producing, and as large raindrops started pelting him on his back, he eagerly dropped his head and took his first long drink in over three days.

CHAPTER 7

A massive low-pressure system had come in off the Pacific Ocean and stretched from just above Arroyo Grande, California, up to Beaver, Oregon. It moved onshore slowly, dumping several inches of rain on the coast, causing massive mudslides and flash flooding in its wake before laboriously making its way inland. It moved so slowly and was so large that it took nearly four days for the leading edge to get over Nevada, while at the same time still dumping rain on the coast of California. Days later, a high-pressure system began building in behind the storm over the Pacific and pushed the behemoth eastward. By the time the storm marched over the Rockies and out onto the plains, it had dumped over eight inches of much needed moisture in the drought-stricken west.

The seven days of rain brought life back to the valley with the river running through it. A little at a time, grass began to grow, sagebrush and bushes began to green up and wildflowers were sprouting everywhere. By the time the rain stopped and the sun returned, the valley was well on its way to recovery, and the gray colt was recovering, too.

The blood that had mixed with red dirt and had dried and caked on his coat had all but washed away. The eggs the flies had laid in his open wounds had hatched into maggots, and the maggots had been feeding on any rotting flesh that developed, leaving the healthy tissue and keeping the colt free of infection. Having successfully completed their job, they too, had been washed away during the unrelenting downpour. To help relieve some of the pain in his legs, the colt had taken to standing for hours on end in the coolness of the now knee-deep river, grazing on the grass that was sprouting in abundance along the bank. The water calmed him, and there were times he would completely submerge himself in the river, often leaving only his eyes, nostrils and ears exposed. This submersion was also something he did when the insects, which were also in abundance now, would bother him too much.

After several weeks of recuperation along the riverbank, most of the colt's injuries were healing nicely. Even the worst cuts and gashes had granulated in and begun to close. However, one injury that wasn't making much progress was his right shoulder, the one the stallion had kicked, and the one he had landed on while tumbling down the slope. It still had severe pain and swelling, particularly up high near his withers and into his neck. The pain was so bad it caused him to limp when he moved, and made it difficult for him to turn his head and neck to the right or to get his head down to graze or drink for any length of time. It didn't stop him from grazing or drinking, but he would have to bring his head up after only a few minutes of doing either to relieve the pain before putting his head down and resuming.

The colt stayed primarily on the south side of the river and never ventured too far from where his herd left the banks during their journey to the top of the mesa. Often during the many long days he spent there he would stand in the shade of one of the cottonwood trees along the bank and stare in the direction of the mesa, as if waiting for the band's return.

About a month after he had arrived in the valley with the river running through it, the colt was standing under one of those cottonwood trees. He had been staring in the direction of the mesa for nearly two hours when he let out a long sigh, glanced upstream to the east, then downstream to the west. He glanced briefly back up toward the mesa, lowered his head, turned and slowly began walking west, along the river's bank. It wasn't so much that something drew him in that direction as much as nothing drew him the other. He didn't even know where he was going. All he knew was something was telling him he could no longer stay where he was.

The gray colt's shoulder was still bothering him and his travel was slow. He kept to the bank of the river, stopping frequently to graze, drink and nap. He seemed to be napping a lot lately, more so than since he'd gone off the ledge of the mesa. While outwardly his cuts and bruises had nearly healed, it seemed to be the inward trauma that he was struggling with—the attack of the stallion, the fall from the ledge, the loss of his herd, and nearly dying in the dry riverbed. These were not things he would spend time agonizing over as individual events. In fact, he couldn't really recall much detail of any of the experiences individually. To the colt, these were all things that just happened in life. They weren't good or bad, necessarily, just things. Still, their cumulative effect seemed to be weighing him down like one massive weight sitting on his heart.

In the thirteen days since he left the cottonwood tree and headed west, the colt had traveled a little under seventy-five miles, never venturing too far from the river or the good grass that grew nearby. The landscape had gradually changed from flat, coarse ground surrounded by steep cliffs and few trees, to rolling hills dotted with sporadic stands of small and large evergreens, and of course, the occasional cottonwood growing by the river. It hadn't rained much since the big storm and the hills on either side of the river were beginning to turn brown once again, although the grazing was still very good next to the river.

The colt's cuts and gashes from the attack and subsequent fall were now nothing more than a number of black scars in his otherwise dark gray coat. There was a scar over his right eye, one on his flank and another on his hip. There were several on his legs, one on his neck and one on his chest. A couple of the bigger wounds, like the ones on his flank, hip and shoulder, still had a small strip of pink running down the middle of them where the skin hadn't completely come together yet. None of the wounds were really a source of pain for him anymore, and with the exception of the limp he still had from the shoulder injury, his movement was beginning to develop more of a natural flow to it, rather than the stilted and labored way he had traveled while the wounds were healing.

Since the fall the colt had also lost nearly one hundred pounds. With all the good grazing in the last few weeks, the colt had gained nearly all of it back, along with some of the muscle mass he'd lost due to the inefficient way his injuries had forced him to move.

Even though his body was healing and he wasn't in as much pain, he still found the need for taking several naps during the day. It was during one of these afternoon naps under the branches of a large Douglas fir tree near a bend in the river, that he awoke to a familiar scent floating on the breeze. The scent was faint and in an attempt at discerning what it was, he curled his top lip back toward his nostrils, raised his head and inhaled. Doing this helped expose the vomeronasal organ at the base of his nasal passages and drew the scent molecules back toward it. The scent was suddenly amplified in his brain and gave him an explosion of information.

He had picked up the fading odor of a band of horses. As far as he could tell there were the scents of at least ten different horses in the little herd, with three, maybe four of the animals being mares, and one of them smelled to be at the end of her heat cycle. He laboriously trotted toward the river, stopped, and repeated the behavior, which allowed him to gain more information about them. They had passed by no more than three days before, crossed the river somewhere near here and headed for the tall rolling hills off in the distance.

He curled his lip and inhaled one last time, picking up on something else that was immediately confusing to him. The mares were relatively easy to single out; they smelled more or less like any other female horse he had ever come in contact with. But there was something different about the males. There was no question in his mind that they were males, but even at that, they didn't smell like any male he had ever come in contact with. There was something about the intensity of the odor—that part of the odor that made a male a male—that seemed to be missing, somehow, and that was what puzzled him.

The colt called out loudly, then raised his head and held his breath to make sure he would be able to clearly hear any return call. He waited for several seconds, then snorted loudly and called out again. Nothing came back. It wasn't surprising to him. After all, the band had a three-day head start on him and even if they were only moving at a slow walk, they were almost certainly out of earshot of even his loudest calls.

The colt crossed the river and with renewed energy coming out the other side, broke into a trot in the direction he estimated the band had traveled. Moving on mostly adrenaline, the colt trotted for the better part of an hour before the muscles in his right shoulder finally gave out. He slowed to a walk but kept moving for the rest of the afternoon and late into the night. He rested for only a few hours before starting out after the band once again just before dawn. He forced himself into a painful trot, stopping only occasionally to check the air or ground for evidence of the band and to make sure he hadn't lost their trail. By mid morning, he had come across an area where the band had stopped to graze and bed down. There were plenty of manure and urine spots in the grass, and more than once he made the effort to smell the urine spots of the males to try to figure out why they were so different. But even with smelling their urine, it gave him no more information than he already had.

By mid afternoon, he had come across a small creek with little more than a trickle of water running through it. Still, he stopped and drank his fill having not had any water in almost twenty-four hours, and not knowing when his next drink would come. He also took time to graze along the creek bank on the short grass that grew there before starting out after the band once again. He was spending more time walking now than trotting and even though he wanted to go faster, his body simply wouldn't allow it. Following the scent of the herd that seemed to get stronger with every step he took, he walked long into the night.

About an hour before dawn, hungry, thirsty and totally exhausted, the colt finally stopped just below the crest of a hill covered in pine trees. He rested there until mid morning when, with some of his energy returning, he lowered his head and grazed until he wasn't hungry anymore. Having eaten his fill, he continued on his way. It took him less than an hour to get to the top of the hill he was on, and another half hour to get to where the hill started to drop down into the valley below. As the colt emerged from the trees and began his slow descent to the valley, suddenly, the band of horses he'd been following for the past two and a half days came into view, grazing quietly down in the valley.

The colt stopped dead in his tracks, raised his head, pricked his ears and called as loudly as he could. In unison every horse in the band came to attention and looked up at the gray colt standing by himself on the hill, but none called back. He called again, this time even louder than the last, and the band instinctively let out a chorus of calls back to him. Out of curiosity more than anything else, one by one the horses in the band started toward him, walking at first, then trotting and finally cantering as a group, calling and nickering as they went. The colt started toward them about the same time, picking up a painful canter before falling back to the trot.

The horses of the band got to the colt before he made it off the hill and swarmed around him like bees around a hive, some of the horses were trying to smell his flanks, others were trying to exchange breath with him. Some squealed and pawed at him, and he at them with nobody ever really making contact. Necks were arched and tails were raised and everybody seemed to be posturing, but nobody really doing anything about it. The colt had never seen this kind of behavior in horses before. He had come from a band where anytime an intruder showed up near the herd, the stallion went out alone to challenge or run him off. If the intruder posed a danger, the lead mare would take the rest of the herd to safety. He hadn't ever seen an entire herd approach an intruder before, and had certainly never seen this kind of posturing from a group before. It was as if nobody knew who was supposed to be protecting the herd, or leading it for that matter.

After about five minutes of this strange ritual, three of the males and one of the females, a dark brown mare with a wide blaze down her face, turned and kicked at him, moving him first one way, then the other. Because of his bad shoulder it was everything he could do to get out of their way, but three of the kicks made contact, although none did any damage. As quick as he could, the colt retreated back up the hill with one of the males and the mare with the blaze on her face following close behind. Neither one seemed too interested in hurting the colt, and even though they could have easily outrun and overtaken him, they simply moved him up the hill a few hundred feet and left him alone.

The strange thing was even though it was clear the herd didn't want the colt in amongst them, they also didn't go too far away from him once the two horses had moved him up the hill. The band seemed perfectly happy to let him graze only one or two hundred feet away, and let him go down to get water in the little stream near the bottom of the hill when he needed to drink.

The colt was unsure of what to think of this strange little band. While there was no question these creatures were horses, there was still something very different about them. They had a completely different feel to them than any of the horses he had ever encountered during his short lifetime out on the range. There was an unfamiliar energy to them. Not bad, necessarily, but very different. In the band he came from there had always been a sort of sharpness to life, an alertness that never went away. Everything was always very clear to all members of the band and everyone had a defined place within the herd and that place was adhered to with strictness. But with this band, there seemed to be a sort of dullness to their life, a lack of urgency in everything they did. Things were much slower here and much less refined. Everybody still had a place in the herd, but that place seemed to be negotiable depending on the day, or even the time of day. That was never the case in his previous band.

Another thing that troubled the colt was he had never seen so many adult males and adult females living together, and he certainly had never seen a herd without babies and youngsters. There was something unnatural about this little band, and it made him uneasy.

These concerns alone were enough for the colt to keep his distance, these along with the knowledge that though his body had gotten stronger, he was not at all strong. If one of the members turned on him and attacked, he wasn't confident he could defend himself so he stayed away, never approaching the herd directly, but still always within sight of them.

In the weeks that followed several members of the band would cautiously approach him, one at a time, and slowly introduce themselves. Their cautiousness only made him more nervous, and even though it was clear to him that he could join them at any time, he still kept enough distance from them to feel safe. He moved when they moved, ate when they ate and slept when they slept—all from two hundred feet away. He had become part of their band, but did not allow himself to become a member.

Days with the little band turned into weeks, and weeks into months. Eventually the cold weather began to set in on the high country they were passing through, and the herd, in one of their more decisive actions, moved to lower, more sheltered ground. The gray colt moved along with them, staying always at their flank, and always two hundred feet away. After three days of nonstop travel, the little band came out of a pine forest and into a large open grassy field surrounded by barbed wire fence with an open gate in one corner. The colt had never seen fence before and didn't know what to think of it. As the herd quietly walked along the wire barrier and headed for the open gate, the colt followed, snorting warily at the horizontal wire attached to vertical posts and staying far away from it.

The little band walked through the gate single file and went directly to a large round tank filled with water and a tall windmill standing next to it—also something the colt had never seen—and began drinking. The colt was thirsty too, having not had anything to drink for the past thirty-six hours since the herd had decided to take a route that didn't include any water sources. The band of horses drank their fill, and then meandered off, spreading out inside the fenced in area and grazing on the tall grass that was there. The colt stayed outside the fence for the rest of that day, watching as the little band drifted farther and farther away from him. Occasionally, one of the horses would nicker at him, but other than that, they didn't seem too interested in his coming or going.

The colt slept outside the fence that night, and in the morning, with thirst overtaking him, he very cautiously slipped through the gate, went to the tank and began to drink. It had taken thirteen men on horseback, four more operating the gates and a helicopter to capture the band of horses the colt grew up with. For the colt, it had simply taken a tank full of water. He didn't know it at the time, but the gray colt, a direct descendant of the stallion ridden by Raúl Gómez Mendoza in 1532, had just begun a life in captivity.

CHAPTER 8

Jessie put the phone down gently after speaking to Mrs. Rodriquez and knew she was going back home. Although she had been away from the ranch since she was 19, the ranch had not been away from her. For ten years she had lived in Denver, Colorado, where the only sign she had of horses or cattle were on the billboards sprawling by the freeway, showing a Hollywood cowboy tugging on a cigarette. Ten years of nonchalant jobs and several equally nonchalant boyfriends could not erase the throbbing she felt in the middle of her chest for the endless azure skies and the earth that rose up to meet it. At the same time, ten years of festering anger would not let her loose from the city.

She had grown up caring for and following cattle, much as the seasons followed one another. She knew when a cow was ready to give birth, she knew when one of the calves was ill and she knew where to take them for grazing. She liked the cattle, their large brown eyes and their wet noses. She could inoculate them, ear tag them and doctor them but could not watch when they were shipped off for slaughter. Her father, Jed, made sure she knew they weren't pets, but it didn't stop her liking them any less.

It was the horses, though, that mystified her. As a child, she would question her father for hours about them, always beginning with, "Why?" until smiling in exasperation, he would throw up his hands, and tell her to go ask the horses themselves. When she was older, he showed her where to find the mustang herds that roamed the land bordering the farthest outreaches of their ranch. She would ride out on her chestnut gelding Rocky and together they would hunt for the wild ones, as she liked to call them. Those were her favorite days, although it gave her mother fits until she arrived back home in the fading light of the sun, as dusty as her horse and ready for supper.

All she ever knew about horses came from her father or watching the mustangs. It wasn't that she didn't know that other people treated their horses differently than she did, she had just never seen it, or sought it out. Shortly after her fourteenth birthday, her father took her with him to do business with another ranch nearby. After they had introduced themselves to their neighbor and walked around his place, she saw a large man atop a screaming, scrambling horse in a dusty pen with a blindfold on. The man was hollering, and digging his spurs into the mare's sides that were already bloody. The horse, spent after long minutes of throwing herself into the air, staggered to a halt. Even after she stood, legs trembling, heaving for air and running with blood and sweat, the cowboy spurred her again. She put her head down and when the blindfold was ripped away, Jessie saw in her eyes that the horse that had been there had disappeared and all that was left was a bloody, sweaty imitation.

She cried all the way home. She was sobbing so hard her father took a hold of her shoulder and shook her.

"You can't be this upset, Jessie. That is the way some horses are broken, it's been going on for a long time and you can't change it."

Jessie, who had been starting colts under saddle since she was ten, gave him her sharpest blue-eyed gaze (the same gaze he often got from her mother), and said in a voice rough with crying, "I am not ever going to treat my horses like that. I don't care who tells me different, and I don't care how long it takes. They may as well have killed that mare for all the use she is going to be to them."

From that day she was more thoughtful, quieter and less hurried when she worked with horses. Even when their cattle business started to decline, the ranch was gaining a reputation for good-minded, settled, saddle horses. Jessie and Jed spent more time gentling horses, and less around the cattle. It wasn't too much of a surprise when they started gentling mustangs to pack guests around the ranch. These horses were cheap, plentiful and needed homes. Jed and Jessie would often find small groups of these wild horses in amongst their own herds, so it wasn't very difficult to drive the whole herd to the ranch and sort out the ones they wanted to keep and let the rest of the wild ones back out to roam. They would work with the mustangs in their quiet way, keep some and sell some to folks in states as far away as New Hampshire and Maryland. The horses were quiet, sound-minded and sturdy and were a large part of keeping the ranch afloat.

Jed soon decided that it was easier to focus on giving rides to "guests" (so they called them when they were out among the people who would pay for a ride—"dudes" when the staff was talking out of Jed King's hearing) than to keep the cattle. Their herd had been whittled down to a couple of bulls that were easy to look after and some older, well-producing cows. Even at that, Jed was surprised if they turned any kind of profit in a given year.

It was, oddly enough, the cattle that drove Jessie to leave for Denver. That spring, her father had finally sold off the prized bulls and cows. He had not sold them to another ranch, however, but to slaughter. When Jessie found out, she had stood toe to toe with her father, shouting up at him at the top of her lungs. She berated her father for selling the cattle to a slaughterhouse, for letting them get on a crowded truck reeking of filth and fear. Why couldn't they drive them to slaughter themselves? Why couldn't he consider that maybe they were afraid, after having lived on the ranch their whole lives? Why did they have to betray them? Why, why, why? This time, Jed King didn't throw up his hands in exasperation and smile. This time he told Jessie she was over-stepping her bounds, and that if she kept going that way, she may as well move to a city. So she did.

In between the odd jobs waitressing, or clerking or being a secretary to faceless executives (some of them boyfriends), she thought of her parents as though she was reading a book about someone else's life. They had met quite naturally. Gloria was the daughter of a successful cattleman and Jed the youngest son of a newly rich rancher.

Owen and Edith Taylor, distressed once they realized how serious their only daughter was about him, pleaded with her to slow down, and let these city folk have their ranch fantasy and go back to their office buildings. How would she be supported by a man who had spent the early part of his life riding pavement on his bicycle, and playing cowboy with other boys in a dirt lot? But Gloria didn't see what they saw. All she saw was a strong, supple young man who's blue eyes danced every time they saw her. All she saw was Jed King, a once city boy who had now been ranching for over twelve years and ready to handle it as easily as he guided her through the weaving cattle trails that criss-crossed his parent's land. They were married in a quiet ceremony, both in their late twenties, and five years later had Jessica, their only child. By that time they had been running the ranch for a year. Though it was hard going, and uneasy at times, they called it their own.

Jed was especially good with the horses. When they had first moved to the ranch from town (his father renamed it the Lazy K as a joke, because neighbors gossiped that he had gotten the ranch through sheer laziness), there had been an old man there, weathered, wrinkled and spare of talk. Except when he talked about horses. Jed drank everything he said in. He watched as this crumpled, faded man took horses bucking to turn themselves inside out and calmed them merely with his presence. He watched as these same horses came to look for the man, and would nicker when they saw him approach. He watched as their eyes went from glassy and white-rimmed to soft as the sky after a summer rain. He never thought taming a creature so prone to flight could be as much a work of art as the paintings he saw in the many museums he had visited. Without realizing it, he knew he wanted to be an artist like this old man someday.

So while he raised cattle for money, he had horses for pleasure. That didn't mean that they didn't work, too, but Jed knew that there was something more than just getting them ready to work cattle that he enjoyed. He was after that summer sky look in their eyes, the way they would approach him even in endless acres of pasture. He liked to think that his art was made of manes, tails and soft nickers.

Jed and Gloria would often ride out on their ranch, sometimes taking Jessie, sometimes going out on their own. Jessie would smile to herself as she saw her father reach for her mother, and they would hold hands while riding their horses side by side. This was Jed and Gloria's way of taking a vacation, the only vacation either of them wanted. It stayed that way until Jessie was fifteen, and her mother became too ill to ride. It had happened quickly, her mother fading like a photograph until one day she didn't wake up in the morning. Jessie and her father, already close, grew closer. She stubbornly insisted on doing the same chores that the hired help did—struggling to push a wheelbarrow through mud, straining against bales of hay that weighed more than she did and fixing fence when she was allowed to ride out.

So it wasn't her mother who tracked her down and called and gave her the news of her father's diagnosis and his insistence on ignoring it. It was Mrs. Rodriquez, a middle-aged widow who had come to them after Gloria King had died to help out with keeping the house in order. This feisty, quick-witted woman had grown into part of their family. Jessie had come to rely on her solid figure and her even more solid, wise ways. Mrs. Rodriquez was not a woman to waste much, and words were no exception.

"Jessie, it is time for you to come home now," she had said as soon as Jessie answered the phone. "Your father has a cancer. If you do not stop being foolish, he will be gone and you will regret being mad for so long. Come home, and stay awhile mijita. We have missed you here."

She had packed a suitcase for one week. But by the time she pulled into the ranch's long driveway that led to the barn, she had decided she wasn't going back to Denver. She got out of her car, and stood in the clear night air, the sky dappled with millions of points of light, the dusky smell of sagebrush and the dust that rose from her car's tires. She no longer was angry with her father. In its place there was only regret, and a hope for some time to spend with him. Now ten years away from nineteen, she realized what a foolish mistake she had made, and how much it had cost her. She hoped it wasn't too late, and that she could somehow find the words to tell her father how much she had missed him, and missed being home. She wondered when had she stumbled so far off track, and what it would take to find her way again.

She saw her father the next morning as she was making coffee. She had risen even before Mrs. Rodriquez arrived, the pinks, oranges, and purples of sunrise urging her out of bed.

"Don't make that too strong, Jess. My stomach isn't what it was." Jed, now also a fading photograph, was leaning on the counter, smiling a weary smile at his daughter. She looked at him, his once tanned and leathery face now pale and wrinkled, took a deep breath and smiled back.

"Don't worry, Dad, I can't drink it that strong anymore either. I guess we're both getting older." Her eyes, cautiously meeting his, showed sadness he didn't remember. He shuffled around the counter, hugged her close to him, his daughter, who was once again where she belonged.

"It's good to have you home, Jessie."

She held her body stiffly, even within his frail hug. She knew she should drop the anger she still felt toward him; it was a child's anger. To carry it around while she reacquainted herself with him and the ranch would only make things more difficult. Part of her, the nineteen-year-old that tenaciously clung to the old betrayal, told her that she could let go once he apologized to her. Another part of her, a part that sounded suspiciously like Mrs. Rodriquez, said that twenty-nine years old is old enough to realize that her father had acted in the best interests of the ranch, not looking to hurt her. If he could forgive her ten years of being away, then she could forgive him his loyalty to the ranch. Sometimes being an adult was a pain in the ass, as one of her ex-boyfriends used to say. Right now, she would have agreed with him.

Right now, however, her father was making his way back around the counter, saying over his shoulder that he had to get ready for the day. The sight of his retreating back comforted and angered her, all in the same moment. She wondered if all daughters found their relationship with their fathers so confusing sometimes. Before she could get too caught up in her thoughts, Mrs. Rodriquez came into the kitchen.

"I thought this morning I would make your favorite breakfast. You still like huevos, bacon and pancakes, mija?"

CHAPTER 9

It was the end of the day for Jessie; though it was hours after the horses were untacked, brushed and fed, she continued on her rounds. It had been an especially difficult evening because one of the guests ("stupid dude," a newly-hired-and-subsequently-fired-wrangler had said) had come in from the last ride with a broken arm. While Jessie tried to get a straight story from someone, she took care of the woman, called the medical clinic in town to arrange for them to send the bill to the ranch, soothed the woman's husband and then fired the big-mouthed wrangler.

Though it was a time when she would normally be finished with dinner and thinking about going to bed, she found herself staring out the kitchen window into the darkness, drinking a cup of coffee and thinking about something her father said to her before he died. "Don't ever stay here because you have to, Jessie. I don't want that for you..." she had interrupted him, protesting before he could finish his sentences, which took a long, wheezy time those days. "Listen to me," he insisted. "It isn't any good you being here if you don't call this home. I know why you came back, and I am glad of it. But don't think that you have to stay here for me or your mother or even your grandfather. If you aren't here because you belong, this is going to be a jail cell, not a life."

After days like these, she was tempted to feel caught, trapped by everything that needed her. But then she would remember her time in Denver, idly strolling through worn out and useless memories. After comparing that life to this one, it was easier to chalk her feelings up to needing a hot bath, a hot cup of coffee and a long night in a soft bed.

That was her way of coping for many months after she watched her father die. "He's comfortable," the hospice nurses told her, which looked comatose to Jessie. While he laid gasping for breath and then taking longer and longer to inhale again, she started repeating the phrase in her head, a mantra fueled by her grief and fear. "He's comfortable."

After the doctor had breezed through in the morning to pronounce Jed King dead, he tried to make arrangements for the body to be taken to the nearest funeral home, which was over an hour away. Jessie told him, her arms hugging herself and her blue eyes giving him a look her father would have recognized, that she would make the arrangements, and thank you for coming by. When he tried to convince her otherwise, he found himself being escorted out by the elbow by a woman half his size and was repeating the same words, as if he were a child being corrected. The screen door slammed behind him, and he wandered off the porch, into his car and drove away. Jessie buried her father in a remote corner of the ranch, where they would ride together to watch the wild ones graze in the evening light.

She rinsed out her coffee cup and set it in the sink. Jessie was forty-two now, a long way away from nineteen and glad of it. She had never been afraid to get old. Never contemplated facelifts, facials and personal trainers the way some of her city friends had. She didn't particularly care what other women did to their bodies, but she knew that keeping seventy-plus head of horses, over twenty staff members and endless miles of fence and trails in good repair kept her too busy to contemplate how the years had used her body for a canvas. She would rather rise early in the morning and walk among the horses. It's a sanctuary, her church, home and place of belonging contained within the horses' soft wuffs as they nuzzle her hair, the way their hooves raise small puffs of dust as they mill around her, and she in the center of this equine universe.

Jessie was in good shape, the same size she was when she returned to the Lazy K thirteen years ago. She had a few more wrinkles, mostly around her eyes from being in the sun, and a few more freckles on her arms. She was more confident with people, having had to take over being the boss once her dad had been forced to bed by his illness. Then, she had the comfort of being able to go to him for direction with the staff. Now, she made her decisions by herself, sometimes doubting that she did the right thing. The horses and guests were, by comparison, easier. She was polite to both, listened to what they had to say, and then tried to find a way to get along with them while directing them the way she needed them to go. She had often wondered why it was not this easy with her staff, but she didn't wonder long before she started thinking of Chad, again.

He came to the Lazy K three years before, a cocky thirty something who didn't look or act his age. He claimed to have just gotten off the rodeo circuit. She hired him because she needed help, and it was plain he could ride as well as entertain the guests. Most of her help could do one or the other, but not both very well. Chad was different and he knew it. He had dozens of bronc stories, told with as much flourish as his bright, knee-length, red-topped buckaroo boots. He had all of his original teeth, rare in a bronc rider, not much hardware in his lean body, though he would boast of all the bones he had broken, and an infectious charm with the guests. She never heard him complain, and she found that she had less work to do because Chad had already taken care of whatever chore needed doing.

It took two years before he was having dinner with her, usually because he was the last one at the Lazy K finishing up with the work. He was more subdued then, helping her with dinner, carrying the plates to the sink after they were done eating, offering his compliments on her ranch and all she had done with it.

It wasn't long after that she took him to her bed, ignoring the voice that told her getting involved with an employee was a very bad idea. That voice didn't bother her much, though, because unlike the faceless lovers of her city past, she remembered every moment of their time together. She had only ever really been interested in horses, but being with Chad showed her that there was a lot she had missed. For the first time she found herself daydreaming during work— thinking about their night together, vaguely bothered that he was a member of her staff. And then he would catch her eye, and the only thing she could think about was being alone with him. It didn't matter that they kept their affair a secret from the rest of the staff, she enjoyed having him to herself and enjoyed the privacy of their relationship.

She was so blinded by this new world that she didn't realize when his questions about the ranch started taking a more specific turn. Was the place paid off? How much did they (he was already talking as though they were business partners) bring in every month? How many rides did they usually do in their busy season, and how many horses did she need to sell in her off-season? She answered his questions honestly, never seeing how he calculated her worth in dollars, how he distracted her with his kisses.

Mrs. Rodriquez, however, saw everything, and even some things Jessie didn't. After six months of the affair, she approached Jessie in the kitchen one afternoon when she came in for coffee.

"I know you are fascinated with this boy, mija," she had said unapologetically. "But I don't think he is all he says he is."

Jessie sighed. She knew this was coming. Mrs. Rodriquez had known her longer than anyone else who was on this ranch, and wouldn't let her alone if she thought something wasn't going well.

"I know, I know. But he's fun for right now!" She tried to brush off the seriousness of the conversation with a laugh, but her faithful housekeeper would have none of it.

"He may seem to be funny, and he may even be all he thinks he is," she said knowingly. "But he is not right for you. He walks around by himself sometimes, looking at everything like he is putting a price tag on it. And he looks at you the same way. Maybe it would be good to be careful with him, a little bit?"

Jessie smiled and agreed, hugged this honest woman who wanted to protect her, and went back to work, secretly looking for the cowboy in tall boots. As she did, it occurred to her that the fascination with Chad was very like looking at the bright lights of an oncoming truck: the question was, did she want to get out of the way?

Despite her better judgment, the voice that was getting faint with disuse anyway, and Mrs. Rodriquez's frequent warnings, Jessie asked Chad to stay with her during their off season in the summer. This wasn't something new. She had always kept the best wrangler on during the hot summer months to help with the horses, and other chores that needed doing. But with Chad, she thought it might be a little deeper. He might be someone to keep her company during the days that were so hot all she could do was sweat or sleep. Someone who could rise early with her and get the work done before the hottest part of the day rolled over them. Someone who could work again at night, finishing what needed finishing in the cooler part of the evening.

Another voice, this one connected to her body, said that it would be good to not sleep alone anymore. She didn't listen to that voice, because if she did she would know that Mrs. Rodriquez was right, and that meant that her days would go back to the way things were before him, and she was having too much fun seeing where this new thing with Chad would take her.

The first month, a May that started out being unusually warm and dry, she didn't regret her decision at all. They worked side by side, Chad always a step ahead of her in getting the work done. He worked sometimes in the hottest part of the day—filling the water troughs, repairing the shelters the horses sought out for shade, or even cleaning the bunkhouse he and Jessie agreed he should stay in.

In June it occurred to Jessie that he was working like he owned the place. When she finally asked him why he worked so hard for the same paycheck, he replied that the Lazy K was like a home to him and he guessed he should treat it like it was. At the time, this fell on her ears like the rain that was needed for their pastures. She was so taken in by him that the bunkhouse was soon just a place to store his stuff, and he moved in to her house and made that his own, too.

It was a month before they were to open for guests that fall that Jessie broke it off with Chad. And while he seemed upset, he found her alone a week later and told her that she wouldn't be able to resist him for long, and once she came to her senses, she would see how good it was for him be a part of her life. She was too angry to talk with him, because the incident that had spurred her decision was still raw.

For most people, the trip from the ranch to town would take close to forty-five minutes. Jessie drove it, as she usually did, in thirty. Once in Grant, she stopped to get ten bags of grain, and then she swung over to the market and picked up two steaks and a bottle of wine for dinner. Jessie returned to the ranch earlier than she had planned that evening, singing along to a song about a pony and a boat by Lyle Lovett that was playing on the truck radio. She couldn't find Chad anywhere near the house. From the kitchen window, she saw a bulging cloud of dust that spiraled up in shimmering heat waves. When she got down to the corral, she saw Chad in the middle of a tornado of horses, their manes tangled with sweat and dust and their eyes brimmed white. One of the three-year-olds, a colt out of her favorite Mustang mare, was caught on the end of a rope and almost down because the noose was so tight around his throat. Chad, smiling grimly, was on the other end.

She didn't remember how she got to Chad so quickly, but before she knew it she had shoved him aside, taken hold of the rope and started walking slowly toward the colt, giving him slack as she did. The colt let her approach him, even as he was shaking with his feet splayed apart, sweat and foam running from his body in rivulets to be taken by the dry earth around him. She was quiet, not even murmuring soothing words, until she was close to him and he could turn his glazed eyes to her and smell her. She said his name, and touched him gently on his neck, while loosening the noose even more. After a few minutes, when his trembling had almost stopped and his breathing was less labored, she slipped the loop over his head in one smooth motion and dropped it to the ground. She had raised this colt; she was the first human he saw after he entered the world early one morning. Yet his eyes were still rimmed in white, and he blew hard at her as he sidled away to rejoin the herd.

She didn't look at Chad as she left the corral, leaving his rope in the dirt. She didn't even turn around when he yelled her name. "Jessie!" He shouted as she stormed toward the house. "It was just for fun! I was only..." and then he had to duck because she threw a rock at him, slinging her arm back and letting loose with all the muscle and anger she had. He moved quickly aside, surprise and anger changing his face from the jovial mask he usually wore.

She continued walking, and once in the house went straight upstairs to their bedroom (her bedroom, now) and picked up his fancy dress boots, his jeans, shirts, belt and, bringing them all downstairs, opened the screen door, and flung them onto the porch. By now Chad had reached the house but stopped once he saw her, and for perhaps the first time in his life had the sense to keep his mouth shut.

Out came his toothbrush, landing squarely in the dirt at his feet, his comb, mirror, shaving kit, aftershave, and mouthwash. Next were his CD's, some of the cases cracking as they hit the porch, dirty clothes, his custom black felt cowboy hat, which joined the toothbrush in the dirt, and finally a fancy western saddle that he claimed he won in a poker game. Even though it weighed over half of what Jess did, she managed to heave it down the stairs of the porch, where it landed upside down in the dust before him.

She stood on the porch, breathing hard, glaring at him and visibly trying to control herself. "I can't fire you because I have everyone hired for this next season, and I need you around to do the work. You can stay in the bunkhouse. And from now on *you* can call me Ms. King."

Before he could think to say anything in protest, she had turned, shut the screen door with a smack and left him alone; his fancy felt hat, toothbrush and saddle at his buckaroo-booted feet.

CHAPTER 10

A little bell attached to a spring jingled as Henry went through the front door of the Teamster Café, and it jingled again as the door closed behind him. He hadn't had a decent meal since he left the Rafter Seven, and now with the cash he had gotten from Sam Mitchell he figured he might just go ahead and treat himself to a plate of steak and eggs for his breakfast. He had hoped it might help him feel better about his situation, although he doubted he could feel any worse.

In front of him was a long wooden counter built from stained knotty pine boards that had darkened over the years, and line of stools with red vinyl seats and chrome legs squatting in front of it. Two of the stools on the left end of the counter were occupied by men, one heavyset, one thin, both dressed in well-worn jeans, cowboy boots with spurs strapped to them, dusty shirts and even dustier cowboy hats. They were both locals by the sound of them. They were discussing the weather, which had been hot, and the apple pie they had just finished, which had been good.

The walls of the place were constructed of the same knotty pine boards as the counter, and were also aged to the same smoky light brown hue. All the walls were dotted with numerous framed black-and-white photos of men driving teams of draft horses. A dusty, stuffed black bear hung on the wall to the left, just above three of the photos, looking as though he was attacking an imaginary prey with his mouth opened, teeth bared and front claws exposed. On the wall to the right hung the head and shoulders of a small bull moose with old Christmas lights, the big screw-in ones, wrapped around his antlers. He also wore an old pair of sunglasses and a well used green-and-white baseball cap that read Fairbanks Construction on the front. Henry didn't like it when people did that. He understood killing for meat. He didn't understand killing for sport. As far as he was concerned, it was bad enough to have a dead animal hanging on the wall. It was even worse to take its dignity by hanging crap all over it.

There was a row of four booths along the wall to Henry's right, next to the front windows on that side of the door, and another set of four to his left, also next to the front windows on the other side of the door—all with the same red vinyl seat covers, matching salt and pepper shakers, an upright napkin dispenser, and a bottle each of ketchup and mustard. The tabletops were also of wood, and nearly the same color as the walls and counter. An old window-mounted air conditioner hummed loudly, and two ceiling fans with little chains hanging from them wobbled as they spun overhead. The place smelled of coffee, bacon grease and old leather, and from the kitchen, a radio playing country music could barely be heard.

"Hello there, hon," a slim redheaded waitress in her early forties said as she breezed by him carrying two plates heaped with food. "Sit anywhere you want. Plenty of room at the counter."

Henry looked at the stools with the red seat covers and decided he'd been spending enough time sitting on stools lately, so he opted for the corner booth on the right, one of only two booths in the place that wasn't already occupied by customers. He sat facing the door, a habit his father had gotten him into when he was just a boy. "Better to see trouble coming," his father had told him on more than one occasion. "Then wish you had."

Henry took the plastic-coated menu from between the napkin dispenser and the salt and pepper shakers, and looked at the front. It had a sepia-colored photograph of the Teamster Café building from 1901, although the name on the sign read Roman's Hotel. There was a brief printed history of the café and the building underneath the photo, that included a paragraph about the Donner Party, which had camped only a few hundred feet from where the building now stood just weeks before they were caught in a blizzard up in the Sierras.

"Ready to order there, cowboy?" the redheaded waitress quipped, "Or do you need a little more time?"

Henry was a little surprised that she got to him so soon. How did she sneak up on him? But it didn't matter, he knew what he wanted before he even walked in the door. "Steak and eggs," he said quietly without making eye contact. "Rare...over easy. Coffee—black—hash browns and some wheat toast if you got it."

"We do," the waitress smiled, taking a pencil from behind her ear and jotting everything down on a small green and white pad she had pulled from the pocket on her apron. "Orange juice or anything else to drink?" Henry looked up. It had been years since he'd had orange juice. In fact, he had almost forgotten it existed. He sat for a second, staring into the waitress's face. "Best juice in town," she smiled. "We squeeze it ourselves."

Annie had a saying about orange juice, and he was trying to recall what it was. "Yeah," Henry nodded. "I'd have some orange juice, if it ain't too much trouble."

"No trouble at all," the waitress smiled. "And if you don't like it I'll buy it for you. How 'bout that?" A bell rang back in the kitchen, sounding like one of those they use in hotels to summon a bellboy. "Oops, I've got an order up." She stuck the pencil back behind her ear. "I'll get this right in for you. We'll have you full up in no time." With that, she turned and breezed back toward the kitchen.

"Thank you," Henry said to the back of her head as she walked away. But she was already on to the next thing and didn't hear him. He glanced back down at the front of the menu. What was it that Annie used to say about orange juice?

While he waited for his food, Henry watched as customers who had finished their meals and conversations went up to the counter where the old copper-coated cash register sat. They would pay their bills, chatting with the waitress happily as the register gave a loud ring and the cash drawer pushed outward, exchanging pleasantries with the waitress whose name he heard someone say was Audrey, then walk out with the bell on the spring above the door jingling their departure. When everyone had gone, Audrey brought Henry a cup of coffee and left the pot, smiling but not saying anything, then returned to her work.

Henry spent time taking a little closer look at some of the old photographs hanging on the walls, pictures of hard-working men with hard-working horses. In one of the photos there was a man and a young boy bundled up against the mid winter cold and standing next to a large sled piled high with hay. It reminded Henry of his team back home, Jim and Joe, two big blond Belgians that he and Josh used for feeding in the wintertime. He used a sled much like that one in the picture, too, when there was too much snow to use the pick up truck. The only difference between what Henry fed and what the boys in the photo were feeding was Henry fed small square bales that he and Josh would break open and toss off the sled to the cattle, instead of piling the hay loose on the sled like they did in the picture. The practice of feeding loose hay like that hadn't happened in years, not since automated hay balers came along.

The smiling redheaded waitress brought Henry his breakfast on a large, white oblong plate. The tenderized rump steak hung slightly off the edge on one side, and the over easy eggs sat on top a massive pile of hash browns on the other. Two pieces of wheat toast, already buttered, were sliced diagonally and sat in between the steak and the pile of hash browns. It was more food than Henry had seen all at once in years and as she sat the plate down in front of him, he couldn't help but stare at it.

"Everything okay?" She asked, setting a glass of fresh squeezed orange juice next to the plate.

"Yeah," Henry said without looking up. "It's a lot of food."

"Don't want anyone to go away hungry," she smiled. "Any hot sauce or anything?"

"No," Henry looked up and smiled slightly. "I believe this will do."

"I'll check back in on you a little bit," she said already turning. "I'm interested to see how you make out."

Henry's eyes were drawn to the glass of orange juice. He reached over, picked it up and held it up in front of his face, staring into the glass and rotating it ever so slightly. For a very long time his life had been filled with dull colors—the pale greens of sage, the browns of leather, tree bark, Hereford cattle and withered grass, the grays of stone, rocks, gravel and pavement. The color emanating from the glass was none of those. It was bright and vibrant and full of life. He wasn't used to it.

He took a slow sip from the glass, and found he wasn't used to that, either. The alcohol he drank over the years seemed to have singed his taste buds to the point where everything he either ate or drank was just as dull as the colors he surrounded himself with. As the juice flowed over his tongue and down his throat his mouth suddenly came back to life, and it brought a genuine smile to his face. "You can always tell how good a restaurant is," he finally remembered

Annie saying. "By how good their orange juice tastes." That made him smile, too.

Henry began eating his breakfast in the same fashion he'd eaten every other sit down meal over the last several years. He leaned his head and upper body far over the table, wrapped his left arm around his plate and shoveled food in his mouth as quickly as he could with the fork in his right hand. It was a habit some cowboys would get into from time to time while having a meal with others of their like. It wasn't uncommon in some camps to turn to talk with the cowboy next to you, only to turn back to your plate and find food missing. That had never happened to Henry, and he wasn't about to let it. His good meals were far and few between and he wasn't going to let any of it go to someone else.

He had quickly shoveled several mouthfuls in this fashion when he heard Audrey's voice. "Its just me and you in here, cowboy," she called from across the room. "And I already ate." He stopped shoveling and slowly looked up to see Audrey standing by the cash register, wiping out the inside of a drinking glass with a white towel and giving him a wry smile. "Honest, I won't take it."

Feeling more than a little silly, and looking a lot like a ground squirrel with its mouth full of pine nuts, Henry came to a little more upright sitting position and very slowly began to chew his food. Audrey nodded her approval, placed the glass she was wiping under the counter, took out another and began cleaning it. "There," she smiled. "Isn't that a little better?"

For the first time in a long time, Henry slowly ate the rest of his meal. Between bites he would look out the window and watch cars go by, most probably heading to I-80, which was only a half-mile or so to the north. From there the drivers could be heading to Reno, Sacramento or San Francisco to the west, or Wendover, Salt Lake City, or Cheyenne to the east. Henry had even heard once that if a man went far enough east on I-80, he could end up clear over in New York if he wasn't careful. That wasn't something Henry was likely to do anytime soon.

Over the past several years, Henry realized, he had been eating simply because he needed to stay alive. Enjoying the meal never entered into it, not that he ate many meals that were all that enjoyable in the first place. Once in a while he had run across a camp cook that took pride in what he did. But for the most part, the cooks were old, broke down cowboys who couldn't ride fence anymore. In order to maintain their way of life they became the cook for whatever outfit they worked for at the time, and usually with no more training in culinary arts than the horses they used to ride. So in a sense, getting through a meal as quickly as possible was actually something a lot of hands did almost in self-defense.

But Audrey had been right. There was no need to hurry here. Henry took his time and in doing so found that not only could he taste the food he was eating, but each item on the plate had a separate flavor and texture, and all of it was good—very good.

"I don't think I've seen you in here before." Audrey walked up just as Henry was finishing the last bite of his steak. "New in town?"

"Just passing through," Henry said as he chewed the rest of his steak, wiped his mouth with a napkin, and then put the napkin on his plate. "Actually, maybe you could help me. I'm looking for work. You don't know of any outfits looking for help around here, do you?"

"Not around here," she said picking up the plate. "The drought really hurt a lot of the ranches in the area. Then that storm hit and nearly wiped out all the little guys." She took the plate over to the counter, and placed it in a plastic tub already full of dirty dishes sitting on a chrome cart. "Sorry."

"That's all right," Henry said as he took the last sip from his coffee cup and set it down softly on the table. He was used to hearing there wasn't any work. All it meant to him was he'd have to go a little farther down the road before the day was over. "What do I owe you?"

Audrey pulled the green and white pad from her apron and the pencil from behind her ear. "Steak and eggs, one coffee and one orange juice," she said to herself as she wrote down the prices next to each item and added them up. "Looks like the damages are six dollars even."

"Fair enough," Henry said getting up from the table and taking the fresh wad of one hundred dollar bills from his shirt pocket. He pealed one off as he got to the cash register and handed it to her. "I'm sorry," he said sincerely. "I don't have anything smaller."

"Hey," Audrey gently took the bill from his hand. "Money's money, right? It all spends the same in my book."

"That it does," Henry replied.

Audrey pushed the wide, round typewriter-like buttons on the old cash register, and a yellowed tab with the number six with a decimal point after it popped up in the window at the top of the antiquated machine. At the same time the register dinged loudly and the money drawer popped open. Audrey pulled four twenties, a ten and four ones from the drawer and counted them back to Henry as she placed them in the palm of his calloused, open hand. "Six," she pointed at the bill still attached to her pad. "Seven, eight, nine, ten, ten is twenty, and forty, sixty, eighty, one hundred." She slipped the hundred-dollar bill Henry had given her in the slot under the rest of the twenties, and closed the drawer with her hand.

Henry took the four one-dollar bills from his change and started to hand them to Audrey but stopped himself mid way. He drew them back, then took one of the twenties and handed it to her instead. "What's this for?" she accepted money from people all day long, and when Henry handed her the twenty, she took the bill almost out of instinct.

"It's a tip," Henry nodded. "I know what it's like to have to work hard for a dollar."

"I can't take this," she protested.

"You already have," Henry smiled. "Thank you for the breakfast." He tipped his hat ever so slightly, nodded his head and turned for the door, jamming the wad of bills she just handed him deep down in his jeans pocket.

"Wait," she said, opening a drawer under the counter. "There's something here, somewhere." She dug around in the drawer, shuffling small pieces of paper around, pulling one out and looking at it, then putting it back and shuffling again. She did that several times before she found what she was looking for. "Here it is," she pronounced. She came out from behind the counter and handed Henry one of the small pieces of paper. "These folks were in here a while back. I think they were delivering some horses to the Wiley place or something. Anyway, they said they were looking for help. They were from down south somewhere. Grant, I think." She glanced at the piece of paper she had just given Henry. "Yup," she pointed at the bottom of the paper. "Grant. I don't think it was a cattle outfit, though. Sounded like they just ran horses."

"Horses?" Henry said almost under his breath. "Why not? I sure ain't had much luck with cattle lately."

"Well, there you go then." Audrey smiled, putting her hands on her hips. "I hope it's of some help."

"It is," Henry smiled. "Thank you."

"You're welcome," Audrey held up the twenty-dollar bill Henry had given her. "Thank *you*."

Henry nodded, took one last look around at the photos on the wall, the bear and moose, and the wooden counter with the stools squatting in front of it, tipped his hat again, and left the Teamster Café with the little bell on a spring above the door ringing goodbye.

CHAPTER 11

It was a dull, incessant pounding that started at the base of his skull near his spine then rolled forward until it crashed mercilessly into his forehead, causing a devastating pain to radiate through his eyes, cheekbones and sinuses. As he struggled to roll himself over in the bed of his old pick up truck and push himself up on his hands and knees, he couldn't be sure if it was the pounding in his head that woke him or if it was the nausea. Either way, he had made it through another night, albeit unceremoniously by the way he was feeling.

He rolled over and slid his backside underneath himself to get to a sitting position. He shielded his bloodshot eyes from the early morning sun with his beat up cowboy hat that he had been using as a pillow, and did what he had always tried to do on mornings like this. He tried to brush the alcohol shroud aside and put together the events of the previous day—and night. It was harder to concentrate than normal due to the fact that for the first time in a long time, he thought he might actually throw up.

He vaguely remembered eating a big meal the day before. He put his forehead in the palms of hands and closed his eyes. *It was at a steakhouse*, he thought. *No, that isn't right.* He slowly picked his head up but didn't open his eyes. It was too painful to do so just yet. *It wasn't a steakhouse; it was a steak—steak and eggs...at a café. There was a waitress.*

He put his head back in his hands. The nausea caused his body to shudder. *It wasn't one big meal,* he remembered, *it was two—one in the morning and one in the afternoon.* He raised his head and with one eye squinted against the daylight, the other eye closed, he scanned his surroundings. Through his one blurry eye he could make out that his truck was parked at the very back of a large gravel parking lot. About two hundred feet to his right and up by the road was the Downtowner Restaurant. Two hundred feet to his left, and also up by the road was Torchy's Bar.

He put his head back down. *I had had two big meals yesterday, and I drank all night. How could I afford that?* He remembered only having thirteen dollars and some change when he got to town. But why did he come to Elko in the first place? Henry rubbed his eyes with the heels of his hands. It was difficult to focus. He came there to see someone...

A breeze came up and blew gently past Henry. As it subsided, Henry could smell the strong odor of stale whiskey and cigarette smoke on his clothes. It had been there the whole time, but because he had been immersed in it for over twelve hours, he simply hadn't detected it before. The breeze had blown the odor away from his body, bending it like tall grass on a windy day. And just like when the wind stops and the grass stands up straight again, so did the odor rise back up when the breeze stopped. Henry gagged.

He forced himself to focus. *I came to Elko to see someone... about a job. I came to see...Sam Mitchell.* Henry raised his head again. That was where the money for the meals had come from. *Sam had given me some money and I put it in...* Henry reached his hand up to his shirt pocket. No money. He checked his other shirt pocket...no money there either. *Six months pay,* he thought. As soon as he could, Henry climbed out of the bed of the pickup and staggered the two hundred feet to the front door of the bar, which, according to the sign on the door that Henry had trouble reading, wouldn't open for another six hours. He scoured the area around the door, and then retraced his steps all the way back to his truck. He nearly tore the cab, his satchel, rope bag and bedroll apart, but the money was nowhere to be found. What Henry didn't know was the money he had received from Sam Mitchell for six months worth of work he hadn't yet done, had already been found.

Henry had stumbled out the front door of the bar just after closing time with the wad of one hundred dollar bills in his hand, minus sixty dollars which he had spent at the bar buying drinks for himself, and nearly anyone that sat next to him, and ten dollars he'd left as a tip for the bartender. Once outside, Henry put the bills in his shirt pocket, or so he thought. He had missed his pocket all together, and dropped all fourteen hundred and thirty dollars on the sidewalk and simply walked away from it. Three minutes later, Bud Stevens, one of the patrons Henry had been buying drinks for during the night, stepped outside and stopped to light a cigarette. He thought he'd hit the lottery when he looked down and found the wad of bills lying there on the ground, and he wasted no time at all in scooping them up and silently claiming them for his own.

Henry checked his shirt pockets again, as if the somehow the money would have miraculously reappeared since the last time he checked. It hadn't. He let out a deep sigh, and in an act of hopelessness, jammed his fingers into his jeans pockets. It was then Henry found the change he had gotten from Audrey, the waitress at the Teamster Café. At the time he had simply crumpled the money up and pushed the wad down in his right front pocket. Now, Henry gently pinched the bills between his fingers and painstakingly pulled them from their hiding place as if he was doing some kind of surgery.

Henry slowly peeled the bills apart and counted them. Seventy-four dollars. It wasn't fifteen hundred, but it was something. As he coaxed the bills from one another, a small, white piece of paper fell from the wad and floated to the ground. After he had finished counting, Henry bent over, causing his head to feel as though it swelled three times its size, and picked the paper up. It had writing on it, but the writing was so small he had to hold the paper at an arm's length to see what it said. In smeared pencil, it said simply, Jessie King, Lazy K Ranch, Route 17, Grant, Nevada. There was also a phone number, but because of the way the paper had been folded in his pocket, three of the numbers were unreadable. In bigger, more legible letters at the bottom, it read: Reliable Wranglers Wanted.

Henry tried to rub the pain from behind his left eye away with the heel of his hand, and then glanced back at the paper. "Reliable," he grimaced. "Why does it always have to come to that?"

CHAPTER 12

The day he had picked up the scent of the domestic band of horses by the river, the gray colt had unwittingly crossed over onto Tom Essex's forty-seven-thousand-acre ranch. Part of the hundreds of miles of fence line that bordered the Essex property crossed the river near where the colt had been resting. But three days into the massive rainstorm that covered the west, the river, swollen by its many tributaries dumping thousands of gallons of water into it, flooded. The flash flood easily removed a quarter mile section of the fence on either side of the river, and washed it miles downstream. The barbed wire fencing snapped as easily as a child breaks a twig and what wire didn't wash away coiled back on itself like a spring. The metal T-posts that held the wire disappeared altogether, ultimately leaving a huge gap in the boundary fence, and allowing the colt to walk onto the property, never knowing a fence was ever there.

The owner of that fence, Tom Essex, wasn't born into ranching, nor did he have any kind of ranching background. In fact, it seemed that Essex had grown up a million miles from the central Nevada ranch he now owned. Tom had been born the second of three sons to the wealthiest and high-powered attorneys in Chicago. And while Tom wasn't born a cowboy, he had been fascinated with the cowboy way of life ever since his father dropped him off at the Bijou movie theater in downtown Chicago one rainy Saturday afternoon in the summer of 1951.

There was a double feature on the bill that day, a B-Western titled *Storm Over Wyoming*, starring Tim Holt, and another movie with a dog in it, of which he could never remember the name. Six-year-old Tom sat with his older brother Jack and Jack's friend Tony in the back row of the theater, eating popcorn and staring at the enormous black-and-white screen that flickered in front of them. The plot had been a little hard for his six-year-old mind to follow, but it didn't matter. The larger-than-life cowboys on fast horses, and endless expanses of wilderness enveloped him like a huge black-and-white glove that he slipped into as easily as he slipped on his Keds that morning.

From that point forward, he was hooked. For the next five years, if a Western was on the Saturday bill at the Bijou, Tom was there. Sometimes Jack would go with him, other times he wouldn't. Tom actually liked it more when Jack didn't go because then he could sit as close to the screen as he liked—Jack always wanted to sit in the back row, too far away from the action, as far as Tom was concerned.

In 1957 the Essex family got their first TV set. It was a consol made by Admiral that not only came with a remote control, but also contained a radio and phonograph. It was massive, and squatted in the family room where the old RCA Victor radio used to be. The picture tube was in the right side of the consol; speaker on the left and it seemed as big as the Cadillac his father drove.

It didn't matter to Tom, though, because now instead of having to go all the way downtown on Saturdays to watch his favorite cowboy stars riding in and out of danger, the cowboys came right to him in his living room through the screen of the colossal Admiral TV. To his parents' consternation, Tom would sit cross-legged on the floor, toy six guns strapped to his sides, watching one Western after another on Saturday mornings. Roy Rogers, Gene Autry, Hop Along Cassidy, The Lone Ranger, and even Sky King, which was a show about cowboys that flew around in airplanes. By the time he was in his early teens Tom was so enthralled by the TV and movie cowboy he had taken much of his allowance and invested it in a sizable collection of TV and movie memorabilia, such as the old posters for movies like *Rollin' Plains, Phantom Rider, The Red Rider, The Crimson Trail,* and of course, *Storm over Wyoming.*

He didn't grow out of his love of the cowboy way of life and interest in the West. Even when he went to college at Princeton, and later made his fortune in commodities trading, his draw to all things western continued to grow. He eventually began collecting western art by Remington, Russell, and Bierstadt, and old firearms made by Winchester, Colt, and Schofield. He also collected antique chaps, cuffs, spurs, stagecoach driver's coats, boots and hats, shirts, trousers and even buttons off of period garments. He collected tack such as stirrups, bridles, saddlebags and bits. He collected old branding irons and cooking utensils. But the most prized possessions in his collection were always his saddles. Over sixty of them all together by the finest saddle makers of the era—Gallatin, Meanea and Williamson were just a few of the names stamped or carved into the old and worn leather of the saddles he owned.

Even though his collection of western artifacts was of museum quality and one of the finest private collections in the country, the one item he wanted the most was the one he couldn't ever seem to find. It was a saddle built by an almost mythical maker down in Texas by the name of Jingles Wexler. From what he could find out through his years of research, Jingles was a cowboy in West Texas who built very high quality working saddles for himself and just a few of his close friends between the years 1876 and 1881. The closest Tom had ever gotten to one of Jingles' saddles, however, was a faded sepia photograph he had from the early 1900's of a young cowboy sitting in one. There was no name on the photo, and from the looks of the landscape it could have been taken nearly anywhere in the western U.S., so trying to trace the photo had proven to be impossible. Still, for all his looking and all his research, it unfortunately appeared as though none of these saddles existed anymore.

By the time Tom was in his mid forties, he had made enough money in his commodities business to take his retirement early and ultimately purchase the forty seven thousand acre ranch he now lived on with Terri, his wife of nearly thirty years. Tom and Terri were very lucky in that, not really knowing a thing about how to run a real working cattle ranch, he had a acquired an excellent ranch foreman by the name of Tug Caldwell who came with the place when Tom bought it, having been the foreman for the previous owners, Carl and Edna Johansson. Along with Tug came a group of ten hard-working and dedicated ranch hands and together they all took Tom and Terri under their wings and taught them about ranching from the ground up, a process they were both still working on years later. The Essex's renamed the place the Diamond Bar T, and it had been called that ever since.

It had been Tug Caldwell that sent a couple of the ranch hands, Ben Stuart and Cat Jones, out to repair the hole in the fence down by the river. He had not been out to inspect the fence but knew by years of experience that anytime a big rain fell, that stretch would go down. It was important to keep the ranch fences in good repair because Nevada, like many western states, practiced open range grazing. This meant that a rancher didn't build fences so much to keep their livestock in as much as they were keeping someone else's out. And while forty-seven thousand acres may sound like a lot of ground, when one considers that in that part of Nevada it took nearly one hundred fifty acres to feed one cow/calf pair for a year, and the Diamond Bar T had just over four hundred pairs, along with thirty good saddle horses, not to mention that one thousand acres of the land was irrigated for hay and not for grazing, suddenly forty-seven thousand acres didn't leave much room for any extra livestock.

Tug had also mentioned to the two hands to keep an eye out for the older saddle horses he had turned out that spring. There had been four mares and six geldings, all in their mid teens that were still good using horses but too old for steady, day in and day out ranch work, in Tug's eyes. Had it been up to him, he would have just hauled them all off to the sale barn the previous fall, like he used to do with the old horses when the Johansson's owned the place. But Tom and Terri both had a soft spot for those old horses, most of which were born and raised on the place. And not quite understanding the tradition, as well as the practicality of ridding the ranch of old livestock, they wouldn't let Tug haul them off. Rather he had been ordered by Tom to literally turn them out to pasture.

Cat and Ben didn't come across the herd until they were nearly back to the ranch headquarters almost a week after they had finished repairing the river fence. They had taken a much more direct route back to the ranch, and had come out of the pine forest and into a large open grassy field surrounded by barbed wire fence with the open gate in one corner just four days after the horses had. The field was a welcome sight to the two men after being out on the range for nearly two and a half weeks. It meant they were only two hours from home, good grub and a soft bed. The men, riding their favorite horses, led three pack mules—one loaded with their camping gear, one with food and medical supplies and the third with fencing materials and tools—through the open gate. As had been instructed before the two men left,

Cat got off his horse and closed the wire gate behind them before watering their animals at the tank near the windmill and continuing for home. If some of the neighbor's livestock or any of the wild horses that surrounded the ranch did wander through the opening by the river, Tug didn't want them on some of his best pasture, which is what the fenced in area was. He wanted that two-mile square piece of irrigated ground left for an emergency, mostly in case he had to bring the pairs in during the winter due to exceptionally bad weather. Those times were thankfully rare, and Tug knew it. But he also knew from experience that it was better to be safe than sorry.

Over the last three days, the gray colt had watched the members of the domestic band disappear one by one over a little rise to the north, like watching ships disappear over the curvature of the earth when going out to sea. Even though the herd had wandered out of sight, the gray colt still had not moved very far from the water tank and the open gate. After initially going through the gate, for three days and three nights the colt stayed. He didn't like the look or the smell of the place. The fence, water tank and windmill were one thing, but there were too many odd sounds and too many strange odors hanging in the air for him to feel comfortable. There was the faint odor of food cooking, of diesel and gasoline fumes, grease, oil, leather, cattle and more worrisome than any of the rest, the smell of humans. When the wind was right, he thought he could actually hear the humans talking, and he could hear vehicles driving down Highway 318, just a mile and a half over the little wooded ridge to the east. All of this was not only new to the colt, but it made him even more uneasy than he had even been around the little herd of horses he'd taken up with, and he had been *plenty* uneasy around them.

Instinct had told him to be wary of this place. Not to get too far from the opening in the fence he had come through, as it appeared to be his only way back from where he had come. Instinct also told him to not get too far from the water, and to be cautious about the sounds and smells he was experiencing. Fifty million years of evolution was alerting him to stay with the herd because there was safety in numbers.

Before the stallion attacked him up on the mesa, the gray colt was starting to grow into himself. He was brave, confident and outgoing and had started to learn the skills he would need to be responsible for a herd of his own some day. But since the attack and the subsequent injuries, all that had changed. Since then the colt had become leery, cautious and guarded. Much of it was no doubt due to his new life and surroundings. But much of it was also due to the fact that he now understood he wasn't invincible. All living creatures know on one level or another that they will die, but because of what had happened to him, because of what he had experienced, the colt *understood* it, and that was different. Ultimately it would be for that reason that, after three days and nights of being by himself near the water tank, the colt chose to go find the herd. Three and a half hours before Ben and Cat brought their pack string out of the pine forest and through the open gate, the gray colt took one last drink then limped away from the tank and toward the little rise to the north.

Having passed over the rise an hour later, the colt stopped dead in his tracks, raised his head, pricked his ears and let out a loud warning snort. Off in the distance beyond the herd that was spread out and gazing quietly some two hundred yards from where he stood, a number of large buildings stood—something the colt had never seen before. To the east, the tree-covered hill had casually dropped away exposing Nevada State Highway 318, which was now less than a mile away. On the highway an occasional car, pickup or semi zipped past.

The colt let out another loud snort. The horses of the herd raised their heads, and with pricked ears turned toward him. One by one they began trotting to the gray, just as they had the first time they saw·him. They nickered and called to him, but this time, instead of approaching him as a stranger, they approached him as one of their own. Upon reaching him they gathered around more trying to be a source of comfort to him rather than with the suspicious nature in which they had approached him the first time they met.

The herd swarmed around the colt, nickering quietly, sniffing at his flanks and nostrils, then slowly dispersing, but staying nearby. The herd went back to grazing, as if to say there is nothing to be afraid of here. The colt, not convinced, watched the buildings and the road cautiously for a good long while before he too, finally felt confident enough to try to graze. He dropped his head, took a few mouthfuls of grass, then raised his head and snorted at the buildings. He would take another mouthful of grass, and then snort at the vehicles on the road. Over time his worry, and so the snorting, subsided and he relaxed enough to graze quietly for several minutes at a time before feeling like he had to check the status of the buildings and the road. After about an hour, the colt had finally relaxed enough to simply drop his head and graze quietly in amongst the others. The quietness would last only a few minutes before, from over the little rise to the south, back toward the water tank and windmill there came two riders on horses towing three pack mules.

No sooner had the heads of the pack string peaked over the rise, than all of the horses came to attention and looked their way. The colt, immediately alarmed by the string's presence, snorted loudly, then turned away from them and tried to run. He went only a short distance before realizing he was running straight for the buildings. He turned to the east, but then was heading for the road; he turned west but within a few yards came up on the west fence line. The fence was only about four and a half feet tall, a height he could have easily jumped had he been healthy, but as he came up on the fence, something told him he wouldn't make it if he tried. He didn't have enough strength in his hindquarters to get him over the fence, and even if he did, he didn't have enough strength in his shoulder to allow him to land without hurting himself more than he already was. The colt stopped at the fence, turned and snorted at the pack string, which by now was coming up on the herd.

"That ain't one of ours," Ben said matter-of-factly pointing at the colt.

"Mustang," Cat said. "Had a rough time of it, by the looks of him."

The horses of the herd curiously gathered around the pack string and then began following as they passed by.

"Guess we'd better gather him up," Ben handed the two mules he was leading to Cat. "See what the boss wants to do with him." He quietly loped his horse off toward the colt. The colt, in a panic, turned toward the fence and ran into it, producing a sizable gash in his chest that immediately started to bleed. He then turned away from Ben and ran toward the buildings, then back toward the herd, then toward the road and back toward the herd. Ben loped easily behind the colt, trying not to scare him any more than he already was, rather trying to gently move him in the direction he wanted him to go. "Keep 'em heading toward home," he called to Cat, who, along with his pack string had turned the herd and was calmly driving them toward the ranch buildings. The colt was beside himself with worry and fear and couldn't find a way to turn. Everywhere he looked there was potential danger, and possibly death. He thought about making a run back toward the open gate, but instinctively knew the man on the horse would easily overtake him. He just didn't have enough left in him to make it. Finally, in an act of desperation and with the pain and weakness in his shoulder and hips getting the best of him, he was forced, almost out of natural intuition, to turn and fall in behind the herd. It was the one thing centuries of evolution told him would be safe. The colt slowed from a panicked gallop to a canter, to a trot and finally to a limping walk. Ben and his horse followed suit, also dropping down to a walk, and remained a comfortable distance behind the colt.

From inside the old truck heading slowly south on Highway 318, Henry McBride looked out across the open field at the herd of horses being driven by a man on horseback leading a pack string of three mules. Some fifty yards behind the herd was a solitary gray colt, limping heavily on his right front and being quietly followed by another man on horse. It was clear to Henry the horses in the main body were well bred Quarter Horses by their refined heads, well muscled bodies, slick coats and easy way of traveling. It was equally easy for Henry to see the limping colt bringing up the rear was a wild horse, more than likely of Spanish breeding with his heavy legs, rough coat, long mane and tail and roman nose, even though it was more refined than most of the mustangs he'd seen. *Probably got hooked up with that herd of Quarter Horses somehow.* Henry thought. *Ain't gonna be a wild horse no more.* "Poor bastard," he said under his breath, as he put his attention back on the road and took a small pull from a bottle wrapped in a brown paper sack.

CHAPTER 13

It was the breeze blowing gently through the slightly open window next to her bed that woke her, not the alarm clock on the nightstand. But then, waking before the alarm was nothing new for Jessie. Every night before going to bed she'd set the time she'd want to get up, push the button on the clock that turned on the buzzer, and then the next morning she'd get up forty-five minutes before it was set to sound, and turn it off. Unlike her time in the city where she needed an alarm next to her bed to wake her, and another set across the room to make sure she actually got out of bed, here Jessie could never stay sleeping once the first rays of light started peeking in through her bedroom curtains. Here she wanted to get up and get involved in the day, to be part of it, and let it be part of her.

On this morning, the breeze carried with it a hint of rain. Not rain to come, but rain that had already fallen. Somewhere off in the desert there had been a downpour during the night and its smell had gotten caught on the current that drifted across the parched region like a wave. This wave traveled outward in every direction from its source until quietly, part of it passed over her ranch and a small portion slipped through the open window into Jessie's bedroom. The air it brought with it was cool, certainly cooler then that in her room, and as it brushed across her bare arms, shoulders and face, Jessie unconsciously drew the blankets over herself and smiled. She breathed the freshness of the scent in deeply before stretching, yawning and opening her eyes. It was going to be a good day.

Seventy-five miles to the north, Henry was waking up on the floor of a cheap motel room he rented for six dollars and fifty cents the night before. He hadn't planned on spending the money on a room, but after having a meager supper and then bedding down next to his fire out in the desert, it had begun to rain. Lightly at first, then heavier and heavier until the raindrops were the size of golf balls. He had climbed into the cab of his pickup to try and sleep there, but it was raining so hard he couldn't even do that. He had barely gotten himself and the old truck out of the desert before getting stuck, and stopped at the first place he could find which was a run down, fleabitten excuse for a public inn on the side of the road called the Tall Pines Motel.

The Tall Pines had been closed down by the Nevada Health Department just two months earlier because of a rodent and insect infestation, but that didn't seem a good enough reason for the owner to actually want to keep it closed. It was that owner who had met Henry when he rang the bell the night before, dressed in a dirty T-shirt, boxers and wrapped in what was quite possibly the oldest bathrobe Henry had ever seen.

"What?" the man had grunted upon answering the door.

"Got a room for the night?" Henry asked, rain dripping off his hat.

"Yeah," was his answer. "$6.50 a room."

Henry pulled a small wad of bills out of his jeans pockets and counted what he had. Not including the coins he had also pulled out, there was a total of seventeen dollars out of the seventy-four he'd gotten from Audrey as change from his breakfast at the Teamster Café. Thunder rolled ominously out of the darkness behind him. Henry looked up. "Got anything any cheaper?"

"Cheaper?" the man in the robe scoffed. "Jesus, mister! You want cheaper, go live with your mother." He was about to close the door, when Henry stopped him.

"Okay," Henry shouted over another boisterous clap of thunder. "I'll take it."

"Fine," The man in the robe jutted his hand out, apparently for Henry to place the money in. "Running water's extra."

Henry passed on the running water, and as it turned out, he might as well have passed on the bed as well. In order for him to sleep in it he would have had to share it with a mouse that not only had built a nest there, but also had apparently recently given birth.

Even so, Henry was able to get some rest by sleeping on the floor. That morning, less hung over than he'd been in a while since he'd run out of whiskey when he was still out in the desert, he climbed out of his bedroll. He went to his satchel and pulled out a clean shirt and jeans. He had found a coin laundry two days before and had washed everything he had for a dollar in change. He didn't spend money on soap, nor on drying the clothes, but rather he secured the wet shirts and jeans to the tailgate of his pickup and drove through the desert until they were dry.

Henry was feeling more and more like he was at a crossroads. He had known for quite some time the way he was living his life wasn't working for him, not that it ever had, but since the night he pulled the gate down—the night he'd heard Annie's voice cheerfully telling him it was "time to change"—it had been on his mind a lot. He now knew he *wanted* to change. But before he could, he'd need a job. Any job, doing anything. He had to prove not only to himself, but also to an employer that he was worthwhile. He understood he needed to be responsible again, but more than that, he needed to be reliable. It was the one word on the little piece of paper with the information for the Lazy K ranch that stuck with him. It was also the one that worried him the most. The way he looked at it, the last time people he cared about relied on him, he drove them over a cliff and killed them. Somewhere in the back of his mind, subconsciously perhaps, he had decided being reliable wasn't all it was cracked up to be. He wasn't sure if he could do it. Maybe it was too late for him. But still, he decided it was time to try.

This job at the Lazy K, a horse ranch instead of a cattle ranch, might just be the catalyst he'd need to turn things around. But first, he'd need to land the job. He was going to make an honest effort, or so he told himself, to do what he could to make a good first impression. That meant clean clothes, clean-shaven, and not smelling like he'd just crawled out of a whiskey bottle. So far, so good.

Staring up at the gate of the Lazy K later that morning, however, Henry was thinking life was playing some kind of cruel trick on him. That was when he found out the Lazy K wasn't just a horse ranch, as he had been led to believe, or perhaps as he had led himself to believe. The sign above the driveway he was staring at read: *Lazy K Guest Ranch, Established 1979. Welcome.*

In the entire world there may not have been any job more demeaning for a real working cowboy than to end up "packing dudes" on a guest ranch. In fact, in Henry's book, packing dudes was even worse than being a sheepherder, which he had already considered doing out of sheer desperation, but then came to his senses at the last minute. Had Henry not made what now looked like a very poor decision back in town just an hour or so before, he would have turned his truck around right then and there and drove off. But the decision to buy a quart of whiskey instead of a couple gallons of gas for his truck sealed his fate. Henry looked at the gas gauge on the truck, which read E, then back up at the sign, then back at the gauge. He reached down and tapped the gauge to see if it would move, but it didn't. With so little gas it was clear he had gone as far as he was going to go, and the only way back to town now would be to walk or hitchhike, and neither prospect seemed terribly appealing to him.

Henry sat for a very long time before finally slipping the old truck in gear and driving through the gate. He hated the prospect of getting this job. But he hated the prospect of not getting it even more. As much as he didn't want to work on a dude ranch, he also understood he was just about out of options, and all the way up the driveway he was trying to convince himself that working there might not be that bad.

After a half mile Henry came to a large open area surrounded by the ranch's main set of buildings. To the right was a dining room and next to it appeared to be an office. To the left was a small gift shop and set back away from the main buildings and down a little hill was a bunkhouse. Not far from it were a set of square and round corrals, some with horses in them, some without, and nearby those was an open-sided barn full of hay, a large tack room and the mounting area for dudes to get on the horses. Set off from the corrals and barn and up on a little hill were the cabins that housed the dudes, a small dormitory for staff, and just past those was a modest two story house that appeared to have been built in the early nineteen hundreds. It was in very good repair, and looked as if someone had been looking after it. It had two well-used hitch rails standing nearby, one in front near the porch and one on the east side. The owner's place, Henry concluded.

He pulled his truck to a stop in an open area used for parking near the dining room.

"Jesus," he said, shaking his head. "A dude ranch."

Henry sat for quite a while, looking at folks coming and going, some with kids, some without, and not quite being able to muster the gumption to get out of his truck. He looked again at the gas gauge.

"Can I help you?" a friendly voice came through his open window.

Henry, a little surprised, looked up to see a young, clean-cut college kid, dressed in wrangler jeans, a long sleeve heavy cotton shirt and well worn felt cowboy hat smiling in on him. "What?" He said to the smiling face.

"Can I help you?" the kid repeated, still smiling.

"Um," Henry was still trying to figure a way out of his predicament, but with nothing coming to mind… "You need any help around here?"

"Help? I don't know for sure. I guess you'd need to talk with Jessie about that."

"Yeah," Henry pulled a small piece of paper out of his pocket, unfolded it and read the name from it. "Jessie. I reckon that's who I need to see."

"Hold on," the kid said, stepping out in front of Henry's truck and calling to another college age kid dressed almost exactly like he was who was walking toward the dining room. "Hey Jake, you seen Jessie anywhere?"

"Out back, working on the corral," Jake yelled without stopping or looking toward the truck.

The kid came back to the window. "Just follow that path there, around back, past the bunkhouse. Ask for Jessie."

"Much obliged."

The kid nodded, then turned and walked toward the dining room himself. "Good luck," he called without looking back.

Henry looked down at the gas gauge, tapped it one last time to see if it would move, then finally shut the truck off when it didn't. He sat for several seconds shaking his head in disbelief that he was actually going to go through with it, forced the door open, and started down the little path that led past the bunkhouse and toward the corrals. He hadn't gone far toward the corrals when he saw a small woman, dark from the sun wearing a large, weathered cowboy hat made from palm.

She was pushing a wheelbarrow full of manure; sweat dripping off the end of her nose and strands of hair that had escaped her long ponytail were sticking to the side of her face. From a distance, Henry thought she was just a small man, but on getting closer he realized his mistake and briefly removed his hat.

"Excuse me, ma'am," he nodded, as she pushed past. "I'm looking for a fellow named Jessie."

Jessie looked up, but didn't stop. "I'm Jessie. What can I do for you?"

From the first time Henry saw Jessie's name on the crumpled little paper way back in the café, he had just assumed the name belonged to a man. Now, not only had he felt as though he'd just made a fool of himself, he was about make a bigger fool of himself by asking her for a job. He didn't know if he could go through with it and seriously considered simply turning and walking away. In fact, he was just about to do that very thing when she interrupted his train of thought by asking, "Looking for someone a little more masculine, Mr...." Jessie called as she pushed the wheelbarrow toward a ramp that jutted out over a manure spreader.

"Um, McBride, ma'am. Henry McBride." Henry slowly started following her.

"Well, Mr. McBride. What can I do for you?"

"Actually," Henry shook his head slightly, still not believing he was getting ready to say it out loud. "I was wonderin' if you needed any help around the place." He winced.

"Looking for a job, are ya?

"Yes ma'am. I guess I am."

Jessie pushed the wheelbarrow out on to the ramp and tipped it up against a stop nailed to the end of the board so the wheelbarrow wouldn't fall into the spreader. The wheelbarrow was nearly as heavy as Jessie and she struggled to get it dumped. After heaving it into place, she dropped it back down onto the ramp, wiped the sweat from her nose with her shirtsleeve, and scraped some of the remaining manure from the bottom of the wheelbarrow with her hand. She threw it into the spreader as well. "You must not be from around here. I don't believe I've ever seen you before."

"No ma'am, I'm not."

"Where are you from?"

"Most recent, up near Elko."

"That's all cattle country up there."

"Yes, ma'am. It is."

Jessie extended her now slightly manure-covered hand for Henry to shake, and Henry, undaunted, reached out and shook it. "So you're a cowboy?"

"Yes, I am."

"You any good, I mean as a cowhand?"

"Yes ma'am. Real good."

Jessie pushed the wheelbarrow back the way they had just come, and Henry followed. She'd seen hundreds of broke-down cowboys in her time at the ranch, all of them coming around, hat in hands looking for work when no one else would have them. She'd even given a few of them a job, only to find she shouldn't have. If they weren't trying to steal from her, they were off getting drunk and coming in the next day late, if they came in at all. Some would just disappear, slinking off into the night about the same way they came slinking in.

"If you're a real good cowboy, then what are you doing hunting up a job at a guest ranch? Why aren't you out chasing cattle?"

Henry stopped in his tracks and let out a tired, deep sigh. She was right. If he was the cow hand he thought he was, or if he hadn't been living out of a bottle for the past seventeen years, he'd be trailing cattle out in the big wide open some-where, not begging a job that meant watching a dudes fall off horses his grandmother could have rode.

"Sorry for taking your time, ma'am. I'll just be on my way."

Henry tipped his hat, turned and started to walk back toward his truck. There was something in Henry's voice that struck a chord with Jessie. With the other cowhands that came around looking for work, no matter how down and out they seemed to be, they always had an arrogance about them, as if their presence on her ranch was some kind of gift they were giving her. This Henry McBride was different. There was no arrogance to him, but rather what seemed to be a profound sadness. Her last question to him had been chosen carefully. It was meant to cut the cowboy and discourage him from wanting him to stay. She had enough trouble with the help she already had this season, not the least of which was Chad, who she regretted not firing when she had the chance. Still, she realized her words discouraged the cowboy even more than he already was, and almost as soon as she had asked him the question, she was sorry she had.

"Dang," she said putting the wheelbarrow down and turning toward Henry. "Must not want a job that bad, eh?"

Henry stopped, turned halfway toward her, and looked her in the eye. "I could use the job, ma'am. But to be honest, I'm just too tired to jump through hoops to get it."

The statement struck a chord with Jessie. She knew about being tired and jumping through hoops. She had done it day in and day out when she lived in Denver. She knew what it was like to be at the end of your rope and be looking for one safe place to stop and take a breath. Standing there in the late morning sun, looking into Henry's tired eyes, and against her better judgment, she suddenly found herself considering giving this cowboy a job. "That's fair enough, Mr. McBride. What kind of work are you looking for?"

Henry was a little taken aback by the woman's seemingly abrupt change in attitude toward him, but there was something in her voice that struck a chord with him, as well. There was suddenly a genuine kindness to it that caused him to turn the rest of the way toward her. "I can turn my hand to most anything," he said quietly. "So I guess I'd take any honest job you'd have to offer."

"We do need some help right now. But I doubt it'd be anything you'd be interested in."

"Much as I hate to say it ma'am," Henry forced a smile. "I ain't in much of a position to be choosy. I'd be happy to take whatever you got, especially if it meant a steady paycheck for a while."

"*I'll* be honest with *you* Mr. McBride," she said moving closer. "The job doesn't pay much. $100 a week. But we can give you a place to sleep and three meals a day. After all, you don't look like you eat too much."

"Actually, ma'am, I'm a pretty good eater. I just ain't had much of a opportunity to prove it, here lately."

"Well," Jessie nodded. "We can't have that, now can we?"

"No Ma'am," Henry smiled. "I guess not."

"Just one more question, though," Jessie stopped just short of getting ahead of herself. Her father had always told her to never hire any cowboy who smoked or wore gloves. Cowboys who smoked were always off somewhere having a cigarette when you needed them, and if they wore gloves, they were always putting them on before they could get anything done. As much as she hated to admit it, he had been right... at least with the cowboys she'd hired in the past.

"Do you smoke, or wear gloves when you work?"

Henry thought the question a little strange, but answered it anyway. "No ma'am," he said. "Neither."

"All right," Jessie smiled reaching her hand out to shake his again. "Why don't you go ahead and unload your gear in the bunkhouse, then come see me and I'll show you around the place."

"Yes ma'am."

The bunkhouse was nicer than most Henry had been in. Cleaner and more spacious for sure, as well as having indoor plumbing, which was rare. The facilities at most of the outfits he'd been on usually consisted of a one-hole privy some two hundred feet from the bunkhouse that was easy to smell when the wind was right, or perhaps just a grove of trees somewhere in the distance. The shower, if there was one, was often little more than a hose on a stick. Not only did this place have a shower, it had four of them with hot and cold running water in separate stalls in a separate room off the back of the bunkhouse. It also had four toilets in separate stalls in the same room, as well as two sinks, also with hot and cold running water, with real mirrors hanging above them.

The building itself was sixty feet long and thirty-five feet wide, with six beds along the back wall, a large footlocker at the end of each one, and another six beds with footlockers along the front wall. A pot-bellied, cast-iron wood stove was in the middle of the room, it's smokestack jutting out through the roof and a small stack of mesquite wood split and piled nearby. In the corner there was a well-used wooden round table with several wooden chairs around it, an old deck of playing cards and some poker chips sitting on it. On a smaller table nearby there was a coffee pot on a hotplate with several coffee cups scattered about. There were two large windows on either side of the front door, two smaller ones in the back wall, and one each in the sidewalls.

Outside, a large covered porch stretched from one end of the front of the building to the other. On it sat four cane rocking chairs, two on either side of the door, and a small table, also made from cane sat between each pair. It was a nice place by anyone's standards, but by Henry's it was a palace. Upon entering, Henry noticed three empty beds, one in the corner by the poker table, and one each on either side of the door. If he'd had to guess where the empty beds would have been, those are the places he would have chosen. The last bunks to fill were always the ones next to where the most late night activity might take place, like a poker table or a door. Everyone wanted to be involved in the late night goings on but nobody wanted to sleep next to it. Henry dropped his satchel, rope bag and saddle on the bed just to the left of the door. He didn't figure to be sleeping much anyway, so folks coming and going wouldn't bother him. Besides, if he needed to sneak out at night to drain a bottle, it would be easier for him to get out unnoticed if he were close to the door.

Henry took a minute to look around the place. He found it interesting someone would use heavy, rough-sawn wooden beams to hold up the roof and make up part of the ceiling, hold the hardwood floor down with brass screws, and use quality cedar for the window frames and door jams, while at the same time leave the corner joints in the place with gaps, some of the beams out of plumb, and cracks in some of the windowpanes. Still, the place was much better than anything he was used to, and as he started for the door, he nodded his approval.

The fresh-faced college kid he had spoken to earlier came bounding through the open screen door and almost ran headlong right into Henry's chest. "Whoa!" the kid squeaked as he stopped just short of crashing into Henry. "Hey, she put you on, huh? Good, we could use the help right now. We're short 'cause she fired Ben about a week ago. He was a good hand, but kind of a jerk to the guests. Jessie, she don't like that much. I'm Jim. Jim Thorson. I'm from Minnesota, originally. Moved here at the end of the summer. I was going to go back to school, but decided to take a year off. What's your name?" The kid jutted his hand out.

Henry looked down at it, and not being used to having that much chatter spewed at him all at once, wasn't quite sure what to do. He looked at Jim, and then at his outstretched hand, then back at Jim. "Henry," he said taking a firm grip on the boy's hand. He didn't see the need to offer his last name. "'Scuse me," Henry eased past the kid and out the door.

"Glad to have ya around," Jim said, following Henry to the door. "I look forward to working with ya."

Friendly guy, Henry thought. *Kind of like a Labrador retriever. Ain't got much use for one of them right now either.*

CHAPTER 14

It was something he had heard Annie tell Josh a million times—
be specific. She would remind him of it whenever he was doing
his homework. When he was preparing for a test at school, and
when he played his guitar. She insisted on it when describing
where he'd last seen the cattle during his turn to check them,
and when he did the head count on them. "Always be specific,"
she'd say. Now, only three-and-a-half hours into his new job at
the guest ranch, Henry was wishing he'd followed that advice.
He had told Jessie he'd take any honest job she had to offer. It
was clear to him now; he should have been more specific.

As promised, Jessie had taken some time to show him
around the place. She showed him the dining room, the
office where he'd need to go to fill out his paperwork, the
laundry room, which was behind the dining room, and the
horse facilities. Henry was impressed not only with the place,
but also with the ease at which Jessie switched from playing
cordial host to him, back to owner/manager of the ranch.
She would switch whenever an employee would come rushing up to her with some urgent catastrophe that was going
on in some respective department.

"Miss Jessie…we're out of guest towels!" a young girl said
breathlessly after running up.

"In the laundry room, to the left of the door, top shelf," Jessie replied calmly. "They're new, so you'll need to wash them first."

"Jessie, do we have anymore feed pellets anywhere?" one of the wranglers asked.

"There are two extra bags in the tack room, next to the saddle blankets, up against the wall. I'm going to town either today or tomorrow to get some more."

"The Hamilton's shower isn't working…"

"I'll get to it in a minute…"

"We don't have enough chicken for dinner…"

"Use the steaks instead, we have plenty of them…"

"The phone's for you, it sounds important…"

"Take a message…"

In between catastrophes, she'd point out this or that tidbit of information about the ranch. The main house, where she lived, had been built in the late 1800's. Many of the corrals had originally been holding pens for cattle. The ten guest cabins had been built by her father and could hold fifty people, give or take. Her father also built the bunkhouse. There were roughly twenty employees on the place when it was open for the season, twelve of which were wranglers. This year, including Henry, she only had ten.

The ranch sat on twenty-six thousand acres of land, and Jessie was grateful to her grandfather who had the foresight to buy as much as he could when land was cheap in Nevada. Most of the ranch was used for trail riding for the guests and grazing of the herd, and it butted up against an additional one hundred fifty-four thousand acres of BLM land, some of which they also used for grazing and trail riding. There were seventy-two horses and two ponies on the ranch, all trained right there on the place, most by Jessie herself.

It would be the two ponies, however, that would need to be of interest to Henry. The job Jessie had apparently needed him for would be giving pony rides to the children who were too small to ride the big horses. Three-and-a-half hours after he had been hired, he was leading a pony with a screaming four-year-old girl, the child of a beaming New Hampshire couple, sitting on top. Henry was wishing for all he was worth he'd been more specific about the kinds of jobs he would agree to do.

It was the second pony ride he'd given in thirty minutes and already he was figuring how much time he'd have to put in at this place to get enough money to fill the tank in his truck (which had run completely dry when he moved it from the parking lot by the dining room, down to the one near the bunkhouse), and have enough to sustain him while he made his way to New Mexico, or perhaps Colorado in search of a *real* job. At $100 a week, by his estimation, it would be a minimum of two and a half weeks, seventeen days total, eighteen at the outside. A lifetime away from this narrow pony trail that lead down into a sand wash, around a number of large barrel cacti—some with holes that seemed to form faces that smirked knowingly at him—back up the side of the wash, through a small grove of Joshua trees, then back to the little covered pens where the ponies were kept. Here, three more kids were dancing around, squealing and waiting not too patiently for their rides. It was going to be a long afternoon.

Jessie wasn't sure about the cowboy she'd just hired. But that wasn't really a surprise to her. Judging character didn't seem to be one of her strong suits lately; evident by the way she'd been struggling with making the right choices as far as her help went. The season was only a few weeks old and already she'd fired two wranglers and one housekeeper. As she sat at her kitchen table eating lunch, she was hoping the new cowboy would make it through the season, especially if he ended up being as good a hand as she thought he'd be. It would be nice to have some competent help around the horses for a change. Not that the help she had already wasn't competent, because they were. Its just that they were all pretty young and not terribly self-sufficient, and as a result, she was spending more time than she wanted overseeing things at the barn—especially when Chad was away, like he was that week. Jessie had gladly sent him out to guide a group of guests on a five-day fishing trip to the Azul River. She was surprised at how good she felt after he was off the property and on his way with the guests. She was starting to think it would be nice when he was gone for good, after the end of the season when she could cut him loose and hopefully never see him again. But for the time being, he was handy to have around the place. Chad knew the workings of the ranch almost as well as she did, and kept things at the barn running smoothly. It was one less thing for her to have to worry about when he was around, but lately she was wondering if the trade-off was worth it.

It was for that reason she hoped the new cowboy would work out. He had the maturity she was looking for in her help, and although he was plenty rough around the edges, there was something about him she liked. He was sure of himself and of his abilities. Not cocky sure like Chad and some of the others she'd had around the place, but rather he had a wise assuredness that only comes from living the life of a stockman. Her father had it, and her grandfather on her mother's side. She knew the look when she saw it, and knew it couldn't be faked. She also knew if a cowboy had to tell you how good he was around stock, it was usually because nobody else would. She had seen the look of a stockman in Henry by the easy way he moved around the horses when she took him in the corral, and by the way he handled the ponies, even though it was obvious he didn't want to be doing it. She hadn't realized how much she missed having a fellow stockman around the place. Henry McBride was the real deal, and that was something she didn't know she needed—but she did now.

She regretted putting him on pony ride detail almost as soon as she did it. She knew it was way below his skill level, but the truth was she needed it done and everybody else was busy with other things. Her father had always told her the boss might not always be right, but the boss is always the boss. The quality of an employee can be measured by the willingness to do something for you the employee'd rather not be doing. She saw by the look in Henry's eyes doing pony rides wasn't his first choice of jobs but was again impressed when he did it without complaint.

By the end of that day Henry was tired, more tired than he'd been in a long time. But then he had walked more than he usually did, too. Ten pony rides during the hot and dusty afternoon and all along the same three-hundred-yard path through the desert. Total, he'd walked nearly two miles. Near dinnertime and after the last child came around looking for a ride, he unsaddled the ponies and put their tack in a small shed near the covered pens they stayed in. He tossed them each a flake of alfalfa hay, checked their water tank, and then went up to the dining room to get his dinner.

The help on the ranch ate the same thing the guests did. On this day it was a T-bone steak, fried potatoes, green beans and corn, salad and lemonade, water or ice tea to drink. For dessert, which Henry skipped, it was ice cream sundaes. It was a good meal by anyone's standards, but by Henry's it was a feast. Still, he ate it much faster than he probably should have, and was in and out of the dining room in less than fifteen minutes.

After dinner he went to the bunkhouse and put his things away. Along with the footlocker at the end of every bed, there was also a small closet next to the head for hanging shirts and jackets. Henry wouldn't need the closet. In fact, he didn't need much room in his footlocker either. Rather, instead of taking his clothes out of his satchel and putting them in neat piles in the locker, as the others had done, he kept everything in the satchel and simply dropped it in the locker instead. *No sense in unpacking*, he thought. *Ain't gonna be here that long anyway.*

Henry carried his saddle over to the tack room by holding on to the cantle, and propping the pommel on his right hip. By carrying it this way, the majority of the saddle's weight was transferred to his hip rather than his arm and walking long distances with it became much easier. He slung his rope bag and bridles over his left shoulder and easily made his way across the dusty trail to the tack room.

He was immediately impressed by the construction and organization of the tack room, as he had been by the bunk-house. Directly in front of him as he walked in the door were two large piles of saddle pads stacked next to each other, laying on a heavy table that was six inches off the floor. Just behind the saddle pads and facing the back wall were four wooden saddle racks, each holding four pegs on which sat saddles. The saddle pads and four racks made an island of sorts in the middle of the room. Along the back wall were ten more saddle racks with pegs that held four saddles each, and along the wall to the left, on either side of a door that led to a fully equipped leather repair room, were two more similar saddle racks also holding saddles for a total of sixty-four saddles. Each individual saddle peg had a small piece of leather nailed to it on which was stamped the name of the horse the saddle belonged to. All were in alphabetical order and went from left to right, starting with the name Abby on the first peg on the left, wrapping around the back wall then finishing with the name Zephyr on the last peg of the racks in the middle by the saddle pads. Along the wall on either side of the door Henry came in were two rows of bridle hooks, one above the other, and each one holding a separate bridle. Again, each bridle was in alphabetical order from left to right.

On the wall to the right were three saddle racks, again with four pegs each. Not all of these pegs had saddles on them, but the saddles they did hold were of higher quality than the ones on the other pegs. Those pegs also had nametags on them, but instead of horse names, they held the names of the wranglers...Jim, Jake, Ted, Little Steve, Dan, Todd, Will, Big Steve, and Chad. Chad's saddle was missing. There were three other empty pegs, all of which were the top peg of each rack and none having a name on them. Henry flung his saddle into position on one of those. He suspected the more seniority the wrangler had, the lower his saddle was on the rack. That way that wrangler wouldn't have to heave his saddle up on the peg when putting it away, or pull it down when getting it out. The lower the saddle, the easier and quicker it would be to handle. Chad's was on the bottom right peg, Jim's was on the bottom of the middle rack and Josh's was on the bottom, left. Now he understood whom he'd be answering to when it was not Jessie.

Sitting off by itself near the door to the leather repair room was a worn but clean and well-used woman's saddle that no doubt belonged to Jessie. He was glad to see she rode. At the very least she wasn't just a businesswoman, but apparently knew something about livestock, as well. He liked that. He also liked the smell of the room: well oiled leather, old wood and horse sweat. He tipped his head back slightly and inhaled. He could tell just by the smell of the sweat in the air that the horses in the herd at this place were fed alfalfa, like the ponies. The odor from sweat of a horse fed on alfalfa smelled different, sweeter somehow, than a horse that was fed on grass or grass hay. It was a very distinctive aroma that he had always been able to distinguish, even when others just as experienced or even more than he, couldn't. He was so sensitive to it he could often know when someone was feeding alfalfa to their horses simply by the odor in the air as he drove past their place. He inhaled again.

The first night at a new place was always difficult for Henry. Not necessarily because if the newness of the place or the fact he was starting a new job, but because not knowing the place or the schedules of the people, he never knew where he could go to drink where he wouldn't be found out. At this place, however, it ended up being surprisingly easy. As it turned out, all of the employees on the place would traditionally stay in the dining room after the evening meal and visit with the guests. Most were still in the dining room for an hour or more after dinner was finished. As a result, Henry found on that first night he was able to sit on his bed and swallow as much as he could while looking out the windows and watching for anyone who might be approaching. Before the wranglers started filing in just after dark, he had already drunk his fill, had the bottle tucked safely in his footlocker and was curled up in bed.

For the most part, Henry's night was quiet. It may have been because of all the walking he'd done during the day, or maybe it was the first comfortable bed he'd slept in in a while. Either way, the familiar and constant nightmares stayed away and his sleep was sound and deep. Just before dawn an old memory gently began to push its way into his consciousness, triggered by a gentle breeze that crept in through the open window next to his bed and brushed across his face. He was riding the fence line in the high meadow the day after the lightning strike that killed his old, well producing cows. He was on his good ranch horse, Jack, and next to him was eleven-year-old Josh riding a little bay gelding named Wisp. They had ridden a long way in silence, partly because Henry was trying to decide what to do about losing so many good cows, and partly because Josh was wanting to talk to his dad about something and didn't know how to approach him about it.

"Jasper's dad just got a new saddle up in Winnemucca the other day," he finally said.

"What's that?" Henry snapped out of his thoughts about the herd.

"Jasper's dad got a new saddle," Josh repeated. "At that new tack shop up in Winnemucca."

"Oh yeah," Henry nodded. "I did hear somethin' about that."

The two continued to ride on, with Josh occasionally glancing in disgust at his father's old saddle. "When are you gonna get a new saddle?"

Henry chuckled to himself at the question. "I don't need a new saddle. I got this one, here. Nothin' wrong with it."

"But it's old," Josh protested.

"It was your grandfather's. And his father's before him, and his father's before him," Henry smiled.

"I know," Josh shrugged. "That's what I mean. It's old!"

"I used to think of it that way too," Henry said. "But it's more than an old saddle. It's part of who we are. My grand dad gave it to my dad, he gave it to me, and one day it'll be yours, and hopefully your son's after that. You might see it a little different then."

Josh looked at the saddle, looked at his dad then turned forward and shook his head. "I doubt it," he mumbled. Henry smiled, remembering having the exact same conversation with his father when he was Josh's age. He turned his gaze to the fence line, and the memory faded into the soft light of the morning drifting in through the windows of the bunkhouse. Through the ragged snoring of the wranglers around him, Henry opened his eyes and found them filled with tears. He wiped them away with his weathered hand, took a deep breath and rolled himself out of bed, bracing himself for yet another day.

CHAPTER 15

"What the hell is that?" Tug Caldwell growled as he walked up to the wooden catch pen.

"Mustang stud colt," Cat replied throwing the lead rope to his pack string over the top rail of the fence and swinging down from his tired and sweaty mount. When he did, the colt skittered off across the pen, nearly running into the fence. "Followed the herd in, I reckon. He was out in the pasture, there, when we come off the hill."

"Dammit boys, you gotta get him outta here." Tug climbed on the second rail of the five-rail fence to get a better look at the colt. "We already got a pen fulla horses here ain't earnin' their damn keep. Damn sure don't need no mustang stud colt to look after, too. Hell, he'll have every mare on the place in foal with a damn roman-nosed, lop-eared mongrel inside of six months. If Tom sees him he'll want to keep him around as a damn pet or some damn thing. Y'all need to cut him outta there and push him back up the hill."

"Hell boss, we ain't gonna be able to do nothing with these horses," Ben said riding up. "They're both played out. The mules, too."

"Dammit," Tug seethed. "Get a couple others and get that damn thing the hell outta here. Take him down to the gulch and put a damn bullet in his brain. I don't want to see him around here again!"

"Yes sir," the men said in unison. They knew better to question anything Tug said when he was in that state. He meant business, and talking to him was only going to make him madder. Both men quickly scaled the fence, vaulted to the other side and trotted off toward the corral near the barn where four extra saddle horses were always kept. That, too, sent the colt running. It seemed the two men no sooner disappeared around the corner than Tom and Terri drove up to the catch pen in their pickup truck.

"Dammit," Tug mumbled.

The truck pulled to a stop next to Tug, and Terri pushed the button that rolled the passenger side window down. "Hi Tug," she chirped.

"Ma'am," Tug tipped his hat slightly, then looked across her into the truck and acknowledged Tom. "Boss."

"Tug, we've been thinking about throwing a little barbeque up at the house on Saturday for you and the boys," Tom said, leaning toward him. "Everybody's been working pretty hard lately, and we thought it might be a good time to take a little break. Have you got anything planned for the crew on Saturday?"

Tug positioned himself in the window so as to block as much of the view of the catch pen as he could. "We got a couple little things we need to do, but nothin' we can't put off till Monday."

"Sounds good," Tom nodded. "Let's plan on about two o'clock. Tell the boys they don't need to bring anything, and we mean it this time." Tom and Terri both smiled. The last time they invited the crew to a meal, they all pitched in and bought them a gallon of wine in a box with a spigot and a handle for carrying it. It was appreciated, but not necessary, as Tom and Terri had an entire cellar full of wine, all in glass bottles.

"Yes sir," Tug nodded. "I'll tell 'em."

"We'll see you all on Saturday, then."

"Yes sir," Tug nodded, tipping his hat to Terri, and stepping back from the truck, still trying to keep their view of the catch pen blocked as well as he could.

Tom put the truck in gear and pulled away about the same time Terri pushed the button that brought the power window back up. Just as Tug felt he'd gotten away with keeping the colt a secret, the truck pulled to a stop a few feet from where it had been sitting during their conversation.

"Dammit," he mumbled.

The driver side door popped open, Tom stepped out and walked to the back of the truck, looking over at the catch pen. "Whose gray is that," he asked.

"He's a stray," Tug said bluntly. "Came in with the old-timers. The boys are fixin' to get him outta here pretty quick."

"A stray? Is he a mustang?"

Tug hesitated. His boss was a good man. As good as any *new* rancher he'd ever seen or been involved with. But if he had one weak spot, as far as Tug was concerned, it was his penchant for wanting to give every animal he came across a home, whether it could earn a living for him or not. Tug could never seem to get his head wrapped around that way of thinking. An animal that couldn't earn it's living was no good to anyone as far as he was concerned, and this gray colt was just one more of those. "Yeah," Tug finally said. "Looks like it."

"What happened to him?" Tom walked around the truck and up to the fence. "He's pretty beat up."

"Could be anything, I reckon." Tug walked over to him. "But if I had to guess, I'd say he got run off."

"Run out of his herd?"

"That'd be my guess." Tug leaned against the fence, propping his foot on the bottom rail. "As beat up as he is, I'd say he didn't have enough sense to get out of his own way, much less the stallion that was trying to run him off. He's lame, there, on his right front, not much good for anything I reckon. The boys will be here directly and they'll run him back up the mountain."

Terri stepped out of the truck and over to where the two men were standing. "Whose is he?" she asked.

"He's a mustang," Tom was still looking at the colt. "He came in with the old-timers. He doesn't belong to anyone."

"He's hurt." There was concern in her voice. "If he doesn't belong to anybody, can we get him out of there and into a pen of his own?"

This was the very thing Tug was trying to avoid. The last thing he wanted to do was to be playing nursemaid to a crippled, wild horse right in the middle of all the fall chores. "Well, now ma'am," he said in the most diplomatic voice he could muster. "That there's a wild animal, and he's hurt to boot. Most any wild animal will turn on you when injured like that, but them mustangs is the worst. It'd just be a matter of time 'fore someone 'round here gets hurt. Keeping him around, well, we'd just be askin' for trouble. I believe the best place for him is up in them hills, yonder, not cooped up in a stall. Besides, we ain't really set up to doctor no mustang."

"He's got a point, hon," Tom nodded.

"He doesn't look that vicious to me," Terri shrugged. "Besides, we wouldn't really need to doctor him. Just put him in a pen by himself where he didn't have to fight for his food and water. I bet given a chance he'd heal himself just fine."

Tom knew by the tone of her voice that this was already a lost cause. One way or another, the gray colt was going to need to stay with them, or Tom wouldn't hear the end of it. Terri understood the workings of the ranch better than anyone gave her credit for, including Tom. She knew how much land they had, how many acres it took to feed one cow/calf pair, and how many it took to feed their horse herd. She knew how much hay they made every year, and how much they needed to feed the stock year round, even in the years of drought. She understood about equine nutrition, tooth, foot and eye care and she understood about horse behavior and temperament, although she seldom rode.

Terri had done her homework long before they bought the place, not just when it came to land and livestock, but also when it came to the help. From everything she could gather, Tug Caldwell was one of the best stockmen around. He may have been "old school" but when it came to any and all ranch animals, there were few better or more knowledgeable. She knew even though he didn't want the horse around, he'd take good care of him. Yes, Terri knew the answer before she even asked the question. Of course they had a pen. Not only that, but they had the means to feed and care for the colt indefinitely if they so chose. She looked at Tom and smiled harmlessly. Tom gave a weak smile back, then turned to Tug. "Have we got an extra pen?"

Tug replied, "Yes sir," but was thinking, *Dammit.* "I'll get him moved as soon as we get the feet on these horses trimmed up and get 'em turned out again."

The colt was pacing the fence line the farthest he could get from the humans. He had already worked himself into a lather, and despite the questioning looks from his adopted herd, he couldn't calm down. It was one thing to be caught in such a small enclosure with a band of horses he barely trusted. But just when he thought he had one thing he was seeing or smelling figured out, it would suddenly change. He had never seen a horse with a human on its back before, and so his initial assumption was it was one animal, not two separate ones. When the rider dismounted, it gave the impression the animal suddenly split in two, and he panicked, turned and ran, nearly crashing headlong into the opposite fence. Having already done that in the pasture when he first saw the riders approaching, he knew better this time and veered off at the last minute, before going back to pacing the fence line, throwing his head over the top rail and trying to find a way out.

While things looked much different than anything he had ever seen, it was the smells he was experiencing that were even more troublesome. He was used to dealing with and being around horses, and even though all horses have a slightly different body odor which allows them to be distinguished one from the other, they also smell relatively the same. When a horse comes across another horse, there is no question he is encountering another horse just by the way the animal smells. In fact, the difference in odor from one horse to another is so subtle, it would be like comparing the sound of water in a creek going around a soccer-sized rock, as opposed to a basketball-sized rock.

But here, not only were there horses that smelled a little different than anything he had ever encountered before, but there were also mules, which smelled completely different, although relatively the same from one to the other. The most disturbing odors, however, came from the humans. The humans smelled so completely different his mind was having a hard time processing the information. As far as he could tell, each individual human had the same odor—the one that was specific to the species—but it could barely be distinguished over the individual human's completely different odor that nearly covered it up. While horse's individual odor was subtle, like the sound of water moving around different sized rocks, human's individual odor was more like the difference between a tree falling and a clap of thunder. Both of which were extremely overbearing to the colt when he experienced them in close proximity to the source.

For the colt, it had always been the subtlety of the individual animal's odor that allowed him to process the information about it quickly and smoothly in his brain, causing him the least amount of stress, effort and energy in the gathering of that information. It was what he was used to and what he understood. Being bombarded by one over-powering odor after another was almost more than he could handle, and he did everything he could to stay as far from the humans as possible.

He stood in the far corner of the pen, his hindquarters up against the fence and watched as humans came and went. Eventually, one of them came in the pen and one by one, caught the horses that were there, tied them up to a post, and trimmed their feet. When the man had finished, he took the horse he had trimmed and turned it back out into the large pasture with the windmill and water tank, although from the catch pen the colt could see neither. At one point, the man had left the gate to the pasture open while he turned one of the horses out, and the colt thought about making a break for it. Had he been healthy, he could have covered the distance from the corner in which he was standing, to the gate easily and before the man—who was outside in the pas-ture—could have gotten back to get it closed. He even took a quick step in that direction, but the pain in his shoulder made it clear it would just be a waste of energy to try. So he returned to the corner.

It took some time, but before long the only two horses left in the pen were the colt and one old gelding that wasn't quite as fit as all the others. The rest of the herd had already begun to move away from the catch pen and disperse out into the big pasture with the windmill, grazing quietly as they did. The horses had been turned out and moved away from the pen so gradually, the colt didn't worry much about them leaving, like he naturally would have had they been turned out all at once. Instead, as the human who had been trimming feet finally left the pen, the colt made his way over to the old gelding and stood as close as the gelding would allow.

The two stood quietly in the middle of the pen until the sun began to go down. It was then another human came in the pen and made his way to the old gelding. The colt immediately bolted for the far corner and watched as the man put a rope around the gelding's neck and quietly led him through another gate…one that led to an alley with tall wooden fence on one side, and several pens smaller than the catch pen on the other. The man left the gate open as he led the gelding away. Neither the man, nor the gelding came back, and as darkness fell the colt found himself standing alone in the corner of the catch pen, which seemed much bigger now than when all the horses had been together.

The colt didn't move from the corner for a long time and it was only when hunger overtook him that he ventured out. He slowly and meticulously scoured the catch pen for something to eat, but found nothing. The man who had trimmed the horse's feet earlier in the day had cleaned up everything, even the manure the herd had left behind. He had also drained the water tank the horses had been drinking from during the afternoon. Finding nothing to eat or drink, the colt eventually made his way to the open gate, where the man had taken the old gelding earlier that evening. He stopped at the opening and sniffed the air, trying to get a bearing on where the old horse was. The light breeze coming from behind him made that impossible, so he then held his breath to hear more acutely any noise or sounds coming from the alley beyond. Out of the dark, but not too far away he could hear the quiet munching of the old gelding. He nickered softly, and the old gelding answered with a gentle blowing through his nose.

Nervous, on shaky legs, and with every muscle ready to spring into action, the colt slowly moved into the void using the old geldings chewing to guide the way. It was a cool, moonless night and as the colt closed in on the sound he was following, he could make out little more than the old horse's silhouette toward the back of one of the pens, head down and eating from a large pile of hay. In an attempt at getting close to the gelding, the colt moved into another opening, only to find he was in a smaller pen than the one he had just come from, and the gelding was in the pen next to him. His instinct told him to retreat back the way he came, something wasn't right, and he knew it. But hunger was guiding him now and as he inched his way closer to the back of the pen and nearer the old gelding, he found a large pile of hay sitting there, as if waiting for him. Torn between going and staying, the colt moved toward the opening he had come through, stopped, and went back to the gelding and the pile of hay. Cautiously, he lowered his head and took a quick bite from the pile, then moved back toward the opening.

Standing near the open gate of the pen, he was suddenly surprised by the flavor of the dry grass in his mouth. He was used to foraging on dry grasses with little flavor and even less nutrition, except in the spring when the grass was lush and green. That seldom lasted long though and usually within a month or so into the summer, with little rain in the region to keep the grass nourished, it would begin to dry up and turn brown, losing much of its flavor. The hay in the pile was dry, but he could tell by the smell it was still green, and with the one bite the richness of it instinctively told him it was still packed with nutrition. He chewed what was in his mouth then returned to the pile, then back to the opening. For several minutes he repeated this pattern before finally settling near the pile, dropping his head and relaxing enough to enjoy the food in front of him.

The whole thing had been Tug's idea. He absolutely didn't want the mustang on the ranch, but when it became obvious the colt was going to be staying, Tug wanted to make sure to cause him as little stress as possible. It would be hard enough to deal with a wild horse, but one that was unduly stressed would be a nightmare, and he knew it. It was he who instructed Cat to trim the old horses and turn them out one at a time. Normally, the herd would be kept together while their feet were trimmed, and when the last one was finished they would all be turned out together. The colt's instinct to want to be with the herd during a stressful time would force him to want to stay bunched up with them, and if all the horses left at once it would no doubt panic the colt. But if they left slowly—one at a time—the transition would be so gradual he may not notice the shift in numbers and even if he did, it would give him time to get used to the idea.

It was also Tug who chose the old gelding to stay in the pen with the colt after the others were gone. The gelding, a nondescript bay named Zip, was born and raised on the place and had proved to be one of the most solid working geldings Tug had ever seen. Anytime a job needed to be done on horseback on the ranch, like dragging a calf to the fire, roping and doctoring a sick cow out in the open, sorting, moving a bull from one place to another, or even just repairing fence where a horse might need to stand hobbled for hours at a time, the first choice for most of the cowboys on the place had always been Zip. He was quiet, reliable and stout enough to hold nearly any steer or cow once roped.

Unfortunately, because he had been used so hard for so long, at twelve years old Zip began to develop arthritis in his hips, and by fifteen he had been all but retired from any and all work on the ranch. Tug had always been of a mind that horses that had outlived their usefulness on a ranch should be sold, plain and simple. Maybe go to some middle-aged lady looking for a safe trail horse, or a kid looking for his first rope horse. But even Tug had a soft spot for Zip. From day one Zip had always been a good, honest-working horse. He never quit and never complained and if the Essex's would have allowed Tug to get rid of the old-timers, Tug believed he would have found a way to keep the old bay gelding.

The cold months were hardest on Zip, and Tug noticed him having more and more trouble getting around out in the pasture during the winter. He had planned on keeping him up by the barn this year anyway instead of letting him run with the herd, so it wasn't difficult to make the decision on which horse to keep in so the colt had some company.

Tug had instructed Cat to take the old horse from the pen while it was still light so the colt could see him go, and then leave the gate open. He also told him to clean every scrap of feed out of the catch pen, and drain the water tank. In doing so, he knew it wouldn't be long before the colt would start looking for food and water, and soon enough he would make his way through the open gate, into the alley and toward the pen that held Zip. Tug knew the one thing that most horse people fail to understand. Horses are born followers. Given the opportunity and the right motivation, a horse—even a mustang—will follow another horse just about anywhere. He also knew if you try to drive a mustang somewhere they don't want to go, things can, and often do, get very messy, very quickly. By setting the situation up the way he did, Tug allowed the colt to move into the pen he ultimately wanted him in, rather than trying to make him go into it, as many less experienced horsemen might do.

Now that the colt was in the pen, the only thing left to do was get the gate closed and that was one task he wasn't willing to leave up to anyone but himself. Just after sunset, Tug eased himself into position behind the small shed at the end of the alley opposite the open gate. Less than an hour later, the entire area became pitch dark with the absence of a moon or nearby yard light, and Tug was forced to rely on his hearing to determine when the colt had first entered the alley, then gone into the pen next to the old gelding. He had heard the colt nicker before entering the alley, and the old horse blow in response. He heard the colt cautiously move down the alley and enter the pen next to Zip and he heard him pacing in the pen. Finally, he heard the colt settling in to eat on the pile of hay Cat placed there earlier.

Tug waited nearly a half hour more before he started taking his slow and measured steps down the alley and toward the colt's pen. He had been lucky in that he was upwind from the colt, which would make it difficult, if not impossible for the colt to smell him. He was also lucky in that the three-inch-diameter lodge pole pine rails that made up the five-rail, nearly six-foot-tall fence of the pens would block most, if not all of his movement from the colt's sight. The one thing he was concerned with was the colt hearing him. So, like a thief in the night he would take one painfully slow step, and then wait to listen for any reaction the colt gave. Then he would take another step, and another until he had covered the thirty-six-foot distance to the open gate of the colt's pen.

Even though Tug's eyes had adjusted to the darkness, it was still nearly impossible for him to see anything unless he was right on top of it. As he neared the gate, which opened into the alley, as did all the other gates on the other five pens on that row, he became even more cautious. He moved slowly, but even as slow as he was moving, he still didn't want to accidentally run into the gate, which would no doubt spook the colt before he could get it swung into place. Mustangs can be extremely unpredictable, especially when they're frightened, and while a domestic horse will almost always run away from a noise that scares them, a mustang may not. Knowing the only way out of the pen was the gate he came in, any noise, even if it were coming from the direction of the gate, could send the colt bolting headlong toward it. If Tug bobbled in any way, it could mean a big problem for both him and the colt.

He had walked the distance from the shed to the gate on the third pen hundreds of times over the years, as he had with all the other gates on all the other pens. He never counted how many steps it took to get there, but somehow he knew when he was getting close. When he got to within four or five feet of the gate, Tug began silently sliding his feet along the ground rather than taking full steps, and he reached his hand out in front of him so as not to bump the gate with his body. He was so cautious, it seemed as though it took nearly as long to go the last four feet as it had the first thirty-two.

Most people in a similar situation would get excited and shove the gate closed as quickly as they could, so as not to give the colt a chance to run out before it latched. Tug didn't. His fingers touched the large wooden gate first and he knew it would swing easily—all his gates did. But instead of pushing the hefty gate quickly, he slowly walked it closed as if the pen's occupant was an old broke ranch horse. He heard the colt snort a warning and jump around a bit near the back of the pen, but he didn't bolt or panic. The metal latch slid into place with a metallic "clack," and that was that. Tug's task for the night having been accomplished, he quietly retreated back the way he came.

The movement at the gate took the colt by complete surprise. He had sensed something wasn't right since even before he entered the alley…but then, nothing at all about the day had been right. He had been on alert and worried since first seeing the men on horses in the pasture with the water tank and windmill, and by the time he got to the pen next to the old horse he was exhausted. No longer knowing what he should be concerned about and what he shouldn't, he let his guard down and decided to take his lead from the old gelding in the pen next to him. The old horse had shown no concern whatsoever while they both ate in the darkness, no warning that there might be a problem or impending danger. The only thing the colt heard before the gate closed was the rhythmic munching of the gelding next to him as he chewed his hay.

The movement at the gate worried him, but because it was so slow and deliberate, and because the old gelding next to him didn't react at all, his own reaction had been minimal. He snorted out of instinct and moved quickly away from the sound and movement, but he felt no need to run or defend himself. Then, as quickly as the movement by the gate came, it also went. After a few seconds, the colt warily approached the area where the opening used to be and sniffed. There was a lingering odor of a human, one he had detected earlier in the day, and he felt the wood of the gate with his nose. He gently pushed on it, but it didn't budge. He pushed again with the same result, and then scraped his teeth across the dried wood. He was locked in, and now he knew it. Oddly, his worry began to dissipate. His instinct had told him to keep moving and not to get caught in a small space. The more open the area, the better his chances of escape, should he need to. All day long the space he was in kept dwindling and he became more and more worried.

But now, finally, it seemed his space had stabilized. When the gate was still open he was on constant alert in case he should need to retreat to it, as it was his only way back from where he'd come. But now that it had been closed, it was one less thing for him to worry about. Things were quiet and peaceful in the pen with the old gelding eating nearby, and he slowly started to find being enclosed actually made him feel better, at least for the time being. He wandered to the pile of hay at the back of the pen, took a mouthful and chewed lazily. Suddenly he was very tired. His chewing slowed until it stopped, and with hay still in his mouth he lowered his head and began to doze. He felt better in that moment than he had in months and the colt let out a long, relaxed breath. The old gelding nextdoor slowly raised his head and nickered softly. The gray colt's day had come to end.

CHAPTER 16

In the four days he'd been on the Lazy K, Henry hadn't seen much of the woman who had hired him. He'd been splitting his time during the day between giving pony rides for hours on end, and scooping manure out of the holding pens, hitch rail areas and the area where guests got on horses so they could go on trail rides. He'd pick up the manure with a large aluminum scoop shovel, trying not to pick up too much dirt along with it, pile it in a wheelbarrow and dump it in the manure spreader out back where he first met Jessie. The work was hot, tedious and unrewarding and as far as he was concerned, his existence now was only slightly less mundane than when he was sitting on a bar stool for hours on end and sleeping in the bed of his pickup.

Shortly after lunch on that third day, however, an incident occurred that seemed to generate a spark in Henry that he thought had long ago vanished. It started harmlessly enough, with an honest mistake by Jim, the young wrangler from Minnesota Henry met on the first day. As far as Henry could tell, Jim was a fair hand and apparently second in command under a fellow named Chad, whom Henry had not yet met. He had spoken with Jim on a few occasions over the past couple days, and as much as he tried *not* to like the affable young man, he actually found it difficult to do.

Henry had just come out of the dining room, and was making his way to the pony ride area when he glanced over to where the wranglers were mounting guests on horses for an afternoon trail ride. For some reason, every guest on the place had decided to go on a ride that afternoon, and because of that, every horse on the place was saddled. During this particular week, Jessie had expanded her guest capacity by three people to accommodate a family reunion. The problem was that while she had the three extra horses to accommodate those three extra riders, what she didn't have were the three extra saddles for those horses. Over-booking horses was extremely rare on the ranch, but it did happen from time to time. When it did, Chad had mandated that the wranglers who weren't guiding or helping out on the ride were expected to volunteer their personal saddle for guest use. It had never been an issue for most of the wranglers that passed through the place, as most "amateur" cowboys don't have the same strong attachment to their gear as a working cowboy does. But with a real working cowboy, that's different. Most working cowboys wouldn't even allow their good friends to use their equipment, not that a good friend would ask to use it in the first place. So allowing a stranger to use their saddle would be out of the question, and allowing their saddle to be used for a "dude" to ride in would be unheard of.

It was for that reason Henry had to do a doubletake when he saw a heavyset man in shorts, t-shirt and tennis shoes, a camera draped around his neck, over in the mounting area getting ready to climb on a horse that was wearing Henry's saddle. Jim was standing next to the man ready to help him get in the saddle. It had been rare in the past seventeen years that Henry had gotten angry at anything or anybody but himself. But knowing that someone had not only touched his saddle without permission, but then had put it on a horse and was getting ready to let a stranger use it, lit a fuse in him that had been extinguished for a very long time. He covered the seventy-five yards from where he'd been standing to the mounting area in seconds. He reached out and grabbed the heavy man's ankle just as his toe was about to reach the stirrup, and jerked it away.

"Hey," the man grunted, losing his balance and falling slightly backward.

Henry's abrupt appearance caused a surprised Jim to step back as well. "Henry," he said, shock apparent in his voice. "What are you doing?"

Henry didn't acknowledge his presence. He flipped the stirrup leather up over the seat of the saddle and quickly untied the T-knot, which secured the latigo to the cinch and held the saddle to the horse's back. He undid the back cinch in one effortless flip, reached under, unsecured the heavy trigger snap holding the bottom strap of the breast collar to the cinch, and the nearside strap of the breast collar to the ring on the saddle a few inches down from the saddle horn. In less than five seconds since he'd shown up on the scene, the saddle was loose, and in one smooth movement, Henry jerked it from the horse's back, turned and started for the bunkhouse. Jim grabbed Henry by the arm.

"Henry," he blurted. "We need that sad…"

Jim stopped in mid sentence when he saw the look on Henry's face as Henry snapped around to look at him. The anger in his glare was so visceral, it was as if electricity shot through Jim's body, and he immediately released his grip on Henry's arm and stepped back. Henry turned without a word and continued toward the bunkhouse.

"Hey," the heavyset man exclaimed. "What's going on? How am I supposed to ride without a saddle?"

"Just a minute, sir," Jim smiled. "We'll get all this straightened out in a minute. I'll be right back."

Jim quickly followed Henry, making sure not to touch him this time. "Henry, we're overbooked this afternoon, and could really use that saddle."

"You or anybody else on this place touch this saddle again," there was an ominous growl in Henry's voice, "I'll cut your hands off and send them to your mother." It was clear to Jim at that point the conversation was over.

Several of the wranglers would go into the bunkhouse later that afternoon to get a cup of coffee, or grab a jacket, or pick up something they forgot and see Henry's saddle sitting on his bunk just inside the door. On it, in big bold letters scribbled on a piece of paper was a note that read simply: TOUCH THIS SADDLE = WORST DAY OF YOUR LIFE! Nobody did.

As had become his custom in the short four-day period since Henry had been at the ranch, he would sneak in the back door of the kitchen at dinner time, grab a quick plate and cup of coffee and eat sitting on the garbage cans just outside the door. When he was finished, he'd return the plate to the kitchen and go straight to the bunkhouse where he'd mix his whiskey (which was running dangerously low) with coffee. He'd usually sit on his bunk and look out the windows for anybody that might be approaching so he could hide what he was doing. The last couple nights, however, he decided drinking from a coffee cup was much less conspicuous than the bottle, and besides nobody ever stopped to chat with him anyway. For that reason, he'd started going outside to sit in one of the rocking chairs on the porch.

On this evening, oddly enough, it wasn't getting a drink that was foremost on his mind. The reason he wanted to finish dinner so quickly was the fact he felt he needed to get back to his saddle. Ever since he'd pulled the saddle from the horse's back he'd had an overwhelming urge to clean and oil it, something he hadn't done in too long of a time, and the saddle showed it. It seemed dirtier somehow, than it had the last time he'd seen it. Maybe it actually was dirtier, and maybe it was simply because people had handled it who shouldn't have. Either way, it needed to be cleaned and he didn't want to waste any time getting to it.

About the time Henry flung the saddle over the railing of the bunkhouse and started washing the dust from the leather fenders with a damp cloth, Jessie found Jim in the dining room finishing his dinner.

"What happened today with the horse George Springs was going to ride?" she asked as Jim stood up from the table.

"Yeah, about that," Jim nodded, wiping his mouth with a napkin, and then placing it on the table. "Mr. Springs. Well, what happened was we had his horse all saddled and ready to go, but then Henry came and took it."

"Took what?"

"The saddle. He just came right up and took it off the horse." Jim shrugged. "I never even saw him coming. He was just there all of a sudden and pulled it right off and walked away."

"Whose saddle was it?"

"Well, it was Henry's saddle."

Jessie smiled slightly, and then raised one eyebrow. "Don't tell me you were going to use his saddle for one of our guests."

"Sure," Jim shrugged again. "We do that kind of thing all the time. Chad says…"

Jessie put her hand over her mouth and slowly shook her head side to side as if in disbelief. She knew how working cowboys felt about their gear and how big a breach of etiquette had transpired. "What did he say…I mean Henry? What did he say?"

"He said if I ever touch his saddle again, he'll cut my hands off and send them to my mother."

Jessie chuckled a little and nodded knowingly. "Next chance you get, you make sure you go and apologize to him for taking his saddle," she said, patting Jim on his shoulder. "Then never touch it again."

"Oh, I hadn't planned on touching his saddle again, or anything else that belongs to him, for that matter."

"Good," Jessie nodded as she turned and walked away. "Good."

It would be another hour before Jim had gathered enough courage to walk over to the bunkhouse and talk with Henry. When he finally did, he didn't really walk up to him, but rather he sort of slunk with his head down, hands in his pockets, shuffling his feet, and acting as if he had forgotten where his final destination actually was. Henry watched in amusement at the boy's jittery and indecisive gait, and knew just by looking he'd made his point.

"Hi Henry," Jim's voice was a little shaky. "Did you get some supper?"

Henry nodded, but otherwise didn't respond. He figured Jim had probably come to apologize but didn't want to look too eager to accept it. As far as Henry was concerned, Jim had already gotten off easy. What he had done wouldn't have been tolerated at all on any real outfit. All things being equal, the same blunder on a working ranch might have at least cost him a couple teeth, and at most, some broken bones.

"I'll say this about the place, they sure have good grub." Jim forced a smile. "Good grub and good horses. Usually, a place like this either has good horses, or they have good food. But this place has both." He smiled again. Henry spit in the dirt, and then wiped his mouth with his sleeve. Jim's smile faded a little as he watched the little puff of dust rise from the dirt. "Um," he started again. "Sure is dry...ain't it? They're sayin' it might rain tomorrow. But then, that's what they said about today. And look. No rain. Not even a drop." He smiled again.

"You're wearin' on me boy," Henry growled. "If you got something to say, then go on and say it. I ain't in the mood for no chit chat." He spit again.

Jim gulped. "Um…well…actually, I just wanted to come by to tell you how sorry I was that we used your saddle today." He winced a little, as if getting ready to be hit. "That's something we do around here all the time—borrow each other's saddles. Nobody ever minded before…"

"I mind," Henry interrupted.

"Yes sir," Jim nodded. "And I can see that. It won't happen again. You don't have to worry about that."

Henry could see the boy was sincerely sorry for what happened, and he also understood Jim probably knew nothing about the unspoken code of ethics between cowboys when it came to their equipment. After a few moments hesitation, Henry slowly nodded. "Fair enough," he said as he reached his open hand toward Jim. A little surprised, Jim slowly reached back and shook it. "Fair enough," Henry repeated.

Both men's attention was suddenly drawn to the trail that came up out of the wash on the other side of the holding pens where the herd was kept. Henry stood to get a better look at the string of riders and packhorses slowly filtering up out of the dust. The rider in front was dressed in old-time cowboy garb, led the pack horses loaded with gear, sat his horse pretty well and appeared as tired as he did dirty. The three men on horses in a row behind him were obviously less experienced riders, evident by the slouch in their backs, lack of structure in their bodies, and the fact they all had to hold on to the horn of the saddle as the horses they were on climbed the barely substantial grade from the bottom of the wash up to the flat area by the holding pen. They were also wearing light tan fishing vests with numerous pockets and small floppy hats with fishing lures attached to them. The rider in front brought the string to the hitch rail closest to the catch pens, dismounted, tied his horse and pack animals to the rail, then helped the other riders dismount. It was a process that looked extremely painful for all but one of the riders.

"Looks like Chad's back," Jim said matter-of-factly, his voice much clearer now that the threat of death or serious injury by Henry's hands had apparently been removed. "He's the head wrangler. Been here a few years, I guess."

Not terribly interested, Henry sat down and went back to oiling his saddle.

"He took a fishing trip out about a week ago," Jim continued. "He says nobody else knows the country well enough to do 'em, but the truth is the tips are real good."

Almost as if on cue, Chad went to the three men, shook their hands, and all three of them, smiling and slapping each other on the back, pulled money from their wallets and handed it to him. Chad smiled and shook their hands again, stuffing the money in his shirt pocket. The three men turned and headed toward the guest housing, while Chad turned and headed for the bunkhouse, his smile fading as soon as he did.

"Looks a little mad," Jim said under his breath.

Chad stopped abruptly at the foot of the steps and looked up and Jim and Henry.

"Chad Collins, Henry McBride," Jim said making the introduction. "Henry's been helping us out these last few days."

Henry barely acknowledged Chad's presence. He'd had his fill of men like Chad Collins, and he could spot their type a mile away. They usually had just enough skill to get by, but not much more. Probably tried rodeoing but wasn't talented enough to make it very far in the sport. Don't know enough about stock to work a cattle outfit—not for long anyway—and their gift of gab usually overshadows their substantial personality flaws. It was already obvious to Henry that Chad was not someone he needed to spend time getting to know.

"Ain't you a little old to be wrangling dudes?" Chad's tone was intentionally condescending. Henry didn't bother to look up. "Not much of a talker, 'eh? Well, no matter. I don't know if Jim here has told you, but I'm the boss on this outfit. And if you're workin' here, that means I'm your boss, too." Henry continued oiling his saddle as if Chad didn't exist.

Chad walked up the steps and stopped next to Jim. "Them horses need to be untacked and fed," he grunted. "You better get to it."

Jim nodded and walked down the steps and toward the horses about the same time Chad turned his attention back to Henry. "There is one other thing you might want to keep in mind. I'm a man of few words, so when I say come, you better come."

Henry finally stopped oiling his saddle and looked Chad in the eye. "Well, Chip," he said, equally as condescending as Chad had been to him. "I'm a man of few words, too. So if I shake my head, I ain't comin'."

Chad was incensed that Henry pronounced his name wrong. "The name is *Chad*. And I'll tell you something, pard. The quicker you lose that attitude, the quicker you and I can become friends."

Henry nodded and went back to oiling his saddle. "I got all the friends I can stand just now," he said quietly.

"You a troublemaker Henry?" Chad's tone had turned threatening. "I sure hope not. I can't stand troublemakers and I can tell you right now, I won't tolerate it."

Henry slowly looked up. Chad's threat was idle, and Henry knew it. Chad was a talker and very little more, and Henry had been dealing with "talkers" pretty effectively for over thirty years, and he was good at that. It started back in his rodeo days. Even though Henry didn't drink much at the time, he and Annie would usually go to the bar to socialize with friends after the rodeo was over. Once in a while, some local wannabe cowboy would decide to pick a fight with one of the competitors to prove he was just as tough as the competitor was. Usually, these fellows were "talkers." Henry hated fighting. He always had and always would. However, if a fight was inevitable, it had always been his philosophy that it should be over as quickly and painlessly as possible.

Henry realized very early on that many men who had wanted to fight had to literally talk themselves into it. Usually goaded on by their friends or drunkenness, they would beat around the bush so long that by the time a punch was actually thrown it would come out of nowhere and that's when things would become dangerous. If one of these "talkers" would pick a fight with Henry, they'd get so focused on telling him how bad they were going to beat him, they never saw Henry's thundering right fist collide with their forehead, and just like that, the fight was over.

During the past seventeen years, Henry had used the same defense no fewer than nine times against "talkers" who tried to pick fights with him in the bars where he was drinking. Inevitably, some young kid would want to fight the old drunk cowboy sitting at the end of the bar, and would begin his talking. The last time it happened was only six months earlier when Henry was getting ready to leave the bar he'd been in for several hours. He stood up and staggered for the door when a kid in his twenties stepped in front of him and began telling him what a washed up old man he was. He made some off-color remark that Henry could no longer recall and turned toward his friend to laugh. When he turned back, Henry's jackhammer-like right hand caught him between the eyes and he was unconscious before he hit the floor. The kid's friends parted like the Red Sea, and let the washed up old drunk cowboy go along his way.

"You will do well not to try to ride roughshod over me, *pard,*" Henry growled. "That is something *I* will not tolerate." The two men locked stares for several seconds, and Chad, understanding a real threat when he heard one, chuckled to relieve the tension, then turned and walked into the bunkhouse.

For the next three days, Chad kept Henry busy doing little more than scooping manure. It was a gross waste of Henry's abilities, and the longer he was around the place, the more that had become evident to everyone that worked there, especially the wranglers. Henry's easy way around the stock, and general knowledge of the operation after only a few days on the ranch made that very clear. Normally, having been relegated to such a menial task for such a long time would have been all it took for Henry to up and leave, particularly when it was a job he didn't particularly like or want. But he didn't leave. In fact, oddly enough, he found himself feeling more and more at home on the ranch with each passing day.

There was something about the place and the people that seemed to be slowly bringing life back to his existence. For years he had been emotionally numb, doing little more than sleep-walking through his days, without anything or anybody able to bring up any feeling, good or bad, in him whatsoever. Even when he would have to punch one of the "talkers" in a bar, it was always more business-like than anger- or fear-based. Still, in the week since he'd arrived at the Lazy K, he had felt two strong emotions that had been absent in him for as long as he could recall. The first one was the unabated anger that came over him when Jim took his saddle without asking, and the second was the absolute disdain he felt for Chad, the mealy-mouthed head wrangler who was obviously pretending to be more than he really was. There was just something about Chad that rubbed Henry real wrong, and oddly enough, it was that disdain that was keeping Henry from leaving.

As far as Henry was concerned, it was going to take more than a would-be dime-store cowboy to run him off a job that even on his worst day he could do with his eyes closed. That simply wasn't going to happen. Almost as soon as he met Chad, Henry had unconsciously resolved to stay at the ranch no matter how demeaning the job, how miserable the conditions got or how many hours he had to work, just so Chad wouldn't be able to best him. In short, Chad had unwittingly done something for Henry that no amount of drinking, altercations with "talkers," arguments with surly bartenders, or the loss of one good job after another had been able to do. He had brought out the fight in him.

At the end of Henry's first week, Jessie approached him as he was entering the dining room to get his breakfast and handed him a hundred dollar bill.

"Ma'am?" Henry questioned, looking at the bill.

"It's your first week's pay," she smiled. "You've been doing a good job and I thought maybe you could use it. I heard your truck is out of gas."

"Yes ma'am, it is."

"I'll tell you what," Jessie smiled. "You can get a couple gallons out of the bulk tank, back by the maintenance shed, to get you to town. Once you get to town you can fill up."

"Why, thank you, ma'am," Henry nodded. "I appreciate it."

"All right then," Jessie nodded. "Have a good day, Mr. McBride." With that she turned and headed for the door. She stopped short and turned back. "You will come back, right?"

"Ma'am?"

"You aren't going to take the money and run off, are you, like some of the fellas who worked here?"

"No Ma'am," he said simply. "I won't run off."

CHAPTER 17

During his first week at the ranch, with his whiskey supply running low and everything that had been going on, Henry's urge to drink had been slowly dissipating. By the time he'd gotten to town, he had told himself he didn't really need to be drinking anymore, and even though he had a little money, he was going to stay out of the bars and the liquor stores. In fact, he found it pretty easy to stay out of the bar, as there seemed to only be one in town and the parking lot was full. But he found it a little harder to stay out of the liquor store. As if drawn like a magnet, Henry found he couldn't keep himself from going in the first one he passed—a little mom-and-pop place just as he came into town. He bought a fifth of Windsor, a Canadian Whiskey, that the older woman behind the counter stuffed in a plain brown paper sack before giving him change from a twenty.

He told himself he just wanted to have a little on hand, which was why he only bought a fifth instead of a quart, and that he'd only have a mouthful at a time. He filled his truck with gas, and on the way back to the ranch, with the bottle seemingly calling to him from its place on the seat beside him, he pulled off the road and into the desert. He had the bottle drained in less than an hour, then went back to the same store where the same woman was behind the counter and bought himself a quart of the same whiskey, figuring he couldn't have too much of a good thing.

Henry missed breakfast the next morning and moved slowly while on his rounds scooping manure. He moved slowly the rest of the day as well, missing lunch altogether and eating very little for supper, before going to bed even before the sun went down. Had anyone stopped to talk with him they would have realized he had been drunk the entire day from all that he'd had to drink the night before. He was still drunk when he went to bed, and only became hung over around midnight, when he woke with a splitting head-ache. As quietly as he could, which wasn't very quietly, he dug around in his footlocker for the remainder of the bottle he'd been sucking on the night before, and drank out behind the bunkhouse until his headache subsided.

He missed breakfast again, and stumbled his way through scooping manure for the first three hours of the morning. Around 10:00 a.m., he finally began to feel somewhat nor-mal, which was about the time he was summoned to the mounting area to help mount an outgoing ride. By the time he arrived, the rest of the wranglers were already there and Jessie was standing on the porch near the barn with a clipboard in her hands. There were a number of guests all standing around waiting for her to assign them horses for the upcoming ride. Henry stuffed himself in behind all the other wranglers and tried to hide himself as best he could. So far, this was the worst part of his job. Deal-ing with and helping inexperienced riders get on horses anybody could ride, except maybe the people he was putting on them.

"Okay Linda," Jessie said with a smile to a woman stand-ing in front of her. "We'll put you on a horse named Tonka. Jim here will go get him for you."

Jim, who was standing in front and just to the right of Henry, tipped his hat, and then trotted off to the hitch rail where a number of horses were tied.

"Well, who's next here?" Jessie was still smiling. "Let's see. Oh yes, Lindsey. Where's Lindsey at?"

An eight-year-old girl slipped out from behind her mother and sheepishly raised her hand. Jessie squatted down to get to the little girl's eye level.

"Hello Lindsey," she said quietly. "Have you ever ridden a horse before?"

"No ma'am."

"You're not nervous, are you?"

"A little."

"Well, don't worry. " Jessie assured her. "We have just the horse for you. She's a real nice little mare named Buttercup. How does that sound?"

"Fine, ma'am."

Jessie rose from her squatting position and looked over at the wranglers, whom were all standing nearby. She scanned the group and found Henry standing in the second row. He saw that Jessie was about to call on him and he tried to step out of sight behind one of the other wranglers.

"Mr. McBride," there was still a smile in her voice. "Would you mind going over and getting Buttercup for Miss Lindsey, here?"

Henry squinted as if he'd been stepped on by a draft horse, hesitated for a second then stepped out to the front of the group.

"Yes ma'am, but maybe one of these other fellas would be more inclined…"

"Buttercup is the bay mare on the end, there," Jessie interrupted.

Henry hesitated again, and then noticed that all the guests were looking at him. "Yes ma'am," he said grudgingly. "I'll get her." He walked to the hitch rail like he was going to the gallows, untied the little bay mare, led her past where the guests were standing, glanced down at the little girl and halfheartedly motioned for her to follow, which she did. Side by side, they walked the rest of the way as slowly as they both could walk, neither one really wanting to be there. They reached the spot where Henry was to help the little girl mount. He tightened the cinch, and then motioned for her to get on. The little girl hesitated, and with sad eyes looked up at the weathered, slightly hungover cowboy. "I'm afraid of horses," she said so quietly he almost didn't hear her.

Henry wasn't sure what she meant. He had never heard of anybody being afraid of horses. Especially one that seemed to have one foot in the grave, as this one apparently had. He quickly looked around trying to find someone to help deal with what he had just been told, but nobody was available and he was left to deal with the little girl on his own, something he wasn't entirely sure he was capable of doing.

"Afraid?" He slowly rubbed the stubble on his chin. "Hell there ain't...I mean, *heck*, there ain't no reason to be afraid. This here is a real nice mare."

"Horses scare me though."

Again, Henry looked for help, and again, none was to be found. He took a deep breath and bent down to her level. "There are two things in this life I know to be true. The first is that I've never lied to a kid. The second is that this mare would never hurt nobody."

Jessie, who had by now finished assigning horses and had seen Henry was struggling with the little girl, headed his way to see if she could help. When he bent down, she stopped just within earshot and listened to what he had to say.

"Now if you're too scared to ride, I ain't gonna be the one to make you do it. But you can take my word when I tell you this mare won't hurt you."

Lindsey looked into Henry's eyes for a moment, then at the horse. "You're sure she won't hurt me?"

"You got my word."

"It's only for an hour?"

"Yes ma'am, only an hour."

"Maybe I could go," she said sheepishly. "As long as it's only an hour."

"That's the girl!" Henry smiled. He helped the little girl into the saddle, and explained how to use the reins to stop and turn. "I expect by the time you get back you'll like riding so much you'll want to go out and be the new rodeo queen or some dang thing like that." The little girl looked down at Henry and smiled. "You have a good ride, now, hear?"

"Yes sir," she smiled back.

Henry stayed with the little girl until the horses started moving down the trail. He walked a short distance by her side then patted her on the leg. "There you go," he said reassuringly. After traveling a few more yards on her own, Lindsey turned back, caught Henry's eye, smiled and waved at him. Henry smiled and waved back. Jessie, who was still standing behind Henry, silently nodded her approval, and then turned and walked back to the porch.

At first, Henry felt good about helping the little girl overcome her fear of horses. But as the day wore on, a profound sadness began to overtake him until by the end of the day he was struggling to hold himself together. As soon as his work was finished, he went to the bunkhouse and dug through the satchel in his footlocker until he found a small, slightly yellowed envelope. He carefully put the envelope in his shirt pocket, and drove to town, stopping first at the liquor store, and then driving on to a secluded spot in the desert. Henry spent the next two-and-a-half hours sitting on the tailgate of his pickup and drinking until he felt he was sufficiently numb. He then reached in his pocket and drew from it the yellowed envelope. He took a labored breath, then peeled the flap back and gently took from it a weathered black-and-white photograph of Annie and four-year-old Josh, who was sitting on a pony. Both were smiling into the camera. Seeing the photo in the fading light of day filled Henry with emotion, and as he tried to force a smile, his eyes filled with tears.

The next morning, a hungover and slightly bedraggled Henry stood next to a big red horse named Champ in the mounting area, waiting for the person who would be riding him. He stood for what seemed like a very long time, the early morning sun beating down on him, his mouth dry and a dull ache behind his eyes, before an obviously wealthy woman in fancy western attire approached and placed her foot in the stirrup. Suddenly, the woman stopped and turned toward Henry with a sour look on her face.

"What is that smell?" she questioned. Henry didn't answer. "That smells like liquor! Have you been drinking?"

"No ma'am," Henry said flatly. "It's my hair cream. I believe it went bad." A confused look crossed the woman's face. "It happens all the time. I really should switch." Then as if that was simply the end of the conversation, he helped her on her horse and went to get his own mount.

It was the first time in the month-and-a-half since Henry had first arrived that he'd actually gotten a chance to ride. It was "breakfast ride morning" and all the guests on the ranch were going. Normally, Henry wouldn't be riding, as Chad always made sure all the wranglers but him did, but on this morning, Big Steve had come down with a nasty case of the hives and was still in the bunkhouse scratching himself silly. As a result, and with no other alternative, Henry ended up going in his place. The ride had actually been pleasant enough by going down into the sand wash, along a dry creek bank, through a spotty grove of Joshua Trees, then back down into another wash, and finally ending up in a grove of cottonwoods near a creek where a chuckwagon breakfast was already set up and waiting. All the wranglers, including Henry, took care to tie the horses to a long wooden hitch rail built some distance from where the guests would be eating, loosen the cinches and then go to the back of the line, where they would wait until all the guests had gotten their food before they got theirs.

It would take nearly twenty minutes from the time they first got in line until they were able to get their plates full, but when they did, all the wranglers migrated to a small area off to the side and under a tree where they stood eating their breakfast off of tin plates, and drinking coffee out of tin cups. Most of the guests were sitting on fallen trees, stumps and rocks, also eating off of tin plates, and Henry had found himself a rock a short distance from where the guests were sitting, and opposite the campfire from where the horses were tied.

Henry had only gotten a few mouthfuls of food down when he heard a commotion over by the horses. Two of the mounts standing next to each other apparently got into a kicking contest, when one of them pulled back, breaking its reins and becoming loose in the process. The wranglers, having all saw what happened, dropped their plates and ran to the area. Henry looked up briefly, but didn't move from his spot. He was hungry, and this was surprisingly a very good meal. Besides, there seemed to be plenty of help there already, considering they only had to catch one horse, which one of the wranglers did without incident.

Chad was quickly on the spot to assess the damage, and when he saw the broken reins, became unusually angry. Moreso, Henry thought, then the situation allowed.

"Which one of you idiots tied this horse with the reins?" he shouted. Nobody answered. "I see," he ranted. "Nobody's man enough to take responsibility for this. Is that it? Well that's just great!" Chad's voice rose to the point where he had gotten the attention of all the guests, who were looking in his direction. Henry also looked up to see what the commotion was about, but was uninterested.

"I don't suppose any of you illiterate bastards thought to bring any extra reins, did you?" he yelled. The wranglers all looked at each other and sheepishly shook their heads no. "Well lucky for you, *I* did. Dan, go to my saddlebags and get that spare set of reins."

Dan, a nice-looking young man with a quick smile and easy demeanor trotted over to Chad's horse and dug through his saddlebags. First looking in one side, then the other, then back to the first side.

"There aren't any reins here, Chad," Dan smiled from his place next to Chad's horse.

"What do you mean there aren't any reins?" Chad blurted. "There's got to be!"

"Well, I sure can't find them."

Chad angrily handed the broken reins to Jake, stomped over to his horse, pushed Dan aside and dug through the bags himself. He, too, came up empty. "Dammit! Who took those reins out of here?"

Jessie had been casually watching the entire ordeal while visiting with one of the guests, and suddenly took more interest. "Would you excuse me?" She smiled to the lady she'd been talking with. She walked over, placed her plate in a washtub by the fire and walked over to Chad.

"Chad," she said quietly, trying to hold her own temper at his unnecessary outburst. "Let's not make a scene here."

"Dammit Jessie. I'm tired of this crap! Every time I turn around I've got to fix something that one of these idiots screwed up."

"Chad, this is not that big of a deal."

"The hell it ain't!" He turned to the wranglers. "One of you, and I don't care who, is going to ride back to the barn and get another set of reins. Now who's it going to be?"

"Oh for Christ's sake," Henry mumbled. He let out an exhausted sigh, stood up and very deliberately walked toward where the wranglers and Chad were standing. As he passed the campfire, he dropped his plate and coffee cup unceremoniously into the washtub, then pulled out his knife, which was in a sheath on his belt. All the wranglers, including Chad, saw Henry with his knife drawn and coming toward them, and a look of concern crossed all their faces, but it was Chad who seemed the most concerned.

As Henry drew nearer, Chad casually stepped behind Jessie. Henry walked right past him and went to Jake. He grabbed the broken reins from his hand and went to a nearby tree. Henry placed the broken ends of the reins against the tree and cut a small slit in the middle of each rein near where they had been broken. He then went to the horse and took the remaining broken pieces of reins from the horse's bit. Again, he cut slits near the broken ends. He then slid the good ends of both broken pieces through the slits he had made and pulled the ends taught. By doing this he had quickly and effectively repaired the reins, which were once again in one piece.

With a look of disgust, he walked over and tossed the now fully repaired reins at Chad, then went back to the fire and poured himself another cup of coffee. Impressed by how Henry had just handled himself, Jessie smiled ever so slightly in approval, and then headed back toward the guests. The wranglers went back about their business, and Chad was left standing by himself, the repaired reins clenched in his fist.

After the ride had returned to the barn, guests were dismounted and horses watered and fed. Henry pulled his saddle from the horse he'd been riding, took it to the tack room and heaved it up to it's place on the top saddle rack. He turned to see Chad standing in the door of the tack room.

"Pretty cute, what you did out there this morning," Chad said in disgust. "You trying to make me look bad so you can get my job?"

Henry barely acknowledged him.

"Well, I can tell you right now," Chad continued. "You'll be in for a fight if that's the case. Nobody's gonna have this job. Not you, not Jim. Nobody." Henry turned and walked past him on his way out the door. As he passed, Chad grabbed him by the arm. "Hey! I'm talking to you, you damn drunk!"

Henry stopped in his tracks, and with a look of contempt stared at Chad's hand, and said quietly, "Turn me loose boy, or you'll lose that hand."

Chad swallowed hard, and then slowly released his grip. Henry shook his head in disbelief at the childish behavior of the man, turned and walked out the door.

CHAPTER 18

The first few weeks in the pen next to the old gelding had been hard on the gray colt. There was always a lot of activity by the humans, which worried him. So much, he never knew which way to flee when they came around. Even if he thought he knew where to run, he couldn't go far before running into one solid five-rail fence or another. The pen itself was large as far as pens go, nearly thirty feet long and twenty-four feet wide with a slanted cover over the far end. But it was small for the colt—very small. He was used to having hundreds of thousands of acres that he could roam at will. Now he was down to just a few feet in any direction. That, in and of itself, took some getting used to.

But it was the humans that worried him most. They seemed to always come out of nowhere, and in the beginning there appeared to be so many of them. It was weeks before the colt realized there were really only a few humans coming around and it was just that they looked so different from one day to the next that he *thought* there were more than there actually were. They were an odd species, and one that took some getting used to because of how much their bodies seemed to change. When it was cold they looked bigger, and when it was warm they looked smaller. Their color would be different from one day to the next, as was their odor. Sometimes their odor would change from the beginning of the day to the end of the day. On bright, sunny days, their eyes were very big, and on cloudy days they were small. They seemed to be able to peel their hide off whenever they wanted, or put more hide on. The colt had never seen anything like it.

Another thing that worried him was when he first found himself in his pen there had been plenty for him to eat. It was in a big pile in the back of the pen near where the old gelding was eating in the pen next to him. But once that pile was gone, which took less than a day; a human started bringing his food around, usually just tossing it over the fence at the front of the pen, near where the tank for his water stood. At first, seeing the hay come flying over the fence would terrify him and send him panicking to the back of the pen. Food wasn't supposed to fall from the sky. As the days went on, however, he not only got used to seeing the human with the hay, he actually started to look forward to seeing him. Each time the hay would arrive there would be just enough for him to eat, and about the time he would finish that pile and start getting hungry again, the human would show up and toss him another pile. It happened every day, twice a day, like clockwork.

In a little over two weeks, the colt had gone from panicking and cowering in the back of the pen whenever a human came around, to standing near the front of the pen and watching in anticipation. And Tug Caldwell had carefully planned it all. He knew about wild horses, that the herd they lived in was actually very structured, and it was the structure and stability of the herd that kept the members in a settled state of mind. It was why the colt attached himself to the old-timers instead of wandering alone in the mountains after losing his own herd. He was searching for structure and stability. In captivity, all that changed. The structure of the herd was gone, and he was by himself again. Tug knew just being in a pen instead of out in the open would worry the colt for a while. He knew he would naturally be looking for structure, and he also knew he would need to get used to being around people.

The way the colt was being fed was designed to do both—put structure in his life, and get him used to seeing and being around people. Every morning, at exactly the same time every day, Tug had instructed Ben to toss the colt exactly the same amount of hay. Then, in the afternoon, at exactly the same time every day, he had instructed him to do it again. He knew the colt would worry about the hay being tossed over the fence at first. But he also knew over time, the colt would begin to pick up on the pattern, and thus begin to see the structure in it. At the same time, he could begin to see the usefulness of people, and that they could be a benefit to him, if he allowed them to be.

Two weeks into his captivity, the colt was beginning to settle in and look forward to the human with the hay. It was the same human that would come around every other day at the same time and fill his water tank with a hose. However, up to that point, all of the colt's contact with humans had been with them on one side of the fence, and he on the other. No sooner had he begun to get comfortable with the human with the hay, when one day the human actually came in the pen with him, pushing a large yellow wheelbarrow and carrying a manure fork. This, of course, sent the colt panicking to the back of the pen, as he had when the hay first started flying over the fence. The human completely ignored the colt and acted as if he didn't even exist. No matter where the colt went or how fast he ran around in the pen, the human simply picked up manure, tossed it in the wheelbarrow, then hauled the wheelbarrow away when it was full. The next day, at exactly the same time, the human pushed the wheelbarrow in the pen, filled it with manure and hauled it away. He repeated this every day until the pen was clean of the first two weeks of manure, then he continued to come in every day after that to keep the pen tidy.

Ben's behavior inside the pen had also been mandated by Tug. He had been instructed to completely ignore the colt, no matter what he did or where he went, unless, of course, the colt tried to attack him—which Tug felt was highly unlikely. If that should happen, then Ben had been instructed to defend himself at all costs. At first, the colt kept his distance from Ben, seemingly terrified of his presence. But as the days and weeks passed, and with curiosity getting the better of him, the colt slowly started closing the gap between the two of them. This was also something Tug knew would happen. He understood the two emotions that control horses from the day they're born to the day they die are fear and curiosity. He knew a fearful horse couldn't be curious, and a curious horse couldn't be fearful. By instructing Ben to ignore the colt no matter how the colt behaved, he figured eventually the colt would get curious and want to get close enough to Ben to smell or maybe even touch him.

The colt had been carefully watching the human that would come into his pen with great interest for over two weeks. His instincts had told him to be afraid of anything that was foreign to him, anything that might be able to cause him harm or death, and there were very few things in his world to date that were any more foreign to him than the human species. For that reason when the human first started coming in his pen he would get extremely stressed and feel as though all he wanted to do was run, which he did.

However, as the days passed it became clear to the colt the human wasn't there to harm him, and the urge to flee began to dissipate greatly. Eventually when the human came in pushing his wheelbarrow, the colt would walk to the back of the pen and stand quietly to watch the man's odd behavior. Sometimes the colt would go back to his hay pile and eat, keeping one eye on the intruder. Two weeks after the human first came into his pen, curiosity began to get the better of the colt and in an attempt to understand better what he was dealing with, he haltingly began to make his way over to the human as he scooped up the manure and put it in the wheelbarrow.

A month and three days into his captivity, with the human standing with his back to the colt in the pen, the colt had finally gotten close enough to the human to reach out and touch him with his nose. The texture of the human's faded Carhartt jacket took the colt by surprise, and he snorted and quickly retreated to the back of the pen. The human's behavior never changed. He simply continued what he was doing without acknowledging the colt. A few minutes later, the colt had approached the human again, and this time he reached out his head and neck as far as it would go, keeping the rest of his body a safe distance in case a hasty retreat would be in order, and smelled the man without actually touching him.

Later that day, Ben would relate the story of what transpired between him and the colt to Tug.

"I knew he was coming up on me," he said excitedly. "I could see his shadow on the ground, there. He come up real slow and cautious, like. You know, like he was sneakin' up on me or somethin'. Then he touched me and scared himself, I guess, 'cause he sure run off. I just kept on doin' what I was doin' like you said to do, and before long he come up again. This time he just sniffed but didn't touch me. Stayed with me, though, and went along wherever I went. He sure enough followed me like a puppy dog and when I left the pen, he just stood there by the gate and watched me go." Ben shook his head. "I gotta tell ya boss, I know you said that'd happen, but if I hadn't seen it with my own eyes, I wouldn't a believed it."

It was about this same time when the colt began to notice the constant pain in his right shoulder had slowly begun to dissipate. He was moving better and feeling stronger, as well as gaining weight, and it was all due to the rest he'd been getting, along with the quality grass/alfalfa hay mix he'd been eating. The dry brown grass he'd been feeding on in the wild had been extremely low in nutrients, and it didn't afford the nourishment his body needed to heal itself properly. But that had all changed, and even though he couldn't move very far or very fast in his pen, he was actually healthier now than he'd ever been.

Two months into his captivity, the colt had become content with his life. He had been happy to see other horses when a human would ride or lead them past his pen, but he never approached to introduce himself. The lesson he learned when the stallion drove him off the ledge had become a part of him—acting out around others was not a good idea, and doing so had severe consequences. He was not going to make that mistake again, and because of it, was always on his best behavior around other horses, no matter if they were mares, geldings, or even other stallions.

The humans didn't cause him the anxiety they used to, either, and even when two or three of them would come to the fence to look in on him, he would stand quietly looking back at them. On occasion, he would approach, but when there was more than one human at a time, he couldn't talk himself into getting too close. That was the case on this day. Tom and Terri had come to the pen along with Tug to see how the colt was getting along, and talk over options on what to do with him.

"He looks like he's moving better," Terri commented.

"Yes, ma'am," Tug nodded, pulling a toothpick from his mouth. "He started coming around about a week or so ago."

"Seems much calmer, too," Tom added.

"I'll tell ya, boss," Tug shrugged, putting the toothpick back in the corner of his mouth. "He's dang sure the quietest stallion I've ever been around. Horses come and go up this alley all the time and he's just as quiet then as he is right now. He shows interest, but that's as far as it goes."

"That was actually my next question," Tom said. "You think we should geld him?"

"Well, I'll be honest," Tug propped his foot on the bottom rail of the gate, "when he first showed up here, I didn't want this horse on the place at all. When y'all decided to keep him, I didn't think we could get him gelded fast enough. Last thing I wanted around the place was a mess of half mustang babies. But ya know, the longer he's here, the more I'm thinkin' we might want to keep him entire, leastways for a while. Hell, if'n we could get the stamina of the mustang with this guy's temperament, and cross him with our good mares, why, we'd really have us a nice little remuda to work off of."

"Really?" Terri smiled. "You like him that much?"

"Yes ma'am, I do."

Tom and Terri turned and smiled at each other, then turned back to Tug. "So," Tom said. "You want to just keep him around as a breeding stallion, or do you want to get him broke, too."

"Oh, I expect we should get him broke, all right," Tug said flatly. "He's gotta earn his keep if'n he's gonna be on the place."

"How soon before you'll get around to it, then?" Terri asked.

"Actually, I been givin' that some thought." Tug stepped back from the gate and stuffed his hands down in his jacket pockets. "I ain't so sure I'm the one to start this colt."

"Why not?" Terri sounded surprised. "You've started nearly every colt on the place."

"Yes, ma'am." He pulled the toothpick from his mouth again and looked at the ground. He was ashamed to say it, and never would out loud, but he had tried to break a mustang back in his younger days and made a complete mess out of the deal. He had been so hard on the colt he ended up crippling the horse, and hurting himself pretty bad to boot. He told himself then that he'd never start another mustang as long as he lived. So far he had managed to keep that promise, and he intended to not to break it on this horse.

"But this here's different," he continued. "These mustangs take a sort a hand like I ain't got; even one as quiet as this one. He may be quiet but he's still a wild horse."

"Who would do it, then?" Terri asked. "Cat? Ben? *Not* Matt."

"No ma'am, I don't believe I'd give him to the boys here. Not that they're bad hands, you know that. It's just that, well, he needs somethin' a little different. He needs someone that understands horses like this." He put the toothpick back in his mouth. "I reckon if'n it were me, I'd jump him in the trailer and run him on over to Jessie King, near Grant. She's the best I know of when it comes to critters like this."

"Yeah," Tom nodded. "She'd sure do a nice job with him, wouldn't she."

"She's the best I know of," Tug repeated.

"Well then, Tom, why don't we give her a call and see if she could take him?" Terri added. "How soon would you want him to go, Tug?"

"He'll need a little more time to let that shoulder heal up." Tug leaned back on the fence. "Maybe another month or so, I reckon. After that I expect he'd be good to go."

"Fair enough," Tom nodded. "I'll give her a call in the morning and see if we can set something up." Tug nodded his approval.

Feeling good about the map they had chosen for the colt's future with the ranch, the three humans stood quietly in the fading afternoon sun looking at the colt, still standing calmly in the middle of his pen. After several seconds, Tom and Terri turned and eased away from the pen. Tossing his toothpick aside, Tug followed. The gray colt lowered his head and let out a long, soft sigh.

CHAPTER 19

The light from the kitchen shone through the screen door and splashed out onto the back porch, creating an odd-shaped yellowish rectangle on the wood in the quiet darkness of early evening. Jessie sat at the kitchen table still dressed in the clothes that got her through the day, sipping on her last cup of coffee. Normally she would put a teaspoon of sugar and a little milk in the cup before drinking, but on this evening she had slipped into her unconscious habit of drinking coffee black whenever she was trying to work out some sort of problem.

The guest season was going by quickly. But then, that was how it seemed to go the last several years. She was amazed at the fact she would no sooner be greeting the first guests of the season, then turn around and seem to be locking the gate behind the last. She remembered when her father first started taking in guests to help supplement income. It seemed the season lasted forever, even though back then it was really only four months, instead of the eight she was open now. Still, back then time dragged on. As a young woman she hated the fact strangers were running all over her home. Not that they ever actually went in her house, but rather that they were traipsing all over the ranch.

She couldn't wait to see the season end so she could have the ranch to herself again.

But things were different now. She was able to see things from a perspective that only comes with time. Where before she hated having people on the place, now she enjoyed it. She loved the fact the ranch brought so much joy to so many people. That would make her father happy, and the thought of it made her smile as she brought the steaming cup to her lips. Those thoughts were slowly pushed aside, however, as a list of projects that needed to get done gradually took over. There was fencing that needed to be replaced—a *lot* of fencing—maybe as much as three miles, as far as she could figure. The barn was going to need a new roof, the septic system for the guest cabins was getting old, and she was looking into replacing it with a leach field. That maybe could wait another year, but not much longer. She wanted to build some feed bunks so the horses wouldn't have to eat off the sandy ground anymore. None of the horses had ever suffered from sand colic, not yet anyway, but she knew it was just a matter of time before one did. There were some hitch rails that needed to be repaired, several of the trails needed maintenance, and then of course, there were the horses. She had no fewer than ten colts of her own to start, and on top of that, she had just taken in a mustang colt to start for Tom Essex.

There was no question she was going to need help again in the off-season, and while she wasn't quite sure which of the wranglers she might ask to stay on, she was certain about who she wouldn't. Chad had steadily been wearing out his welcome ever since he'd gotten back from the last fishing trip, and as far as Jessie was concerned, as soon as the season was over he would be leaving and would not be coming back.

Of the rest of the wranglers, most had summer jobs they'd be going to on guest ranches up north, in Colorado, Utah and Wyoming. She knew there were three that didn't have summer jobs lined up, not yet at least. Little Steve, Jim and

Henry. Of those three, Jim seemed to be the most likely candidate. Little Steve was good with horses, but not too handy when it came to maintenance type work. Henry was good at everything, as far as Jessie could tell, but he was a cattleman at heart and more than likely wouldn't stay on if he could find a job on a cow outfit. Besides, he was a drinker, and she'd already had complaints about the smell of liquor on his breath during the day by guests. The last thing she wanted to do in the off-season was play nursemaid to a drunk. So by process of elimination, Jim seemed like the most logical choice. He was a hard worker, good with the horses, and was pretty handy in general. She had briefly mentioned the idea to Jim in passing a few days before, but at the time he hadn't said much, and the truth of the matter was, neither had she. Still, as the thumbnail-shaped moon began to grudgingly show itself on the horizon, she decided to wait a couple more days before she'd make the final decision. With fatigue suddenly setting in, she found herself staring blankly at the back door. She blinked her eyes twice to bring her back to consciousness, then rose from the table, set her half-finished cup on the counter, and called it a day.

Later that night in the dark bunkhouse, the only light in the room the dim moonlight streaming in through the window, Henry woke from a semi-drunken restless sleep to see Chad quietly pulling on his jeans near his bunk. He picked up his boots, and then snuck out the front door. After several seconds, Henry heard the faint sound of a gate opening, and a few seconds after that, the sound of horses running. A couple minutes later, Chad reappeared, sneaking back in the door with his boots in his hand and, without taking his jeans off, climbed back in bed.

Henry wasn't able to get back to sleep, which wasn't uncommon, and he laid in the darkness with his eyes closed trying to fend off an impending hangover that was pressing on the back of his neck and creeping toward the front of his head. Just before sunrise, the pounding in his head began to subside enough to where he actually started to doze. For a time he was vaguely aware of his surroundings, as one is during that instant between consciousness and unconsciousness, then as sleep overtook him, the awareness drifted away. It seemed as though no time had passed whatsoever when he was jarred awake by the sound of thundering footsteps on the bunkhouse porch and the door next to his bed opening, and then slamming closed.

"Jim!" Chad yelled. "Dammit, Jim, Wake up!

Everybody in the room stirred in their bunks as Chad flipped on the light switch.

"Jesus, Chad," Jim was groggy. "What?"

"You left the gate open again last night, and now we got horses scattered all over the country, that's what!"

Jim sat up in his bunk, rubbed his eyes and squinted against the light.

"That ain't right, Chad," Jim protested. "I closed that gate, I know I did. I even checked it before I came in the bunkhouse."

"Sure you did. Just like you did the last time, and the time before that! I told you what would happen the next time horses got loose. You get your gear packed and be out of here by noon. You hear me?"

"Chad, that ain't right. I closed that…"

"Jake," Chad blurted, turning away from Jim. "You, Dan and Henry. You get mounted and get them horses gathered. We still got rides to take out today." He turned back to Jim. "Your check will be ready by the time you leave." Chad turned and stomped out the door, slamming it behind him as he went.

"I closed that gate," Jim said looking around at the faces looking at him. "I know I did."

Henry pushed the heel of his hand firmly into the socket of his left eye, trying to stave off the painful pounding just behind it. He was trying hard to recall clearly what he'd seen and heard during the night, but was having trouble. He knew he'd heard horses running, and he thought he saw and heard Chad leave the bunkhouse and come back, but he just couldn't be certain. He knew it wasn't like Jim to leave a gate open. He was too good a hand to do something like that. But Henry wasn't also certain he hadn't and because of that, Henry had no alternative but to get dressed, get mounted up and go gather the loose horses.

The three men headed out from the ranch while it was still dark, and branched out in three different directions. Dan went west, along the dry wash, Jake went east toward the hayfield that was a little over a mile and a half away, and Henry went south toward the open desert. Along the way Henry racked his drink-fogged brain trying to sort out fact from fiction about what happened during the night. It was only after he had drunk nearly two canteens full of water that things began to sort themselves out. The cobwebs slowly started falling away and the certainty of what happened became very clear. Chad had snuck out during the night; there was no question about that. Henry hadn't actually seen him turn the horses loose, but he wasn't a fool either. It wasn't much of a stretch to put two and two together.

The thing Henry couldn't figure, though, was why he did it. Jim was a hard worker, a good hand and as far as Henry knew, never caused any trouble for anybody. Why would Chad want to scuttle him like that? It didn't make sense. As Henry and his horse scrambled up a steep, rocky trail to the top of the mesa that loomed in front of them, he may not have understood why Chad did what he did, but he knew he didn't like it. Still, Henry had lived his life making every effort to stay out of other people's business, just as he wanted them to stay out of his. And this was clearly none of his business.

Henry crossed the mesa and gently pulled his horse to a stop near its edge. He looked down into the small valley below at fifteen of the seventeen ranch horses that had run off during the night. He stopped for a few minutes to admire the day's sunrise and warm his cheeks in its heat. He then eased his horse down into the valley and gathered the herd. It wasn't difficult. By all appearances the herd seemed to want to go back anyway and all Henry had to do was get behind them, turn them for home and the whole bunch picked up an easy trot and went straight back to the ranch. The herd and Henry kept the trot up until they rounded the bend that took them through the sand wash, up the little rise, through the yard and straight into the corral they left some four hours before.

A genuinely surprised Chad closed the gate behind them. "You're the first one back," he said. "How'd you get 'em gathered so fast? Where were they?"

Henry dismounted, ignored Chad's questions, and led his horse away. While he was walking away, Henry thought of something he had heard in a bar somewhere. Chad was a "step over." Meaning, if Chad had been lying in the dirt, having a heart attack the most Henry would have done is step over him so he could continue with whatever it was he was doing. Henry didn't think he would have ever thought of another human being in these terms, but with Chad, he was inspired to it.

Jim had been busy, angrily packing his clothes and other gear in a large duffle bag when Henry came in, walked to the little table toward the back of the room and took a tin cup from the shelf. He blew the dust out of it, and then took the coffee pot from the little stove and filled his cup. He placed the pot back on the stove and sat in a chair next to the table.

"I didn't forget to close that gate, Henry," Jim said. "I know I didn't. Something's going on here. This is the fourth time this has happened to me."

"Mr. Head Wrangler out there. Has he got something against you?"

"Not that I know of. Why d'ya ask?"

"No reason in particular," Henry shrugged. "Just wonderin', I guess."

"I don't know." Jim pulled up a chair and took a seat. "I heard he was mad that Jessie said somethin' to me about staying on in the off season."

"Stay in the off season?"

"Yeah. Jessie'll be closing the place down soon for the summer. Nobody wants to come to a guest ranch in the middle of the desert in the summertime. Every year when the season is over, she usually asks one of us to stay on to give her a hand with things. The last few years it's been Chad. This year she said something to me, but I can't do it because I got a summer job up in Colorado. I was actually going to tell her that today."

Henry finished his coffee, then stood up and slung the last few drops out on the floor before putting the cup back on the shelf. He then walked to the door, but stopped short of leaving. Henry wanted to tell Jim about what he'd seen and heard during the night, but couldn't seem to bring himself to do it. "Bad luck all the way around," was all he could say.

"It's been good working with you, Henry. If you ever get up near Durango, look me up."

Henry nodded, and without looking back, walked out the door. He stopped on the porch. There was something that told him he should go back, even if it was only to tell Jim that he knew he didn't leave the gate open. It wouldn't make any of it right, but it might help Jim feel better. Henry stood a long time, but in the end, all he could do was shake his head in disgust at himself and step off the porch.

The morning dragged on forever, and a heavy cloud hung over the atmosphere at the barn. Jim was well liked by everyone and the crew hated to see him go. On top of that, however, everyone found they needed to fill in and do the things Jim would have normally done during the day.

Nobody really understood all the work he had been doing until he wasn't there to do it, and by lunchtime, everyone was ready for a break.

Henry had eaten half a barbeque sandwich, some coleslaw and drank a cup of coffee. He hadn't been very hungry. Normally he would take his plate back to the kitchen himself, to save the dining room staff the extra work of cleaning up after him. They already had their hands full taking care of the guests and he didn't want to add to it. But on this day, a little blond waitress named Sue came to his table just as he was getting up.

"All done Henry?" she smiled.

"I am," he said, picking up his hat, which had been sitting on the chair next to him. "But I can get it."

"I know," she said, scooping up his plate and coffee cup. "I don't mind. Have a good afternoon."

"You too," Henry said as she scurried off to the kitchen.

He put his hat on his head and turned for the door, nearly running headlong into Chad who had come up behind him. "Hey there, cowboy. Can you fix wire fence?"

A stupid question, Henry thought. But then, what else could he expect from someone like Chad.

"Well Chet," Henry said flatly. "It ain't my preference, but I've fixed a few over the years."

"The name's *Chad*," he blurted. "And we got some fence for you to mend. About two-and-a-half miles worth toward the back of the property. You can get started on it right now."

Just then Jessie walked up. Henry took off his hat. Chad didn't.

"Say Chad, do you mind if I steal Mr. McBride for the afternoon? I need some help with that new corral."

"Actually, Henry here was just heading out to fix that fence in the back pasture. I'll be happy to give you a hand, though."

"Thanks anyway," she forced a smile. "But I know you've got more important things to do." She turned to Henry. "Unless you'd rather get out and string wire all day."

"No ma'am," Henry smiled. "I'd be happy to give you a hand."

"Good then. I'll see you out back in, say, ten minutes?"

"Yes ma'am."

Jessie continued on her way, saying hello to a few guests sitting at a nearby table as she breezed past.

"Don't worry," Chad said walking past Henry, "we'll save that fence for you."

Chad had to jog to catch up with Jessie, which he did once she got to the dining room porch.

"Say Jess," he called. "Have you got a minute?"

"A minute," she said coldly. "What?"

"I didn't know if you heard, but I had to let Jim go this morning. He left the dang gate open again. I had half the crew out hunting horses all morning. We got them all back, but it took a little doing."

"Were any horses hurt?"

"Luckily, no," Chad said. "But I thought I'd better let him go just the same. After all, that was the fourth time it happened, and I figured it'd just be a matter of time before one *did* get hurt."

"I guess it's for the better, then," she sighed. "Too bad."

"Yeah, it is," he said with mock sympathy, which Jessie saw through immediately. "Say, I was wondering. Now that Jim won't be able to stay on after we close for the season, would you reconsider having me stay?"

"We talked about this, Chad." She looked around to make sure no one was watching or listening. "I just don't think it would be appropriate."

"Dang Jess. I know it's over between us. That's not why I want to stay."

"No? Why then? You sure haven't been doing a very good job these last few months, or shown any interest in any of the young horses, have you?"

"Well now," Chad nodded in fake agreement, "I can see

how you'd think that. But I've had a lot on my mind lately. Personal stuff. I have it worked out now, though. What d'you say? Give me a chance?" He was grinning slightly and he reached gently for her. No sooner had his hand reached her shoulder then she angrily brushed it away.

"No, Chad." There was no question this time that she meant it. "Now, is there anything else?"

Chad's grin quickly faded. "No. I guess there isn't."

"Good. Then get back to work."

Henry met Jessie by the unfinished round pen close to the barn ten minutes later. The pen had been an ongoing project for nearly five months with either Jessie or one of the wranglers working on it as time allowed. The only problem had been that over the past several months, there really hadn't been much extra time to dedicate to it. As a result, the pen had been going up in fits and starts. Four months earlier, after the sixty-foot round pen had been measured and laid out, the holes were dug for the posts to go in. But then it had been weeks before the posts were able to be set. When they were, it was usually only two or three at a time. Two months later, once all the posts were set, the rails that would make up the fence needed to be nailed into place. Since this was a project that only got attention when two people were free to work on it, the rails went up three or four at a time. On a sixty-foot diameter, six foot tall, five-rail fence, that had proven to be time consuming.

However, after four months there were finally only six more rails to be hung before the pen would be finished, and Jessie was adamant about getting it done before the end of the season. It would be one less thing for her to have on her ever-growing list of things to do once the place closed down. On top of that, with Jim now out of the picture, it was looking more and more like whatever projects she had going into the summer were projects she would have to do on her own. Although she wasn't afraid of hard work, she also didn't see the need to work herself into the ground, either.

Henry could see what needed to be done, and without any direction from Jessie he grabbed one of the eight-foot long, three-inch diameter pine rails and brought it to the fence. Jessie climbed to the top of the fourth rail and straddled it while Henry propped the rail he had brought over into place just above the rail Jessie was astride. With Jessie holding one end of the rail, Henry nailed the other end into place.

Still upset about her conversation with Chad, and having detected alcohol on Henry's breath in the dining room, Jessie couldn't help herself.

"You smell like alcohol," she said bluntly. "Have you been drinking?"

Henry stopped what he was doing, and looked over at Jessie. The question took him by surprise. "No ma'am." He paused. "Not today anyway."

"I see," she was aggravated. "That smell is from drinking last night?"

"You'll excuse me for sayin' so, ma'am. But I reckon what I do on my own time is my own business."

"That's true enough. Except when it starts hurting my business. This is a family ranch and I can't have my help smelling of liquor during the day."

Henry let out a deep sigh. He hadn't had this exact conversation with the people he worked for in the past, but he'd had similar ones, and he could see where it was going.

"If you're goin' to fire me," he said, taking the last two swings at the nail. "I guess you'd best go on ahead and do it. I found this job, I reckon I'll find another."

"I don't want to fire you or anybody else," Jessie said, letting out an exhausted sigh of her own. "But I do need to do what's best for my business. If you're drinking continues, and I keep smelling liquor on you during the day, I will have to let you go."

Henry nodded in agreement. After all, what else could he do? It was her place and her rules were her rules. Besides, he wasn't so much of a drunk that he couldn't see the practicality in what she was saying. He would have said the same thing to one of his employees if the shoe were on the other foot. He went to the end of the rail Jessie was holding up and started driving a nail into place. Jessie, seeing the two of them were in apparent agreement, decided to change the subject. "I liked the way you handled that situation a while back, by the way."

"Ma'am?"

"The broken reins. At the breakfast ride," she reminded him. "You saved one of those wranglers a lot of time by not having to ride back to the barn."

Henry shrugged, and then finished pounding the nail into the rail.

"You're a pretty fair hand. Where you headed after you leave here?"

"No offence, ma'am." Henry headed over to the pile of rails, but stopped and looked back at her before pulling one out. "Because you sure got a nice place. But to be honest, I'll probably just see if'n I can find a job chasin' cattle somewhere."

"I see," Jessie nodded.

Henry pulled a rail from the pile, brought it back and put it in place at the bottom of the next section. Jessie grabbed the other end to steady it as Henry began to pound the nail that would hold his end in place.

"This place used to be a cattle outfit years ago," she said with a smile. "Turned out my father liked horses more than he liked cattle, though."

Henry went over and pounded the nail in the other end of the rail near Jessie. It went in quickly.

"He started gathering and training mustangs about forty years ago," Jessie continued. "In fact, when my father first started to bring guests on the place to help pay the rent, mustangs were all we had, so that's what they rode. Our neighbors found out dad's horses were safe enough for near beginners, so they began to come around and buy them up from us, to use on their ranches or for their kids. To keep up with the demand, he started teaching me how to do the training."

After the rail was secured, she walked over to where a canteen was hanging on the fence, took a drink and wiped her mouth with her sleeve. She then offered the canteen to Henry, who was still somewhat dehydrated from the night before, and took a long drink, as well.

"What about you?" she asked as he handed the canteen back to her. "Ever done much horse training?"

"Some." Henry shrugged. "Mostly I just got on till they quit bucking, then we'd go to work." He retrieved another rail from the pile and positioned it above the last.

"The cowboy way, eh?" Jessie asked knowingly.

"It always worked for me." Henry set the nail in one end and began pounding.

"Let me ask you this," she said, positioning the other end of the rail for him. "Would you ever be interested in learning an easier way? I mean, if the opportunity presented itself?"

"I'm always for findin' an easier way to do *anything*." He started a nail on the end she was holding. "When it comes to horses, I been doing it the same way for so long I don't know if I *could* do it any different."

"I bet you never thought you could ever work on a guest ranch either," she said glibly. Henry stopped and looked at her. She was right—that *was* something he never thought he could do. Quietly, he turned and went back to the pile to gather another rail.

The remainder of the rails went up easily and quickly, and before long the project was finished. Jessie thanked Henry for his help and they went their separate ways, Jessie to take care of the next impending crisis her staff was experiencing, and Henry scooping manure out of the other corrals. Henry wasn't sure what to think about the conversation he and Jessie had, and it weighed on his mind the rest of the day and into the evening. He was having trouble figuring if Jessie had been making idle conversation with her questions about working with horses, or if she had something else in mind, like asking him to stay on after the season was over. Finally, while sitting on the trashcans out behind the kitchen and having his supper, Henry decided it'd be best just to let it go. Whatever was on her mind, if anything, he'd probably find out soon enough.

Henry took his plate into the kitchen, thanked the kitchen help for his supper, and went back to the bunkhouse. His first thought was to pull the bottle out of his footlocker and start his nightly self-medication process. But it was such a pleasant evening, with a slight warm breeze coming from the south and the beginning of a beautiful yellow, orange sky developing in the west, he decided to have a seat on the porch and just sit for a few minutes.

He had been sitting in a rocking chair, gently rocking back and forth for nearly a half hour when he noticed Jessie walking across the yard toward the corral, where some fifty horses had their heads down and were eating from the piles of hay that were scattered about. He watched as she climbed between the wooden rails of the fence and stood quietly inside the corral. The horses all stopped eating and one by one, slowly made their way over to her. Like the conversation the two of them had earlier in the day, he wasn't sure what to think about what he was seeing, and he stopped rocking and leaned forward, as if that would somehow give him a better vantage point. Soon, Jessie appeared to have been consumed by the herd as they circled around her, and Henry, becoming concerned for her safety, got to his feet to get a better look at what was going on.

If Jessie could have seen the worry on Henry's face, or if she would have even known he was watching, she would have laughed. This was something Jessie had been doing with the horses since she was a little girl. It worried her parents at first, too, seeing their little girl all by herself in a pen full of (at the time) wild horses, and them milling around her to a point where she disappeared. They had warned the young Jessie about going in with all the horses, and at ten years old, even threatened punishment if they caught her doing it again. But it didn't stop her, and eventually they realized what she already knew: the horses weren't going to hurt her. Even back then, anytime things got to be a little too much for her, she would go spend time with the horses, and before long, her worries would fade like the last note of an old song. There had even been times back when she lived in the city when she longed for her herd, even for just a minute or two, when she could stand amongst them and draw from their strength.

Of course Henry had no concept of what she was doing, or why. He had always loved horses, as most stockmen do, and had even had pretty special relationships with a couple of them during his lifetime. But mostly, horses were tools to get a job done, and in some cases, just a necessary evil. So of course as he watched Jessie disappear in the mass of horse bodies that surrounded her, he was concerned. It was easy to get hurt around horses, especially that many all at once. All it would take is one of them kicking at another and missing, and just like that somebody'd be hauling her off to the hospital.

Instinctively he started heading for the porch steps but stopped when a few of the horses moved just enough for him to see Jessie's head and shoulders, and the smile on her face. He saw her talking to each horse as she pet them on the head, or neck or shoulder, and the horses all responded quietly to her touch.

Jessie moved slowly through the herd, and talked to each one as she made gentle contact with them. "Hello Fancy.

Dakota, how are you? Well, there's Zephyr. I haven't seen you in a month. Amigo, how are you today?"

Dust rose from under the horse's feet as they moved in a slow circle around her, and the setting sun gave the entire scene a crimson hue Henry had never seen before. He continued to watch for several minutes, almost in awe at the relationship Jessie had with her horses, and it was only after she had made contact with each one that she made her way back through the herd, climbed through the fence and walked slowly back the way she had come.

As soon as Jessie was out of sight, Henry stepped off the porch and nonchalantly made his way over to the pen she had just vacated. He stood outside the corral for several seconds, looked in every direction to make sure nobody was watching, then climbed through the fence and in with the horses. He stood in the same spot Jessie had when the horses first approached and waited for them to respond. The horses barely acknowledged his presence, and then turned their backs to him and walk away as if he weren't even there.

"I'll be damned," he said to himself. He turned and looked in the direction Jessie went when she left the pen, and wondered what kind of magic she used on the herd. He looked back at the horses, and found they had dispersed all over the pen and gone back to eating the piles of hay scattered on the ground. "How the hell'd she do that?"

CHAPTER 20

Most people seem to have one or two landmark days in their lives—days that shape them in some dramatic way, or perhaps send it off in a direction they weren't expecting. Henry McBride had three such days. The first was when he met his lifelong sweetheart, Annie, the second was when his son Josh was born, and the third was when he lost them both. Henry didn't know it at the time, but the day after he saw Jessie in the pen with the horses would be yet another.

That day, he and Dan had been picked to go to town and pick up a load of grain from the local feed store. They were nearly finished loading the twenty, fifty-pound sacks of grain in the back of the ranch pickup when Henry noticed a construction worker coming from the café next door. At first, the man's face looked familiar, and then as the man got closer, Henry realized he actually knew him from his days working a ranch up near Sand Point, Idaho. His name was Dick Reynolds, but everybody called him Sunny Dick. This was because he had lost all his hair from a childhood illness and the kids he grew up with said his bald head was as bright as the sun. Sunny Dick had been a fair hand with cattle and horses, but his real strength was drinking hard liquor. He could hold more whiskey than men twice his size and had drunk Henry under the table on more than one occasion.

"Sunny?" Henry shouted. "Sunny Dick?"

Henry jumped down from the loading dock and quickly made his way over to his old friend.

"Who the hell's that callin' my name?" Sunny yelled back.

"Hell, Sunny, it's me, Henry. You goin' blind in yer old age?"

"Well, I'll be damned." Sunny turned and headed for Henry. "How the hell are ya, Henry? I ain't seen you in years."

"I'm getting' by, Sunny," Henry grinned as he shook his hand. "How about you? What the hell's with this git-up? You a nail-bender now?"

"'Fraid so," Sunny nodded with a smile. "I got drunk one night a few years back and shot old man Breecher in the foot. I'll be damned if he didn't fire me the very next day."

"That old booger. He never could take a joke."

"Ain't that the truth?"

"So you ain't cowboyin' at all no more?" Henry sounded disappointed.

"Hell no. I couldn't find no work. The only place I could get a job was on a dude outfit up in Wyoming."

"Damn, Sunny," Henry said, forgetting for a moment *he* was working on a dude outfit.

"Yup," Sunny grinned. "Well, I remembered how we used to say that if one of us ever got so stupid we went to work on a dude outfit, the other one was supposed to put us out of our misery. Hell, I was afraid you'd find out where I was and come up there and put a bullet in my brain. So I got out."

"Damn. Construction? You ain't no nail-bender. You're a top hand. You should be trailin' cattle."

"Not no more, Henry." Sunny crossed his arms in front of himself. "Hell, I guess I just got tired of lookin' at the south end of northbound cattle. Not only that, but this sure beats the hell out of wranglin' dudes. I just couldn't stoop that low. What about you? What are you doin' these days?"

Embarrassed to actually say, Henry hemmed and hawed a bit before finally making up a story about having picked up some day work on a cow/calf outfit forty miles south of town. Henry had chosen forty miles because he knew it would have been close enough that, if the story had actually been true, he would have traveled that distance for feed, but it wasn't so close Sunny would have wanted to go out and have a look at the place. They spoke long enough for Henry to find out Sunny was just passing through on his way to Las Vegas, where he had been hired as part of a crew to work on a new casino that was getting ready to go up. They also talked a little about the "good old days," that for Henry, hadn't actually been that good. It had been back when the wounds of the accident were still fresh, and when he kept himself drunk all day long, instead of just at night, as he did now.

The two men quickly found they didn't really have that much to talk about after all, mostly because the relationship they had in the past had been based around both of them being drunk. While they seemed to have had an unbreakable bond back at the time, it hadn't really been a relationship with any substance, and the longer the two of them talked, the more uncomfortable, and even embarrassed, they both became. Finally, mercifully, Henry broke the conversation off by saying he needed to get back to the ranch, and the two men parted ways, never to see each other again.

Henry's chance meeting with Sunny stirred something in him he wasn't expecting. Seeing him had been like putting Henry right back at that time in his life when the emotional wounds from the accident were still raw and deep and as Henry went through the rest of his day he began experiencing one unstoppable flashback after another. At the beginning, most were pleasant memories: of his days with Annie before Josh came along, then of he and Josh working on the ranch together, or of he and Annie listening to Josh practice his guitar, or of Annie helping Josh with his homework. Later in the day, the memories turned more sinister: of Annie breaking her leg on the step of the tack room, of him waiting at the clinic for it to be set and have a cast put on, and of him sleeping though Josh's talent show. Finally, near the end of the day and just before the bell rang signaling it was time for dinner, Henry was making his way to the bunkhouse to search out his whiskey bottle when, as if it were happening all over again, a visceral flashback of the accident flooded over him. He heard the screams, he saw the flames, and smelled the burning wood, metal and flesh.

It wasn't the first time he'd had this flashback. He'd had it many times before. But this time was different. It was so real he actually felt the heat from the fire on his face and hands, and felt the pain on his head where he'd been cut. The smell from the accident followed him no matter where he went, and the screams rang in his ears over and over like the whining of a siren. Henry ran for his footlocker, only to find the bottle he'd been drinking from the last few days was too close to empty. He quickly chugged what remained, then sprinted for his truck and headed for town as fast as he could.

By the time he got to Mona's bar, his face was ashen white, he was sweating profusely, and his hands were shaking so hard he had trouble pulling the money from his shirt pocket to pay for the first of seventeen rounds of whiskey he would consume during the next five-and-a-half hours. The bar's regulars, men and women who would usually show up between three and five in the afternoon and have a few drinks before heading for home, had all cleared out by ten o'clock, and by half past, the only ones left in the place were Henry and the bartender. Henry had been drinking all night on an empty stomach. This caused the effects of the alcohol to intensify nearly three times what they normally would have been, and with the amount he had already consumed, would have been enough to put any normal person close to unconscious. Still, it hadn't been enough. In the past, the memory would have faded long before now, at least to a point where it would have been manageable. But even as drunk as he was, the memory continued unabated to a point where he felt he might actually be going crazy.

He reached for his half empty glass but misjudged the distance and knocked it over, spilling the contents all over the bar. The bartender calmly came over with a rag, picked up his glass, and wiped up the mess. Henry tried to talk, but no words came out of his mouth. Seemingly unable to speak, he motioned for a refill.

"Sorry man," the bartender said, putting the now empty glass under the bar. "That's it."

"I'll take 'nother," Henry slurred.

"Can't do it, buddy. You've had enough."

"I'll take 'nother," Henry repeated.

"Nope." The bartender shook his head. "That's it for tonight. Go on home and sleep it off. You come back tomorrow and I'll serve you all you want."

Henry was visibly upset, but in no real shape to do anything about it. He tried to get off the stool and lunge for the bartender, but lost his balance and fell face first on the bar, then slid off and fell on the floor. It took every bit of effort he could muster to scramble to his feet and steady himself on a nearby table. The bartender was unimpressed. He'd been in the business a long time and Henry wasn't the first drunk he'd seen fall off a barstool. He looked at Henry and pointed to the door. Henry, barely able to keep his balance, motioned that he understood, turned and stumbled out into the night.

Henry slowly staggered to his truck, which was in the parking lot next to the bar, and upon reaching it, swayed back and forth uncontrollably while he dug in his jeans pocket for his keys. Suddenly, and out of nowhere, he was struck hard from behind with a heavy closed fist. He staggered forward and fell onto the hood of the truck, then slid off and onto the ground.

Chad walked out of the shadows and stood over the now nearly unconscious Henry. "Ain't so tough now, are ya, you old son of a bitch." He began kicking Henry relentlessly and after several vicious blows to Henry's torso and face, Chad was out of breath and had to stop. He looked down at the now fully unconscious Henry, and then spit on him before finally slinking back into the shadows from where he'd come.

Henry was unaware of how long he'd been unconscious and had only slightly come to his senses when he heard the faint sound of what seemed like a dog sniffing. He had been lying on his left side and groggily opened his eyes in time to see a small, mangy dog sniff his legs and boots, then lift its leg and urinate on him. Henry lowered his head back to the concrete and closed his eyes, knowing the taste of total defeat.

Henry's next conscious memory was stumbling out the front door of the liquor store with a bottle in a paper sack and staggering down the street. Beaten, face swollen and bloodied, he climbed into the driver's seat of his old pickup truck, and after several attempts, got it started. He jammed it into gear and the truck leapt and jerked from the curb and headed off into the darkness. He drove out of town and veered off the road and into the desert, going another three miles before finally coming to a stop.

He shut off the truck's motor and headlights and sat for several minutes doing nothing more than stare out into the desert. There was a bright full moon that illuminated everything in sight as if it were nearly midday. Any other time, Henry might have looked around him and marveled at the beauty of the night, how everything was bathed in a bright blue hue, and how the stars seemed so close he could have reached out and touched them. But not on this night. On this night, Henry had reached the end of his will to endure any more pain. The overwhelming grief, guilt and sadness he'd been trying to keep at bay for over seventeen years had finally caught up with him, and he understood now, there was no escaping it.

He clumsily reached over and flipped open the glove box, pulling out the holstered .45 caliber Colt revolver he kept there. He pulled the weapon from its holster and checked the chambers, making sure it was loaded, and then set it next to him on the seat. He rummaged around in the glove box again, this time finding a scrap of paper and a pencil. With the moonlight streaming in the truck's windows, he painstakingly scribbled his last will and testament on the paper. He spoke the words as he wrote them.

"I, Henry McBride, being of sound body and weak mind, do herewith give-ith all my belongings to anybody who can use them. Not that son of a bitch Chad, though." He paused, trying to remember how a will and testament should end. "Amen," was all he could come up with.

Physically and emotionally unsteady and numb, he pulled the old yellowed envelope he'd been carrying around with him out of his shirt pocket, folded the note and placed it inside, along with the black-and-white photo of Annie and Josh. He took the pistol, along with the bottle of whiskey he'd bought, and climbed out of the truck, staggering around to the front. Holding the bottle in one hand and the pistol in the other, he raised the bottle to his lips and took a long swig, then wiped his mouth with his shirtsleeve. Henry stared blankly at the ground for several seconds, wanting nothing more than to have all the hurt and pain go away once and for all. He was tired, very tired, and on that beautiful moonlit desert night, he had finally come to the understanding the only way the pain would go away for good, was for him to make it go away.

He closed his eyes and then slowly raised the pistol barrel to his temple. Several more seconds passed before he very deliberately pulled the hammer back with his thumb. He placed his finger precariously on the trigger and had all but surrendered that final moment on earth when, through all the fog and pain and anguish that had been thundering in his head for so long, came a quiet, soothing voice. "Henry." The voice was as familiar to him as if it were his own. "Henry," the voice whispered. "Not yet." Out of his overwhelming despair and grief, Annie had somehow found him. "Time to change, Henry," her smiling voice told him. "It's not too late. It's never too late." The voice hummed softly a tune Henry recognized but didn't know the name of. The humming faded and Annie returned. "Everything is okay, Henry," she said in the most reassuring voice he'd ever heard. "Now it's time for you to be okay, too. It's time to change."

Henry's entire body began to quiver and tears fell from his tightly closed eyes. He began shaking uncontrollably, and he found himself opening first one eye, then the other. "Time to change, Henry," the voice repeated kindly. Suddenly coming to his senses, he lowered the gun while at the same time raising the bottle up in front of his face. He stared at it for a long time, his mind racing through all of the bars, all of the bottles, all of the jobs and all of the time he had wasted. A feeling of overwhelming anger shot through his body and all of it was aimed at the symbol of his agony: the bottle he held in his hand. He tossed it with all his might, raised his pistol and began shooting at it as it flew.

"You son of a bitch!" he yelled at the top of his lungs. On the third shot, the bottle exploded in midair, but Henry continued to fire the weapon until all six rounds had been expended. The hammer clicked on several empty chambers before Henry finally quit pulling the trigger and lowered the gun to his side. Out of breath and exhausted, he fell backward against the front of the truck. The desert was quiet now and as much as he longed to hear it again, Annie's voice had gone quiet, as well.

A peacefulness slowly washed over him, and he suddenly felt as though the weight of the world had been lifted from his shoulders. He glanced up at the sky and for the first time, saw the beauty of the full moon above him, and it brought a genuine smile to his face. Henry hadn't realized until just then, but the day's date was March eleventh—it was his birthday. He was fifty-two years old.

CHAPTER 21

The old horse had been in a lot more pain lately than anyone really knew, but because nobody ever took the time to watch him move around inside his pen, nobody ever noticed it. While Tug had been looking out for Zip's well-being by keeping him in the pen for the winter, limiting his movement was the worst thing he could have done. The overall lack of movement the pen provided was causing the gelding's joints, already limited in movement by the debilitating arthritis he suffered from, to become even less active, and thus more painful. In the past month, things had gotten so bad he began limiting himself to trips to and from his water tank and feed pile, and very little else. Even his manure ended up in one small area of the pen, a fact the men cleaning the pen took for him consciously wanting to keep it relatively unsoiled, rather than the old horse not being able to go elsewhere to defecate.

To the casual observer, the old gelding had looked perfectly normal that day. The people passing by or looking in on the colt in the pen next to him saw nothing at all out of the ordinary. In one instance when Tug went past, Zip had been eating. In another instance when Ben came by to toss hay, he was standing with his eyes closed, resting. In reality the pain in his hindquarters that day had been so bad his gut had begun to shut down. A gas bubble had developed in his large intestine, and another in his small intestine, which wasn't allowing the digested waste matter coming from his stomach to ultimately be expelled. Waste matter backed up behind the gas bubbles, which made him acutely uncomfortable, and in an attempt to relieve the pain in his gut, the old horse got down and rolled. It had been everything he could do just to get down on the ground and back up, but by the time he did, he had signed his own death warrant. The act of rolling caused a section of his bowel to loop around the gas bubble, and when he stood, the weight of the full intestine behind the bubble pinched the looped intestine and closed it down completely. As the sun began to set, the final hours of the old gelding's life painfully started ticking away.

The colt instinctively knew something was wrong with the old horse, but he could only watch helplessly as all during the night he threw himself down on the ground and thrashed violently in the dirt of his pen. From time to time Zip would stop long enough to let out a breathless groan as he lay on his side, caked in sweat-soaked dirt, then he would begin thrashing again. Just before dawn, after a full night of tortuous suffering, the gelding's thrashing quieted, and then stopped altogether. By seven-thirty that morning, when Ben came by to toss the two of them their morning ration of hay, the old horse had already been dead for three-and-a-half hours.

The smell of death and the fact the colt was unable to get away from it made him uneasy, a fact made worse by the steady stream of humans that came by to gaze upon the lifeless body of the old horse in the pen next to him. It was strange to the colt that the humans that passed by the old gelding's pen day in and day out when he was alive, without so much as a glance in his direction, would now come and gather around his corpse, standing for long periods of time, sadly looking down on him and talking amongst themselves in hushed tones.

Eventually, everyone from the ranch showed up. Tom and Terri, Tug, Ben, Matt and several humans the colt had never seen before. They all came into the pen, shook their heads, then left. As the sun rose higher in the sky, the stream of people coming to see the old horse's body stopped and all was eerily quiet. The colt, now more nervous than he'd been since the first day he'd arrived, stood as far away from the body as he could get, clear in the far back corner of his pen. He couldn't even bring himself to go and eat from the fresh pile of hay Ben had tossed to him just after seeing the old horse's body for the first time that morning. He stood in that corner for a long time, until the sun was at its highest point in the sky, when down the alley came the sound of a large machine—a yellow tractor with a big hydraulic bucket on the front, and a back hoe at the rear. It belched heavy black smoke out of the stack that jutted upward from just in front of the cab, in which a sat a man working the machine's controls—a very unnerving sight for the colt. He had never seen such a machine, and he wasn't sure if what he was seeing was a different, gigantic, angular, and loud form of human, or if what he was seeing was actually two separate beings, one inside the other. The machine grunted and belched its way down the alley, then swung into the old gelding's pen and stopped a short distance from where he lay.

Ben climbed out of the cab and grabbing a heavy chain from inside the bucket, looped one end around Zip's hind legs, and the other into a heavy hook welded securely onto the bucket. He climbed back into the cab, and then cautiously and respectfully lifted the old horse off the ground. Once the gelding was completely off the ground, Ben backed the machine out of the pen, and slowly drove off down the alley, the old horse's body swinging gently with each movement of the bucket.

Not only did the gray colt suddenly feel very alone, but he also began to see humans in a completely different light.

After watching what they were able to do with the old horse's body, he was beginning to understand humans had much more power over horses than he could ever imagine, and it worried him. If they could pick a horse right up off the ground, there was no telling what they could do to him, should they choose.

That afternoon, the colt began nervously pacing his pen along the fence opposite the pen where the old gelding had lived. The colt took eleven steps, turned toward the fence, took eleven steps back, turned again, and repeated the pattern for hours on end, stopping only briefly to get a mouthful of hay or a drink of water. Tug had Cat bring one of the saddle horses over from the barn and put him in the pen the old gelding had lived in to see if that would help settle the colt. It did seem to help some, but not much.

After three weeks of nearly non-stop pacing by the colt, Tug finally decided maybe the best thing to do was to get the colt over to Jessie King and get him started on his training. Now that the youngster was feeling better, physically, Tug just assumed he was going a little stircrazy from being cooped up and not having anything to do, and getting him to a new place and new challenges might be just the thing to snap him out of his worry. After talking the idea over with Tom and Terri, Tom agreed with Tug's assessment and made the call to Jessie to set up a day they could bring the colt over.

As it turned out, the day the colt was to be delivered was the same day Henry had put the finishing touches on the three-week project he had been involved in since his exhaustive night in the desert. As promised, Chad had saved the two-and-a-half miles of fencing that needed to get done in the back of the ranch property for Henry, and with his face having been so badly bruised and cut from the beating he took in the parking lot of the bar, nobody thought it prudent for the guests to see him for a while.

While Chad was hoping the fencing project, a demeaning job for someone with Henry's skills, would be enough to get Henry to want to quit, for Henry the project had just the opposite effect. Getting out on his own and away from the ranch, people, and even more importantly, away from town where liquor was easily accessible, was just what he needed. In fact, while it would have been easy for Henry to make the four-mile ride from the fence he was working on back to the ranch at the end of every day, he chose to take a couple packhorses loaded with supplies, and he stayed by himself for the three weeks it took to repair the fence.

Admittedly, he wasn't able to get much work done the first five days he was out. His body had to suffer the very painful, but necessary detoxification process it needed to go through to rid itself of the poisons Henry had been pumping into it for the past seventeen years. By the time he had ridden out to the fence the day after his time in the desert, his symptoms had already started.

Without having any alcohol to drink for nearly ten hours, his head began to ache and his stomach turned sour. A day after not drinking, he craved alcohol so badly he thought about trying to ride his horse all the way to town to get some. After two days of not drinking, hallucinations began to develop. They started innocently enough with him seeing rabbits and squirrels where there weren't any. Over time they started turning more dramatic and frightening, with him seeing snakes, bears and at one point even a dragon. He also began hearing sounds that weren't there and detecting odd smells, both of which he would spend hours during the day searching out the source he would never find. Three days after quitting, mild convulsions and seizures began to occur, along with migraine headaches, vomiting, and sweating while he was cold and shivering when he was hot. By the fourth day, Henry shook uncontrollably, and was unable to stand or even crawl because of it. He felt as though ants were crawling over his skin, he retched uncontrollably and his nose bled as if it had been broken. Finally, he lost control of all bodily functions and at one time even felt as though he was having a heart attack. But by day five, his body had once again begun to stabilize, and for the first time in years, he fell into a quiet and peaceful sleep that lasted nearly sixteen hours.

On the sixth day Henry woke up with some muscle soreness, but otherwise feeling better than he could ever remember. His head and eyes were clear, his breathing was easy and his natural energy had returned. By midday, Henry had eaten a full meal of canned chili cooked over an open fire, bread and coffee. Immediately after eating, he was up and starting to string wire on the two-and-a-half mile stretch of fence that had been assigned to him by Chad. Henry would continue on the project for the next two weeks, stopping only to eat, drink, sleep and tend to his horses.

By the time he got back to the ranch, Henry was a different person. Much of the bruising from the beating he took from what he believed to be an unknown assailant was fading, and the cuts and scrapes were also healing well. He had gone a full two weeks without even the hint of a flashback or nightmare, and had been sleeping through the night without any trouble. Even though things were beginning to turn around in Henry's life, things were still the same at the ranch. No sooner had Henry ridden up to the corral and got his horses and equipment put away, than Chad put him to work scooping manure from the corrals and pens.

Henry was dumping the last wheelbarrow full of manure of the day into the spreader when he heard the sound of a truck and large enclosed stock trailer rattling its way up the driveway and into the yard of the ranch. He quit what he was doing to watch the rig pull around the bunkhouse and stop at the new corral Jessie and Henry had finished several weeks ago. There was sporadic loud banging and the panicked whinnying of a horse emanating from the trailer as the rig backed up to the open gate of the corral. Jessie was waiting near the gate and as the rig pulled to a stop, she opened the trailer's back door and the dark gray mustang colt jumped from the trailer and into the corral. Jessie closed the trailer door, then swung the corral gate shut and latched it. She then turned to look at the horse, which was running frantically around the inside of the round pen, looking for a way to escape.

It had already been a confusing and frightening day for the young colt that had begun shortly after dawn. He noticed an unusual amount of activity in and around the alley just outside his pen. Tug, Ben and Matt had opened several gates, and closed others to create a path through the four-hundred-foot-long, twelve-foot-wide alley that ulti-mately ended with the alley narrowing into a three-foot-wide chute. At the opposite end of the chute was a sliding metal gate that opened into a large catch pen. Cat had pulled the ranch truck and stock trailer into the catch pen and backed it up to this gate, with the trailer's sliding stock gate also opened and lined up with the chute's open gate.

As the commotion in the alley subsided, Tug came back to the colt's pen and opened the gate. No sooner had he done that when Cat climbed over the fence on one side of his pen, and Ben climbed over the fence on the other, and both men were at the back of the pen and behind the colt, leaving the only place for him to go was to the gate Tug had just opened. Feeling as though he needed to run for his life, the colt bolted for the opening and turned to the right. He went only a short distance before running into what looked like a fence across the alley that blocked his way. He turned around and saw an opening for him to flee back the way he had come, so he took it. He went clear to what he thought was the end of the alley, only to find another opening that went off to his left, so he took that, too.

After making the turn, he had gone only about a hun-dred feet when he noticed the end of the alley he was in narrowed down to what looked to him to be a small black hole. He stopped dead in his tracks, wheeled back around and tried to go back the way he'd come, but found it closed off by another fence. He knew he had just come from where there now was what seemed to be a solid fence. He charged up to the fence and frantically paced back and forth in front of it, dropping his head low, looking for an opening big enough for him to get through, then rearing up to try and find an opening somewhere above.

Finding neither, he wheeled back around and headed back toward the hole, only to turn back again. When he did, he found once more that the fence had moved closer to him. This worried him even more and he turned and ran toward the hole again. Again he turned back and again, the fence had moved closer to him. He realized then that the moving fence was forcing him into the black hole.

It had been a technique stockmen used for nearly as long as there was stock that needed to be moved from one place to another. Alleys were set up with a number of gates hung at different intervals throughout, so animals could be moved simply by getting them headed in the direction they needed to go, then as soon as they got past a certain point, someone would close a gate behind them. Doing this effectively shortened the distance one ultimately needed to travel with the stock, and also got them closer to the destination without them being able to go back the way they came. Every time the colt passed one of the gates in the alley, one of the ranch hands would simply swing a gate shut behind him, moving him closer to the trailer by twenty-foot intervals. If he got stuck and refused to move closer to the trailer, either Cat, Ben or Matt would take off their hats and wave them around in the colt's direction. That was always enough to get him moving again. After an hour, the men had worked the colt past the final gate in the alley, and like the others, it, too, swung closed behind him.

The colt was consumed by worry and ran in circles, whinnying and snorting and doing everything he could not to go any closer to the black hole. At one point he even tried to scale the fence by climbing up the rails, but all that did was skin up his legs and cause him to fall backwards landing first on his hip, then on his back. He quickly scrambled to his feet and began circling the other direction.

Tug understood the reason the colt wasn't going any further was because of the way the inside of the trailer appeared to him. Being so early in the day, the inside of the high-sided, covered stock trailer was all in shadows and was very dark. He knew instinct wouldn't allow the colt go into something that looked so unnatural, and he also knew he'd have a better chance of getting him inside if there was more light in there. After nearly forty minutes of the colt circling, scaling the fence and circling some more, Tug did what he wished he would have done to start with. He went to the passenger side of the trailer, up by the front, and opened the escape door, which allowed sunlight to fill the nose of the trailer. Almost as soon as the interior of the trailer lit up, the colt turned and looked toward it.

Light at the end of a dark tunnel means the same to a horse as it does to a human—a way out. The colt, extremely wary of the narrow chute he would need to pass through to get to the apparent opening, chose to go forward rather than stay. No sooner had he entered the chute than another gate closed behind him, blocking any escape other than the one directly in front of him. The metal chute clattered loudly under his feet and caused him to nervously scamper across it all the way to the step he would need to take to get inside the trailer. Every eight feet or so, another gate had closed behind him, this time sliding in from the side as opposed to swinging closed, as the others had.

Finally, he stood in an eight-foot-long, six-foot-tall, three-foot-wide opening with the light of the escape door nearly twenty feet away inside the trailer. The last gate to close behind him began sliding back and forth, six inches at a time, making a loud clanging noise as it did. The noise heightened the colt's worry, and he tried to go over the top of the chute rather than go into the trailer and toward the light. Finally, after six attempts at going over the top, and seeing nothing he was doing to try to escape was working, he sunk his whole body down about as low as it would go, and with the gate behind him banging and clanging, he launched himself into the trailer. He no sooner landed inside than the light from the escape door went out.

The men had tried as hard as they could not to overstress the colt any more than he already was during the process, but the bottom line was, they needed him in the trailer. As Tug had directed, once the colt got to the back of the trailer Matt was to open and close the sliding gate behind him, intentionally making a little noise and trying to encourage the colt to move forward. As soon as the colt decided to jump in, Tug closed the escape door. Now it was just a matter of getting the colt to Jessie King. The rest was up to her.

The trip to Jessie's place was supposed to take a little over an hour and a half, one way. If everything were to go right, Tom (who would be driving) would be back to the ranch before lunchtime. Unfortunately, on this trip it seemed nothing would go right. Tom hadn't gotten more than ten miles down the road when the left rear tire on the trailer blew. It wouldn't have been that much of an issue, but the trailer jack, a piece of equipment that is always with the trailer, wasn't. Tom was forced to unhitch the trailer and leave it on the side of the road with the colt still inside, while he drove back to the ranch and retrieved the jack. An hour later, Tom had removed the flat tire, put on the spare, and was back on the road. He hadn't gotten another five miles when the right rear trailer tire blew. With no spare, Tom was forced to once again, unhook the trailer, this time drive to town, get the tire replaced at the local tire store, drive back and replace the flat. All of that took an additional two-and-a-half hours.

Worried that he still had no spare for the trailer, he hooked the trailer back on to the truck, drove to the tire store in town and bought a spare. Another hour was shot. By this time Tom was beyond hungry. He accidentally overslept that morning and had to skip breakfast. Figuring he'd be home in plenty of time for an early lunch, he hadn't thought it a big deal. But now his blood sugar was running low and he was getting cranky. He was already late, and he figured a quick stop in the local diner wasn't going to hurt a thing. Unfortunately, he got to the diner for his lunch about the same time everybody else got there, and just like that, another hour and a half had been added to his day. Then there was the road construction, which he wasn't expecting, that added an additional hour, and the jackknifed semi tractor-trailer that blocked both lanes of the two-lane highway for another two-hour delay. When he finally got to Jessie's place it was nearly a quarter to five in the afternoon.

By the time they reached their destination, the colt was beside himself. For nine hours he had been stuck in the smallest enclosure he'd ever seen, much less been in, and if it wasn't moving, it was rocking side to side or throwing him forward or back. He tried to understand how he was going to live his life in the dark box that thoughtlessly threw him around, as for all he knew, he would never get out of it.

It was for that reason when the dark box stopped moving and back door of the trailer swung open, he instinctively bolted. Once outside, however, he found he was only slightly better off than he had been in the box. Without thinking, he had simply jumped headlong into another enclosure, and frantically looking for a way out, he ran for all he was worth, only to find the fence of the corral kept turning him in one circle after another. He had gone in circles so fast he didn't even notice that the opening to the box he'd come in had closed, and in it's place was just another part of the fence. Unlike his pen next to the old gelding, in this one there didn't appear to be any way out, or any way in.

Jessie climbed to the top rail of the fence and lifting first one leg, then the other over it, she sat down and watched as the colt galloped around the inside of the pen. Tom, tired after a long day on the road, also climbed the fence and swinging one leg over the top rail, took a seat next to her. "Well, here he is, Jess, in all his glory. My wife named him Tico, but I guess he'll answer to anything."

"He's a dandy, Tom," Jessie said without taking her eyes off the colt. "Do you know anything about him?"

"He came in with our old-timers when we brought them off the hill." Tom shrugged. "Tug thinks he might be out of that south valley herd that was captured last summer."

"Might be," she nodded. "A lot of grays come out of that band. Probably got separated or pushed out during the drought."

"That'd be my guess, too," Tom agreed. "He's been like this for a few weeks now. When he ain't running in circles, he's been pacing his pen looking for a way out. He barely takes time to eat and sleep."

The colt continued to run frantically, blowing hard through his nose and called loudly in every direction.

"He's definitely a little worked up," Jessie commented. "We'll give him a few days to settle in before we try to do anything with him."

"Whatever you think, Jess."

Henry, who had been watching everything from his vantage point near the spreader, walked over to have a look at the new horse. As he got to the pen, he tipped his hat to Jessie and peered through the rails.

"Hello, Mr. McBride," Jessie smiled. "What do you think of our new boarder?" The colt shook his head and bucked while he circled the pen at top speed.

"I believe I'd keep the amateurs off him for another day or two."

Both Tom and Jessie smiled.

After dinner that night, Jessie skipped her time visiting with guests at their respective tables and walked out in the fading sunlight to the round pen that held the gray colt. He was eating nervously on the pile of hay she had placed in the pen just before Tom left for home, and he quickly raised his head and snorted a warning as she walked up. Jessie smiled at him, but didn't say a word.

"Evenin' ma'am," Henry said, tipping his hat as he quietly walked up next to her.

"Good evening, Mr. McBride," she said, briefly turning toward him. "Looks like he's trying to settle in."

"Yes ma'am," Henry nodded. "He has quieted down some. I'd still pity the fella that takes the first ride on him, though. I expect it won't be a pleasant one."

"Oh, I don't know," Jessie shrugged. "He might just surprise you. I've seen horses a lot worse off than him that did just fine when someone first got on their back. No bucking or carrying on at all."

"I have, too. But usually it was because they'd been drugged up or because someone had tired 'em out first in the sand wash before getting on."

"Well," Jessie nodded knowingly. "I'd be willing to bet this horse doesn't pitch any kind of fit whatsoever the first time someone gets on his back. Even *without* having to tire him out or drug him."

The possibility of what Jessie proposed seemed silly to Henry, even impossible, and he unknowingly shook his head and smiled at the thought of it. "I'll be honest with you, ma'am. If I had somethin' to bet, I'd dang sure take up that."

Jessie turned back to the colt and stood quietly for a few seconds. "Maybe you do," she said without looking back at him.

"Ma'am?"

"Maybe you *do* have something to bet."

Henry had no idea what she was referring to, and turned to her as if questioning what she meant.

"You know the ranch is closing soon, right?"

"Yeah." He still wasn't sure where she was going with all this.

"Okay. Do you have another job lined up?"

"No, ma'am."

"All right then." She turned to him. "I'm going to need someone to give me a hand with things during the off season. Would you be interested?"

"Well," Henry smiled. "My other prospects ain't lookin' *real* good right now. I guess I could see clear to…"

"Okay then," Jessie interrupted before he could change his mind. "Here's the bet. I'll give you the same deal you have now. One hundred dollars a week plus room and board for as long as you want to stay and work. If this horse bucks or pitches of fit of any kind the first time someone gets on him, I'll pay you double for the entire time you're here." This brought a very small smile to Henry's face. "Now," she continued. "If he doesn't pitch a fit or buck, you work for the next whole month for free. How does that sound?"

"Are you sure you want to do that?" Henry's smile was bigger now.

"The question is…" Jessie was smiling now, too. "Do *you* want to do it?"

In the distance, a coyote howled and the colt suddenly jumped and ran a small circle before stopping and giving a loud warning snort in the coyote's direction.

"I believe I could see my way clear."

Jessie looked at the horse and smiled knowingly before turning back toward Henry.

"Good. Then it's a bet?" She offered her hand. Henry looked at it, and as sure as he could be he was in for some easy money, he took her hand a shook it.

"Yes ma'am," he grinned. "A little one-sided, but a bet just the same."

"Funny," Jessie nodded. "I feel the same way."

Both turned and briefly looked at the colt before Henry stepped back from the fence. "Well, I guess I'd better get to bed. I got a pretty busy day on the end of a scoop shovel tomorrow." He shook his head in disgust. "I swear, you'd think Chet could get a little more creative when it comes to finding chores for me nobody else wants to do."

"You mean Chad?"

Henry turned and started walking away. "Whatever," he shrugged. "Good night, ma'am."

"Good night, Mr. McBride."

Henry walked only a few paces before he stopped and slowly turned back toward her. He took off his hat and held it with both hands. "Ma'am," he started. "If it wouldn't be too much trouble, I was wonderin' if you might could call me by my given name…it's Henry. Only lawyers and bankers call me by my proper name."

Jessie turned and faced him, and suddenly, standing there in the ginger-colored light of the fading day, Jessie's rugged beauty slowly washed over him. It was something he hadn't really noticed before.

"I'd be happy to, Henry," she said with a smile. "Providing you call me by *my* given name. It's Jessie."

"Yes ma'am, I know," he stammered. "I mean, I will. Thank you ma'am. Jess. Jessie. Ma'am." Henry felt as if someone had just stepped on his foot, and the look on his face showed it. "Good night, ma'am."

"Good night, Henry."

CHAPTER 22

Originally, Jessie planned on letting the colt be alone in the pen for a few days to let him settle into his new surroundings before she tried to work with him. What she quickly found, however, was a few days wasn't enough. Not only was he not settled in a few days, the colt continued to move nonstop for nearly two weeks, pausing only briefly from time to time to eat, drink or take a short catnap before getting on the move again.

The colt was understandably disoriented and confused. Until the last several months, the only world the colt had known was the one he was born into. That of wandering a one-hundred-sixty-mile radius of open country with a small band of horses he'd known all his life. Since then, however, he'd come as close to death as any creature should and still come out alive; he'd become part of a band of horses so foreign to him there were times he wasn't even sure they were horses. His freedom had been taken from him, and now, just as he had been getting used to the quiet routine of his new, smaller surroundings, even that had been taken from him. He had been forced into a metal box that transported him farther and faster in one day than he could have traveled on his own in a month, and then been placed in the middle of a whirlwind of activity with no way to get away from it. There were humans of different shapes, sizes and ages everywhere, and more horses than he'd seen in his lifetime. Not only that, but both horses and humans were coming and going so often he simply couldn't keep up with all the commotion, and it caused him a great deal of anxiety.

But the thing that worried him the most was that a different human came to his pen each day to feed and water him, and then a completely different human would unexpectedly show up to clean the pen later in the day. It was the not knowing who to expect or when to expect them that kept the colt emotionally off-balance the most, and it was a huge struggle for him to keep up with it all. At the tender age of three years old, the colt simply had no life experience that could help him deal with what he was going through, and without being able to emotionally sort things out very well, he instinctively felt the need to keep himself moving. He didn't know why, or for how long he would need to move, only that he felt better when he did.

Still, the time Jessie had given him to get used to the place *had* helped him. Even with all the commotion and the different people coming and going, after a while the colt was able to see it was all just that: commotion and people coming and going. Nobody appeared to want to harm him in any way, and in fact, two of the humans he had actually begun to feel relatively comfortable with, over time. One was the lady that came by every evening to quietly watch him through the fence; the other was the man who came to clean his pen every day. Most of the others that came around he could either take or leave as far as feeling comfortable with, with one exception. Of all the humans he came in contact with, no matter how fleeting, there was one he didn't like at all, and in fact would run from any time the man came around. There was something about that human that told the colt he couldn't be trusted, and probably never would. As a result, while the colt was starting to feel a little better about some of the humans he came in contact with, as well as his situation in general, he remained extremely wary of the man in the big hat.

The fact that the colt was extremely uneasy around Chad didn't escape Jessie, and in an odd sort of way, she knew exactly how he felt. Jessie was getting more and more uncomfortable around him herself, and she found herself counting down the days until the ranch closed for the season, not so much to be rid of the guests, but more to be rid of Chad. As the season wore on, she could finally see what Mrs. Rodriguez had been so worried about. Chad was no good, maybe not to the bone, but no good nonetheless. She found she was kicking herself nearly everyday for allowing him to get so close to her, for inviting him into her home and for sharing that most intimate part of herself.

The longer the season went, the more distant she had gotten from him until, near the end, she was unconsciously doing everything she could to avoid speaking with him altogether. If she needed to get some information to him, she relayed it through one of the other wranglers. "Steve, could you please tell Chad I need him to… Jake, if you see Chad, could you let him know… Dan, could you ask Chad to…" was the best she could do. If she saw Chad coming, she would go the other way; if he spoke to her, she would try to give one-word answers, if she spoke at all. If she could get away with nodding or shaking her head, she preferred to do that.

It wasn't that Jessie was afraid of Chad, because she wasn't. She wasn't really afraid of much of anything. It was just that there were things in her past she wasn't proud of, whether leaving the ranch and her father when she did and for the childish reasons she did, or some of the things she'd done when she lived in Denver. Jessie understood she was a much different person at forty-two than she had been at twenty-two. But still, nobody likes being reminded of her life's failures, disappointments or bad decisions. For Jessie, Chad's continued presence on the ranch had become exactly that—a bad reminder of all those things in her life that she probably could have, and should have, done differently.

Still, as much as Chad was a reminder of all those things she wanted to forget, the colt was a reminder of all the promise life could hold. It was clear, even at the colt's young age, he had already lived a life full of struggles and bad decisions. The only difference was the colt carried the scars of his missteps on the outside of his body, while most people, including Jessie—and from all indications, Henry—carried them on the inside.

Yet, the colt stood in the round pen every day trying to find a way to move through his life in a way that helped him feel better. No matter how worrisome things were for him, Jessie was aware of how the colt would face them, literally, and try to figure them out. Every day since he'd arrived, the young horse's courage in his situation began to grow, slowly at first, then with more confidence. Lately, she even noticed the colt had taken to following Henry around in the pen as he cleaned it, a feat that, for the colt, would have been unheard of when he first arrived just a couple weeks before.

The final weeks of the season passed quickly and before anyone knew it, closing day had arrived. The last guests had actually left the week before closing day, and with them went the majority of the staff. The only help Jessie kept for the final, non-guest week, which was primarily used for closing the guest cabins and cleaning the big kitchen and dining room, was a skeleton crew of housekeepers and kitchen staff. She also kept as many wranglers as could stay to help clean and oil saddles and tack, move the horses to summer pasture, and generally close things down in the big barn. As it turned out, all but three of the crewmembers were able to stay for the last week. Ted, Todd and Little Steve all had jobs they had to get to up north and had said their goodbyes the day after the guests left. That left Jake, Will, Dan, Big Steve, Henry, and of course, Chad to close the place down and get it ready for the off-season.

While the rest of the crew was cleaning tack, moving horses and closing things down, Chad kept Henry on clean-up duty, scooping manure and hauling it off. It was about mid afternoon on the last day when Henry pushed his fifteenth wheelbarrow full of manure toward the ramp to the spreader. He was almost to the ramp when from behind him he heard Jake call, "Hey Henry, wait up." Henry looked around to see who it was, but kept on going.

Encumbered by his chaps, high-heeled cowboy boots and spurs, Jake broke into an awkward jog and quickly caught up. "How's it going' Henry?"

"Best day of my life," Henry responded unenthusiastically, the dry axle bearing of the wheelbarrow chirping like a bird as he pushed it along the dusty path.

"Yeah," Jake shook his head as he broke from his jog and walked alongside Henry. "Well, just so you know, the rest of us think you got a bad deal, what with Chad makin' you do all this shit work every day."

"No matter," Henry shrugged. "It all pays the same."

"Still, it ain't right." Jake shook his head in disgust. "Anyway, seeing how this is our last day together, a bunch of us are getting' together in town tonight…you know, have a few beers, maybe shoot some pool. We're wonderin' if you wanted to come along."

Henry pushed the squeaky wheelbarrow to the edge of the ramp, out over the spreader and dumped it. "I appreciate the offer, but I believe I'll pass."

"You sure?" Jake smiled, and rubbed his hands together as if just finding a hidden treasure. "They got shooters on special. Two for a buck."

"Thanks anyway," Henry shrugged.

"Don't you know, Jake?" Chad had quietly come up behind the pair and was standing at the edge of the ramp leaning on a scoop shovel. "Old boys like this have trouble holding their liquor. After a couple beers they all start howlin' at the moon and gettin' into fights."

"For once Chub," Henry nodded. "You may just be right."

"Dammit," Chad grunted. "How is it you get a simple name like *Chad* wrong every damn time you say it?"

"Actually…it ain't easy."

Jake couldn't hold back a snicker, which sounded more like a quiet sneeze than a laugh of any kind.

"What the hell are you laughin' at?" Chad yelled. "Get back to work!"

"If you change your mind, Henry," Jake grinned as he walked past Chad, "we'll be at Mona's around eight."

Chad tossed the scoop shovel in Henry's direction, but Henry let it fall to the ground at his feet, kicking up a small puff of dust when it landed. "The mustang's pen needs cleanin'." Chad walked off, trying to strut but only managing to show how intimidated by Henry he was.

With most everybody in town celebrating that night, Henry decided to take a walk around the ranch, clean his saddle and turn in early. He had been sleeping well since his night in the desert, most nights all the way through until morning, and on that particular night he dozed off almost as soon as his head hit the pillow. He slept peacefully until just after one in the morning when he awoke to the creaking of a gate opening and then closing. With eyes open, he lay quietly in his bed, listening.

There was the sudden but unmistakable sound of a horse running in the dirt and loud but undistinguishable whispering of a man's voice in the night. Henry climbed out of bed and made his way to the window. Peering outside he saw a shadowy figure in the round corral chasing the mustang, who was running frantically inside the dark pen, dust rising up in the corral with every worried step. The unsteady figure in the pen threw a rope at the colt, but missed, then gathered the slack for another attempt.

Unbeknownst to Henry at the time, what he was witnessing was the culmination of Chad's frustration with being unable to manipulate the situation—and Jessie—in the direction he wanted them to go. The frustration began to boil to the surface three hours earlier in the poolroom of Mona's bar, when an already heavily intoxicated Chad held himself up with a pool cue, waiting for his turn to take a shot.

"He's a son of a bitch," Chad slurred. "That's why I don't like him."

Dan lined up his shot on the pool table, drew back his cue, and skillfully sent the cue ball the length of the table. It grazed the seven ball, driving it toward the corner pocket, only to have it hit the edge of the bumper, just off target. The seven ball bounced off the bumper and skittered back out toward the middle of the table. "Damn," Dan said under his breath. He stood up and looked at Chad, who was barely able to stand. "Who's a son of a bitch?"

"Did ya know Jess axed *him* to stay a'the ranch 'stead a *me*?"

"Jesus, Chad," Dan shook his head. "Get over it. It's your shot."

Chad stumbled to the table, bent down and did his best to line up his shot, the thirteen ball in the side pocket. "I'm ten times th'hand that ol' fool is. Wha' the hell's she thinkin'?" He hit the cue ball much harder than was necessary, spraying balls all over the table.

"Yeah," Dan said sarcastically. "Nice shot. Maybe its time for you to call it a night."

Chad turned abruptly, losing his balance and almost falling over backward. At the last second he caught himself and with a great deal of effort was able to get righted. "You don't tell me wha' ta do," he grumbled. "I'm the boss 'round here. You son of a bitch. Maybe I'll just kick yer ass."

Jake got up from the nearby table, and having seen and heard enough, walked over and took hold of Chad's arm. "Nobody's going to kick anybody's ass," he said calmly. "Come on Chad, I'll give you a ride home."

Chad pulled away, again losing his balance and falling into a nearby table, then sliding unceremoniously to the floor. He quickly struggled to get on his feet, and after what seemed like a monumental effort, he finally did. He pointed a finger at Dan. "You don't tell me wha' ta do."

Jake came over and helped Chad steady himself. He then gently, but firmly started ushering him toward the door. "All right Chad." Jake was only slightly patronizing. "He won't tell you what to do. Come on, let's go home."

"I'm done for the night, too," Big Steve said getting up from his chair at the table. "I'll give you a hand."

With Jake on one of Chad's arms and Big Steve on the other, the two men half dragged him out the bar door and over to the pickup truck. Big Steve climbed in behind the steering wheel, Jake sat in the middle and Chad poured himself in the passenger seat. Together, the three men started for the ranch.

"I'm ten times the hand tha' ol' son of a bitch is," Chad mumbled to himself. He then turned to Jake. "I'll tell ya one thing. I'm ten times the hand tha' ol' son of a bitch is!"

"Well, it's too late now," Jake said flatly. "He's stayin' and you ain't."

"I'll prove it, too," Chad grunted.

"You ain't gonna' prove nothing," Jake told him.

"The hell I won't. I'll show her wha' kind a hand I am. Once she sees wha' I can do, she'll run tha' ol' son of a bitch off fer sure."

"Don't be stupid, Chad. Just leave it be."

"Don't call me stupid'r I'll kick yer ass!" Chad fumbled for the door handle. "Now pull ov'r so I can puke."

Big Steve would need to stop the truck three more times so Chad could be sick before they got back to the ranch. In between bouts of throwing up, Chad formulated his plan for how he would make Henry look bad, win back his job, and get back in Jessie's good graces all in one fell swoop. He was so drunk he didn't even realize he was vocalizing every step of his plan rather than just working it out in his head, and after hearing what he planned on doing, Jake and Big Steve thought it best to simply drop him off at the ranch gate and head back to town. Both men knew if Chad actually went through with his alcohol-induced plan, not only would he *not* get back in Jessie's good graces, but most certainly his life at the Lazy K would come to an abrupt and irrevocable end. Neither wanted to be around to get caught up in the wake of Chad's self-destruction, or to have Jessie think they had been part of it. The men felt absolutely no loyalty or allegiance whatsoever to the head wrangler, so if Chad was going down, he was going down by himself, simple as that.

The colt had eaten his fill of hay that had been placed in his pen early in the day and had been dozing in the relative coolness of the starlit night when he first detected there was something wrong. A terrible odor drifted past him on the breeze, and as hard as he tried, he couldn't pinpoint where it was coming from. There was the strong smell of cigarette smoke mixed with stale alcohol, beer and the sweat of a human. Not just any human, though. It was the smell of the man in the big hat, the one he didn't like and didn't trust. There was some noise in the distance, the sound of the man in the big hat mumbling to himself, and suddenly there he was, standing near the colt's pen, a coiled rope in one hand and saddle in the other.

The colt snorted a loud warning, then started running furiously in the pen looking for an escape from the foul-smelling human. The heavy wooden gate creaked loudly as the human opened it, entered the pen, and then closed it behind him. Chad staggered to the middle of the sixty-foot enclosure and built a loop in his forty-five-foot lariat. He swung the loop over his head a number of times before finally throwing it toward the colt.

The loud whirring sound the rope made as the human swung it over his head scared the colt to the point where he could no longer think, and in a panic he crashed headlong into the tall wooden fence, bounced off, wheeled around on his hind legs and galloped off in the other direction. The rope zipped loudly as the man threw it toward the colt and hit him hard on his neck and side of his face. It stung, which caused the colt to duck toward the fence, turning and running wildly the other direction. The human built another loop and threw it at the colt but missed him completely. Then another, and another before suddenly the loop dropped over the colt's head and down around his neck.

"I got you now you son of a…" Chad yelled just before the slack came out of the rope and he was jerked off his feet. The rope tightened near the base of the colt's neck and right over the scar he received in his encounter with the stallion. A severe pain shot outward from the scar and quickly enveloped his entire body. He felt a heavy tug on what had now become a noose around his neck and the human suddenly lunged toward him at the same moment.

Henry, who had been leaning on the windowsill in the bunkhouse, watched as the figure in the round pen threw loop after loop at the colt before finally catching him with one of the sloppiest, and luckiest throws Henry had ever seen. One of the first things Henry's father taught him about roping way back when he was just a kid was, you never throw a loop at anything you're not prepared to catch. Obviously, the fellow in the pen had never heard that piece of advice because he no sooner got his loop around the colt's neck than he was yanked off his feet and dragged through the dirt.

Henry was impressed with the fellow's stamina (as well as his stupidity) as he held on to the rope with both hands while skidding along on his belly. Finally, after two-and-a-half laps, the man was apparently unable to hold on any longer and let go. He tumbled, rolled and landed hard against the bottom rail of the corral fence. The colt made one complete revolution around the inside of the pen at top speed and was blindly bearing down on the man in the dirt, when, at the very last second the man rolled out through the space between the bottom rail and the ground.

The noise emanating from the round pen, through the yard and into Jessie's open bedroom window didn't wake her, because by the time all the commotion started she still hadn't gone to sleep. Jessie had gone to bed at her usual time and was just as tired as normal, but for some reason sleep escaped her. She was unusually restless that night and from the time her head first hit the pillow she found herself alternating between tossing and turning, staring at the dimly lit ceiling and glancing at the orange numbers on the alarm clock that sat on the nightstand next to her bed. The sound of the colt crashing into the round corral fence was enough to jolt Jessie from her bed. In one effortless motion she was on her feet. She grabbed the bathrobe from the bedpost and flung it around herself. In seconds she was out of her bedroom, down the steps, out the front door and running barefoot across the yard and toward the mustang's pen.

She barely felt the gravel of the driveway as she sprinted over it, or the softness of the desert sand that made up the area by the barn, holding pens and round pen. Her mind was solely on the mustang and what could have happened that would have made him crash into the fence like he did. As she neared the corral she was shocked to see the shadowy figure of a man lying in the dirt next to the pen, and the colt running frantically inside. She quickened her pace and finally reaching the corral, found that not only was the colt in a full blown panic, but that he had a rope around his neck and was dragging it behind him as he ran.

With her full attention on the horse, Jessie barely noticed Chad getting to his feet and brushing himself off. "What the hell...?" Were the only words she could come up with as she stared at the scene playing itself out in front of her eyes. Instinctively she sprinted for the gate, but before she could get it unlatched, Chad stumbled his way toward her with open arms.

"Hi Jess," he slurred, smiling broadly. "I got yer horse caught up fer ya."

"You idiot!" Jessie yelled. "What have you done? He's got a rope around his neck!"

"Tha's okay... it wan't mush of a rope an'way. He kin keep it long as he needs it."

Chad reached out for Jessie and tried to give her a kiss, but just as he got within arm's length she reared back and slapped him hard across the face. The force of the blow knocked Chad off balance and sent him tumbling backwards in the dirt.

Henry, who was still watching from his vantage point in the bunkhouse, turned from the window and walked back toward his bunk. "Ain't none of my business," he said to himself.

Jessie went back and fumbled with the gate latch, trying to get it open. "It's all right," she said in a voice that was quiet, yet full of emotion. "It's okay. I'll get that off..."

She barely had enough time to feel the tight grip of two hands on her shoulders before she was yanked backward away from the gate and thrown to the ground. She hit the back of her head as she landed, which stunned her briefly, but she came to her senses in time to see Chad standing over her and glaring down at her menacingly. "Who do you think you are?" he growled.

Jessie began to scramble backward, but Chad followed, kicking her in the legs as she tried to escape. "I was just tryin' ta help. An' this is how ya repay me?"

"Chad, listen to me." There was firmness in Jessie's voice as she continued crawling backward, Chad continuously thumping her with the toe of his boot. "Don't do this."

"Hey lady, I don't work fer you anymore. I can do any damn thing I want."

"No Chad." Jessie's voice was more commanding now. "You've done enough for one night. Go sleep it off. You're drunk!"

"You know what…I don't think so." Chad reached down to grab Jessie, but before he could, the flat end of a scoop shovel hit him squarely in the face with tremendous force, sounding very much like a cast iron fry pan being dropped on a hardwood floor. Chad flipped over like a rag doll, landing hard on his back. He found himself senseless, but conscious, and through slightly blurred vision, he recognized the form of Henry McBride standing over him, holding the shovel and smiling down at him.

"Well Chuck," Henry said. He held the shovel in front of Chad's face, "that's the other thing this can be used for."

Chad did his best to get to his feet and try to make an ill-advised fight of it, but before he could get to a full sitting position Henry's thunderous right fist crashed down squarely between Chad's eyes and everything went black.

CHAPTER 23

Henry woke at his usual time the next morning, but found he was quite tired from the overall lack of sleep. After his encounter with Chad during the night, and acting on Jessie's request, he had gone and found the keys to Chad's pickup truck among the belongings Chad had packed and set at the foot of his bed the previous day. Henry drove the truck to where Chad still lay unconscious and with Jessie's help, flopped him in the bed of the truck. He threw Chad's saddle and bridle in next to him, then went to the bunkhouse, retrieved Chad's belongings and tossed them on top of the saddle. With Jessie following in her truck, Henry then drove Chad and his belongings ten miles from the ranch and parked the vehicle on the side of the road. Jessie gave Henry a ride back to the ranch, relieved that she was finally rid of the man who had been a painful thorn in her side for over a year.

The way Jessie saw it, drunk or not, Chad's behavior and actions that night had been completely unacceptable and were the last straw. She had unconsciously wanted him off the ranch almost since the season started, and as time went by that feeling had been creeping ever more into the forefront of her mind. Admittedly, it had taken a while, but eventually she had been able to see through Chad's elaborate façade. Nonetheless, on a number of levels she felt more than a little used by him, and she had been upset with herself for a while now—not just for keeping him on at the ranch, but also for falling for him in the first place.

Jessie King was not a vindictive woman by nature, and she knew a good part of the blame rested on her shoulders for not looking out for herself better. Still, if the truth were known, more than just a small part of her was actually happy things ended with Chad the way they did. As far as she was concerned, he deserved nothing better than to wake up hungover, battered and bruised on the side of the road with the hot desert sun beating down on him.

That next morning, Henry had sleepily pulled himself from his bed just as the sky was getting light, got dressed and brewed a fresh pot of coffee. The wranglers who'd been out partying the night before had gotten back to the ranch just a couple hours earlier and were passed out in their bunks, three of them still with their clothes on. Henry poured himself a cup, shrugged into his threadbare canvas jacket, slipped on his hat and stepped outside onto the porch. Steam rose up to great him as he brought the tin mug to his lips, and a perfect sun breached the horizon in the east. He stood quietly, watching as the sky slowly turned from dark blue to a soft yellow-orange, and for the first time in a long time, he found himself welcoming the beauty of a new morning.

He thought about taking a seat in one of the nearby rocking chairs, but in the distance he heard the faint sound of the screen door on Jessie's house opening and closing. Rather than sitting down, Henry moved closer to the steps and leaned on the wooden upright supporting the roof that hung over the porch. Across the yard he could see Jessie heading his way dressed in her faded jeans, large brimmed cowboy hat, denim jacket that was beat up nearly as bad as his own, and her long light brown hair in a thick braid hanging down the middle of her back. He took another sip from his cup.

"Morning, Henry," Jessie smiled while still several yards away. Her smile seemed different somehow—happier, more open, perhaps, than Henry had seen before. It caught his attention and held it for several seconds before he straightened himself up and tipped his hat.

"Mornin', ma'am."

"The others ever get back from the bar last night?" she asked.

"Yup," Henry nodded, stepping down the steps as she walked up. "Sleepin' like babies in there. I expect at least a couple of 'em will be wakin' up somewhere between 'oh lord' and 'my god' in a few hours."

"Happens every year," Jessie smirked. "Last day of the season comes and the first thing everybody does is run down to Mona's bar and blow half their last check drinking too much and spending the rest of the next day wishing they hadn't."

"Yes, ma'am," Henry nodded. "I know what that's like. Been more than one mornin' when I woke up wonderin' if I'd found a rope or lost my horse."

Jessie didn't comment. Instead she changed the subject. "I wanted to thank you again for coming to my rescue last night. I wasn't entirely sure I was going to get out of that by myself."

"*Believe* me, ma'am, I was happy to do it."

"I'm sure that's probably true," Jessie smiled. "But thank you just the same." There was a sincerity in her voice that Henry wasn't accustomed to, and as he stood looking at her in that early morning sun, he felt himself blush.

"Ah," he stammered. "Can I get you a cup of coffee? I just made some. I don't guess it's much good, but it is warm."

"No, thank you. I've already had mine." She turned and looked in the direction of the round pen where the colt, lariat still around his neck, stood with his side to the sun to help warm his body from the chill of the night. "I guess we should see about getting that rope off that little horse over there."

"Yes, ma'am," Henry said, flinging the few remaining drops of coffee from the bottom of his cup out on to the ground. "I've been giving that some thought. I've seen similar predicaments before, and the best way to fix something like this is for me to get a-horseback and drop a loop on him. I'll get him dallied up, slip a halter on him, then take both ropes off." He glanced in his cup to make sure it was empty. "Once the ropes are off you can leave the halter on so's he'll be easier to catch the next time."

"I see," Jessie said. "You feel roping him *again* is the best way to go? Even after the panic it put him through last night?"

"No offence, ma'am, but I believe it's the *only* way."

Jessie stood quietly for several seconds as if going over Henry's suggestion, then nodded in apparent agreement. "And you wouldn't mind doing the roping?"

"Not at all," Henry shrugged. "It's what I'm good at. I've done this a hundred times."

"Well," Jessie smiled. "I guess if you think it's the best way, then you might as well give it a shot."

"Yes, ma'am." Henry placed his empty cup on the porch railing. "Now, do you have one horse on the place that might work better than another? As far as being a good rope horse, I mean."

"Oh yes," Jessie nodded, then turned and pointed toward the back pasture. "Out back, there, is a big sorrel gelding. He's got a star on his forehead and a sock on his left hind. He'd be the best bet."

"Yes, ma'am. I'll get right after it then."

With that, Henry tipped his hat, turned and walked toward the tack room. Jessie couldn't keep herself from smiling. She fully expected Henry to come up with that type of solution to get the rope from around the colt's neck. It was method typical of a working cowboy whose focus was almost always to get a job done as quickly and effectively as possible so he could move to the next task at hand. Jessie also knew the method Henry proposed was not without merit, and on any other horse she may have actually allowed him to do it. But she had something different in mind for the colt, and rather than trying to take the time to explain what she was going to do, or perhaps get into some big long, drawn out discussion about it with Henry, she simply sent him out to get one of the horses she knew would be a little difficult for him to catch. Between Henry trying to catch the horse, grooming and saddling, then getting back over to the round pen, she figured it might just give her enough time to get the rope off the colt before he got back.

The colt smelled Jessie coming toward his pen before he saw or heard her. He thought about moving but had come to understand during the night that every time he moved, the rope that hung from his neck and stretched out in a line on the ground next to and behind him, appeared to chase him. It took him a couple hours during the night to figure it out, but eventually he realized if he didn't move, the rope didn't chase him. So even though he wanted to move when he smelled Jessie coming, he decided to stay still instead.

The decision to stay still may have been more difficult for the colt had the person approaching been anyone other than Jessie. Unlike most of the humans the colt came in contact with, Jessie didn't worry him as much as the others did. There didn't seem to be the underlying edginess in her that most seemed to carry with them, and even though she *was* a human, he didn't feel the need to be as wary of her as he had with the others. As a result, he stayed alert but quiet as she unlatched the gate, entered the pen, then closed and latched the gate behind her. She stood at the gate for a while, watching the colt and his reaction to her presence, before slowly making her way to the center of the pen. Once there, she put her hands behind her back and looked down at the ground in front of her, the brim of her hat blocking her eyes from the colt's line of sight.

What little worry the colt had when Jessie came into the pen started to disappear, and in its place curiosity began to build. He dipped his head slightly to try to get a glimpse of her eyes, but her hat was just too big. He nodded his head up and down in an attempt to get a reaction from her, but none came. Then, as he stood, quietly looking at her, a foggy picture began to form in the back of his mind. It was hard to make out at first, and he wasn't sure where it was coming from. Then, he realized the longer he looked at Jessie, the clearer the picture got, and soon the entire image came into focus. It was a simple picture of Jessie removing the rope from around his neck...nothing more nothing less. It was a picture that was not only visually understandable for him, but there was a feeling to it as well. Along with the picture came an overwhelming sensation that no harm would come to him if he allowed her to take the rope from his neck.

It was something Jessie had been doing with horses since she was a little girl. She never told anybody about it because she doubted anyone would believe her if she did tell them, and besides, there were times when she didn't even believe it herself, so how could she possibly ask someone else to? It was a simple thing, really. She would stand quietly in one spot and develop a very clear picture in her mind as to what she needed or wanted from the horse. Sometimes—in fact more times than not—the horse would replicate through its actions the picture she held in her mind. Other times, the horse might offer something close to what she had pictured, and still other times the horse wouldn't do anything at all. In this case, Jessie pictured herself gently removing the rope from the colt's neck in the spirit of helping him, not hurting or worrying him further. Initially, the picture would form over and over in her mind, like the individual frames of an old hand-cranked silent movie. Then, eventually, the image would begin to hold for longer periods of time until it would finally become clear and vivid, like a full-color photograph.

Instinct told the colt to stay where he was, away from the human, but something deep inside urged him forward. He began moving toward Jessie, one hesitant step at a time, keeping one eye on the rope that dragged on the ground beside him, the other eye trained on Jessie. Jessie continued to keep her head down and hands behind her, in a passive posture until the colt was within arm's reach. At that point, Jessie let out a long, relaxed breath and began bringing her head up so he could once again see her eyes. She let out another breath and lowered her hands to her sides.

"Well, there you are," she said quietly. "Ready to get that thing off?" The colt seemed a little surprised when she spoke, tightening the muscles in his neck and raising his head. Jessie stood quiet for a couple seconds, smiling at the colt and after a few seconds, he warily lowered his head back down and let out a nervous breath. "I know," Jessie whispered. "You're okay."

Out in the pasture, Henry wasn't having quite as much luck with the horse he went to catch. He went out feeling better than he had since he arrived at the ranch, mostly because his day was going to have a purpose other than scooping manure. But as he got closer to the horse he was looking for, he began to see things might not work out as smoothly as he had hoped. First, the big red horse he was trying to catch was caked with mud from a recent roll on the bank of the little creek that ran through the draw the gelding, as well as a number of horses, were standing in. Once Henry reached the draw, he began to build a loop with his lariat as he moved down into it, only to have all the horses move away from him. The big sorrel gelding stayed behind, and at first, Henry thought he was going to have an easy time catching him. As Henry got to within twenty feet of the horse, he slowed his pace and began to talk to him in a low, relaxed voice. "Easy boy. That's it; stay right there for me. I ain't gonna hurt you."

Henry was almost up to the gelding when the side of the tall heel of his boot caught a small rock, causing Henry to stumble. "Dang it," he grunted. Henry's sudden movement and the change in the tone of his voice startled the horse and he turned and started walking after the rest of the herd. "Whoa Red." Henry stumbled again. "Damn it." He regained his balance and continued after the gelding. "Red... Whoa!"

Henry ended up following the gelding, along with the rest of the herd, for another twenty minutes before they all stopped to graze on some new spring grass down by the creek. It was there he was finally able to slide the loop of his lariat over the gelding's head and snug it high around the geldings neck, just behind his ears. He then fashioned it into a halter by slipping a coil of the rope between the loop and the horse's bottom jaw and slipping the coil over the horse's nose. With the makeshift halter, Henry then led the gelding back to the hitch rail by the tack room, tied him up and groomed him, which took another half hour. After over an hour since he and Jessie went their separate ways near the bunkhouse, Henry was finally saddled, mounted and heading toward the round pen. He moved the big, smooth gaited gelding into a slow jog, while at the same time building a loop with his lariat, which he planned on using to catch the colt. Jessie met him half across the yard and Henry pulled to a stop next to her.

"I see you found him," she said, petting the gelding on his shoulder.

"Yes ma'am, I did. But he sure must have found one heck of a mud hole to roll in. Took me nearly half hour get him brushed off." It was only then that Henry noticed the dirty lariat Jessie was holding in her hand. "Oh, thank you ma'am," Henry nodded. "But I'll go ahead and use my own rope for this."

"Yes, I know," she smiled kindly. "This is the one *he* was wearing." She nodded her head in the direction of the round pen.

A little puzzled, Henry bent down in his saddle and looked through the gaps between the rails to the colt's pen. He was able to see the colt standing quietly without the rope around his neck and eating from a pile of hay Jessie had placed in with him.

"I guess we didn't need to rope him after all." She shrugged her shoulders knowingly. Henry straightened up in his saddle and looked back at Jessie. "I was just going in to fix some breakfast," she smiled. "Would you like some?"

"Yes, ma'am." There was a hint of confusion in his voice. "I believe I would. Thank you."

"Come on up to the house after you put your horse up." She turned and headed toward her front porch. "Just come on in. No need to knock." Jessie had no sooner walked away than Henry again leaned forward in his saddle to look at the mustang. He sat for a second in disbelief, not understanding how a feat like that could have been accomplished, and then climbed down from his horse. "Damn." He scratched his head. "How the hell does she do that?"

Even without Henry moving very quickly, it only took a fraction of the time to put the big gelding away than it did to get him out. After turning the horse back in his pasture and closing up the tack room, Henry made his way over to Jessie's house. He was still several yards from her back door when he caught the pleasing odor of bacon frying as it drifted toward him on the morning breeze. Walking up the steps to her back porch Henry had to stop for a second as the sound and smell of breakfast cooking, and Jessie humming to herself in the kitchen triggered a brief flashback of Annie and Josh. Unlike the flashbacks he would get back when he was drinking—the ones that would last for several minutes and send him running for the closest bar or bottle—this one washed over him like the breeze that carried the aroma of breakfast out across the yard.

He knew Jessie told him he didn't need to knock, but he did anyway.

"C'mon in," Jessie chimed. She was standing at the stove scrambling eggs in a pan, and the bacon was cooking in another. As Henry entered, he removed his hat and wiped his feet on the mat just inside the door. "Have a seat." Jessie turned and pointed briefly at the chairs next to the small wooden kitchen table. "This will be ready in just a minute."

"Thank you, ma'am."

"That's quite a saddle you have," she commented without taking her attention off the eggs she was stirring. "How'd you run across it?"

Henry had never been in Jessie's home, and so felt somewhat tentative as he walked over to the table.

"It was my father's, and his father's before him," he said as he gently pulled a chair from the table and sat down. He went to flop his hat on the table next to his plate, then stopped himself and got ready to put it on the chair next to him. That didn't seem right either, and as Jessie, still stirring the eggs in the pan, turned and began to come to the table, Henry quickly dropped the dirty and battered old thing on the floor at his feet.

"Well," she said as she breezed across the floor. "Don't let Tom Essex see it."

"See what, Ma'am?"

Jessie stood next to Henry and scraped half the eggs from the pan onto his plate. "Your saddle." She scraped the rest onto her plate, which sat on the table directly across from him. "He collects those old ones. I swear he must have two hundred of them." She went back to the stove and brought back the pan with the bacon in it.

"I doubt he's got enough money to buy *that* one." Henry's tone was matter of fact. "I expect I'll be buried with it."

She placed several pieces of bacon on his plate. "Well, if he starts hounding you about it, don't say I didn't warn you." Jessie placed the bacon pan on a hot pad in the middle of the table, and then took her seat. Henry had been patiently waiting, refusing to take a bite of anything on his plate until she did first.

"Oh, please, Henry," she said scooting her chair to the table. "Go ahead and eat. You don't have to wait for me."

Henry smiled but waited for her to take the first bite. Once she did, he picked up his fork and dug in. It was about that time it dawned on Henry he was having breakfast with his boss in her kitchen, and he suddenly felt a little self-conscious. Several uneasy seconds passed before Henry finally broke the silence. "Ma'am," he said, swallowing a bite of bacon. "I just gotta ask. How did you get the rope off that horse?"

Jessie swallowed, and then placed her fork on the table next to her plate. "I just tried to show him I wasn't there to hurt him," she said after giving the question a few seconds thought. "Once he understood that, it was easier for him to come to me for help."

The answer made no sense to Henry whatsoever, and he felt himself looking blankly back at her. "Yes ma'am," he finally said. "But how did you get the rope off?"

Jessie sat for a second looking back at him. To her, the answer she already gave was as clear as could be, but it was obvious that its clarity had escaped Henry. "I just slipped it over his head," she shrugged.

Henry waited for her to say more, but after a few minutes, and when it became clear there was no more, he went back to eating his breakfast. He couldn't understand how she could have possibly done what she had. It didn't make sense to him. How could she go in with a wild horse and touch him, much less have the horse come to her and allow her to take a rope from around his neck? He had seen her in with the herd and the way they all gathered around her, and now this. There was something about this woman, something in the way she was with the horses that intrigued him. He had been around horses all his life, been riding almost before he could walk and still he had never seen or heard of anything like what Jessie was apparently able to do with them.

Henry's focus for most of his life had always been cattle. They had been his passion and he prided himself in his knowledge of the animal and the ease at which he could handle them. Horses, on the other hand had simply been a means to an end, almost a second thought. He realized, eating the breakfast of bacon and eggs his boss had made for him, that for Jessie, horses were much more than a second thought. They were not only her livelihood, they were also her life, and she understood them as well or maybe even better than Henry understood the cattle he worked. Henry was a top-notch stockman and he appreciated the fact that he had gotten that way partly by paying attention to other stockmen better and more knowledgeable than he. It came to him then sitting at that breakfast table, that if he paid attention, the small, handsome woman across from him was going to teach him something about horses.

CHAPTER 24

The early summer storm blew in just after midnight, pushing ahead of it the unmistakable smell of rain, snapping spectacular jagged white lines of electricity across the starless night sky like a horizontal spider web. Each crack of lighting was quickly followed by a powerful blast of thunder so loud it shook the bunkhouse where Henry slept. Within minutes of the storm's assault, the rain began to fall—lightly at first, and then heavier as the west wind drove the squall across the desert and over the ranch.

The grand demonstration of light and sound, wind and rain lasted for over an hour before the power locked in the leading edge of the storm crawled eastward, leaving behind a soaking rain that was still falling when Henry rolled out of his bunk just after dawn. He knew about freak storms and the damage that could be done to livestock by them, so without making himself a pot of coffee, he threw on his clothes, clamped his hat down on his head, swung into his old slicker and went out into the weather. Within minutes he'd checked all the horses he and Jessie had brought up to the holding pens the day before after hearing the storm was on its way, and where they had cover under the three-sided loafing sheds scattered throughout the pens. All the horses were standing under the shelters, upright and healthy. He also checked on the mustang, which unlike the horses in the catch pen, had no cover from the weather. The colt was soaked and standing with his head nearly to the ground in an effort to keep his face as dry as possible, and other than being very wet, he was no worse for the wear.

Henry went back to the catch pen and pulled out the buckskin gelding named Mic that three weeks earlier Jessie had given him to ride. He was young, barely four years old. Jessie had started him the past summer, but she hadn't had time to work with him much since. The gelding was Henry's first project after the ranch closed and all the other help left. Jessie had asked him to ride the young horse every chance he got, mostly just to get some miles on him, but also to get him some experience with working for a living instead of sitting out in a pasture grazing all day. Henry had taken her request seriously. He caught the young horse every day, saddled and bridled him and rode him everywhere he went on the ranch. Whether he was going to the back of the property to check fence, a distance of several miles, or if he were simply going from the barn to the bunkhouse, a distance of only a hundred yards, he rode the gelding. Henry grew up in a culture where a cowboy never walked when he could ride, and the young horse he'd been assigned was finding out just what that meant. If the man worked, his horse worked, too, which meant if Henry was doing a project near the barn for the day, the young horse was with him, saddled and bridled and standing tied to a hitch rail.

Henry saddled the young horse in the rain, placed his lariat over the saddle horn, and with water pouring off the brim of his hat, mounted up and headed out across the yard to the open country to start a big circle and do a head count on the horses he and Jessie didn't bring in the day before. It was a quarter after five in the morning.

The storm had kept Jessie awake most of the night and early morning. Realizing she had probably gotten all the sleep she was going to, she grudgingly tossed the covers aside and placed her bare feet on the hardwood floor next to her bed. Rubbing the sleep from her eyes, she looked out the window and saw Henry and Mic, both soaked to the bone, trotting out across the yard and heading for the desert. She glanced at the alarm clock, then back out the window, suddenly remembering something her father told her about cowboys when she was a little girl.

Eight-year-old Jessie and her mother had been in town when she overheard someone refer to a fellow walking down the street as a *dime store cowboy*. When she got back to the ranch she asked her father what it meant, to be a dime store cowboy. Her father said the term referred to someone who wasn't a real cowboy, but just acted like one. "A dime store cowboy will always quit when the going gets tough, or the weather turns too cold, too hot or too wet." He put his gnarled hand on her shoulder and smiled down at her. "The real ones never quit no matter what. They look after their animals before they look after themselves, and they go till the job is done. That's a real cowboy."

"I'll be darned," Jessie whispered to herself as she watched Henry and the horse disappear into the gently swirling mixture of rain and fog at the edge of the yard.

Henry started by heading due west along a wash that was normally dry, but now had two feet of swift running current in it from the storm. He found a good place to cross about a mile or so upstream where the bank was gradual on both sides and the water wasn't too wide, and he brought the young horse to its edge. The buckskin gelding hesitated for a second, watching the fast-running water before stepping quietly across the creek and scrambled easily up the other side. The pair continued along the opposite side of the wash for half a mile, then turned southwest toward a large, lone tree. As expected, Henry found a small band of horses huddled beneath its branches and he stopped to count noses. There were seventeen total, and although he didn't know all the horses names, he did recognize colors and markings and make a mental note of the horses he saw. He turned the gelding due north and headed for another place he figured horses might be holed up, a spot near the river where a large rock outcropping would provide shelter.

With very little wind, the rain was falling almost straight down and limiting Henry's visibility to less than one hundred fifty yards. He scanned the horizon for horses from time to time, but for the most part kept the brim of his hat tipped toward what little wind there was to keep the rain out of his face. After an hour Henry reached the river and followed its bank to the outcropping another half mile up stream. There he found another fifteen head standing dry and quiet in the sand under the rocky roof. With forty-one horses back in the catch pen, seventeen under the trees and the fifteen he found under the outcropping (along with the one he was riding), he figured he was still missing two.

Henry and Jessie had covered most of the ranch on horseback over the past three weeks as a way for Henry to get a feel for the country, learn where the fence lines and gates were, and where the watering holes and places were the horses go to feed were. Along with seeing all of that, Henry also noted places like the two he had just visited, places where horses—or other livestock for that matter—might go to seek out shelter in bad weather. He sat across the river from the band under the rocks and ran through all the places he could remember that might afford a dry, safe place in a storm like the one that had passed through.

There were three spots he could think of off-hand. One was a half-mile-long box canyon lined with trees and rocks, another was a grove of trees a little smaller than the one he had already checked, and one was a shallow ravine with a deep cut into the red rock that lined it. The only problem was all three were over on the other side of the ranch; at least two hours ride to the east. Henry looked up at the gray sky for any break in the clouds that might hint the rain was coming to an end, but found none. He took a deep breath, tipped his head to let the water drain from the brim of his hat, and urged the buckskin forward.

Before going out into the weather that morning Henry had put on several layers of clothes under his slicker. There was the woolen long-sleeve undershirt, and over that he'd slipped a heavy flannel shirt. Then came a light denim jacket, and over that a heavy waterproof canvas jacket. He then pulled on his slicker. As he turned east to head to the other end of the ranch, he realized not only were the seams of his slicker leaking, but the unrelenting rain had caused water to penetrate every layer he was wearing and he was quickly becoming wet all the way to the skin. The situation would have been uncomfortable in a warm rain, but it was near unbearable in the cold rain that was dousing him. Still, he had two horses unaccounted for and a lot of ground to cover before he would feel comfortable about going back. *It's going to be a long morning*, he thought to himself.

To say that Henry was making a big circle around the ranch was an accurate description. He had begun the morning by heading due west, away from the barn. Once he found the small band of horses in the grove of trees a few miles away, he turned and rode north. After a couple more miles he came across the horses near the rock cut. There, he turned and headed almost due east. It wasn't quite nine in the morning yet. He wasn't expecting to find the two missing horses out in the open, which was why he was a little surprised when, after a couple miles of eastward riding, his horse stopped dead in his tracks and his attention suddenly snapped to the right. The gelding snorted once, then called into the rain and fog. In the distance, two separate and distinct whinnies answered. Henry couldn't believe his luck. He had no sooner turned Mic in the direction of the calls when, out of the dim trotted the two horses he had been looking for. The pair excitedly circled he and Mic a few times, and after determining they were both fine, Henry pointed his mount to the west and headed for home, thus completing the circle he had started earlier that morning.

The two stray horses followed Henry and the buckskin all the way back to the ranch. After arriving, Henry turned them in with the others in the catch pen. He then pulled his saddle and bridle from the buckskin and turned him in with the others as well, before carrying his tack back to the bunkhouse. Henry knew that after getting as wet as it had, if his saddle dried without being oiled first the one-hundred-and-twenty-five-year-old leather it was made from would dry and immediately start cracking, ruining the saddle. If he could help it he wouldn't let that happen. *Looks like my day isn't done yet*, he thought ruefully. He was going to spend some time that rainy morning getting oil on his old working partner.

Less than twelve hours earlier, dust would have risen under his feet with each step he took. Now, he was slipping and sliding in the muck and stepping over wide streams of water running down from the yard. After finally negotiating his way to the bunkhouse, he swung the saddle over the porch railing, which was covered by the overhang of the roof and out of the rain, and went in to get out of his waterlogged clothes. It was colder in the bunkhouse than it had been when he'd gotten up five-and-a-half hours earlier, or maybe it just felt colder to him because of the dampness. Either way, he decided a fire would be in order and still in his slicker, he went to the pot-bellied stove in the middle of room and opened the cast-iron door, which made a sound a like a small metallic mule braying.

He loaded the inside of the stove with old newspaper, which he'd wadded up, then placed some small and medium-sized dry twigs on top of the paper. He struck a match on the stove and lit a corner of one of the paper wads, which burned slowly at first. Within seconds, however, a long low whooshing sound emanated from the opening as the rest of the paper caught fire. Henry kept the stove door open for several seconds, allowing enough oxygen in to ignite all the paper, as well as the twigs that sat on top. When the twigs began popping and snapping from the fire lighting the sap pockets trapped inside, he then slipped in a few bigger pieces of split mesquite that sat in a pile next to the stove. He watched until he could see the edges of the mesquite turn black as they kicked up yellow flames. Assured the fire would stay lit, he closed the door.

Layer by layer Henry peeled off his rain-soaked clothes, starting with his slicker and ending with his woolen under-shirt, and hung them all on the backs of the wooden chairs he had placed around the stove. He shivered uncontrollably in the cold dampness of the room. As he rushed to put on some dry clothes he cursed himself for not starting a fire *before* he left to check the horses. He knew better.

Between rubbing his hands together and blowing into them to try and warm them, he poured water into the coffee pot and added the grounds. He then placed the coffee pot on the stove, its smokestack ticking and creaking as it expanded from the heat being generated inside. Henry stood only inches from the stove warming first his hands, then turning around and warming his backside, then turning back to warm his hands. His shivering finally subsided about the same time he noticed steam slowly beginning to rise from each of the wet garments hanging on the chairs. *It could be worse*, he thought to himself, as one last shiver rushed through his body.

Through the din of the rain on the roof, Henry heard footsteps on the bunkhouse porch. Just outside, Jessie stopped at the door, tipped her head and dumped a long stream of rainwater from the brim of her hat. She then shook the water from her slicker and reached up and knocked on the bunkhouse door. She waited several seconds for a response from inside, then knocked again.

"Come in." She could barely hear Henry's voice over the rain hitting the porch roof, and it dawned on her then that he had probably answered her the first time she knocked, but she simply hadn't heard him.

This had been somewhat of a strange day for Jessie. Almost as soon as she finished watching Henry ride out in the early morning rain and fog, she found herself fighting an overwhelming urge to want to talk with him. She didn't know why she wanted to talk with him, and she didn't really have anything to talk with him about. Yet, no matter how hard she tried she couldn't seem to shake the feeling. She felt like a teenage schoolgirl trying to get a glimpse of a new boy as she spent the next few hours interspersing her morning household chores with glancing out the windows to see if he'd returned. By the time he *had* returned, Jessie had come up with something to discuss with him, and after waiting what she felt was an appropriate amount of time, she made her way through the rain and muck and knocked on his door.

It was only after seeing Henry standing next to the woodstove trying to warm himself that Jessie came to understand why such a strong urge to talk with him had come over her. She realized then that she knew absolutely nothing about the man. Normally she would get to know a little about the people that work for her before she hired them by reading a few paragraphs on a resume they had submitted, or by checking their references on a job application. But with Henry she had neither. She had hired him more or less as day help, not knowing if he'd be there any longer than it took to get gas money. She didn't think to ask for a resume, and she doubted whether he had one anyway. She hadn't even had him fill out an application. All she really knew about him was what she saw. And what she was seeing was beginning to intrigue her. After all, it was obvious he was well versed in ranching and livestock, but even with that, what Jessie was having a hard time figuring was: what kind of man would go out in the middle of the worst storm in nearly twenty years to check on horses that didn't even belong to him?

"Mornin' ma'am," Henry said with a slight uncontrollable quiver in his voice. The outside of his body was beginning to warm, but the inside was still chilled. "I just put some coffee on, here. It'll be a minute or two before its ready, and I doubt it'll be any good, but I'd be happy to pour you a cup if you're up for it."

"No thanks," Jessie smiled, "I've had my fill for the morning." She hesitated, debating which direction to go with the conversation she was getting ready to start. Did she begin by asking him some innocuous question about his personal life, like where he was from, or if he had any brothers and sisters, or should she stick to the subject she had come up with while waiting for him to return from checking horses? In the end, she decided it probably wasn't the right time or place to be asking any kind of personal questions of a man she barely knew.

"I've got a customer who buys a couple yearlings from us every year," she finally said, her voice raised so that it could be heard over the rain on the roof. "They need to be delivered in the next couple days. I've been thinking that you've been stuck on the ranch pretty much since you got here and I was wondering if you'd like to take them. It would give you a chance to get off the place for a couple days."

"Where do they need to go?"

"A little town up north, just this side of Winnemucca and right off of I-80 called Humboldt."

It had been years since Henry heard anyone mention the name of his old hometown and the spot where Annie and Josh were now buried. He had been trying as hard as he could over the years to forget the little place and had actually talked himself into believing he had. And yet suddenly hearing the name seemed to hit Henry like a giant fist in the gut. It not only caused his heart to skip a beat but for a second he even lost his breath.

"Are you all right?" Jessie asked, noticing the sudden change in Henry's behavior.

"Oh…yes ma'am," Henry said, quickly bringing himself back. Thinking fast, he wrapped his arms around himself and forced his body to shiver slightly. "I guess I got a little colder out there this morning than I thought I did."

"Would you like to come up to the house and warm up for a while?" There was concern in Jessie's question.

"No, ma'am," Henry shook his head. "Thank you though. This old stove'll have the place warmed up in no time, and when I get a little of that bad coffee in me I'll be good as new."

"Fair enough," Jessie smiled. "So, what do you think about taking the colts up north? You up for it?"

"If it's all the same to you, ma'am," Henry said after acting as though he had thought about it. "I'd just as soon stay here. I'm really liking the quiet, and besides, after losing this day to the rain I'm gonna have a few things to catch up on."

"You sure?"

"Yes ma'am, but thanks for the thought. I will take a rain check, though."

Jessie smiled, thinking Henry was making an attempt at a pun. But then, seeing he was actually serious, she nodded in agreement. "That'll be fine," she said, turning for the door. "I'll make this delivery. You make the next one."

"Fair enough."

"See you for lunch up at the house?"

"Yes, ma'am." Henry placed his hands near the stove. "Hopefully it'll calm down a little by then."

"It's supposed to, according to the weather report," Jessie said, looking back at Henry. He didn't seem to hear her, but rather he slowly turned toward the stove and drifted into what appeared to be a blank, faraway stare. Jessie thought about saying something else, but instead she turned and slipped out the door.

CHAPTER 25

The jolt she suddenly felt when the left front tire hit the pothole was enough to shift her focus from the piece of paper she was holding in her hand, back to the narrow road she was driving on. The directions seemed simple enough when Lloyd White, the customer she was delivering the yearlings to, gave them to her over the phone, and she was sure she scribbled them down correctly. Yet as she made her way through the rows of horse barns at the Humboldt rodeo grounds, she couldn't seem to find the one landmark she needed in order to get to the barn where Lloyd was waiting.

After hitting the pothole, Jessie stopped the truck and re-read the directions. *Use the Brine Street entrance*, she read quietly to herself, reading off the piece of paper. *Okay, did that. Then take a right just past the office…did that. Go past the grandstands, then left at the concession stand. Yup, did that. Go a short distance and look for the 4-H pavilion on the right, Barn C is two barns past the pavilion.* She had already traveled what she considered to be a "short distance" but when she scanned the buildings on either side of the road, there was no pavilion.

She read the instructions again, and now convinced she had followed them to a T, decided Lloyd must have accidentally given her a wrong turn somewhere along the line. Jessie figured she'd try to find a place to turn the rig around and backtrack to see if she could find where the mistake was made. She slowly pulled the truck forward another one hundred yards and found what looked like a large parking area big enough to swing the forty-foot truck and trailer she was driving around. As she pulled into the open area, she noticed a sign that had big green letters that read 4-H PAVILION.

Jessie let out a sigh of relief, swung her truck back onto the narrow road of gravel and dirt, and continued on her way. She drove past barns A and B, and finally came upon Barn C. There, Lloyd White and his ranch help were tending to a barn full of Lloyd's horses that he had brought to the rodeo grounds in preparation of an upcoming ranch versatility competition to be held over the weekend. Rather than having Jessie take the yearlings she was delivering out to his ranch, which was an additional fifteen miles away, he had her bring them to the rodeo grounds instead.

Lloyd, a heavyset man with a crooked smile, large nose and big laugh, met her as she pulled her rig to a stop just in front of Barn C. "I was starting to think you might have got yourself lost," he chuckled, stepping up to the window, his deep voice filling the cab of her truck.

"Nope," Jessie grinned back. "Drove right up to the place. You all ready for the weekend?"

"Purty much," The big man smiled. "We got a real good chance of takin' the whole thing. This year we'll even be usin' a couple of those colts we got from you a while back. They sure turned out to be nice horses."

"Nothing but the best for you, Lloyd."

Lloyd burst into a big belly laugh. "Yeah, me and everybody else you sell horses to! Hell, I'm just glad nobody else up this way has discovered you yet! If they do, it'll dang sure make this competition a whole lot harder than it is right now."

"You flatter me, Lloyd."

"Why hell, Jess, flattery is about the only thing I got going for me these days!" He patted his protruding belly with both hands and let out another big laugh. Lloyd's laugh was contagious, and Jessie couldn't help but chuckle along with him.

"Well, you're sure getting a couple of real nice babies this year," Jessie said, opening the door of the pickup and climbing out. "The little stud colt is a beauty, but the filly is going to be something special. She's out of one of my best mares. I think you're really going to like her."

"Why hell, let us just go take a look, then!"

Jessie grabbed two lead ropes off the seat next to her and she and Lloyd made their way to the back of the trailer, where they were met by two of Lloyd's ranch hands. One was a young boy no more than seventeen, with a black, flat-brimmed hat held on his head by a long stampede string, his faded jeans tucked into his tall, high-topped boots and just the wisp of a moustache growing on his upper lip. The other was an older cowboy Jessie had seen before out at the ranch. He never talked much, always had a large chew of tobacco in his cheek and seemed to have a nice quiet way with horses.

As Jessie went to open the trailer gate, she suddenly stopped dead in her tracks. Seemingly out of nowhere, a picture of the front of the 4-H pavilion she had just passed flashed into her mind. She had been so fixated on trying to find the building on the way that all she focused on when she finally saw it were the words 4-H PAVILION. But now, in her mind's eye, she could see very clearly that there were other words on the building, as well. All together, the sign, which had been spelled out in big green letters, read "Josh McBride Memorial 4-H PAVILION."

"Is it stuck?" Lloyd asked, bringing Jessie's mind back to the task at hand.

"Oh…no," Jessie smiled, lifting the latch, which freed the

gate. Still thinking about the sign, she went into the twenty-eight-foot stock trailer, which was much larger than was needed to haul two yearling horses, and snapped a lead rope on each of their halters. Holding the filly's lead rope, she tossed the other over the colt's neck and sent him by himself to the back of the trailer, where the young ranch hand took the rope and led him out of the trailer. Jessie followed with the filly, and getting to the back of the trailer, she handed the rope to the older cowboy who was waiting there.

The two men led the young horses toward barn C, with Jessie and Lloyd following behind. "There was a name on the 4-H pavilion," Jessie said, almost as soon as the two of them started walking. "Josh McBride. Do you know who he was?"

"No, not really," Lloyd shrugged. "I think it was some little boy that got killed in a car wreck or something, but I don't know for sure. The building's been called that since before I got here, and that's been ten years ago, now. I bet old Leon, there would know. He's been here forever. Ask him."

"Oh, that's okay." Surprisingly, Jessie's heart began to ache when she heard how the boy died, and she suddenly felt as though she was prying into someone else's business. "I just thought…"

"Hey Leon," Lloyd yelled ahead to the old ranch hand. "Do you know the story about the boy the pavilion is named after?"

Leon had just walked the filly into an empty stall and slipped her halter off. He came back out closing the stall door behind him, and with the halter draped over his arm, dug the tobacco out of his cheek with his forefinger and dropped it unceremoniously on the ground at his feet. "Little Josh," Leon said, almost wistfully. "Boy, it's been a while since I thought about him."

"I'm sorry." Jessie winced. "I didn't mean to pry…"

"You're not prying," Leon smiled. "He was a great kid. Quite a little ranch hand, too." Leon slowly shook his head.

"He and his mom were killed when their truck went off the road up on the pass. A real tragedy all the way around."

"I'm really very sorry," Jessie repeated. "It sounds like you knew him pretty well."

"I did," Leon nodded. "Knew his parents even better. We went to school together, even rodeoed together for a while. His dad took their passing real hard."

"Oh?"

"Blamed himself for it 'cause he was drivin' when it happened. Fell asleep at the wheel."

"My God, that's awful."

Leon shook his head. "Wasn't his fault, though, and everyone but him knew it. It was springtime and he'd been runnin' himself ragged, what with all the spring chores his ranch had him doin'. He went downhill pretty fast after the accident. Started drinkin', sold off all his livestock and eventually lost his ranch altogether. Me and a couple of others bought up his saddle, truck and a few other things when they auctioned his place off and gave 'em all back to him."

"Is he still around here?"

"Henry?" Leon looked surprised that Jessie even thought to ask. "Naw. He left right after that auction and nobody around here that I know of has seen him since." Leon hesitated. "Too bad, too. Far as I know, he never even knew folks around here donated the money to have that building put up in Josh's name. I think someone tried to find him at the time so he could be at the dedication, but it was like he just fell off the planet. Far as I know, he may even be dead somewhere." He hesitated again. "I hope not, though. Henry was a hell of a nice fella, the best kind, ya know? The kind of man that'd give you the shirt off his back, and tell you to keep the money that was in the pocket."

"I know the kind," Jessie smiled.

"When did all that happen?" Lloyd asked.

Leon took of his hat and scratched his head. "Seventeen or eighteen years ago now, I'd say." He put his hat back on. "Don't really seem like that long, though."

The conversation then turned back to the yearlings Jessie had brought. Lloyd talked of how impressed he was with the looks of the youngsters and wanted to know what their breeding was, how much they had been handled, and if Jessie had any more like them that she wanted to sell. She thanked him for his kind words about the babies, but told him that was all she had for now. They discussed the weather for a bit, and Jessie asked about a hotel she could stay in for the night before heading back to the ranch in the morning.

As the sun started to set, Jessie said her goodbyes, climbed back in her truck, and drove to the end of the road where she found an area big enough to turn her rig around and headed back out the way she came. She passed barns C, B and A and when she came to the parking area in front of the pavilion, she slowed the truck to a stop and looked up at the big green letters on the front of the building. She felt a profound sadness well up inside her as she read the words "Josh McBride Memorial 4-H Pavilion."

"My God, Henry," she said with quiet sympathy, as if he were sitting right next to her. She looked at the building for a long time, fighting back tears, before finally putting the truck in gear and slowly driving away. She thought about the pain Henry had been living with, and the grief he was still carrying around when he arrived at the ranch. A wave of guilt washed over her for thinking of him as just another drunk cowboy and for being hard on him about his drinking.

What kind of man still grieves for his family seventeen years after they've passed? She wondered to herself. As she got ready to pull the rig out onto Brine Street, something Leon said during their conversation flashed into her mind and answered her question: the best kind.

CHAPTER 26

It was the most comfortable the gray colt had felt since he was first forced into the company of humans some several months earlier. During the past few weeks the man would come in the morning and put feed in the pen, then he would come back a short time later to clean. Soon after, the woman would come around to look in on him. Neither one would hang around long, and the colt usually wouldn't see either one again until later in the day when either one or the other would stop by to give him some more hay, or fill his water tank or check the latch on the gate.

Then, suddenly the woman seemed to disappear. She stopped coming around and the gray colt figured she must have gone to the same place where all the other humans who used to be at the ranch went. He remembered when he first arrived, there were humans everywhere. Then one day they all disappeared, except the man and the woman. Then the woman disappeared, too. It was too bad, because the colt liked her. She was the one that got the rope from around his neck, and she always spoke softly when she was around him. The man never really spoke at all, unless it was to the woman.

Just as the colt thought he was never going to see the woman again, one morning there she was. She and the man showed up about the same time of day the man usually came around to put the hay in the pen. This time, however, the man didn't give him the hay, but rather the woman came in the pen by herself with a halter and lead rope hanging in the crook of her arm. Then she did something she never did before. She slowly, but very deliberately started walking toward him. Her intention was clear: she was trying to get up next to him. The colt, not sure what to think of her behavior, and with no picture in his mind to guide him like the last time she tried to get up close to him, he did the only thing he thought prudent at the time. He ran. As quickly as he could he went to the fence and began making lap after lap around the inside of the round pen, a fine dust rising from under his feet with each step he took. He realized almost immediately that the woman wasn't leaving him alone, which is what he had hoped for. Instead she was slowly walking a small circle near the middle of the pen, always staying parallel to his hip, as he ran a big circle near the fence. In an attempt to try and escape the pressure he was feeling, he turned his gaze to the outside of the pen, so as not to have to look at the woman who was following his every step.

He had just started to feel better about being able to "escape," at least mentally, when, just as he flew past the gate on his tenth lap, the woman with the halter and lead rope in the crook of her arm suddenly appeared directly in front of him. In one rapid, fluid movement, the colt scrambled to a stop, crouched his hindquarters down over his hocks, lifted his front end around toward the fence and through a cloud of red dust, pushed off hard in the opposite direction. "Catty," the man said from outside the pen.

Before the colt could make one full lap around the pen, the woman had already made her way back to the middle and was once again calmly walking a small circle parallel to his hip. For another five full-speed laps, he watched the woman intently as she quietly stayed with him, never getting any closer, but also no farther away. The consistent pressure he was feeling from the woman's mere presence in the pen finally started to get to him, and soon he again felt the need to mentally escape. He turned his head to the outside of the pen and two laps later, his head still tipped to the outside, the woman suddenly appeared in front of him. Again, the colt wheeled and bolted in the opposite direction.

The colt, now operating on pure adrenaline, continued his frantic stampede around the inside of the round pen for another twenty-eight laps, nine of which had been reversed by the woman when she stepped in front of him, and two of which he reversed on his own when he mistakenly thought she was going to. The months of inactivity from standing dormant in pens had taken its toll on the colt's once limit-less strength and stamina. His frantic and mindless running ultimately pushed his lungs to their limit. No longer able to bring in enough air to oxygenate his muscles, the colt's legs became weak and unable to carry him any further and after nearly twenty minutes of non-stop running, the gray colt finally ground himself to a halt.

Dust as thick as fog hung in the air as the colt, sides heaving, nostrils flaring and his once steel-gray coat now a reddish hue from dust sticking to his sweat, turned wea-rily to the inside of the pen. He slowly, almost cautiously, lowered his head to chest level, and with his ears pricked in her direction, took time to study the woman standing just a few feet from him. He was in a precarious situation, and he knew it. He had done the one thing no horse ever willingly wants to do—mindlessly expend all of his energy in the presence of a predator. Yet that was exactly what he'd done and now he was vulnerable. His severely fatigued legs shook uncontrollably under him and he began to under-stand that if he needed to run again, he wouldn't be able, not for long anyway.

The colt stood in that spot, sweat dripping from his belly and his chin and his nose, for what seemed like a very long time. His instinct—the same one that had earlier told him to run until he could run no more—was now telling him to stand. Perhaps if he could stand long enough, he could catch his breath and regain some strength. If he did, he could make another run for it if he had to, or if need be, even fight.

Then the woman moved. It was an extremely small movement for a human, her foot sliding less than an inch to the right. But for a horse, and a nervous horse at that, any movement was going to appear big and that movement appeared to him as if someone had just driven a bulldozer through a wall. The colt's body immediately stiffened. Eyes rimmed in white and bulging nearly out of their sockets, his head shot straight up, and he sucked back on his haunches preparing to flee. The woman slowly shifted weight onto the foot and the colt instantly looked to his left, away from the direction the woman was obviously thinking about going. His head darted back to the woman, then back to the left, then back to the woman.

She slowly shifted her other foot to the right, which put her body ever so slightly out of alignment with the way the two of them had been standing in relationship to one another. This minute, but well thought out adjustment the woman made, caused the colt's thought to change from fleeing, or even fighting to a worried curiosity about what she was doing. The colt quickly, albeit stiffly, adjusted his entire body so that the two of them were back in alignment with one another. Again, the woman shifted, and again the colt adjusted.

It was about then, after his panic began to subside, that an image slowly began to form in the recesses of his mind. It was a picture similar to the one he had received several weeks earlier when the woman entered his pen and quietly removed the rope from around his neck. He had almost forgotten about that. Then, he had received a mental image, apparently from the woman, showing him what her intentions were, and what he could do to help himself. By doing little more than following the image, the colt was able to approach and allow the woman to remove the rope he had been dragging around since the night before. In this image, though, the colt thought he was seeing the woman gently touching him on his shoulder. There was no danger or harm coming to him in the image, although he was still concerned and fearful.

The woman shifted again. This time, however, instead of the colt shifting his entire body to realign with her, he took one small, tentative step in her direction. The woman responded by stepping slightly backward, away from him. This break from the previous pattern once again caused concern for the colt and he raised his head in alert. The woman took in a long slow breath, and then just as slowly let it back out. This one tiny gesture on her part caused the colt to relax slightly and as his head gradually began to lower as he, too, exhaled.

The woman smiled, and the colt, almost as if some unknown gentle force was carrying him, took two easy steps in her direction. The woman shifted backwards, the colt stepped toward her. She shifted to the side; the colt lined himself up with her and stepped toward her again. She let out a long, slow exhale, and the colt lowered his head and quietly walked up to her, stopping just far enough away so that the woman, if she chose to do so, could touch his shoulder.

"I'll be damned," came the man's quiet voice from outside the pen.

The colt and the woman stood next to each other for several seconds before she slowly raised her arm and touched him briefly on his shoulder. The colt exhaled again. The woman lowered her arm, backed two steps, turned and left the pen. The colt tried to follow her, but the man's presence outside the pen presented just enough pressure to cause him to stop. After closing and latching the gate behind her, both humans left, only to have the man return several minutes later with the colt's breakfast that he placed in its usual spot just inside the pen not far from the water tank.

The colt was exhausted. He spent nearly twenty minutes of every hour during the rest of the day sleeping. The other forty minutes of every hour were spent eating and playing hide and seek with the sun, as he tried to keep his face covered by the narrow lines of shade cast by the fence rails as it pivoted from east to west. When night fell, the colt drifted into a much deeper sleep for longer periods, and by the time the man and woman showed up at his pen the next morning, he was awake, but still groggy.

Just as she had the day before, the woman entered his pen with the halter and lead rope in the crook of her arm, and slowly but deliberately approached him. Also just like the day before, the colt bolted for the fence and made several very fast and worried laps. But then, after traveling fewer than ten laps total, and as if someone had flipped a switch, the colt stopped dead in his tracks and turned to face the woman, ears pricked and eyes alert. Ever since the woman left the pen the day before, the colt had thought about what had transpired between the two of them. He came to the realization that he had run a lot farther and faster than he needed, because at no time had the woman really ever posed a threat to him. While he was leery of all humans in general, the woman had proved to him on two separate occasions that she meant him no harm. He wasn't sure what to think of her other than that, but one thing was fairly certain; running from her probably wasn't necessary.

The woman stood facing the colt for several seconds, and then slowly shifted her weight to the right. The colt followed with his eyes. She shifted again, and this time the colt dropped his head and took one hesitant step toward her. The woman took a step back. The colt took two more toward her. At this point, the woman stopped moving and the colt began to receive another image. It was the same picture he had gotten the day before, of him approaching the woman, and her gently touching him on the shoulder. He slowly lowered his head, then raised it, then lowered it again, making a mental map of the woman, the distance between him and her and the escape routes in all directions, should he need one.

He glanced at the man on the other side of the fence, making sure he was staying where he was, and then cautiously walked right up to the woman. The colt stopped near enough to the woman that she could easily reach out and touch him. As she slowly raised her hand, the colt tipped his ear slightly in her direction, as if listening for the sound her hand would make when it touched him. Unlike the day before, he flinched slightly when she made contact with him, but quickly relaxed when he realized she was doing nothing more than what she had the day before. She touched him in the same spot on his shoulder three times before lowering her hand, breathing deeply, then raising her hand and touching him again.

This time, her touch turned into a gentle, one-inch stroke with the back of her fingers. Then a two-inch stroke, and eventually she was quietly running the back of her hand nearly the entire length of his shoulder. The colt wasn't sure what to think of the woman's behavior. It was so foreign to him that his instincts were all at once telling him to stay and flee. He wanted to flee because of the perceived danger the situation provided, and he wanted to stay because of the comfort he was experiencing. He had not had such a feeling since he was young, back when he was still with his mother and long before he was forced out of the safety of the herd into which he was born. He wondered, as the woman's hand slowly moved up toward his withers, if what he was experiencing with this human was in some way the same thing he had back then.

Within minutes, the colt was allowing the woman to work her hand over his withers, down his shoulder and around the front of his chest. She worked up his neck, under his mane, then back down to the spot where she started on his shoulder. She repeated this pattern twice, then lowered her hand and stepped away from the colt. He had become totally relaxed with the woman and as she stepped away from him, he sleepily raised his head and turned in her direction, his eyes soft and his breathing slow and regular.

Over the next six days the woman repeated the process with the colt to the point that by the fourth day he no longer thought about running when she entered the pen, and by the fifth day she could touch him nearly anywhere on his body, with the exception of his lower legs. Being touched low on his legs instinctively told the colt to be on alert. If someone got a hold of his legs, he somehow understood he wouldn't be able to run if he needed to, and while he was relaxed around the woman, he still wasn't totally convinced the situation was completely safe.

Also by the fifth day the colt had become so comfortable with the woman that he would willingly follow her in the round pen anywhere she wanted to go. Wherever she went, he went, without question or hesitation, always quiet and with his head down. On the sixth day, after the woman had been in with the colt for nearly a half-hour going over all of the things the two of them had worked on during the week, the woman asked the man to come in the pen. Immediately upon the man entering, the colt went on alert and quickly moved to the far side of the pen. He stood with his neck and body rigid, ears and eyes focused in the man's direction. The woman spoke reassuringly to both the colt and the man, then stepped out of the pen leaving the two of them alone. The colt snorted a warning, and without moving from his spot in the middle of the pen, the man said quietly to the woman, "You sure this is a good idea?"

"Breathe," the woman said with a smile in her voice. "Move just a little to your right and lets see what he does." The man did. The colt, still alert, dropped his head, then raised it, then dropped it again. He was mapping the man and the area around him. The colt then shot a quick glance at the woman standing outside the pen, then looked back at the man. "Do it again," she said quietly. The man did. This time, the horse shifted his body to get in line with the man, and lowered his head.

"Okay, now take a half-step back." The man did, and much to his surprise, the colt raised his head slightly and stepped toward him, just as he had so many times with the woman. "Good," the woman said. "Now do it again." The man did. It was then the colt began to receive an image. It was a picture of him standing next to the man while the man touched him just like the woman had. But this image was different. In the past when he received an image, the colt was sure it was coming from the person in the pen with him, in other words, the woman. But this image wasn't coming from the person in the pen. In fact, there was very little coming from the man standing before him with the exception of a strong feeling of uncertainty.

"Again," the woman repeated. "Step back again." The man stepped back. This time, the colt lowered his head and took two confident steps in the man's direction. "One more time," the woman said. The man stepped back and the horse, almost as if on cue, walked right up to him and presented his left shoulder to the man, just as he had to the woman on the very first day she had gone in with him. The man slowly turned to the woman and shrugged his shoulder as if to say, *Now what?*

"Pet him on the shoulder, for crying out loud," she laughed. The man reached up and touched the colt so gently that the young horse barely felt it. "You're not going to break him," the woman said. "Go ahead and pet him; he'll be all right."

The man reached up and began to quietly stroke the colt on the shoulder. He had watched the woman carefully the whole time she was with the colt, and to the best of his ability, he mimicked everything he saw her do with the young horse. He started very small, touching the horse on the shoulder, then his neck and withers and slowly branching out from there so that eventually he was touching, petting and stroking the colt all over his body.

The man's touch felt different to the colt than the woman's. Like the difference in their individual odors, which were the same, but not the same. In either case, the colt found it much easier to transfer the information he had been learning from the woman than he ever would have thought. The man's actions were so similar to hers the colt quickly began to relax with him, just as he had with her. It was slowly becoming clear to him that neither of these humans seemed to want to harm him, as he had always thought they might.

Ever since the colt walked into the pen at the Essex place by following the herd of strange horses he had stumbled across out in the wild, he had been frightened by humans. Their smell, their movement and most everything about them kept him on edge. But all that seemed to be changing. Because of the time the woman with the long hair and big hat had spent with him, he was now starting to look at humans in a completely different light. He was slowly starting to understand that being around the humans offered him a certain level of comfort he had never expected, and much to his surprise, he actually liked it.

The man spent the better part of thirty minutes petting and rubbing the colt. Every once in a while he would stop long enough to take a short walk around the pen with the colt following him, just as he had with the woman. Finally, the man reached up and stroked the colt lightly on his forehead, then turned and left the pen. The colt followed him to the gate, and just as he had been doing with the woman, stopped there and watched him step out and latch the gate behind him.

The colt watched quietly as the man and woman walked away from the pen and disappeared around the corner of a nearby building. He let out a long relaxed sigh and cocked a hind foot. It was the most comfortable the colt had felt since he was first forced into the company of humans some nine months earlier.

CHAPTER 27

As the pickup Jessie was driving rocketed down the rutted and washboarded gravel road, Henry could now see why Mrs. Rodriguez had been so insistent that *he* drive to town instead of Jessie. It had started that morning over breakfast when Jessie announced that she and Henry would need to go to town and pick up some supplies.

"Maybe you let Mr. Henry drive today," Mrs. Rodriguez forced a smile as she scraped scrambled eggs sprinkled with jalapenos from a cast-iron fry pan onto Jessie's plate.

"No," Jessie shrugged. "I'll drive."

Mrs. Rodriguez stepped over to Henry and scraped the remaining eggs from the pan onto his plate. "Maybe you drive today," she repeated.

"That's okay," Henry smiled, taking a sip from his coffee cup. "I don't mind."

"Not now, maybe," Mrs. Rodriguez said not too quietly as she turned and walked back to the stove.

"Did you say something?" Jessie asked.

"No mija," Mrs. Rodriguez placed the egg pan in the sink and plucked a pan sizzling with bacon from the stove.

"Five hundred pounds of feed, Chicago screws, leather soap…" Jessie read from the list sitting on the table next to her plate. "Sixteen penny nails, power steering fluid for the tractor…"

"Fencing staples," Henry added as Mrs. Rodriguez slid five pieces of bacon onto his plate.

"Right," Jessie nodded, jotting it down on the paper. "Anything else?" she asked, turning to Mrs. Rodriguez.

"The bolt of fabric I ordered is in," Mrs. Rodriguez said, sliding three pieces of bacon onto Jessie's plate. "Could you get it for me, por favor?"

"Of course." Jessie jotted it down as well. "Is it at Hansen's?"

"Si, mija." Mrs. Rodriguez slipped around behind Jessie, then turned back and faced Henry. "Maybe Henry drives today?" Henry looked up in time to see Mrs. Rodriguez trying to catch his eye. She then glanced at Jessie, shook her head and scowled slightly. She then looked back at Henry and shook her head again.

"You know…" Jessie smiled disarmingly. "If you're not careful, you're going to get Henry here all worried that there's something wrong with the way I drive."

Mrs. Rodriguez and Henry were still looking at each other, when Mrs. Rodriguez tipped her head toward Jessie, and widened her eyes as if to say, *There IS something wrong with the way she drives.*

Henry had gotten the hint, but thought, *How bad could it be?* Now, however, with one hand braced against the dashboard, the other hand braced on the ceiling as Jessie slid the truck around a turn traveling twice the speed of the posted limit, he was beginning to get the idea. The truck fishtailed on the backside of the turn, spraying gravel and dust into the air, and just as Jessie regained control, she hit a three-inch deep, two-foot-wide pothole, which sent Henry's right shoulder crashing into the door handle. Henry was then catapulted upward when the back tire hit the same hole, causing him to whack his head on the ceiling, mashing his hat.

"Ma'am," he said in desperation. "Do you think we could slow…"

"Uh oh…" Jessie said, slamming on the brakes and sliding past the turn she needed to take to get to the main road. Henry lurched forward, sliding partially out of the seat. "I've been driving this road for over thirty years," she said, jamming the truck into reverse and backing up without looking into the mirrors to see where she was going, "and I miss that dang turn every time." Jessie looked at Henry, put the truck into first gear and smiled. "Weird, don't you think?" She floored it.

Henry started digging for his seatbelt, which he was now wishing he'd put on before they left. "Are we in some kind a hurry?" He asked with as much politeness as he could muster.

Henry had always found that it normally took about forty-five minutes to drive from the ranch to town. On this day, however, and as Jessie slid the truck into the parking lot of Lander's Feed Store (which was just inside the town limits) less than twenty-five minutes had passed from start to finish. She jerked the truck to a stop near the loading dock.

"Well, here we are," Jessie smiled. "That wasn't as bad as Mrs. R made it out to be, now was it?"

Henry had never been carsick before, but as he unbuckled his seatbelt and climbed out of the truck, he suddenly felt queasy—as if the inside of his head was still moving, but the outside wasn't. He walked precariously to the loading dock and as nonchalantly as he could, leaned up against it. Jessie, on the other hand, hopped out from behind the wheel and bounded around the front of the truck and over to where he was standing.

"Your hat's crooked," she said, walking past him and into the feed store.

Without moving his head, Henry glanced at the brim of his hat. She was right, it was crooked. He straightened it as best he could.

"Your first time ridin' with her?" Henry heard a voice say from behind him. He slowly turned around to see Hank Lander, the owner of the store, standing on the loading dock.

"Yeah," Henry said, trying to get enough air in him to quell the nausea he was experiencing. "How'd you know?"

"Hell," Hank chuckled, "'cause most folks learn their lesson after the first time."

"I can see that now," Henry said flatly.

Jessie came out of the store and back to the loading dock. "There you are," she said walking up to Hank. "Margaret said you were out here. I must have walked right past you."

"I was inside, there." Hank motioned over his shoulder to the back room of the store. "What can I do for you today, Jess?"

Jessie handed him the list she made from earlier that morning. "Would you mind getting all this together for us? We've got a couple more errands to run."

"No problem," he said, glancing at the list. "We have everything you need, except maybe the Chicago screws. I think we ran out over the weekend. Got a shipment coming in on Thursday, though."

"That's fine," Jessie nodded. "We've still got a few so there's no hurry." She turned to Henry. "Would you like to come along, or stay here with the boys?"

"If its all the same," Henry forced a smile, "I reckon I'll stay here."

"Suit yourself." Jessie waved at the two men, as she turned walked toward town.

"Hell," Hank shrugged. "We got this. It's slow today and the boys need something to do. Besides, a walk might do you some good."

Henry hadn't taken his eyes off Jessie since she started down the street. With the exception of her two-and-a-half day absence from the ranch when she went to deliver the yearlings to Humboldt, the two of them had been inseparable since the ranch closed for the season two months earlier. In fact, the two had been working so closely together that Henry was a little surprised at how much he missed her when she was gone for those two-and-a-half days, and how happy he was when she returned. Watching her walk down the street, away from him, made him feel a little uneasy, almost sad, and he didn't even know why.

"You know," he boosted himself from the loading dock. "You might be right. Takin' a little walk might just be the thing right now." He glanced up at Hank. "We'll be back in a little bit."

"See you then," Hank nodded.

Jessie had stopped briefly to do a little window-shopping at the Valero Mercantile, an old hardwood-floor shop not far from the feed store that carried everything from groceries to nuts and bolts and everything in between. The Valeros, a couple in their early eighties, had owned the store for as long as anyone could remember, and it was Mrs. Valero who always took great pride in dressing the front window. In this particular display, along with the ever-present, pink-skinned mannequins—one male, one female—both dressed in conservative bathing suits and staring blankly across the street at the gas station, the window also had a Fourth of July display spread out at their feet.

The display consisted of fifty-two, one-hundred-year-old small figurines all attending the Fourth of July town picnic on a replica of the lawn of the local park. These figurines (of which there had been well over a hundred) spent most of the year in the mercantile window in one display or another. At Christmas time they stood in sugar, which was meant to represent snow, and gave each other gifts. At Easter they hunted for Easter eggs. Memorial Day, they saluted the veterans. Fourth of July, they had a picnic. Labor Day they worked, Halloween they trick-or-treated, and on Thanksgiving they ate turkey.

Mrs. Valero had lived in New York as a child, and was always fascinated by the window displays in the large stores like Macy's. When the Valero's bought the mercantile, she brought a little of her childhood with her in the form of those window displays. Although most of the holiday displays were all beginning to look the same these days, everyone in town would still stop to see what Mrs. Valero had done with the window, and she would beam with joy whenever anyone paid her a compliment on them.

Jessie's reason for stopping at the window that morning was actually two-fold. Of course she wanted to see what Mrs. Valero had done with the display, as she did whenever any holiday would roll around. But more importantly, she also wanted to give Henry time to catch up with her, as she was hoping he would. Her admiration for the cowboy had grown ever since they first they met. But something had dramatically changed with her visit to Humboldt and her discussion with Leon, watching Henry doing his work on the ranch, and more importantly, the kindness and thoughtfulness he showed when working with the gray colt.

There was a substance to the man unlike any she'd experienced before. Her relationships with the men in the city, the stuffed white shirts with little more than talking heads, the one-night stands, the brief encounters and of course the falseness of men like Chad, had jaded her almost to the point of disgust. She was disgusted mostly with herself, of course, for the poor choices she had made over the years. She had known better, and certainly could have done better. Or at least that was what she told herself. But still, if the truth were known, she'd have to say she was more than just a little disgusted with the men she'd had those relationships with, as well. They lacked the substance of men like her father and the men who worked at the ranch when she was little. It seemed those men had all but disappeared out of her life, and there were times when she grieved for them. They were men of honor and integrity, who did what they said and didn't complain about hard work. Men who thought more about others than they did themselves, and who lived by an unspoken code of ethics. She was as sure as she could be they were all gone. Then Henry showed up.

She couldn't help but look back toward the feed store and felt a rush of happiness when she saw Henry walking toward her.

"They got all that handled back there," he said, shrugging slightly as he got closer. "So I guess if you don't mind, I'd like to go along with you after all."

"I don't mind," Jessie smiled.

Henry had been to town numerous times, but mostly when he was either drunk, or on his way to get drunk. He had never really taken the time to appreciate the simple beauty of the place, its nineteenth-century architecture, narrow sidewalks and tidy storefronts. As they walked down the main street, Jessie pointed out the two-story red brick building near the middle of town where she went to school. She had been in that building from kindergarten until she graduated twelfth grade.

"The young kids went to class on the first floor, the older kids on the second," Jessie said as they stopped in front of the building. "That was my second grade classroom, right there." She pointed to a window on the first floor.

"Is it still a school?" Henry asked.

"Oh, no. About ten years ago they built a new grade school, middle school and high school just outside of town, there." Jessie motioned her hand to the east. "This is the administration building for the school district now." She shrugged. "Kind of sad, you know? It was a great little school…a nice place to learn."

Perhaps it was how she said it, or maybe it was the look on her face when she did, but the statement brought a smile to Henry's face, and as they continued on their way down the main street, he couldn't help but glance back at the building that held so many fond memories for the woman walking next to him.

They made their way past the town park with its raised and stately red-and-white gazebo in its middle and children running and playing on its lawn. They crossed the street and headed back the way they came, past the old bank built of stone that had once been robbed by Butch Cassidy and the Sundance Kid—to date, the town's only claim to fame. "It only had seventy-five dollars in it at the time," Jessie told Henry. "Not a terribly profitable day for them, I expect."

Two doors down from the bank was Hansen's Sewing Shop where Jessie stopped to pick up the bolt of cloth for Mrs. Rodriguez. They spent the better part of a half-hour in the shop, visiting with Joli Hansen, the seventy-five-year-old and not quite five-foot-tall shop owner. She was a colorful old woman with a long, tight braid that hung down the middle of her back, who wasn't afraid to curse, and who liked to watch professional football while drinking beer from a can. From what Henry could gather in the short time they were there, her favorite team was the Green Bay Packers, because Vince Lombardi, the team's coach during the 1960's, "never took no crap from nobody."

"She's a lesbian," Jessie said matter-of-factly as they left the shop.

To say the least, the statement surprised Henry. Even at that, he wasn't sure what surprised him more, hearing Jessie say the word *lesbian,* or the fact that the little woman behind the counter may have actually been one. As far as Henry knew, he had never met a lesbian before, and while he never gave much thought as to what one might look like, he was pretty sure he wouldn't have pictured Joli Hanson. "Why do you say that?" he asked. "Just because she likes football? Hell, I've known women that liked football, and they weren't…um…"

"Lesbians?" Jessie said looking into Henry's quickly blushing face. "No, Henry, it's not because she likes football. She told me. That's how I know."

"Why would she do that?" Henry asked, looking back toward the store and a little shaken by the conversation. "I mean...don't folks usually keep that sort of thing to themselves?"

"You know Henry...you really need to get out more."

The pair continued down the street and came upon the local movie theater, which caused Henry to stop and stare at the show bill that hung inside the window next to the front door. He then went back a few steps and looked up at the marquee rimmed in yellow lights.

"What?" Jessie seemed bewildered by Henry's behavior.

"It's a movie theater," Henry blurted.

Jessie walked back to where he was standing. "Never seen one before?"

"Sure I have. I guess it's just been a while."

"Really? How long of a while?"

"Boy." Henry stopped to think. "Years." He looked back up at the marquee. "A lot of years."

"No kidding?" Jessie grinned, seeing an opportunity that she couldn't pass up. "How about you and I go to a movie some time. My treat."

"Really?"

"Sure." She turned and began walking again. "I think you'd like it. They have sound now and everything."

Henry heard the humor in her voice, and couldn't help but smile.

"We should probably get on back," she said. "I expect they've got the truck loaded by now."

"Okay," Henry agreed. Just as he turned to follow, a flyer in the window of the store next to the theater caught his eye. On a brightly colored ten-by-twenty sheet of posterboard read: *63rd Annual 4th of July Celebration. Fireworks, hayrides, watermelon seed spitting contest, dunk tank, potluck supper in the park. Dance at the American Legion—8pm–12 midnight. Live music by the Clifford County Wranglers.*

The item on the poster that really caught Henry's attention was the second to the last, *Dance at the American Legion—8pm–12 midnight.*

A dance, Henry thought.

The ride back to the ranch wasn't any smoother and only slightly less hurried than the ride into town had been. As they pulled into the yard, Mrs. Rodriguez stepped from the house and walked toward the truck. Henry unbuckled his seatbelt and climbed from the cab, not quite as nauseous as he had been when he'd gotten out at the feed store. Mrs. Rodriguez' glance as she walked past him said *I told you so,* and Henry knew then that if she suggested something to him in the future, he should definitely pay attention.

CHAPTER 28

By the time Henry had finished his dinner that evening and
gotten to the bunkhouse he was feeling much better. Yet,
it didn't help the fact that, as was his nightly custom, he
fought with first one boot as he peeled it off his foot, then
he fought with the other, before dropping them both unceremoniously to the floor. He sat for a minute on the edge of
his bed, shaking his head and cursing the fact that he didn't
have a bootjack, when, through the nearby open window he
heard what was by now starting to become a familiar sound.
Already certain of what he would see, Henry rose from his
bed and looked out the window, across the yard and into
the pasture where Jessie was standing with horses milling
around her as if she were some kind of rock star being surrounded by adoring fans.

It was the third time in as many weeks that he had seen
the horses of the herd come to her like she was the pied piper.
It was the seventh time overall. In nearly every case, as soon as
Jessie had finished with the horses and left the pen or pasture,
Henry would sneak in behind her and try to replicate what
she could so effortlessly achieve. So far, he was zero for seven.

Henry shook his head as one by one the horses reached
for her, and one by one she stroked each one on the muzzle,

chin or forehead. "That is one of the most aggravating things I've ever seen," Henry mumbled to himself. "How the hell does she do that?"

He quickly sat down on the bed and pulled on his boots, which wasn't near the struggle getting them off was. He reached for his hat, plopped it on his head, and then marched toward the door. Once outside he was surprised to see that in the short time it took him to put on his boots and hat, Jessie was no longer in with the horses. He quickly looked around, but she was nowhere in sight. Like some school kid looking for mischief, Henry skittered across the yard and climbed through the fence. He slowly made his way to the approximate area where Jessie was standing when he had seen her through the window, and then straightened himself up, as if to say to the world: *Okay, here I am. Come gather 'round.*

One by one the horses, which were for the most part still standing nearby, simply turned and walked away.

"Damn that's aggravating," he said again.

"It's your attitude," he heard Jessie say from behind him.

Startled, Henry spun around to see Jessie leaning on the fence, very near where he had climbed through.

"Dang ma'am! You 'bout scared me out of my skin!"

"I'm sorry," she said unconvincingly. "I thought you knew I was here."

"Well, I do now!" Henry turned and watched the rest of the horses that were nearby saunter down the gently sloping hill and into the little ravine to get water. When the last one disappeared, he walked sheepishly over to where Jessie was standing. "I was just..." He turned nonchalantly and pointed toward the horses. "The horses were..."

"It's your attitude," Jessie repeated.

"Ma'am?"

"It's your attitude, Henry." She shrugged. "That's why they don't want to be around you."

"Attitude?"

Jessie nodded. "Can I buy you a cup of coffee?"

By the time Henry and Jessie made their way to the old wooden porch swing in front of Jessie's front room window, the sun had just passed below the horizon. The eastern sky had turned nearly black with nightfall, but to the west the heavens were still ablaze with dark red, amber and yellow hues. Henry was noticing the beauty of sunsets like these more lately, and as he sat in awe of the brilliant colors being cast upon the desert, Jessie stepped out onto the porch carrying two steaming cups of coffee and gently sat on the swing next to him.

"Here you go." She smiled as she handed him one of the cups, and took a sip from the other.

"Beautiful evening," he said quietly.

Jessie turned her attention to the western sky. "Isn't it though?" They sat for a while, watching the remaining shards of colored light fade to black. "Is the coffee all right?" Jessie asked, breaking the silence.

"Oh," Henry brought the cup to his lips, having not tasted it yet. "Yes, it is. Thank you." He then took a sip. Jessie smiled.

"You know, Henry," she started. "My father always used to say that every jackass in the country thinks he's got horse sense." She was holding her cup with both hands, and raising it to her lips, took a long sip. "Its like that mustang Tom brought in. The most important thing in the world to him was his freedom. When he suddenly realized he wasn't free anymore, he panicked. Some people would see a horse like that and think the best way to calm him down would be to get rough with him. Bully him into submission. *Make* him feel better." She paused. Henry sat quietly, paying close attention as she spoke, almost as if his very life depended on what she was saying. "The problem with that idea is that horses are peaceful animals by nature. They don't much care to be bullied."

"Well that's fair enough," Henry nodded. "But when you were in with them horses out there, they come up to you like you was their long lost mother. When I went in, they acted like I ain't took a bath in a while. Now I dang sure didn't bully 'em. So why did they quit me and not you?"

Jessie smiled kindly. "That's what I was saying." She shrugged ever so slightly. "It's your attitude. It's not what you say, it's what you do, and it's not what you do, it's what you feel. You have to be connected to yourself, Henry, before you can connect with someone else." She gently touched herself on the chest, above her heart. "It comes from here. If your heart isn't right they'll know it."

Henry heard what she said. He understood the words, but not the meaning behind them. He sat for a long time waiting for her to say more, perhaps something that would clear up the confusion for him, but nothing more came. Jessie smiled again, then turned her gaze back to the now darkened desert and breathed deeply, closing her eyes as she did. "It is truly a beautiful evening, isn't it?"

"Yes, ma'am," Henry agreed, allowing the confusion in his mind drift away. The ranch was quiet now, only an occasional distant nicker from one of the horses in the pasture breaking the silence. Until that very moment, Henry hadn't realized how tumultuous his life had been since he lost Annie and Josh. As he sat there on the porch swing next to Jessie, on that most perfect night, the peace of the evening slowly descended down upon him like a down-filled blanket on a cold winter night. He turned his gaze to the desert. "Yes, ma'am. It truly is."

CHAPTER 29

Shortly after sunrise the next morning, Jessie climbed the stairs to the bunkhouse and knocked on the door. "Henry," she called. "Are you up?"

The door opened and Henry stepped out onto the porch looking worried. "Yes, ma'am. Is everything okay?"

"Yes it is, Henry." She smiled, pleased with his concern. "I've decided that we're going to take the day off and go for a ride."

"A ride? What about the chores?"

"The neighbor boys are here," she said, nodding over her shoulder toward the barn and pens. "They'll take care of the place for the day. Come on, get your gear and let's go." She turned and walked down the steps, stopping at the bottom to look back at Henry, who, still standing by the door, was a little mystified by Jessie's behavior. "Well?" she motioned for him to follow. "Come on! We haven't got all day."

In less than a half-hour Jessie, on her favorite horse Bree, an eight-year-old bay Mustang-Quarter Horse mare, and Henry aboard Mic were heading westward out across the ranch. Side by side, they passed by the red rock overhang down by the river where Henry had found a group of horses that cold, rainy morning. An hour later, they passed through a gate on the backside of the property, leaving the ranch and going on to BLM land that spread out over fifty thousand acres farther to the west and north. After another hour of riding, a slight breeze had come up from the south and began to heat the air, as Jessie and Henry passed through a shallow canyon.

"So ma'am," Henry said, taking a short swig from his canteen. "Where is it exactly that we're headed?"

"There's a little place up ahead here that I wanted you to see."

"With all due respect," Henry put the cap back on the canteen and hung the strap back over his saddle horn. "I've seen the desert before, and we sure got a lot of work to do back at the ranch. Shouldn't we be back there instead of out here?"

"We'll be back soon enough," Jessie smiled.

Just out of the canyon, Jessie eased her mare up into a lope, and Henry and Mic followed suit. They loped until the ground turned too rocky, and then brought the horses back to a walk. For the next four miles the pair alternated between loping, trotting and walking, depending on the terrain they were moving across. At one point, they both needed to dismount and walk their horses down a steep, rocky trail that led into a narrow draw. Still dismounted, they then led their horses back up the other side and once on top, they remounted and continued across the mesa.

By noon, they had come to the base of a large, winding hill where Jessie brought her horse to a stop, and turned to Henry with a finger across her lips telling him to stay quiet. They dismounted, loosened their cinches and wrapped their reins around the limb of a nearby Joshua tree. The horses immediately dropped their heads and began browsing on what little dry grass was in their reach. Jessie pulled a pair of binoculars from her saddlebags and motioned for Henry to follow her. The little game trail they started up was so steep and rocky they soon needed to get down on all fours just so they could make the climb. Near the top of the hill, and after an arduous twenty minutes of climbing, Jessie motioned for Henry to get lower to the ground and slow his pace...which wasn't all that fast to begin with.

As they closed in on the crest of the hill, both of them now crawling flat on their bellies, Jessie pushed her hat off her head so that it lay on her back, still attached around her neck by the braided horsehair stampede string. Silently, she stopped, reached back, took Henry's hat from his head and handed it to him, before motioning for him to follow her to the top. The pair moved so gradually the last four feet of the climb that there were times Henry wondered if they were even moving at all. Soon enough, however, they had reached the summit, and as they slowly peeked over the crest, Henry finally could appreciate why Jessie had brought him all the way out to such a desolate area.

Below was a lush green valley that sprawled out in front of them, rimmed on three sides by rocky hills. Almost directly under where they hid grazed a large herd of wild Mustangs. As far as Henry could tell, there looked to be around forty horses in all. He could see yearlings, two- and three-year-olds, mares with new foals at their sides, and on the edge of the herd stood the band's patriarch—a massive bay stallion with his matted and tangled mane flowing down from a heavily crested neck.

Jessie put the binoculars to her eyes and surveyed the herd for several minutes before handing them to Henry and pointing down toward the herd. Henry placed the glasses up to his eyes, but had to bring them down to adjust them before trying again. He scanned the valley and could see some of the foals running and playing through the knee-deep grass, mares and young horses grazing and the stallion prowling the outskirts of the band, protecting them from a younger stallion who seemed to be trying to work up the courage to challenge him. Henry watched for several more seconds before offering the binoculars back to Jessie. She motioned for him to keep them, and then leaned very close to Henry's ear. "Which one is the boss horse?" she whispered so softly he could barely hear her. Henry looked at her questioningly.

She nodded her head toward the herd and whispered again. "The boss horse. Which one is it?"

Henry turned his attention back to the herd and placed the glasses up to his eyes. He scanned the entire herd several times before finally deciding which one was the boss. Without looking at Jessie, he pointed to a sorrel mare in the middle of the herd that was acting very aggressively toward the other horses. Several horses responded by running away from her, while others simply walked in the other direction as soon as she got anywhere near them. Henry looked at Jessie, who slowly nodded in agreement, before leaning close to his ear again. "Which horse is liked the best?"

A look of confusion crossed Henry's face.

"Which one do the other horses really like?"

Once again Henry raised the glasses to his eyes and scanned the herd several times. He finally decided on another sorrel mare that was away from the majority of the herd. When she moved from one spot to the other, several horses followed her. When she stopped, they stopped. He looked at Jessie and pointed to the mare at the edge of the herd. Jessie smiled knowingly.

Henry shifted his arms to get a better angle with the binoculars and accidentally bumped a rock that began rolling down the hill. The horses in the valley snapped to attention as the rock hurdled toward them. There was one, loud, unified warning snort that went up from a number of the horses and echoed off the three hills surrounding the valley before the entire herd turned and ran. In an instant, with heads and tails in the air, babies and mares calling to one another, and the stallion bringing up the rear, they were all gone from the valley leaving nothing more than an ocean of waving grass in their wake.

"Wow!" Jessie exclaimed. "Aren't they something!"

Henry and Jessie both climbed to their feet. Henry put his hat back on and knocked the dust from his chaps and shirt, while still looking in the direction of the Mustangs. "Yes ma'am, they truly are." He turned to look at Jessie, who was still watching the valley, as if they might return. She was smiling broadly, and it was the sight of that infectious smile that stirred something in Henry that had been dormant for many years. He suddenly found that no matter how hard he tried, he was simply unable to take his eyes off of her, and he couldn't keep himself from grinning because of it.

Jessie turned toward him and their eyes met for a brief second before Henry, still grinning, turned and slowly began to make his way back down the hill.

"What?" Jessie asked, having seen Henry's grin. She began to follow him down the hill. "What are you grinning at?"

"Nothin'." There was a slight chuckle in Henry's voice as he carefully picked his way through the rocks and cacti. "Nothin' at all."

It took less than half the time to get off the hill than it had to get up it, and once back to the horses, Jessie got busy putting the binoculars back in her saddlebags and Henry tightened the cinch on his saddle.

"I could watch a herd like that all day," Jessie said closing the saddlebag cover. "You know?"

"Yes ma'am, I do." Henry hadn't taken his eyes off of what he was doing. "I guess its like ol' Winston Churchill once said...there's somethin' about the outside of a horse that's good for the inside of a man." He went to put his foot in the stirrup, but as he did he glanced over at Jessie who was looking at him with a slightly astonished expression.

"Winston Churchill?" she asked, somewhat surprised Henry knew who Winston Churchill was, much less that he was able to quote him. Most of the cowboys she had been around, particularly lately, bordered on the illiterate.

"Yes, ma'am. He was quite a horseman." Henry slid effortlessly into the saddle. Jessie slid into hers, smiling and shaking her head as she did.

"What?" Henry asked.

"Oh...nothing."

They hadn't gone far when Jessie realized that she would really like to know more about the man she was spending the day with other than his name and what he did for a living. Of course there was the story she had gotten from Leon, about the accident, but it wasn't until Henry's statement about the former English Prime Minister that she realized he'd never really spoken about himself. She didn't know what he liked or disliked, where he was from or anything about his family. She was now understanding there was much more to him than what she was seeing on the surface, and by taking a slightly longer route on the way back to the ranch, Jessie was hoping to perhaps engage Henry in a conversation in which he might open up a little.

There were even a few times during the ride when she thought he might do that very thing, like the time she asked if he grew up on a ranch. He began talking about how he'd learned to rope when he was four or five, and was riding before he could walk. But then, before she knew it, he had somehow turned the conversation back to talking about her and her past. Another time she asked him about his family—did he have any brothers and sisters? He answered no, but that sometimes he wished he did. Then, again he turned the conversation back to her by asking her about her relationship with Mrs. Rodriguez, and how long they'd known each other.

After a couple hours, Jessie realized he probably wasn't interested in talking about himself, which was not an uncommon trait in some cowboys. She had once read an interview years ago with an old cowboy about the disappearance of the west and the cowboy way of life. The interviewer, having had a hard time getting the old man to open up about his past experience, said something to him about it. The old cowboy replied: "It was hard enough going through my life the first time. If it's all the same to you, I'd rather not have to do it again."

Perhaps, Jessie thought, *that's how Henry feels about his life. If so, who am I to try and bring it back out of him?*

By the time they had gotten back to the ranch, their conversations had turned back to the mustangs and how when Jessie was younger, she had loved to go out to the hidden valley her father had once showed her and watch them for hours on end. She told Henry that, with the exception of her father, she had learned more about training horses from watching that herd than from any person. Henry nodded and said he could see how that would be the case.

The sun was an hour away from setting by the time they had unsaddled, fed their horses, and started giving them a good rubdown before getting ready to turn them out for the night. The horses were still tied to the hitch rail with Jessie going over Bree with a soft brush, and Henry doing the same with Mic, when Jessie stopped.

"I want to thank you for riding along with me today, Henry," she said quietly.

"No, ma'am. The pleasure was mine." He stopped brushing and leaned on Mic's back with his forearms, looking across at her. "In fact, I don't believe I can remember ever havin' such a pleasant day."

"It's been a while for me, too."

Henry went back to brushing, then stopped again. "I just gotta ask. Was there some other reason why you took me out and showed me them wild horses today?"

Jessie, having finished, untied the mare and looked back at Henry. "As a matter of fact," she smiled, "yes, there was." She reached over and gently touched Henry on the arm before turning and leading the mare away. "Goodnight, Henry."

Henry watched the woman he had spent the day with walking away from him, and once again, just as he did when they were in town, he found he wanted nothing more than to follow her. This time, however, he didn't. "Goodnight, ma'am."

Henry took his time grooming the gelding, and when he finished walked him to the pen, turned him loose. He stood for a minute watching the buckskin drop his nose to the dirt and walk around the pen trying to find just the right spot to roll in. Once he did, the gelding circled the chosen area several times, getting lower to the ground with each pass until finally his front legs seemed to buckle underneath him and he dropped to the ground. He lay quietly in the dirt for several seconds before rolling over on to his side, then onto his back, exposing his underbelly to the sky. He rolled back onto his side, then over on his back again. He repeated this three times, each time getting more momentum until finally he was able to roll all the way over to his other side, wait for a second and then roll back over again. The gelding, having apparently gotten a sufficient amount of dirt on the area where Henry's saddle had sat, got back up and vigorously shook the excess dirt from his coat, starting at his head, then his neck and finally his entire body. He grunted as he shook, sending a cloud of dust in the air that surrounded him, before it gently floated to the ground. The gelding blew threw his nose several times, shook a second time, and then wandered off to the pile of hay Henry had tossed over the fence for him.

It seemed the perfect end to the perfect day. Henry took a deep breath of the warm evening air as he turned to head to the bunkhouse, and he had only walked a few yards before stopping again. To his right was the pasture that held the herd of horses Jessie had been in the night before. Although

Henry was tired from the long day's ride, it was relatively early, and there was still a sliver of daylight left. Instead of going to the bunkhouse as he had originally planned, he decided to watch the horses in the pasture. There were several horses grazing by the fence as he walked up, and unlike the past evening when he went in with them, this time he stayed outside the fence.

He stood, quietly watching the horses, when one of them, a paint mare named Fancy, raised her head and looked in his direction. Several of the other horses began to walk off, away from him, but Fancy didn't. She stood watching Henry for several seconds before slowly making her way toward him. Henry remained perfectly still as she approached, and she ended up stopping about an arm's length from him on the opposite side of the fence. Henry ever so slowly began to raise his arm toward the mare, and simultaneously, the mare began to reach for him. As Henry's arm reached its full extension, so did the mare's neck, and it seemed they were just a hair too far away from one another to actually touch. Just as Henry was about to lower his arm, the mare reached just a hair more, and ever so softly, touched his hand.

From the dining room window inside her house, Jessie stood watching Henry and the mare. With her arms folded in front of her, she let out a small sigh and smiled.

CHAPTER 30

Henry had a hard time falling asleep that night. He had never really dated anybody but Annie, and even then, he couldn't recall their first date. Everything he and Annie did together since they were kids always just seemed to happen naturally. Because of that, their dates never really felt like "dates." They felt more like two really good friends spending time together. As a result, Henry never really knew what it felt like to be on a date, and specifically, he didn't know what it was like to be on a first date. Still, if he had to guess, he thought being on a first date might feel real close to what he and Jessie had done that day.

And that's what was keeping him awake. Henry had always admired Jessie. Since the first day they met he had seen in her something special. The way she so easily went from one small catastrophe on the ranch to another without so much as a blink of an eye, the way she handled the guests and employees, the way she was with the horses, and most of all, the kindness she showed him. Henry was finally realizing that ever since Annie and Josh died, part of him had died with them, and for the past seventeen years he had done everything he could to make sure that part of him stayed dead.

Yet, because of his time with Jessie, he was also starting to realize there was another part of him deep inside that was slowly waking. He was coming to understand that he was feeling different about her now—as though there might be more between them other than an employer/employee relationship. He wasn't sure, and of course had no real way of knowing, but he felt Jessie might be looking at him differently, too.

He lay in bed, thinking about the poster he had seen in town advertising the Fourth of July dance, and struggled for hours whether or not he should ask her to go with him. The problem was, if he was wrong and she wasn't feeling the same way about him that he was for her, it might make her feel bad or put her on the spot, and he didn't want to do that. But most of all, he didn't want to hurt the relationship they currently had by assuming there might be more to it. Yet, if he didn't ask, he'd never know. It was a dilemma, all right.

Henry finally dozed off two hours before it was time to get up, having gotten no further in the process than when he had started it nearly eight hours before. When he woke, however, he decided he would see how the day went. If there came a time when it felt appropriate to ask Jessie to the dance, he would. If not, he wouldn't...simple as that.

At breakfast that morning Mrs. Rodriguez nonchalantly asked where the two of them had been the day before. "We went to look at the mustangs," Jessie replied.

"Ah...the wild ones. You used to go there with your father when you where just little." She turned to Henry. "All the time, she was with the horses, this one. All the time. Still, all the time, she is with the horses."

Henry smiled. "Yes, ma'am."

"Now she is with you all the time, too." Mrs. Rodriguez smiled knowingly at Henry.

Mrs. Rodriguez had seen the way Jessie looked at him. She instinctively knew Jessie was interested in him, and she also knew after the Chad debacle that Jessie would be in no hurry to jump into another relationship. But unlike Chad, Mrs. Rodriguez liked Henry. She sensed he'd had some trouble in his life, bad trouble from what she could tell. She could also tell Henry was somehow working his way out of that trouble, and she liked the character of a man who could move himself forward even after going through some hardship. Henry was a good man, and if Jessie decided to make some time for him, Mrs. Rodriguez wouldn't be opposed. "And was that all you did?" Mrs. Rodriguez asked slyly, offering a Jessie a slight prod.

"Of course, that's all we did," Jessie said with a look on her face that said, *What else would we be doing?* Henry saw that look, and figured he had spent a sleepless night for nothing. The look on Jessie's face gave him the distinct impression that she wasn't interested in him in any way other than an employee, and that was that.

Henry didn't know it, but Jessie didn't sleep very well the night before, either. She had been tossing and turning with the same thoughts and feelings for Henry that he had for her. In the end, she came to the conclusion that because it appeared so hard for him to talk about his past he still had a very strong attachment to his deceased wife. Any relationship other than the one they currently had with each other was, no doubt, out of the question.

"Too bad," Mrs. Rodriguez shrugged.

"What?" Jessie asked, her cheeks flushing red.

"Nothing, mija," she smiled. "Huevos Rancheros for breakfast today. I get the tortillas." Mrs. Rodriguez headed for the pantry.

Jessie nervously put her napkin on her lap and forced an embarrassed smile in Henry's direction. "I don't know what's gotten into her today." She glanced toward the pantry.

Henry shrugged as if to say, *I didn't notice anything out of the ordinary,* although both of them knew he had. There was an uneasy quiet through the rest of breakfast, with the only sound that of eggs frying and Mrs. Rodriguez humming the way she always did when she was trying to fill a room with something other than silence. Both Henry and Jessie seemed to eat a little faster than normal, as if trying to get ahead of any more uncomfortable conversation. Foregoing the second cup of coffee that usually followed the meal, both of them thanked Mrs. Rodriguez almost simultaneously for breakfast, and like a couple of kids late for the school bus, hurried out the door.

Henry followed Jessie out to the round pen and stood outside of it watching as Jessie slipped a halter on the gray colt for the first time. Up until that point all the work that had been done with the colt had been done at liberty. Nearly two weeks had passed since Jessie had first gone in with him carrying the halter on her arm, but until that day, she had never taken it off her arm, with the exception of switching it to her other arm so the colt knew it was there.

By this time the colt was fairly comfortable with both Jessie and Henry coming up to him, and even touching him. He was still leery of having his feet handled, but that would come with time. On this day, Jessie began by rubbing the colt on his face with her hand, something he actually seemed to enjoy. She then removed the halter and lead rope from her arm and gently touched his face with it in the same areas she had with her hands. Finally, she began sliding the halter over his nose, a little at a time at first, and then farther and farther until she was able slip it over his nose, reach over his neck, take a hold of the strap that would fit just behind his ears, and buckle it in place on his head.

Other than the colt raising his head slightly when she reached over his neck, he seemed to accept the process without any worry. The colt had been following Jessie and Henry around in the pen for nearly two weeks by that time, so when Jessie began walking, the colt followed as he always had. So it was that his first leading lesson went without much of a hitch. She led him around the pen for half a dozen laps, then removed the halter and left the pen. The lesson for the day was over.

It surprised Henry to see how easy Jessie made the whole process look. On any of the other outfits he'd worked in the past, getting a halter on a horse for the first time, particularly a wild horse, was usually quite an ordeal and generally wouldn't end as quietly as this had. Yet everything Jessie did with horses was quiet. And even if it didn't start quietly, like the first day with the colt when he ran mindlessly around the pen for nearly forty laps, it *always* ended quietly.

"We'll do it again tomorrow," she said with a smile as she hung the halter on a peg just outside the pen's gate. "If we can get him leading well, we can get him out of this pen. We'll need to get him moving off the pressure of the rope, which he might struggle with a little. He's done everything so well up till now I can't imagine he'll have too much trouble."

"I don't know when I've ever seen a more willing animal, that's for sure," Henry commented as they turned to head back to the barn.

Both Henry and Jessie had a full day of projects. Henry had some leatherwork he wanted to catch up on. There were at least seven saddles that needed repair, most of which needed their saddle horn caps restitched. Many of the wranglers during the season had set saddles on the ground by propping them up on the saddle horn. It was a common practice by a lot of people in the horse business because it kept the sheepskin on the underside of the saddle out of the dirt. Unfortunately, when done a lot, or when the saddle is dropped onto its horn, the practice has a tendency to pop the stitches that hold the top of the horn to the bottom. It was a practice that Jessie didn't allow for that reason, but inevitably it still happened and every year the caps would need to be repaired. It was a job that would take Henry most of the day.

Jessie, on the other hand, needed to inventory the hay she had on hand. Up till now she fed small square bales of hay that weighed between sixty and a hundred pounds each. The hay would come in on a semi and then would be stacked in the barn. There was a tally sheet that hung on the wall in the barn that was used to keep track of the hay that was fed out. Anytime anybody fed, the amount they took was to be marked down on the sheet so it would be easy to keep track of what was left. Unfortunately, about halfway through the last season, the practice of marking down what was taken was abandoned as their season had gotten busier. Jessie had no idea how much was in the barn.

She had been considering changing the long time practice of feeding small bales, and replacing them with the large, one-ton, round bales instead. The round bales were cheaper and much easier to keep track of. By feeding them, the horses would never run out of hay. Plus with the large bales, the staff would only need to put them out once a week, instead of feeding small bales twice a day. Still, there would be additional up-front costs to feeding round bales, such as buying round-bale feeders for the pastures and pens, and acquiring equipment to move the huge bales from place to place—expenses Jessie wasn't sure she wanted to incur right now.

That was one of the things on her mind as the two of them got ready to part ways after leaving the round pen. Neither one had said much since they left the colt, which wasn't all that uncommon after they worked with him. Both seemed to become somewhat introspective about what they had seen or done with the youngster, and it was often an hour or more before either one said anything at all. But today was different.

"I wanted to thank you again for taking me out to see them mustangs yesterday," Henry said just before they parted. The comment brought a smile to Jessie's face as she immediately recalled the horses from the previous day running through the valley.

"That *was* fun, wasn't it?"

"Yes, ma'am." They both stopped for just a second, waiting for the other to say something more, but when nothing else was said, Henry nodded. "Well, them saddles ain't gonna mend themselves, I guess."

"No, I guess not." There was another second or two of silence.

"Alright then...I better get to it." Somewhat reluctantly, Henry turned and headed for the tack room.

"Maybe..." Jessie started, but then stopped herself.

Henry turned back.

She hesitated. "Oh...nothing."

"Yes, ma'am." Henry turned and started for the tack room again.

"Maybe we could do it again sometime," Jessie blurted. "You know, go find the mustangs."

Henry stopped and looked back. Jessie was smiling tentatively. "I mean, if it's something you wouldn't mind doing," she added.

"That'd be real nice," Henry said with a smile of his own. "I'd like that."

"Okay then," Jessie nodded.

"Okay."

Jessie headed to the barn to count hay bales and Henry went to the tack room to stitch saddle horns. Even though their conversation was a brief one, it affected them both in different ways. For Henry, he wasn't sure if it was what she said, how she said it, or both, but the conversation seemed to breathe new life into his thought of asking her to the dance. At breakfast he was convinced she wasn't very interested in him, but now he wasn't so sure.

As for Jessie, she ended up counting the stack of hay three different times and getting a different total each time. The entire time she was counting, she was also kicking herself for being so forward with Henry in asking him to go see the wild horses again. *Will he see that as me asking him out?* She asked herself. *It's not a date, surely he knows that. I mean, it could be considered a date, I suppose. I didn't mean it that way...I don't think. Maybe I did. He said yes, so he must want to go. Although, I am his boss, and maybe he thought he* had *to say yes. That's probably it. He doesn't really want to go, but thought he had to. I should tell him he doesn't have to go. No, if I do that then he might think I don't want him to go. I should have just kept my mouth shut.*

Throughout the rest of the day, a sort of cat-and-mouse game between the two began to take shape. Every time they were together, whether at lunch or doing chores or just in passing, Henry looked for an opportunity to ask Jessie to the dance, and Jessie looked for an opportunity to tell Henry he didn't have to go look at Mustangs if he didn't want to. By the end of the day, neither had really said much of anything, and at dinner they did little more than talk about how much hay there was, how many saddles Henry had finished, and what the plan was for the next day. No sooner had they finished with dinner when Henry, having once more talked himself out of asking Jessie to the dance, and Jessie, having talked herself out of telling Henry he didn't need to go with her to look at the wild horses, said a polite goodnight, and once again went their separate ways.

Jessie began to realize shortly after Henry had gone to the bunkhouse just how much stress she had put herself through during the day worrying about whether or not Henry was bothered by her invitation. She suddenly felt very silly and to make it up to herself, she decided to make some lemonade, take a shower, and finish off the day by sitting out on the porch swing to watch the sunset.

She took her time with both the lemonade and the shower, lingering in the hot water much longer than usual, so by the time she finally made her way to the porch swing, the sun had already set. It was a beautiful evening and in the glow of the dim porch light above the door, Jessie brought her bare feet up next to her on the bench while her long hair, still wet from her shower, hung loosely about her shoulders.

She had just enough time to settle back on the swing and take three long sips from her glass when she noticed a lone figure walking toward her from the bunkhouse. "Henry, is that you?" she called.

"Yes, ma'am," Henry said moving out of the shadows and into the light at the foot of the steps. He was clean-shaven and wearing a clean, newly ironed shirt and pair of jeans. He took his hat off, exposing his neatly combed hair.

"Good evening," Jessie said, with a genuine smile in her voice. "My, don't you look nice tonight."

"Evenin' ma'am." He was nervous, but trying to smile back. "Thank you. So do you." There was another awkward silence in a day filled with them as Henry fumbled with his hat and debated whether or not he should climb the steps.

"Would you like a glass of lemonade? I just made it fresh."

"No, ma'am. Thank you though."

"Would you like to come up and have a seat?"

"No, ma'am."

There was another awkward pause. "Is there something else, then?"

Henry straightened his posture, closed his eyes momentarily, and took a deep breath. "Yes, ma'am...Jess...Jessie." He paused, shaking his head in embarrassment. "The fact of the matter is..." He fumbled with his hat. "I quit drinking here a while back." He paused again, wanting to head back to the bunkhouse, but knowing it was way to late for that.

"That's great Henry. You should be proud."

"Yes, ma'am." He took another deep breath. "I guess that's why I'm here. See, when we was in town the other day, I seen a poster about this dance comin' up on Saturday night down at the American Legion. They got a live band. Anyway,

I was thinkin' I'd maybe like to go and celebrate a little. I mean, the fact I ain't had a drink in a while."

"That sounds like a good idea, Henry."

"Yes, ma'am." Henry reached up and scratched his cheek. It dawned on him this was the first time in his life he was getting ready to ask a woman out. "Now, I ain't much of a hand at dancin', leastways when I'm sober. But I was thinkin' about maybe goin' on down there just the same." He stopped, took another deep breath and focused his attention directly on Jessie. "I was wonderin' if maybe you'd do me the honor of going along with me. To the dance. I mean, if you want to."

The question took Jessie completely off guard, particularly after all the worry she put herself through during the day about that very subject.

"Why, Henry, are you asking me out on a date?"

Henry winced as if the word *date* was too harsh.

"No, ma'am…well…I…you…you wouldn't have to…I mean it'd be…I…I…"

"Henry," Jessie felt the need to step in. "I'd love to go with you. Thank you so much for asking."

Henry looked blankly in her direction, as if he couldn't believe he asked, nor could he believe she actually said yes. He let out a big sigh of relief.

"*Now* would you like a glass of lemonade?" she smiled.

"No ma'am. Thank you, but I think I better just go lie down."

Henry turned and walked back across the yard, putting his hat back on and shaking his head and thinking there must have been an easier way to do what he had just done.

CHAPTER 31

It was the third time in less than a mile that Jessie felt the need to glance over at the speedometer. She was trying to be discreet about it, but Henry noticed anyway.

"Something wrong?" he asked.

"No, not at all. I was just wondering how fast we were going."

Henry glanced down at the speedometer. "About thirty-five."

"I see." Jessie looked out the passenger-side window. "I guess I've never gone this slow down this road before." She turned to Henry and smiled. "The dance starts at eight. You think we'll make it before then?"

"It's only five-thirty."

"I know," she said jokingly. "You think we'll make it?"

Henry had picked Jessie up when he said he would, at 5:00 p.m., for their date. He didn't like being behind schedule, and especially didn't want to be late this time, either. He had gone to town the day before and bought a new shirt and jeans for the occasion. He wanted to get some new boots, but couldn't find any that fit, so he stuck with his old ones for the night. He cleaned his hat as best he could, shined up and put his old trophy belt buckle from back in his rodeo days, and slipped on his best vest.

He couldn't recall having ever seen Jessie in anything other than her work clothes, and for some reason, he just assumed she would be wearing a cleaner version of them for the dance. He was momentarily speechless when she opened the door and stepped out onto the porch. Her hair, which she normally wore in a long braid, was now pulled back in a silver barrette, hung loose over her shoulders and flowed down her back. She wore a white, long-sleeve, western-style blouse with short white fringe on the yoke, and jeans that showed off her figure quite nicely, or so Henry thought, as soon as he could think again.

"Evenin' ma'am," he said, removing his hat and placing it over his chest.

"Good evening, Henry."

"You look real nice." It was the best compliment he could come up with, and Jessie knew it. It made her smile. "I guess we're ready to go, then?" he asked.

"Almost."

"Ma'am?"

"I'm not putting one foot off this porch until you promise to call me by my first name for the rest of the night." Henry had to stop and think for a minute. He wasn't sure he could do it, seeing as how he hadn't called her by her name the entire time he'd been at the ranch. He had tried to do it the night he asked her out, but it was as if it hurt his tongue when he tried. "Well?" she asked playfully. "I'm waiting."

"I don't know, ma'am…I just…"

Jessie turned for the door.

"Okay, okay!" he blurted. "I promise."

"Okay then. Shall we go?"

"Yes, ma'a…Jess… Jessie." He winced, putting the hat back on his head.

"We'll work on it," Jessie said, gently taking Henry by the hand and starting down the steps. "Rome wasn't built in a day."

"No, ma'am." He winced again.

The drive to town took the normal forty-five minutes. Or at least it was normal for Henry. It was twenty minutes too slow for Jessie. Still it was an enjoyable ride, and soon enough Henry brought the truck to a stop near the feed store, parked, and the couple walked into town.

The main street was busy with foot traffic, including the occasional child running past with a lit sparkler in his or her hand. There was also the sporadic sound of firecrackers going off down the side streets, along with the intermittent whistling of bottle rockets and other small fireworks in the distance. There was an odd odor of gunpowder and cotton candy in the air, and it was all mixed with laughter and cheerful conversations of the folks on the street. All in all, it was a very pleasant experience for Henry, one of community and friendship that he had not encountered in a very long time.

They stopped at the park in the middle of town just as a horse drawn hayride pulled to a stop at the curb. The people who had ridden on the wagon gleefully jumped off, and another group waiting in the park jumped on. Henry and Jessie stood on the sidewalk watching the people get situated on the wagon when the wagon driver saw them. "Come on folks!" he said in a deep baritone voice. "Hop on, we still got plenty of room."

Jessie smiled and turned to look at Henry who was politely shaking his head at the wagon driver. "Oh come on," she said, grabbing his arm and pulling him toward the wagon. Henry resisted the whole way. He had used big horses and wagons like this to do chores on a ranch since he was a kid. Riding on a horse-drawn wagon through the streets of town with a bunch of people singing and carrying on seemed a bit silly to him.

The people on the wagon added friendly encouragement to Jessie as she got him closer, and a man and woman slid over to make room. Jessie quickly vaulted herself onto the vacated spot, still holding Henry's arm and pulling him near. At the very last minute, Henry looked in all directions to make sure nobody he knew was watching, and finally joined Jessie on the wagon. Spontaneous applause broke out as the driver yelled, "Bill and Bob, git up!" and the wagon lurched forward.

They had traveled less than a block when someone in the back started singing "She'll be Comin' Round the Mountain," and before the first line was finished, most everyone on the wagon had joined in, including Jessie. Soon, even Henry, who at first had been so self-conscious about even at being on the wagon, began getting in the spirit and was having trouble keeping himself from smiling broadly and nodding his head to the rhythm of the tune. When the song ended, everybody let out a loud cheer and clapped enthusiastically.

As a loud chorus of "Row Your Boat" started up, the wagon turned right off of Main Street, traveled a block to First Avenue, took a left on First, went two more blocks and took another left on Lincoln Avenue on its way back to Main. It was on Lincoln that the wagon rolled past Mona's Bar, and as it did, a silhouetted figure of a man stepped to the window and watched as it went by. The figure could easily see Jessie and Henry sitting near the front of the wagon, Jessie smiling and singing and Henry sitting next to her holding her hand. Once the wagon reached the end of Lincoln and turned back onto Main, the figure slowly slunk back into the smoky shadows of the noisy barroom.

The dance that had started at eight that evening stopped for fifteen minutes at nine o'clock so the attendees could go outside and watch the annual town fireworks. It wasn't really much of a show, with only one rocket going off every thirty seconds or so. The locals enjoyed it, and after the grand finale, which consisted of seven rockets going off within a three-second period of each other, everyone applauded and went back in to the dance. The band, a talented group of local musicians who played primarily contemporary country music, started up before everyone was back inside. After finishing two popular up-tempo songs, they eased into a soulful version of "The Tennessee Waltz," and the dance floor quickly began to fill.

Henry, who had yet to ask Jessie to dance during the night, sat next to her at the table and watched as couple after couple, hand in hand, headed for the floor. Jessie looked around and seeing they were nearly the only ones not dancing, stood up and planted herself in front of Henry. Smiling down, she reached out her hand to him. "Would you like to dance?"

There was a brief hesitation as Henry glanced at her hand, then back up into her flashing blue eyes and kindly smiling face. He had been trying to work up the nerve to ask her to dance for a while, but feeling he'd embarrass both himself and her due to his rustiness, he kept stopping himself. It was clear to him now by the look on Jessie's face that even if he was rusty, she wasn't going to mind. "I'd be honored," he said, taking her hand, lifting himself from his chair and walking with her to the dance floor.

Much to his surprise, it only took Henry a few steps before he was in rhythm with both the music and Jessie. They began to glide a small circle in amongst the crowd, with his leathery hand nearly enveloping hers, his right hand gently around her waist, and her left hand resting on his shoulder. "I thought you said you couldn't dance." She smiled, looking up at him.

"Oh," Henry shrugged. "This ain't really dancin'. It's more like real slow walkin'."

"You could have fooled me."

They made a quarter of the way around the dance floor when Henry let out a deep breath and looked into her eyes. "I wanted to thank you again for takin' me out and showin' me them mustangs the other day."

"Weren't they wonderful?"

"I believe I know why you took me out there, though."

"Oh?"

"Well," Henry started. "I guess you figure I might be kinda like that boss horse in the herd, the one the others didn't like much." There was a long pause as Henry tried to find the words he wanted to use next. Jessie recognized that he was searching, and waited patiently for him to resume. "I guess that may be true. To be honest, there was a long time there where I didn't really like myself much." He paused again. "I went through a pretty rough patch there for a while, and I'm not real sure I'm all the way through it yet, but I'm workin' on it." He paused, this time a little longer. "You see, I got to bein' pretty hard on myself, and them around me, a little like that boss horse, I guess. Took to drinking because of it. I drank a lot, for a real long time. I didn't like bein' that way, but I'd been doin' it so long that I didn't know any other way *to* be."

The end of the song came, music stopped and the people on the dance floor broke into loud applause, mixed with an occasional shrill whistle. Jessie and Henry stood looking at one another as if they were the only two on the floor. The band struck up another slow song and some of the couples left the floor, but most of them stayed and slowly drifted into the rhythm of the new melody.

Jessie and Henry gradually glided in time with the others on the floor, which created another long pause. Jessie sensed there was more Henry wanted to say, but she also sensed the break in the music and the applause from the crowd had broken the momentum of his words. She wanted him to know that not only had she been listening to him, but that she cared very much about what he was saying and if he wanted to do so, that she wanted him to finish.

"Then?" Jessie finally asked, looking up at him and hoping the one word question would be enough to get him started again.

"Then I come here, and I saw you." Henry smiled. "And you ain't that way—you ain't hard. You're fair. You're fair in your business, to the people and the horses on your place; you're fair to that gray colt. Most of all, you been fair to me." Jessie stopped dancing and looked tenderly into Henry's eyes. "I been thinkin'," he continued. "Maybe its time for me to try to be a little more fair to myself. If I can do that, then maybe I can get this thing in me turned around once and for all." He forced a smile. "Like I said, I ain't all the way through it yet, but I'm workin' on it."

It had been Henry's way of telling her about his past, or as much of it as he could at the time. He had opened up to her, and in his own way, he had invited her into his life. Jessie felt it immediately and as they drifted across the dance floor, she slowly lowered her head until her cheek rested on Henry's chest. "Some things take time, Henry," she said quietly. "It's okay."

The couple made one full turn around the dance floor when Jessie suddenly felt a tap on her shoulder. A bit startled, she quickly turned to see Joli Hansen standing behind her. "You two are getting' way too serious out here for my liking," Joli said with a joking gruffness in her voice. "I can see I'm just gonna have to break you up." Taking Jessie's arm, she moved her aside, and then, standing in front of Henry with her arms out as if already dancing with a partner, she said, "Mind if I cut in?"

Smiling big, Jessie curtsied and put her hands out toward Henry. "By all means," she said. "But you need to have him back by midnight. He's my ride home."

"Well, we'll just see about that!" Joli blurted. Jessie smiled and waved as little gray-haired woman, taking the lead, spun the hapless Henry out across the dance floor in a completely different rhythm than what the band was playing.

"Midnight!" Henry heard Jessie call over the sound of the music.

After two fast dances, Henry, out of breath and grinning, excused himself from the spry little woman and made his way back to Jessie, who had already poured him a glass of lemonade from a large punchbowl near the refreshment table in the back of the room. The remainder of the evening was filled with laughter and dancing and introductions to some of the townsfolk as well as some of the local ranchers. Henry and Jessie never returned to the seriousness of the conversation they had had during their first dance. There was no need. An understanding between them had developed that hadn't been there when the evening began. They were moving in a different direction now, and while neither really knew what that direction was, one thing they did know was that they would be going down that path together—perhaps tentatively at times—but together.

The evening finally came to an end. Jessie gently held Henry's arm as they walked up the steps of the porch and stopped at the door to Jessie's house, the dim light above them casting soft shadows on the wooden floor below them. Jessie stopped at the door, turned to face Henry and gently took his hands in hers.

"I can't remember when I've had a more enjoyable evening," Jessie sighed. "Thank you, Henry. And thank you for talking with me tonight. It meant a lot to me."

"Thank *you*, Jessie." Henry felt like he wanted to say more, but nothing more came out. Jessie wanted to say more too, but like Henry, was suddenly at a loss for words.

"Well," Henry sighed. "I guess I'd better say goodnight."

"I guess so," Jessie reluctantly agreed. There was another moment of silence.

"Well," Henry smiled, gently rocking Jessie's hands back and forth. "Goodnight then."

"Good night, Henry."

Henry continued to stand for a few more seconds before unwillingly letting her hands go, turning and walking down the steps. He had yet to reach the bottom step when he stopped, turned around and went back to where she was standing. He removed his hat and gingerly kissed Jessie on the cheek.

"There," he said, slowly stepping back away from her. "I been worried about that all night."

"Me, too," Jessie smiled.

"I guess I better go now. Sleep well, Jess."

"You too, Henry."

Henry put his hat back on, turned and walked down the steps and into the shadows. "Goodnight," Jessie heard him call from the darkness.

"Goodnight," she called back.

Content and happy, Jessie turned, opened the screen door and went inside.

CHAPTER 32

Something was wrong, and the gray colt knew it. The other horses in the pen also sensed it and had instinctively begun to make their way to the back of the darkened paddock, as far from the gate as they could get. The colt had only been in this larger pen for a day because he had become so easy for Jessie and Henry to catch and lead.

The day after Jessie and Henry had gotten back from their date on the Fourth of July, they started paying more attention to helping the colt give to the pressure of the halter, rather than simply follow whoever was in front of him while he was wearing it. Giving to physical pressure was part of the colt's education Jessie didn't want to skip over, and in fact if done properly, would help later on in his training when they started riding him.

Jessie and Henry both knew that initially most horses, particularly wild horses, will instinctively push into any pressure they feel on their body, or pull against something that they feel is pulling on them. In training, their goal was to get the horse to override that instinct and give to the pressure, whether it pushes on him or pulls on him. That was the idea in getting the colt to give to any pressure he might feel from the halter. If he could give to pressure, he could eventually learn to stand tied to something without pulling back, or not pull away from someone who was handling him. A little further into his training he might be able to transfer the idea so that it would be easier for him to give to the bit when learning how to stop, turn or back up.

The first time the colt actually felt pressure from the halter in the area behind his ears was when Jessie was in the pen with him holding the lead rope that was attached to the halter. Jessie then had Henry walk into the pen just a little faster than he usually did. The colt was not only *not* used to having two humans in the pen with him, he also wasn't used to seeing the quicker movement the second human provided. Immediately, the colt began backing away, which Jessie allowed him to do. However, Jessie also didn't move with him at first. As a result, the slack quickly came out of the rope attached to the halter, which put pressure in the area behind his ears where the halter rested. The colt, upon feeling this kind of pressure for the first time, panicked and instinctively pulled back in order to free himself.

Jessie knew from experience that the worst thing she could do, would be to clamp down on the rope and lean on it with the entire weight of her body. In effect, it would have added more pressure to the rope and caused more panic in the colt. She didn't want to make the situation worse. She simply moved with the colt, softly holding the lead rope, but keeping the same amount of pressure on the halter that was there when he began to pull away. The colt tried to fight the pressure by pulling harder, but every time he did, Jessie simply moved with him.

The colt realized quickly that fleeing from the pressure the halter was putting on him wasn't working. Not only was he *not* getting away from the pressure but the pressure also stayed relatively consistent. Eventually, when fleeing didn't work, he tried something else. He did the one thing his instinct told him not to do: he went *into* the pressure and toward Jessie. Immediately, the pressure went away which caused him to stop fighting. As soon he did that, Henry left the pen, further relieving the pressure the colt was feeling.

Jessie began to back away from the colt slowly, and once again took the slack out of the rope. Again the colt fought the pressure, but this time not as much or for as long before stopping and moving toward Jessie. She repeated this four more times before the colt began moving toward her, instead of away every time he felt pressure. Within less than a half-hour, not only could the colt follow someone that was in front of him, but he could also give to the pressure from the halter.

Over the next few days, both Henry and Jessie spent time reinforcing the lesson with the colt. He became so comfortable with the concept that Jessie was able to finally take him out of the round pen he had been in since Tom Essex dropped him off nearly two months earlier. She took him for very short walks at first in the area of the round pen. But within days she was able to walk him all over the ranch: by the barn, the bunkhouse, tack room and in the yard up by her house. Once she was able to take him in all those areas without much worry on his part, then Henry repeated the process. After a week of leading and giving to pressure, Jessie made the decision to put the colt in with a small band of her geldings in one of the larger paddocks so that he could socialize and get out to stretch his legs; something he hadn't really been able to do since before he went off the ledge up on the mesa over a year before.

Henry went along with Jessie as she led the colt into the two-acre pen and removed his halter. She left the pen and stood with Henry just outside the gate. The colt came to the gate and stood looking at them as if not knowing what to do next, when up the gradually sloping hill from the back of the paddock galloped the six geldings that resided there. In a flash, the geldings had the colt surrounded. With bowed necks and stiff bodies, they smelled his flanks, shoulders and nose. Simultaneously, the colt and the older gelding Jack that was sniffing his nose and mouth at the time, squealed and struck out with one of their front feet, neither striking or coming close to each other. All of the horses milled around, posturing, prancing and snorting when, as if some unseen or unheard command had been given, they all galloped off together, heads high and tails in the air, back down the hill toward the far end of the paddock with the colt galloping right along with them.

They made several laps around the inside of the pen at top speed, squealing, bucking and kicking as they went, never missing a step or breaking stride. Jessie and Henry stood watching. "I guess they were happy to have him," Henry quipped.

"Looks like he's happy to be there, too."

They stood watching for several more minutes as the horses stretched out at top speed, running from one end of the paddock to the other and back. One by one each of the horses began to slow and then drop into a trot, then a walk, then they would stop. It was the older ones that ran out of steam first, then all but the colt were stopped and standing or grazing. The colt continued to run and buck for several more minutes with Jessie and Henry both watching in wonder at the colt's natural athleticism and power, before Jessie turned to Henry.

"Oh, I almost forgot," she said touching Henry on the arm. "I got a call from Ed Wilson over in Lucyville. He's been after me for over a year to sell him that little Ginger mare of ours. He finally offered me what she's worth so I sold her to him. He'd like to have her delivered tomorrow. Seeing as how it is your turn, and all, I was wondering if you wouldn't mind taking her over for me..." she paused. "There'll be a home cooked dinner in it for you."

"Well now, I don't know how I could ever turn down a deal like that." He put out his hand to take the halter from

Jessie, before they both turned and started back. "Lucyville... isn't that about one hundred fifty miles to the south?"

"Yeah, just this side of the Arizona border. If you leave around eight or nine in the morning, it'll probably take you most of the day." A mischievous smile crossed her face. "Especially the way you drive."

"Hey...there's nothin' wrong with the way I drive." Henry feigned indignity. "At least I'll get there in one piece!"

"Yeah, and two years older." Their conversation faded as the colt, who had finished his run, trotted up to the gate and watched as they walked away.

The next morning, the colt once again came to the gate and watched as Henry pulled the truck and trailer into the yard and loaded the mare. Jessie, who had been doing chores, stopped to go say goodbye. The colt couldn't hear what was being said between the two of them, but just before Henry climbed in the truck, Jessie stood on her tip toes to kiss him on the cheek. She stood and waved as the truck pulled away, and Henry waved back.

Henry needed to stop in Grant to fuel up for the long drive. As he pulled up to the pump and got out to begin filling the tank, he got an uneasy feeling that he was being watched. Yet, when he quickly scanned the entire area within his view, he saw nothing out of the ordinary. Not giving it much more thought, he finished filling the tank, paid for the fuel, got in and drove away. Henry passed the diner on the opposite side of the street, and for a split second out of the corner of his eye, he thought he caught sight of a familiar figure standing in the diner doorway. But when he looked back it was gone. He didn't know it, but the reason Henry didn't see anybody was that by the time he looked, the figure had already slipped out of the doorway, around the corner and was heading toward his pickup truck out in the back parking lot.

After Henry left the ranch, Jessie finished the morning chores, and then went to get the colt. The young horse was looking forward to their time together more often these days. He was beginning to understand there was a reason for the things Jessie was doing with him. He was learning new skills that he could have never imagined, like following a human, moving into pressure instead of away from it, and exploring things that he initially found frightening.

On this morning, Jessie led him from his new pen with the geldings and took him to his old pen. Usually Jessie would stay with him in the pen for a while. But on this day, she did something different. She brought him into the pen, took his halter off and then turned and left the pen. At first, the colt was a little confused. He became even more confused when he turned from the gate he had followed Jessie back to and saw a saddle and saddle pad sitting in the middle of the pen. During all the time he had spent in the pen, nothing like that had ever been in there. Immediately, the colt snorted and began taking evasive action from the foreign and potentially life-threatening object by running back and forth. The saddle, of course, sat there.

It wasn't long before the colt began to understand that the object wasn't chasing him, and so at least for the time being, it posed no threat. After slowing down, he faced it, and watched it carefully for a very long time before finally deciding to investigate. He remained alert and cautious as he inched his way up two or three steps at a time, then stopped and retreated, only to try again when he felt comfortable enough. By the time the sun was getting high in the cloudless sky, the colt had made his way all the way up to the saddle, cautiously smelled its leather, the metal-covered stirrups and the saddle pad. It was the pad that smelled the most familiar. It smelled of horse, but not just one. It smelled of numerous horses, too many for him to distinguish any one in particular. The saddle also smelled of horses, but the odor was faint and covered by oil, soap and dust. He lingered by the saddle for several minutes, moving it with his nose and picking the saddle pad up with his teeth, before finally ignoring it completely and going to get a drink of water from the tank by the gate.

An hour or so after she had first turned the colt in the pen with the saddle, and with the day's lesson having been completed, Jessie returned, slipped his halter on and led him back to his new pen with the geldings. The rest of the day passed uneventfully for the colt. He spent it standing in the shade of an oak tree at the bottom of the paddock, eating and sleeping, and things on the ranch felt as peaceful to him as they always had.

It wasn't until after dark that there came a change. Uneasiness began to settle in with the herd as a ripple of alarm passed silently from one paddock to the next. A menacing presence had arrived on the ranch and was slipping through the shadows and toward the house where Jessie lived. Once the presence had passed the pens, an eerie quiet hung over the entire ranch until it was shattered by the sound of voices up by the house. The voices got louder and were soon mixed with screams, the sound of wood cracking and glass breaking. All the horses ran as far from the sound as they could—all of them except the gray colt. The gray colt ran to the gate of the paddock and looked helplessly toward the house. He nickered softly.

It seemed like forever before the sounds from the house finally stopped and the presence the horses had been feeling stepped out of the house and into the dim light of the porch. Even though the house was at least one hundred yards away, the colt immediately recognized the presence as human. Not only was the presence human, it was a human he knew and was afraid of. The colt snorted a warning and ran to join the others at the bottom of the paddock, turning only after he had hid himself behind one of the older geldings and looked back up the hill, waiting for the presence to pass.

The horses could hear the presence talking to itself as it passed their paddock and headed in the direction of the round pen. There was more talking coming from the direction of the round pen, and then suddenly, the presence appeared at the gate of the paddock, a rifle in its hand. It stayed at the gate for a short time before moving on to the next one, and the next one after that. Then, as quickly as the presence had come, it disappeared and was gone from the ranch.

An eerie quiet once again returned to the ranch. As the horses curiously eased their way up to the gates of their pens, a soft, almost inaudible sobbing began to emanate from the house. It was Jessie, lying on the upstairs bathroom floor, bloodied, bruised and racked with pain from the horrendous beating she had tried to fight off. Her mind was trying to remember what happened, and how, but the pieces weren't fitting together. Images floated aimlessly through her consciousness, but none stayed in focus long enough for her to recognize any of them. Then, all went black as she lost consciousness for the second time.

She awoke a few minutes later, groggy, but with a very clear vision of the entire ordeal. It ran as effortlessly through her mind as if she were watching a movie. She had been in the kitchen, checking on the roast she had in the oven, and then went to the dining room to set the table. She had placed the two plates across the table from one another, stood back and looked at them, then went back to move them so they were next to each other. She laid out the silverware next to the plates, the glasses and coffee cups, and as a final touch, put two long yellow candles in the middle of the table. She thought about lighting them, but decided to wait. There was no telling how long it would be before Henry would be back.

She went up to her bedroom and put on one of her favorite denim shirts, tucked it neatly into her jeans, and went into the bathroom to brush the braid from her hair.

She returned to the kitchen, opened the oven to check on the roast and closed the oven door. That is when she heard something outside. She had assumed the sound was Henry. She figured he had probably gotten back while she was upstairs and that she hadn't heard the rig pull in.

Smiling to herself, she walked through the dining room, into the hallway, where she stopped by the hallway mirror to check her hair, before pushing the screen door open and stepping out onto the porch. "Henry? Is that you?"

"Henry? Is that you?" a surly voice from the darkness mocked her. She was startled by the familiarity of the voice, and the image of the man in the shadows. It was Chad, standing by the corner of the house.

"What happened?" he said in a spiteful voice. "That old fool run off on you?"

"Chad! What are you doing here?" Jessie snapped. "I want you off this property now."

Chad stepped out of the shadows and up onto the porch, but Jessie stood her ground. "You don't really want me to leave yet, do you?" There was a sinister grin on his face. "I only just got here."

"Jesus, Chad," she said as he closed in on her. "You've been drinking. You leave right now or I'm going in and calling the sheriff."

"And what? He'll be here in an hour? Two hours?" Chad grabbed her by the arm, and Jessie instinctively swung her free hand and hit him in the face with everything she had until he grabbed that hand as well. "No." He was enjoying himself now. "I'll just stick around for a while. I don't mind telling you, I'm a little put out that you chose that old man over me."

It was then Jessie realized why Chad was there, and a feeling of terror shot through her, almost making her sick with fear. She kicked Chad as hard as she could in the groin, and when he let go and doubled over, she kicked him again on the side of the head and bolted for the door. Her kick didn't land square and only knocked him off balance, and Chad quickly, though agonizingly, chased after her. He caught Jessie just inside the house, and pushed her as hard as he could. She landed hard on one of the living room chairs, flipping it over backwards as she thudded heavily on her side against the wall.

Tossing the fallen chair out of his way, Chad grabbed her by the arm and jerked her to her feet. Jessie hit him as hard as she could in the face with her closed fist, and he momentarily stumbled backward, taking her with him. As soon as he regained his balance, he hit her squarely in the face with an open hand, sending her sprawling on the floor. Jessie scurried across the floor to the corner of the room where her father's old, knurled walking stick still resided. She grabbed it, and holding it with both hands, scrambled to her feet. Chad, undeterred, walked toward her menacingly and as he reached for her, she let out a bloodcurdling scream and swung the stick with all her might, striking Chad squarely on the side of the head.

The blow knocked him to the ground, and Jessie struck him squarely on the back, and again on the arm before he stood up, turned and grabbed the stick from her, then grabbed her by the arm and threw her through the screen door. The force of her body going through it knocked it off its hinges. Jessie landed hard on the porch, and rolled down the steps and into the yard. A bloodied and bruised Chad stepped out onto the porch. "Damn, you're scrappy tonight!"

The image in Jessie's mind suddenly went blank, and she felt herself slipping back into the dark of unconsciousness, when, in the distance, she heard the familiar sound of her truck and trailer pulling into the yard outside. "Henry," she whispered to herself.

The lights from inside the house were a welcome sight as Henry pulled the rig up the long driveway and into the yard.

Since he had left that morning, all he could do was think about being back. He really missed being with Jessie, even if it were only for a few hours, and he wanted to do everything he could to get back to her as soon as he could. He found himself driving the speed limit on the way there and back. He normally drove three to five miles an hour *under* the speed limit. It had been a habit he acquired as a youngster driving farm machinery up and down narrow roads, and it had carried over to driving his trucks once he got older.

Had it been a quick delivery, he would have been back before dark. As it was, however, old man Wilson apparently didn't have many visitors, so when he did get one, he took advantage of it. Henry got hung up at Wilson's place an hour-and-a-half longer than he would have liked. This put him an hour-and-a-half behind when it came to getting back to the ranch. The good news was there was very little traffic, which made the trip go much more smoothly. One of the only vehicles he ran across the last twenty miles of the drive back to the ranch was a pickup truck on the gravel road. It was strange to see a vehicle on that stretch of road, especially after dark. At first, the truck looked vaguely familiar to him, but in the dark it was hard to tell. In the end, Henry figured it was just some kids out joy riding.

As Henry turned the rig into the yard, the headlights shone directly on the front porch and lit up the screen door hanging off its hinges. Confusion then concern shot through him. Jamming on the brakes, he sat for a minute in the truck staring at the door. He climbed out and looked around to see if anything else was out of place, then started for the house—slowly at first, but as he got closer his pace quickened.

On the porch, there was a spattering of blood. Henry's heart sunk and, swallowing hard, he stopped at the door. "Jessie!" he called. "Jessie, where are you?" He looked inside and saw the mess that had been made, and then saw the blood drops leading up the stairs. "Jesus...Jessie," he said to himself. He ran up the stairs skipping two at a time, and upon getting to the top immediately looked to his left in the direction of the blood trail and saw Jessie's crimson-spattered legs sticking out of the open bathroom door. He rushed to her, gently pushing the bathroom door open to reveal her lying on her side, her shirt tore nearly all the way off and her face, arms and ribcage bloody and bruised. Henry knelt down by her side and bent down close to see if she was still breathing. "Jessie," he whispered next to her ear. "Jessie, can you hear me? It's Henry."

Jessie slowly opened her eyes, and forced a smile. "Henry. Could you please call Mrs. Rodriguez? She'll know what to do." She closed her eyes again and drifted into unconsciousness.

CHAPTER 33

Henry was pacing the floor in the living room when Mrs. Rodriguez appeared at the top of the steps wiping her hands with a towel.

"She is better now," she said as she descended the steps. Henry met her at the bottom. "She has some broken ribs and cuts on her face and some bruises, a concussion, too, I think. She is resting now. We need to wake her every hour."

"It's my fault," Henry said sadly. "I should have never left her today."

"This is not your fault," Mrs. Rodriguez said sternly. "This is the fault of the man who did it. It is not the fault of you, not the fault of her. Only he is to blame."

Without warning, the image of the pickup truck Henry saw driving down the road, away from the ranch that night, suddenly flashed into his mind. He thought the truck looked familiar at the time, and now, as the picture froze in his mind, he was certain he not only knew whose truck it was, but also whose fault this was.

"Ma'am," Henry said, anger starting to rise in his voice. "I know it's late, but would you mind stayin' with her for a little while. I got to go to town."

"It is *very* late," Mrs. Rodriguez said bluntly. "Can this thing in town not wait till morning?"

"No, ma'am." Henry turned for the door. "This is something that needs doing tonight."

Henry ran to the bunkhouse, went to the bottom of his footlocker and pulled out his Colt revolver. He loaded each of the six chambers, put it in its holster and headed for the truck. He did not drive the speed limit on his way to town, and didn't stop until he reached the parking lot of Mona's Bar. There were fifteen vehicles sitting in the gravel lot next to the bar, one of them the truck he'd seen on the road by the ranch. Henry drove his truck to the very back of the lot and parked in the shadows and away from the lights of the street. He shut his truck off and waited.

By midnight, all but two of the vehicles had left the lot—a car and the truck Henry was watching. By one in the morning, the pickup was the only one left. Henry climbed out of his truck and took up a position on the side of the bar, in the shadows near a dumpster. At one-thirty, Chad stepped out of the bar and stopped long enough to light a cigarette. His face was bruised and scratched, as were his knuckles. He took a drag from the cigarette and let the smoke roll out of his mouth before heading for the parking lot. Getting to his truck, he pulled the keys from his pocket and dropped them on the ground. He bent over to pick them up, and that was when he heard the cocking of a gun next to his ear.

"Don't do anything stupid," Henry growled. "Or you'll die right here, right now."

"Whoa there cowboy," Chad slurred. "You've got me mistaken for someone else."

"You sorry son of a bitch." Henry cracked Chad on the back of the head with the butt of the pistol, knocking him to the ground. "As you can see, I ain't in a mood for your crap. Now stand up and turn around."

Chad slowly stood up and turned to face Henry. The look on Henry's face was cold and unforgiving, and Chad knew he wasn't going to talk his way out of this situation. Henry raised the .45 caliber Colt to Chad's head until the barrel was only an inch from his right eye. Sheer terror crossed Chad's face.

"The only reason you ain't dead already is because it'd take too much time to get rid of your body." Henry's voice was low and unwavering. "So you better listen real good or by God, I'll make time." He moved the pistol even closer to Chad's eye. "You climb in that piece of shit truck of yours, and you start drivin' and you get as far from here as you can get. If you come back, I'll kill you. If you ever go anywhere near Jessica King again, I'll kill you." He put the barrel of the pistol on Chad's forehead and shoved him with it. "From here on out, you watch your back, because you'll never know where I might show up and you'll never hear the shot. You can consider this your only warning. You won't get another."

Henry briefly glanced down at Chad's jeans.

"Now look at that. You pissed your pants."

Chad looked down, and when he looked back up Henry hit him so hard between the eyes Chad's feet lifted off the ground and he landed four feet from where he had been standing.

Henry stood over the unconscious Chad. "No more warnings," he repeated ominously.

CHAPTER 34

Henry slept in the chair next to Jessie's bed that night, and woke her every hour as Mrs. Rodriguez had instructed, making sure she didn't drift into a coma from her head injury. When the early morning sun shone through the window, it did so directly into Henry's eyes. He woke suddenly and slightly disoriented, looked around the room and remembered where he was. He pushed himself from the chair, but had trouble straightening up. He stretched his neck to work the kinks out, then went over to Jessie and gently touched her face. Her eyes opened slowly, and she smiled, albeit painfully.

"Good morning, Henry."

"Mornin' Jess," Henry smiled. "How you feelin'?"

"Like someone pulled me through a keyhole," she tried to slide herself to a sitting position, but quickly relinquished the thought.

"Well, you had a pretty rough night. You're gonna be all right, though. You've got a few busted ribs and a pretty good knock on the head, but other than that, nothin' too serious."

Jessie reached out, gently took Henry's hand and squeezed it. "Do you know who did it?" she asked quietly.

"I do," he said.

There was a long pause. Jessie squeezed his hand again and tears began to well up in her eyes. "Why did he do this, Henry?"

"I don't know why people like him do the things they do, Jess." He squeezed her hand lightly. "What I do know is, he won't ever be doin' it again."

Concerned, Jessie looked up and wiped a tear off her cheek. "Henry, what did you do?"

Henry smiled reassuringly. "Don't worry about that now. He's still alive, and so are you. That's all that matters." He placed his other hand on hers. "He won't be botherin' you again. That much I know." Normally stoic, Jessie broke down and started sobbing.

Except for taking time to do chores, Henry stayed with her the rest of that day and through the night. He heated up a can of chicken noodle soup in the afternoon that he patiently fed her with a spoon. That evening he read to her from one of her favorite books, *The Sacketts*, by Louis L'Amour, until she drifted off to sleep. As soon as she did, he gently pulled the blanket up to cover her exposed arms, settled into the chair by the bed and fell into a restless sleep until morning.

Henry rushed through his morning chores, gulped down the breakfast of ham and eggs Mrs. Rodriguez made for him, and was back by Jessie's side before she woke. He spent the day with her, helping with meals, walking her to the bathroom and back, and reading to her at the end of the day. That night after she fell asleep, Henry once more spent the night in the chair next to her bed.

On the third morning, Henry awoke to see Jessie smiling at him from her bed. "Good morning, Henry," she said quietly.

"Mornin' Jess." Henry squinted at the sunlight, and pushed himself to a more upright posture in the chair. "How are you feelin' today? Can I get you anything?"

"No, Henry." There was a thankfulness to her voice. "You're going to need to get back to work today."

"I've been keepin' up with everything, Jess. You don't need to worry about that. So, if it's all the same to you, I guess I'd rather be right here until you're feelin' a little better."

"I appreciate that, Henry. I really do." Jessie painfully scooted herself into a sitting position. Henry rose from his chair and gently propped one of the pillows up behind her. "But that gray colt isn't going to train himself."

"The gray?" Henry seemed surprised. "Boy, you don't want me messin' with that colt, Jess. I don't start 'em like you do. Chances are better'n average I'd ruin all that you've done with him." He paused, giving it some thought. "No, I think maybe he should wait till you're feelin' better."

"He can't wait, Henry." Jessie winced as she repositioned herself. "He needs handling every day. He's a good boy, and if we keep up with him, he's going to let us ride him before long." She stopped to catch her breath, something that seemed terribly difficult for her. "Can you do this for me, Henry...please?"

It was evident by the look on Henry's face that he was really struggling with the idea. "I don't know, Jess. I mean..."

"*I* know, Henry," she smiled. "You'll both do fine. Really, you will."

"But who's gonna tend to you?"

"Mrs. R. said she can come by in the mornings for the next few days," Jessie said confidently. "I'll be all right." She paused, and then smiled coyly. "Please?"

"Honest, Jess...I'm not goin' to know what to do with him to not screw him up."

"Don't worry, Henry. We'll do it together, just like we have been since we started," she smiled. "The only difference is now you'll be the one doing the work, and I'll be the one watching. If you have any trouble, or something doesn't look or feel right to you, stop and come and talk with me about it and we'll get it figured out. Okay?"

Henry hesitated for a long time. He had closely watched the kind of work Jessie had been doing and witnessed the results. It was like nothing he had ever seen and certainly like nothing he had ever done. The way he had always worked with horses was much more direct, and faster, but also certainly harder. Because of it, his horses didn't always end the day as soft and quiet as the colt did with Jessie. Her way was different—there was no question about that. Still, the longer Henry thought about it, the more he began to think that different may be just what he needed. In the end, he agreed to give it a try.

The colt was leery of Henry when he entered the paddock carrying the halter and lead rope. Henry had caught and worked with him in the past without a problem, but that was before the night the dark presence showed up on the ranch. Something hadn't been right that night, and it still wasn't as far as the colt could tell. The woman hadn't been around at all since then, and the man had only been around long enough to throw hay over the fence and check the water tank. Regardless of how much handling the colt had had up to that point, his instincts were still firmly intact, and right or wrong, they were now telling him to stay away from the man with the halter.

Henry quickly found he was only able to get within about five feet of the colt before the colt would turn and walk away, always staying just out of his reach, but at the same time not using any more energy than he had to do it. Henry followed him, as he had seen Jessie do, but the colt kept walking. He walked from one end of the paddock to the other and back. He walked up toward the gate, and then down to the bottom of the pen. Finally he walked over to where the other horses were standing and parked himself in amongst them, stopping only to look at Henry as he kept approaching. Seeing that Henry wasn't stopping, the colt turned and, this time, trotted away, taking the rest of the horses with him. Still, Henry followed. The horses made a lap all the way around the sizable pen with the colt before, one by one, they all began to drop off until the colt was the only one moving.

Twenty minutes had passed with no change in the pattern between Henry and the colt, and just as Henry was beginning to get frustrated and think about leaving the pen, the colt suddenly stopped, turned and looked at him. The colt, also a bit frustrated, decided to stop to see if he could bring in an image, the kind he seemed to get from Jessie when she worked with him, to see if he could learn what the man wanted from him. As he stood looking at Henry, who had also stopped, no picture at all came. He waited, but all he got was a picture of darkness, and a feeling of heaviness. Then, just as the colt was getting ready to move, a blurry picture slowly started flashing in his mind's eye.

When the colt stopped, Henry stopped, just as he had seen Jessie do. He watched the colt for several seconds, alertly standing in one spot. Henry subconsciously took the picture of the motionless colt in, and, just happy the colt wasn't moving anymore, took a deep breath and said quietly, "That's it...that's what I'm looking for."

The picture the colt started getting was the picture Henry was actually seeing—the colt standing in one spot, facing Henry. The colt lowered his head slightly, and the picture changed slightly. He moved a foot, the picture changed again. In real time, the colt was seeing everything *he* was doing through Henry's eyes. This was completely different than what the colt got from Jessie. Jessie always showed him what she wanted. Henry was apparently just telling him what he was already doing. This was difficult for the colt because he already knew what he was doing. What he needed help with was what he should do next.

The colt shook his head and snorted, asking Henry to give him a different picture, but he simply got his own reflection back. The colt pawed at the ground, so did the picture in his head. Finally, the colt stopped. He began to think about what he had learned from Jessie, and what she expected from him in a similar situation. When she stood with a halter and lead rope in her hand, the picture he got from her was always for him to come to her so she could put the halter on him. So, guessing that might be what Henry wanted, the colt repeated the behavior by walking over to him. He put his head down, and sure enough, Henry petted him on his neck, then slipped the halter over his nose, and buckled it in place.

Henry had planned on taking the colt to the round pen and putting him in with the saddle and pad, which was the last thing Jessie had done with him before she got hurt. However, because of the hard time the colt apparently had with remembering how to be caught, Henry decided instead to lead him around the inside of the paddock, pet him from time to time, then just turn him loose so the colt could get the idea that was all Henry wanted from him. Henry would come back later in the day and try again to catch him, and then repeat it as many times as necessary until the colt understood how to be caught. The colt, on the other hand, didn't really need the extra reinforcing. He already understood.

Henry checked on Jessie shortly after he worked with the colt, and found her sleeping. He finished his chores, went and caught the colt easily, and then it was time for lunch with Jessie. After lunch Henry set to fixing and re-hanging the screen door that had been dangling off its twisted hinges since the night of the attack. Henry unscrewed the old hinges from the splintered doorjamb, pulled the screen door down and placed it across two sawhorses he had brought up on the porch.

As he repaired the doorjamb as best he could with wood glue, screws and putty, he thought about how lucky Chad had been that night in the parking lot. Things may have been very different if the whole thing would have happened six months earlier. With very little to live for back then, Henry believed he wouldn't have thought twice about actually pulling the trigger on the son of a bitch. Six months earlier, he wouldn't have had anything to lose, and spending the rest of his life in prison, if that's what it came to, would have been fine with him. After all, what would it have mattered if he spent the rest of his life behind the walls of some actual prison, or if he spent it in the prison he had built inside himself. Either way, he was locked up. In his mind, he deserved it. But things were very different now. For the first time in a very long time, Henry felt he actually had something to live for. As much as he wanted to make Chad pay for what he'd done to Jessie, he could also see a lowlife like Chad wasn't worth spending the rest of his new life in jail over.

Henry bent down to put a small screw in the very bottom of the cracked doorjamb and as he did, he noticed three tiny crimson dots between the white boards of the porch decking. It was Jessie's blood that had escaped notice when Mrs. Rodriguez scrubbed the porch with water and bleach the day after the attack. The dots would be virtually unnoticeable for anybody not kneeling in the doorway and looking down at the porch at the angle that Henry was. He couldn't take his eyes off them. He thought about how hard Jessie must have fought to save herself that night. He thought about the force that it would have taken to knock the door off its hinges, and he wondered from which cut on her body those three small dots had come. As he sat staring at them, his own blood began to boil. *Yes,* he thought to himself. *Chad was very lucky that night in the parking lot. But luck won't be enough if I ever see him again.*

CHAPTER 35

Henry, his sleeves rolled up above his elbows, hung laundry on the clothesline outside the back door of Jessie's house in the late morning sun. It was one of the many tasks Jessie hadn't been able to perform since she'd gotten hurt nearly a week before. Back when he and Annie were married, doing laundry was one of the household chores Henry hated to do, and he avoided it all costs. He disliked doing laundry so much that during his drinking days when he rarely had the money, he would rather go to a thrift shop and buy used jeans and shirts then take the time to wash his own clothes. When he did wash them, it was usually in some flea-bitten, coin-operated laundry on the side of the road, or sometimes he used the water in a stock tank or a creek or river.

But like so many things in his life lately, his feelings on doing laundry had somehow shifted; for some reason it didn't seem like such an unpleasant chore for him anymore. It was for that reason he offered to do the wash that Jessie hadn't been able to do on her own since her injury. Once finishing the ranch chores, and spending time with the gray colt that morning, Henry set to doing the laundry. After taking the clothes from the washing machine that stood by itself in the little room off the kitchen, Henry brought the heavy basket to the clothesline and hung each item of her clothing carefully, using the old wooden clothespins that Jessie kept in a bucket near the machine.

He hung several shirts and three pairs of jeans, as well as a number of pairs of socks. After everything else was out of the basket and hanging on the line, he took from it one of the items of clothing he had subconsciously been avoiding—a pair of Jessie's panties. Embarrassed about handling the tiny and frilly things, Henry looked in all directions before putting his hand in the basket. With a pained expression on his face as if it hurt him to handle something as personal as her underwear, he drew the first of four pair out and gingerly held them up between two fingers of each hand. He slowly raised them to the clothesline.

"Good morning, Mr. Henry," came a cheerful voice from behind him. Startled and as if having been caught with his hand in the cookie jar, Henry swung around, quickly hiding the underwear behind his back.

"Dang, ma'am!" His voice seemed higher than normal. "Don't sneak up on a fella like that—you scared me half to death."

"I'm sorry," Mrs. R. shrugged. "I thought you seen me. How she's doing today?"

"Who?" Henry was still a little shaken.

"Jessie," she chuckled. "Who do you think?"

"Oh...um...good. Fine. She's doing good."

"Good, then." Mrs. R. started for the house. "I go see her now. I bring her some things."

"Yes, ma'am. That'd be fine. She's...a...she's just up in the house, there."

"Yes, I know, Mr. Henry. Thank you." Mrs. R. was amused by Henry's fluster. She walked nearly to the back porch before looking over her shoulder back at him. "Mr. Henry, there's no need to hide them. I have seen women's underwear before."

"Yes, ma'am," Henry sighed, keeping the delicate panties in his leathered hand behind his back.

He finished hanging the rest of the laundry, then went inside and started on Jessie's lunch. Today it was a grilled ham-and-cheese sandwich, small green salad, two chocolate chip cookies he had bought at the store, and a glass of milk. He arranged all the items neatly on a tray, placed a small vase with one purple wildflower he had picked, and carried them all up the stairs. He rounded the corner into Jessie's room to see her sitting up in bed and looking much more alert. He eased over to her, making sure not to disturb anything on the tray, and gently set it across her lap. He then took a seat in the chair next to the bed.

"I don't know how I'll ever be able to thank you for all this, Henry." Jessie smiled sheepishly.

"I wouldn't be handin' out too many thank-yous till you try it first," Henry grinned. "I believe I may have overcooked it a bit."

"I don't mean the food, Henry. I mean everything else. Really, I don't know how I could have…"

"Don't think another thing about it," he interrupted. "It's been my pleasure…except maybe for the laundry."

Jessie chuckled weakly, then coughed a little, unable to get any force behind either. "Yes, Mrs. Rodriguez mentioned you had a little trouble with that when she stopped in a few minutes ago."

"Yeah, well…I was doin' all right till she snuck up on me," Henry said in mock defense of himself. "Anyway, everything else is goin' pretty good if I do say so myself. Even the gray colt seems to be warmin' up to me some."

"Yes…the mustang." Jessie repositioned herself. "How'd you do with him today?"

"Well," Henry started proudly. "I can get him caught and haltered, and he lets me brush him and he don't run off anymore."

"Sounds like he's beginning to trust you." Jessie took a bite of her sandwich. "That's good."

"I'm thinkin' it might be time before long to think about tryin' to get him saddled," Henry said, leaning back slightly in the chair. "But I'd sure hate to screw him up by doin' somethin' wrong."

Jessie swallowed what was in her mouth, and then sat quietly for a few seconds. "You know," she said thoughtfully. "I think there might be a similarity or two between that colt and yourself."

"How's that?"

"Well," Jessie started. "Take your saddle, for instance. That saddle means everything to you, right?"

"Yes, ma'am, it does."

"You'd never part with it, and in fact, if someone tried to take it from you, you'd fight with all your might, wouldn't you?"

"I expect I would," Henry nodded.

"On the other hand, if you ever found something that meant more to you than it does, you might *willingly* give it up in trade and feel like you got a bargain in the deal."

Henry sat quietly giving the idea some thought before shrugging his shoulders and slowly nodding in agreement.

"Well," Jessie continued. "The only thing that meant anything to that horse was his freedom. By training him, we're asking him to give that up." She stopped briefly to catch her breath. "Before he'll be able to willingly do that, we'll need to offer him something better in return."

"What could we ever offer him that could mean more to him than his freedom?" Henry asked, more rhetorically than anything else.

"Two things that I know of," Jessie replied. "Respect and understanding. Respect for who he is and who he was, and understanding that he may not be able to do everything right all the time. He's probably going to have trouble with some of the things we're going to ask of him."

Henry looked at her, not fully understanding.

"When he sees that you are giving him the respect he deserves, and the understanding he needs, he will start to trust you in return." She took a sip from her milk glass. "When you have his trust, you'll have the horse. Once he trusts you, putting the saddle on him won't be a problem."

"You're sure of that?" Henry asked, already knowing she was.

"I'm sure." Jessie smiled. She then let out a long, relaxed sigh, and then turned to look at Henry. "The flower is beautiful, Henry. Thank you."

The picture of her smiling at him melted his heart. It was all the thanks he would ever need.

CHAPTER 36

For the past two days, Henry had been bringing the colt into the round pen and turning him loose with the saddle and saddle blanket sitting on the ground near the pen's middle. On the first day, the colt acted as if he'd never seen it before, although Henry knew he had. The second day, the colt went right up to the saddle and pad, and not only put his nose on it, but also began to paw at it and move it around. By this, the third day, Henry turned the colt loose in the pen, and then carried the saddle and pad in with him. Although it was a strange sight for the colt to see the saddle and pad being carried instead of sitting on the ground, it wasn't long before he had approached Henry and tried to get his nose on the items to get a good whiff of them.

Henry then placed the saddle and pad on the ground, and brought in a thirty-foot-long, five-eighths-inch-diameter cotton rope with bull snap braided into one end and a loop braided in the other. He doubled the rope up, and then slowly, but deliberately began rubbing the colt all over his body with it. Eventually, holding on to one end of the doubled up rope, he slipped the other end over the colt's back, letting it hang down on the opposite side from where he stood. Cautiously, he reached under the colt's belly, took a hold of the loose ends that hung down on the other side and brought them under the colt and back to his side.

Henry brought the rope gently snug around the colt's barrel just behind his front legs, and softly sawed the rope back and forth across the colt's hair. When the colt was comfortable with that, Henry then incrementally tightened the ropes a little at a time until they were stretched firmly around the area where the cinch of the saddle would ultimately be placed. The colt scooted around a little at the unfamiliar feel of the tightness around his body, but soon seemed to get used to the sensation and much to Henry's surprise, settled down nicely after only a few minutes.

Henry spent nearly an hour putting the ropes on the colt, tightening them around his barrel, then loosening them and removing them. He did this over and over until the colt was able to accept the feel of it without question and without worry. Once he felt confident the colt understood what he was doing, he haltered the colt up and took him back to his paddock.

Henry then went to the house and fixed Jessie a breakfast of toast, eggs and orange juice and brought the tray to her room. Much to his surprise, he rounded the corner to her room to see her standing by the window, dressed in a working shirt and jeans. Jessie turned slowly toward him and smiled, but not without the unmistakable look of discomfort showing through.

"What are you doing out of bed?" There was a genuine concern in Henry's voice as he placed the tray on the table.

"Loafing around in bed for two weeks is about all I can stand," she said, still very short of breath. "I was starting to feel if I didn't get up soon, maybe I never would." She smiled again. "Don't worry, I'll take it easy."

"Okay." Henry went to her and helped her back to the bed. "But have your breakfast first. Get out of bed later."

Henry stayed with Jessie in her room all morning, chatting with her about things he saw around the ranch. The two of them realized, but never said, how much they enjoyed each other's company. It was something they were beginning to do more of lately, and they each not only looked forward to their daily visits, but also began to rely on them.

That afternoon found Henry back at the colt's paddock, standing by the gate. In the past two weeks since he had started working with the colt, he had grown to like him very much. The colt had a lot of try in him; he worked hard at doing whatever was presented to him, although whatever that might be was often very foreign, not to mention very frightening. After the work they'd done that morning, Henry was feeling confident about the colt accepting a saddle soon. As Henry propped his foot up on the bottom rail of the gate and looked down at the gray colt grazing amongst the geldings, he began to think about how the colt's first saddling might go.

The colt was munching happily on the few sprigs of dry grass down in the bottom of the paddock when the image came to him. The picture was so clear and strong at first he thought it might be coming from the woman. But the more the image came into focus, the more he realized it wasn't her at all, but rather it was somehow coming from the man. What he was getting was a picture of Henry standing next to him in the round pen. Henry was holding the saddle blanket, which he rubbed the colt with several times, then he slipped it up on his back. Henry then got the saddle, let the colt smell it, and then put it, too, on the colt's back. The image was so clear that the colt found he had to raise his head to see if the man was nearby.

At the top of the hill, Henry watched as the colt stopped eating, raised his head, and looked directly into Henry's eyes. The two of them stared at one another for a long moment, and when Henry finally left the pen a half-hour later, he had an overwhelming feeling that somehow, everything was going to be just fine between them.

It had been an interesting day for Henry. By the time he had gotten to the end of it, a subtle but profound change had come over him. Since he'd lost his family, his life had become little more than a dusty, closed book with only half of the pages read. But things were different now, and he knew it. He was back with the living. His book was open, and a new chapter in his life had begun. It was a chapter like no other he had experienced, and he was ready to drink it in. Years later, he would look back and recognize the change he felt that day had not only been helped along by Jessie, the woman he was slowly falling in love with, but it also came from the colt, an animal whose life paralleled his own in so many ways.

Henry was feeling happier and lighter than he had since he could remember as he walked up to the large pasture to check on the big herd before turning in. It was dusk, the sun had set, but it was still light enough for him to be able to scan nearly the entire seven acres where half the herd resided. The rest were still scattered over the property, and would be until the ranch got closer to opening for the season. Henry entered the pen and stood in a spot close to where a number of horses were grazing. One horse lazily raised his head and walked over to him. Another raised his head and came over, and a third horse followed suit. All three horses stood quietly with their heads only inches from Henry. He reached out and, smiling broadly, petted each one gently on the head. Jessie, who watched the events with a knowing smile from the window in her bedroom, turned and settled in for a restful night's sleep.

The next morning, Henry put the colt in the round pen, and then returned later with the saddle and saddle pad. To Henry's surprise, the colt allowed him to not only approach with the saddle pad without running off, but he also allowed

Henry to touch him with it and rub it on his back, shoulders, rump and belly. Within less than ten minutes, Henry was able to gently toss the blanket on the colt's back from a foot or so away, just like he would any "broke" horse. The colt stood so quietly, Henry then backed away a bit and tossed the blanket from two feet, four feet, then six feet and even ten, with the colt looking as though he was going to fall asleep.

All of the work with the pad had gone so well, Henry decided to bring the saddle over and see how the colt would do with it. Again, with the colt standing quietly in the middle of the pen, Henry approached and allowed the horse to smell it. The colt seemed interested, but not at all worried, and when he had apparently sniffed it to his satisfaction, Henry gently touched and rubbed it on the colt's shoulder, then on his side, and finally he placed it up on his back. Again, the colt showed no signs of worry or regard for the once foreign object now sitting on his back, and after leaving it there for several seconds, Henry decided to remove it and call it a day. He thought about cinching the saddle to the colt's back, but then decided against it. *Tomorrow is another day,* he thought.

Henry found himself unusually tired that evening, and after a supper of grilled pork chops, fried potatoes and green beans, he and Jessie moved into the living room to drink their coffee. Henry had planned on reading the rest of *The Sacketts* to Jessie that evening, but seeing how tired he was, Jessie offered to read to him for a change. Henry, settling himself onto the couch, happily agreed. She began reading and had only gotten a few pages into the story when Henry drifted off into a peaceful sleep. Jessie, noticing him sleeping, closed the book, took the afghan from the back of the couch and gently covered him up. She turned to go upstairs, then stopped, came back and kissed him lightly on his white forehead that dramatically contrasted the dark tan of his face. "Good night, Henry," she whispered, touching him softly on his shoulder. He stirred, but did not wake.

Henry woke just before sunup the next morning, and realizing he had fallen asleep while Jessie was reading, wanted to apologize to her. He quickly slipped back to the bunkhouse for a shower, shave and a clean set of clothes, before returning to Jessie's house. By the time he got there, an hour had passed and Jessie was already out of bed and had breakfast cooking. "French toast and fresh fruit this morning," she chimed as Henry walked in the back door. "Go ahead and take a seat, it'll be right up."

Henry sat in his usual spot facing the stove, and placed his hat at his feet, as had become his habit. Jessie, still moving slowly, scooped five pieces of lightly browned French toast onto a plate, brought it over and set it down in the middle of the table. "I'm really sorry about last night," Henry said meekly. "I sure didn't mean to fall asleep on you like that. I guess I was more tired than I thought and I apologize."

Jessie walked over to Henry and kissed him briefly on the cheek. "Good morning, Henry," was her only acknowledgement of his statement. She then turned and went back to the counter to retrieve the bowl of fruit she'd made up. Her gesture immediately put Henry's mind at ease, but it was the kiss on his cheek that made his heart skip a beat.

"Maybe we'll get a chance to finish the book tonight," Jessie said, putting the bowl of strawberries, blueberries, bananas and melon on the table and taking her seat. "I can't wait to see how the Sackett boys will get out of the fix they're in."

"You mean to tell me as many times as you've read that book, you still don't know how it turns out?"

"How many times you read or hear a story has nothing to do with it," she grinned. "Its all in the telling."

"Maybe so," Henry agreed.

Henry placed two pieces of French toast on Jessie's plate, and three on his own, before taking a scoop of fruit from the bowl and covering his toast with it.

"So, I was wondering," Henry said without looking up. "Would you be feelin' good enough to come out to the pen tomorrow?"

"The round pen? Why?"

"Well," there was just a hint of pride in Henry's voice, "I think he might just let me get up on his back, and I'd sure like it if you was there to see it if he does."

"You think tomorrow might be the day?"

"It might," Henry shrugged. "We'll have to see how things go today, but it's sure lookin' that way."

"Then I'll be there." She took a small bite of food. "Besides, I wouldn't want to miss being there when I win the bet."

"Bet?" Henry asked, pretending he'd forgotten about the bet he and Jessie made about the colt not bucking when someone first got on his back. "What bet?"

"What do you mean, *what bet?*" she said in false indignity. "You know what bet I'm talking about, and don't you try to get out of it, either!"

"Now, hold on there. I don't recall making any bet..."

"Don't you give me that!"

"Naw," Henry took a bite of his French toast. "That must have been some other fella you made this bet with, cause I sure don't..."

"You are such a liar!"

It was a mock argument and they both knew it. Before long, both were laughing at themselves, and the silliness continued throughout breakfast with both of them making lame jokes. Nothing either of them said would have been even remotely funny on any other day, but on that particular morning it was. With everything that had happened in the past several weeks, it turned out that they both needed a good laugh, and that morning they got one.

With breakfast and chores finished, Henry went out, caught the colt and put him in the round pen. Just as he had the day before, he brought in the saddle and saddle pad and worked with the colt until he willingly accepted both. This time, however, after Henry had plopped the saddle on the colts back several times, he finally cinched it down onto the colt's back.

Having the saddle on his back didn't bother the colt very much. Henry had been very slow and deliberate about how he introduced things to him, so that by the time the saddle went on, the colt pretty much understood what was happening. Still, it was a very strange sensation for the colt to have the saddle strapped to his back without any way of getting it off. Henry let the colt stand with the saddle on for several minutes before asking him to move. The colt wasn't sure what to think. Henry urged him forward, and after taking just one step, the colt felt something terribly wrong and froze. He humped his back, which did nothing to relieve the pressure he was feeling around his girth, or the tightness over his back and shoulders. He let out a loud warning snort and took one short hop, but it wasn't enough to dislodge the heavy saddle from his back.

Quietly but firmly, Henry urged the colt forward again by raising his hand behind him and making a loud kissing sound. The colt took another very worried step and stopped, head high, eyes showing white and tail tucked between his hind legs. "I know, buddy," Henry said softly. "It's gonna be okay. You'll see. But you're gonna have to move now. I promise. It'll be okay." With that, Henry flapped his arm to his side, kissed loudly, and the colt was off. He took two steps, then, with a loud bawl, he jumped high in the air and snapped both hind feet directly out behind him. He made two jerky laps around the pen, bucking, spinning, bawling, snaking his body and kicking out, before sorting himself out and settling into a gallop.

It was life or death for the colt. His instincts told him that anytime anything clamped onto his back like this thing had, he was not likely to live through it. He fought with everything he had until it became clear he was not going to dislodge the thing by kicking at it. When he came to that realization, he decided perhaps he could outrun it. Unable to kick it off or outrun it, and realizing it wasn't actually harming him in any way, he slowed himself, sweaty and out of breath, and after dozens of dusty laps around the pen, stopped.

As soon as he did, Henry eased up to him and, talking to him quietly, uncinched the saddle and took it and the pad from his back. Henry then placed both items on the fence, and left the pen, allowing the colt time to relax and think about what had just transpired.

Initially for the colt, the process had been terrifying and something he didn't think he would live through. Yet, he also realized he was really no worse for the wear other than being sweaty and a little winded. In fact, living through yet one more thing that at first he thought might kill him, had actually given him a strange sort of confidence. It was for that reason that when Henry came back in the pen an hour later and resaddled the colt, the colt accepted it as if he'd been wearing a saddle all his life, and carried it this time without raising any dust or showing any worry.

Henry saddled and unsaddled the colt three more times in the next two hours, urging the colt to move each time, and each time the colt did without any trouble. The last time Henry saddled the colt that day, he brought his horse Mic into the pen, also saddled and bridled. Henry haltered the saddled colt, climbed aboard Mic, and began ponying the colt around in the pen while he rode. He ponied him first one direction, then the other, then back. He then eased Mic up to the colt's left side so the colt could get used to having someone up above him, then put his hand on the colt's saddle horn and rocked the saddle back and forth so the colt could feel something moving the saddle that was strapped to him. He hung over the colt's saddle, slapping at the leather seat, picking up and dropping the stirrup leathers against the colt's sides, and brushing his hand and arm over the colt's rump. He repeated all of this on the colt's right side, then went back and did it all again several more times on both sides.

When Henry was finished, he opened the gate to the round pen, and ponied the saddled colt across the ranch. For the next three hours, Henry, Mic and the colt rode out toward the back of the property, looped around through the sand wash, up over the mesa and back down toward the river, where they stopped. For the first time in nearly a year, the colt was able to drink from a cool, running stream, just as he had when he was in the wild. The colt enjoyed being out of closed-in pens and in the open again, and he felt a genuine appreciation to Henry and Mic for taking him out into the open, big spaces he so dearly loved.

Henry and Mic took time to help the colt learn how to stop, turn and back up from pressure on the halter, and then practiced it until the colt understood each cue. For the colt, the idea was a difficult one to grasp at first, but soon he began to realize it was really no different than what Jessie had showed him shortly after she put a halter on him for the first time. Within a short time he understood what Henry was asking of him when he applied the pressure and he was able to respond correctly in nearly every instance.

The trio then worked their way back to the ranch, where Henry tied both Mic and the colt to the hitch rail by the tack room, unsaddled and groomed each one, making sure to give the colt an extra long rubdown on his back and in the area where the cinch had been. The colt, appreciative of Henry's attention, started to realize that perhaps living with humans would not be so difficult after all. Henry unhitched both horses, and walked them to their respective pens for the night. The colt was tired but not worried like he had been when the day had started. As he munched on the hay in the paddock Henry had put out for him, with the sun setting and a cool breeze coming up from the valley, the gray colt found he was actually looking forward to what new things tomorrow might bring.

CHAPTER 37

It was a most perfect day. By eight-thirty in the morning, the sky was already sapphire blue and cloudless, and there was just the hint of a breeze coming from the north, which kept the air from being too hot. The gentle wind carried with it the sweet smell of sage, and as Henry looked toward the house, it also seemed to be carrying Jessie toward him. Her movement was very close to being back to the pure and effortless gait Henry had had gotten so used to seeing during his months at the ranch. For him, the way she floated across the ground when she walked had always been part of her natural beauty, and he hadn't really appreciated how well she did move until it became hard for her to move at all.

It was the first time in nearly three weeks that Jessie felt good enough to venture outside, and her normally richly tanned features were now beginning to pale from lack of sunlight. Henry thought about going to her as she walked across the yard to offer her help if she needed it. After all, it would be three or four more weeks before her ribs were completely healed, and she still continued to have breathing problems if she exerted herself. But when he saw the determination on her face, and watched the relative normalcy of that familiar gait, he decided perhaps he should leave her alone for now.

The colt was already groomed and standing quietly in the pen by the time she got there. Henry' saddle, saddle pad and the bridle he would use were sitting by the gate. The colt had yet to carry a bit in his mouth, and so the bridle Henry had chosen to ride him in was a sort of side-pull; a leather headstall with a flat noseband made from two small lengths of old lariat rope laid side by side and attached to a leather chinstrap. The rope was covered in sheepskin so it wouldn't rub or otherwise damage the bridge of the colt's nose, and on either side of the rig, where the rope and chinstrap came together, were two small metal rings braided into place with rawhide strips. Henry had attached the reins he would be using to the metal rings.

"Is he ready?" Jessie glanced into the pen.

The colt, hearing Jessie's voice, looked her way, and then let out a soft nicker.

"I believe so," Henry replied, looking toward the colt.

"Are you ready?"

Henry smiled. "As ready as I will be."

Henry picked up his saddle, pad and bridle, and then turned toward the gate. Jessie pulled the heavy latch that kept it in place, and as Henry went in with the colt, she closed and latched the gate behind him. The colt immediately moved toward him and they met halfway between where the colt had been standing and the gate where Henry had come in. The colt went to the saddle and pad Henry was holding and gave them each a good sniff. While he did, an image began to form in his mind. He could tell by the way it formed that it wasn't coming from Henry. This image had the familiar softness and clarity to it that he knew to be Jessie's. The picture formed slowly, but by the time he had finished smelling the saddle and pad, it was obvious to the colt what it was. In his mind's eye he saw himself wearing the saddle and bridle. Then he saw Henry climbing into the saddle while the colt stood quietly under him.

Henry placed the saddle on the ground and petted the colt on the forehead before swinging the pad up on his back. He then reached down for the saddle, and swung it up onto the colt's back, as well. In both cases the colt stood unperturbed by Henry's actions or the objects. Henry cinched the saddle down, securing it to the colt's back, then slipped the side pull over the colt's head and placed the reins over his neck.

Henry petted the colt's sleek gray neck, head and rump, then took a hold of the stirrup closest to him and gave it a gentle tug. The colt briefly lost his balance when Henry pulled on the stirrup, but quickly got his feet back under him and squared himself up. Henry pulled on the stirrup again. This time the colt was balanced and solid and Henry was unable to move him. Henry looked back at Jessie and smiled, then turned back to the colt, placed his foot in the stirrup, took a hold of the saddle horn and the cantle of the saddle and placed a little weight in the stirrup. The colt was unbothered. Henry put more weight in the stirrup, then a little more, and finally he lifted himself off the ground for a second before returning to the ground. The colt looked as though he would fall asleep.

Henry turned to Jessie, shrugged his shoulders as if to say, *He doesn't seem too bothered,* to which Jessie agreed by shrugging hers. Henry turned his attention back to the colt, put his foot in the stirrup and bounced up and down a few more times before once again lifting himself smoothly off the ground. He stood in the stirrup, but didn't throw a leg over, then let himself down and lavishly petted the colt. Henry then put his foot in the stirrup again, bounced a few times and lifted himself. He stood in the stirrup for a few seconds, watching the colt. Seeing he was comfortable with what was happening, Henry gently lifted his right leg over and just as gently sat in the saddle.

The colt wasn't troubled by what Henry was doing. The work Henry had done with him the day before went a long way to helping the young horse understand what was going on. Between that and the picture he was getting from Jessie, he was actually very clear about what was happening. Not only that, but the colt had been through a lot in his short life, much more than many of the older horses on the ranch. On at least two occasions he had literally faced life-or-death situations and come out alive, and those experiences had given him a quiet confidence that allowed him to see that dealing with something like this was going to be relatively easy. So far it was.

Sitting quietly on the colt's back for the very first time, Henry turned to Jessie and smiled broadly. She returned his smile and pretended to clap, and then pointed at him with a look that said, "You owe me."

Henry, still smiling, slowly bent over and petted the mustang on his neck. "You just lost me a month's pay," he said quietly. He then turned back to Jessie and nodded in agreement.

It was, indeed, a most perfect morning.

CHAPTER 38

The gray colt had no idea how many days had passed since the first time he allowed Henry to sit on his back. Horses don't think in terms of days, or weeks or years. They think only in terms of survival. A day behind them is of no consequence once it has passed, other than how what they learned during it will help them survive. The colt had learned some very valuable lessons of survival early on after being banished from his herd, lessons that were serving him well now that he was living amongst humans. The most valuable of those lessons was that he should first pay attention to what the rules are—whatever the rules are—and not overstep the bounds that have been placed on him, no matter what.

He remembered the freedom he had when he was less than a year old. He, along with all the other foals that had been born that year, were able to play or sleep at will. They could run into, under, over or through any other horses in the herd and almost never get reprimanded for it. They could drink when they wanted and where they wanted, they ate whenever they wanted and they could even dictate to their mothers when they would nurse, and the mare would almost never protest. If they wanted to go investigate something, they could just go do it, as long as it wasn't so far from the herd that they couldn't get back if danger arose.

But then, when he was about ten months old, everything changed. His mother weaned him in preparation for foaling the following year's baby, and it seemed as though the very day that happened the herd took over and began giving him and the other foals born the same year very firm and very strict direction. He and the others learned how to become productive members of the herd, and as long as they adhered to the rules the herd set forth, everything was fine.

The colt hadn't adhered to the rules of the herd, and as a result, he almost paid for it with his life. It was a lesson he would never forget, and it was for that reason that he tried so hard to understand, and then perform, anything and everything the humans showed him. He also realized within days of when the woman, Jessie, first starting to work with him that the calmer he stayed, the easier it was for him to learn. But, then, it was almost always easy to stay calm around Jessie. She exuded strength and confidence, and was always very clear about what she wanted the colt to do and how she wanted him to do it. She had the ability to send pictures to him, which helped him tremendously, and he very quickly gained assurance in whatever she asked.

But then the man, Henry, started working with him, and things were less clear. Still, as much as he could, the colt tried very hard to stay calm and pay attention. Henry didn't send pictures at first, and early on when he did send them, the images were often of what the colt was already doing, not what he needed to do. That was somewhat confusing for the colt. Yet as time went on, something in Henry changed. His thoughts seemed to lighten and the pictures he sent sometimes became clear and helpful; never as clear and helpful as Jessie's, but clear enough for the colt to realize that Henry, too, was trying.

While Jessie's thoughts and intentions were always clear to the colt, it was Henry's actions that brought with them *his* clarity. In their interactions, Henry was direct and to the point about what he was looking for from him, and while Jessie's demeanor gave the colt comfort while he tried to learn from her, it was Henry's deeds the colt understood clearly. It didn't take long for the colt to understand that all humans were as different in the way they dealt with horses as they were different in the way they looked and smelled. Some, like Henry and Jessie, were trying to find ways to communicate with him, while others, like the dark presence that came to the ranch the night Jessie stopped coming around, were not.

Understanding that each human he came in contact with would probably be communicating with him a little differently than the last actually gave the colt a strange sense of comfort. He began to understand if he could figure out how humans were trying to communicate, he could then figure out how he could fit in with them, and thus survive another day. So far, the key to understanding humans in general seemed to be the colt trying to stay as calm as possible no matter the human or what was introduced to him. Of course, it also helped that the two humans he had been dealing with most at this ranch had also been calm when they worked with him. This, too, brought him comfort.

While the colt may not have known how many days had passed since Henry first sat on his back, what he did know was that he had learned a lot from the man since that time. He could recall that just having Henry's weight on his back wasn't too confusing. But the next day when Henry climbed in the saddle, he didn't just sit. On that second day, Henry asked the colt to move, and that was when things became a little worrisome for the youngster. Henry made a kissing sound to the colt and gently squeezed his sides with the heels of his boots. The colt had heard the sound in the past from Jessie and from Henry, and understood that sound to mean he should go forward. However, because of the extra weight of Henry and the saddle on his back, the colt's front feet suddenly felt much heavier than normal. He didn't think he *could* go forward. As a result, when Henry kissed and squeezed, the colt, knowing Henry wanted him to do *something* other than stand, began backing up.

Henry continued to kiss and squeeze, which was a sure sign to the colt that whatever he was doing was probably not correct. He knew this because he had learned early on in his handling that anytime either Jessie or Henry made a noise or applied pressure as a request for him to do something, the noise or pressure stayed on until the colt gave the response they were looking for. As soon as the colt responded correctly, the noise or pressure *always* came off, and it *always* came off immediately.

It didn't take long before the colt had backed nearly all the way across the round pen, and with neither the kissing sound, nor the pressure coming off, he was beginning to get worried. He still wasn't able to see any other option but back because his front end felt so heavy he thought it impossible to move forward. Finally, with Henry still kissing and squeezing, Henry picked up the right rein and gently turned the colt's head to the right. This not only caused the colt's body to bend to the right, but it also produced a slightly off balance sensation and, while still backing, the colt suddenly felt as though he was going to fall over. In an attempt to keep himself upright, the colt picked up his right front foot and stepped it forward and to the right. As soon as he did, the kissing sound stopped and the pressure on his sides was immediately released.

The colt stopped, and Henry reached down and petted him on his neck, a reassuring sign to the colt that everything was all right. Henry let the colt stand for several seconds so that the young horse could relax and catch his breath. The colt hadn't gone far, but he had gone pretty fast, holding his breath most of the way. When he did stop, his nostrils flared and sides heaved as he breathed in the fine dust that hung in the air.

Soon, Henry began making the kissing sound and lightly squeezing again, and again the colt backed. This time, Henry didn't wait so long before he turned the colt's head, and as soon as he did, the colt took an unbalanced step forward. The sound and pressure came off, and the colt got to rest. On the third attempt, the colt took only three steps backward before Henry turned him, and this time, the colt took one forward step, and then another. Henry stopped and heaped praise on him the likes the colt had not experienced from either Henry or Jessie. It was then that, even though the colt didn't really think he could do it, he knew for sure what Henry wanted.

Over the next several minutes, with Henry's patient help and guidance, the colt slowly began to make tentative progress. For the colt, it was very much like the feeling he had when taking his first steps right after he was born. He was completely out of balance and the feeling of something upright on his back was so foreign it was actually a little frightening. But after two steps, then three and finally six and seven steps, the colt began to find his balance and timing, and soon he and Henry were walking comfortably around the inside of the pen.

In another session with Henry, the colt learned how to stop, turn and back up when he felt pressure from the sheepskin-covered noseband of the side-pull he was wearing. That lesson seemed to be simply an extension of a lesson he learned earlier in his training: when he felt pressure, he should give to it rather than fight it. It was an easy concept for him to understand. After this session with Henry, the colt was back to feeling confidant and comfortable. In another session, the colt learned how to carry Henry when the colt trotted and then cantered. In the same lesson, he also learned how to slow down out of the trot and canter when asked to do so. It was during that particular session with Henry the colt began to realize that Henry was asking him to do things that he already knew how to do. The only difference was, Henry was asking him to do those things at specific times and using specific requests, such as a kissing sound, or pressure on his sides with his legs, or the pressure on the noseband of the side-pull.

Once the colt figured out Henry was only asking things of him that he could already do, the training then became extremely easy for both of them. As time went on, the pressure Henry used to ask the colt to move, or stop or turn became so small, it was as if sometimes he was using no pressure at all. Somehow, the colt and Henry had gotten to a point where they seemed to share the same thought, and it was then that the colt's learning really took off. It was also around that time Henry and the colt moved from the smaller round pen into the big arena for their sessions.

It wasn't long before the colt and Henry were sliding to a stop out of a gallop, spinning circles in place, and side-passing across the arena, all things the colt enjoyed doing. He was finally getting a chance to use himself, to free up his body, get air in his lungs, use his mind and most of all, get out in the open. His body was beginning to feel strong again, like it did before he went off the ledge on the mesa, and the stronger he got, the easier the tasks Henry gave him became.

The easier the tasks became for the colt, the more Henry showed him. He was always careful not to overdo any particular session or push the colt too hard. In one such session, Henry had shown him how to move up next to a gate, get in place so Henry could open it, turn and walk through the gate, then turn back and close the gate, all without Henry getting off. In another session, Henry tied his lariat to a log and, dallying the other end around the saddle horn, taught the colt how to drag the heavy thing around the arena. Of all the things Henry had done with the colt, dragging an object was the most difficult for him to grasp. It was initially frightening for the colt to feel the added weight pulling against his shoulders and watch as the log appeared to chase after him. It was only his trust in Henry that kept him from turning tail and bolting away from the log that was not acting like any other log he had seen. But with Henry's help, it soon became understandable and even doable for the colt. Henry showed him, first by facing the log and backing away from it while it was dallied to the saddle horn by the rope, that whenever he moved, the log did, but it never got closer to him, and it always stopped when he did. Eventually, he could turn and go forward for short periods of time with the log following him, and soon he could drag it all over the arena.

The colt wasn't sure when it happened, but one day Henry took the colt out of the arena and began riding him all over the ranch. It was then the colt started to feel good about his new life. There was something about being out with Henry, the two of them moving quietly through the desert, that caused his spirit to soar. He now understood why Henry, and most every other human he had come in contact with, had done the things with him they had. It was to get him to a point where he could once again go back into the wild, to smell the fresh desert air, feel the wind in his mane and be able to look out for miles without any buildings, people or fences in sight. He was doing it under someone else's rules, but then, there had always been rules. These were just different rules than the ones he had grown up with, but he was beginning to see that maybe having rules to go by wasn't such a bad thing after all.

The work they had done together, and the rides Henry took the colt on, created a bond between the two of them that neither one had ever felt before. Every morning the colt met Henry at the gate, and every morning Henry took the colt on some new and exciting adventure. Sometimes the adventure meant going out on one of their rides together in the desert. Another time it was Henry teaching the colt how to accept the swinging of a lariat overhead while Henry roped fence posts, barrels or the a roping dummy Henry had constructed out of a saw horse and a black plastic steer head he had bought in town. On another day, Henry taught the colt how to go quietly in a trailer, stand relaxed inside, and come back out. Henry also taught the colt how to stand when someone picked up and cleaned his feet; something the colt had been terrified to do not so long ago.

One of the colt's proudest moments, however, was the day Henry brought him out and saddled him up, just as he had done so many times before. This time, Henry also brought Mic out of his pen. Mounting the colt, Henry took Mic's lead rope, dallied it around the saddle horn, and Henry and the colt ponied Mic out across the desert—just as Henry and Mic had done with the colt all those weeks before.

While the colt had no idea how long it had been since Henry first threw a leg over his back, he *was* beginning to realize that the hot, dusty months they had passed through were beginning to come to a close. The days were gradually getting shorter, the nights cooler, and ever so slowly, he was beginning to shed his summer coat and a heavier, winter coat was beginning to grow in its place. It was on one of those cooler mornings, when the air was still crisp from the night before, that Henry came to get the colt. He groomed the colt, as he always had, placed the familiar saddle pad on his back, and then the saddle. But almost immediately, the colt realized something was different. The saddle Henry put on him was not the saddle he always wore when Henry rode. It was different, somehow—not at all uncomfortable, really—just different.

Henry bridled and led the colt to the arena where the woman, Jessie, was waiting with a smile on her face. "Are you sure you want to do this," the colt heard Henry say to the woman.

"Yes, Henry. Don't worry. I feel fine," the woman answered.

"I know…but what if he should act up or go to buckin'? I wouldn't want you to get hurt again."

"Has he acted up or bucked with you?"

"Well, no…"

"Then he won't with me." The woman smiled. "For crying out loud, Henry. Have some faith in your horse. He's got faith in you."

Henry slowly moved to the colt's head and held him while Jessie climbed in the saddle. It was a strange feeling for the colt, to have someone other than Henry on his back. He turned and looked at the man standing next to him. "You take care of her, you hear?" Henry said calmly and quietly. "No foolin' around, I mean it."

The colt let out a long exhale, and blew softly through his nose. Henry smiled.

"Well, here we go," Jessie chirped.

An image suddenly appeared in the colt's mind of him and Jessie quietly riding around the arena. At first, he wasn't sure if the picture was coming from Henry or Jessie. He realized with some surprise it was coming from both of them. He let out another relaxed sigh, and began walking forward. Jessie and the colt made several laps before the picture in the colt's mind changed to that of them trotting, and so he did. Two laps later, the image changed again to them cantering, and the colt responded by moving up into a relaxed and easy lope. After another two laps, Jessie gently asked the horse to come to a stop, spin around with his hindquarters over his hocks, and lope off in the opposite direction. The colt liked the way Jessie rode him. It was different than the way Henry rode, but very similar, too. The colt found comfort in the fact that he had learned enough from Henry to be able to work through the differences, and relax in the similarities.

The pair slowed and walked up to Henry, who was waiting by the gate, right where they had left him. "Henry, he's wonderful," Jessie beamed. "You've done an amazing job with him."

"He did all the work, Jess. You know that." Henry walked over and gently stroked the gray colt on his neck. The colt slightly leaned into him as he did. "I swear he's the finest animal I've ever been around."

Jessie placed her hand on Henry's shoulder and smiled. "I expect he probably feels the same way about you."

Just then, the colt softly laid his forehead against Henry's chest, and sighed one more time.

CHAPTER 39

The house seemed too big and empty since Henry had started sleeping in the bunkhouse again. For weeks after Jessie got hurt, Henry spent his nights either sleeping in the chair next to her bed, or on the couch in the living room, always making sure he was close enough that if she needed anything he'd be there. Now that her injuries were almost healed, Henry began drifting back to the bunkhouse in the evenings and Jessie found she missed his company at night.

There had been a number of times in recent weeks when, as he was getting ready to make the walk across the yard in the dark after dinner, she had an overwhelming urge to ask him to stay with her; not on the couch or in the chair next to her bed, but *with* her. Then he would smile, say goodnight, and be out the door and off the porch before she could get up the nerve to do so. This had been one of those nights.

Jessie walked through the house and turned off the lights, leaving only a small lamp in the front window lit, and the light at the top of the stairs so she wouldn't be stumbling up them on her way to her room. The sudden ringing of the phone pierced the darkness. A bit surprised by the noise at this time of night, Jessie hurried to the small table at the foot of the stairs and snapped the phone off its cradle. "Hello?" It was Tom Essex returning her call from earlier in the day. Jessie had put off calling him as long as she could. His horse, the gray colt, was ready to go home. If the truth were known, he had probably been ready for a while, but Jessie had been struggling with the thought of separating him from Henry. When she knew she could wait no longer, and with the new guest season fast approaching, she needed to move the "outside" horse off the place and get back to her own herd.

Tom seemed genuinely happy to hear the colt was ready to come back to his ranch, and even happier to hear the colt had done well with his training. He had done so well, in fact, that Jessie offered to buy him right there over the phone, and told Tom to just name his price. Her thought was to get the colt and give him to Henry as a gift, but in hindsight, she realized that her enthusiasm about the colt did nothing to help deter Tom from wanting to keep him in the first place.

Jessie broke the news to Henry the next morning over breakfast—Tom would be coming by about midday to pick up the colt. At first Henry seemed unaffected by what she said and ate his breakfast and visited with Jessie just as they did every morning. Near the end of the meal he suddenly stopped eating, looked out the back door and said almost inaudibly, "I'm gonna miss him."

Tom, unencumbered by all the traffic hazards that had plagued him when he delivered the colt months earlier, showed up with his trailer at the ranch along about eleven-thirty that morning. He had called Jessie when he stopped in Grant to fuel up, so Henry had plenty of time to get the colt groomed and saddled before he arrived. Henry tried to be as businesslike as he could while getting the colt ready, but still found himself lingering through the process more than he normally would. The colt, sensing something was different, refused to take his eyes off Henry and twice nickered to him when he went into the tack room to retrieve his saddle or put the brushes away.

Jessie brought Tom across the yard and toward the arena, where Henry would bring the colt and put him through his paces so Tom could see what they'd done with him.

"So he turned out to be a good horse after all?" Tom asked Jessie.

"He sure did," Jessie forced a smile. "One of the best I've seen in a while."

"I gave a little thought to your offer to buy him," Tom said, clasping both hands behind his back as they walked. "I'd like to get him home first and see if he'll work for us on the ranch."

"I understand. But please do keep me in mind if you don't think he'll work for you. We'd love to have him around here. I wouldn't mind breeding some of my mares to him sometime down the road either, so if you decide to geld him, I'd appreciate it if you'd give me a call first so we could do that beforehand."

"Fair enough," Tom nodded. "Say, I heard you had some kind of accident. How are you doing?"

"Oh, I got a little dinged up, but I'm fine now. Thanks for asking." Jessie looked up and saw Henry bringing the colt, saddled and bridled toward the arena. "Here they come." She nodded her head in their direction.

As they all came together, Henry extended his hand to Tom, and Tom, looking past Henry at the old saddle on the colt's back, shook it.

"Hello, Mr. Essex," Henry said with a smile. "Here's your horse."

Tom walked to the side of the colt, and with eyes big as saucers, reached out to touch the saddle, then stopped himself, knowing about the cowboy etiquette that prohibited such behavior. "Where did you get this saddle?" He glanced at the saddle's cantle, and on the back he found a nearly indistinguishable stamp in the leather. It read, *JB Wexler, Saddle Maker,*

Texas. "My God! It's a Wexler! I've been looking for one of these for years!"

"It's been in the family," Henry said bluntly, somewhat put out that the man was more interested in his saddle than the horse.

"I don't know if Jessie told you, but I'm a collector. What would you have to have for it?"

"It's not for sale."

"Everything's for sale," Tom smiled. "I'll pay top dollar for it. Just name your price."

"You're right, sir," Henry said. "Everything is for sale. In fact, I'll sell you anything else I own, including my hat, boots and long handles. I just won't sell that saddle and that's my final word on the matter."

It was clear by the tone in his voice that Henry meant what he said, and as much as he wanted to make a deal on the saddle, Tom knew better than to push a cowboy who sounded as serious as Henry. He decided to drop the subject for the time being, but hoped he would be able to get back to it at some point before the day was over. "Well, if you should change your mind…"

"I won't."

"Fair enough," Tom nodded. "Well then," he said, still having a hard time taking his eyes off the saddle. "Why don't you show me how Tico here works."

"Yes, sir." And for one last time, Henry mounted the colt, and together, the two of them breezed effortlessly through everything they had been working on over the past several months. They moved as one through their transitions from one gait to the next. The colt's natural athletic ability shined through in his effortless stops, spins and roll backs, and Henry showed the colt's calmness by swinging a rope over his head and dragging everything from logs to fifty-five gallon drums behind him, and finished by opening and closing the gate of the arena.

"We haven't had him around cattle," Henry said as he brought the colt to a stop near Tom and Jessie, "but I doubt he'll have any trouble workin' a chute or bein' in the brandin' pen. I've made plenty of big circles with him, and he seems to really like bein' out by himself. He's fine around other horses, too. I've even ponied other horses off him and he's done real well with that. He's good with his feet, and he loads." Henry stopped and petted the colt on his neck. "To be honest, I can't find a hole in him." He paused. "I think you'll be real happy with him. I know I sure have been."

It didn't take long for Tom and Jessie to take care of their business after Henry had run the colt through his paces. Tom paid for not only the colt's training, but also his board for the past six months and even a substantial tip for having done such a good job with him. Jessie tried to turn it down, and was as successful as Tom had been trying to once more buy Henry's saddle. Then the colt was loaded in Tom's stock trailer and the rig drove slowly out of the yard.

"Are you okay?" Jessie asked, looking up at Henry as the truck and trailer pulled away.

"I'm fine," he quietly replied. As Jessie reached over and gently took Henry's hand, he found he was having a little trouble breathing.

The colt turned and peered through the open windows at the back of the trailer, and watched as the figures of Henry and Jessie, standing hand in hand, disappeared in the dust being kicked up by the tires as they rolled over the gravel road. He let out one long, loud whinny that echoed through the valley for what seemed like forever, before it, too, quietly faded.

Henry and Jessie stood, watching the road until the rig was out of sight and the dust settled back to the earth before finally turning and walking back toward the ranch that now seemed a bit big and empty to both of them.

CHAPTER 40

"Henry!" A voice boomed from out of nowhere. "Henry McBride! Is that you?" Henry, who was standing on the loading dock of the feed store tossing fifty-pound sacks of feed into the bed of the pickup, stopped to see where the voice was coming from. "Over here!" Henry honed in on the voice, and found it was coming from the gas station across the road. There, sitting at one of the pumps was a brand new Ford F-350 dually, and standing in front of it was the old rancher, Sam Mitchell, waving his arms.

"I'll be right back," Henry said to the feed store clerk as he hopped off the loading dock and trotted across the street. After dodging two cars and a water truck, Henry got over to Sam, who was just putting the nozzle back on the pump after filling his truck with diesel fuel.

"Henry, by golly!" Sam said, smiling broadly and reaching out his ham-sized hand for Henry to shake. The ever-present small patch of stubble Sam always had somewhere on his face had moved since the last time Henry saw him. It had migrated to his right cheek, not far from his earlobe. "I thought that was you. What are you doing way down here?"

"I was gonna ask you the same thing," Henry smiled. "You're a long way from Elko."

"There was a big cattle auction south of here," Sam leaned on the truck, "the boys are loading what we bought as we speak. How about you? What are you doing in these parts?"

"Workin'," Henry said proudly. "I got me a job not far from here. Been there nearly a year now."

"Well I'll be," the big man grinned. "You working cattle?"

"Horses, mostly."

"Well, horses must agree with you, because you sure look a whole lot better'n the last time we talked. How you doing?"

"I'm doin' good."

"You still drinking?" Sam asked bluntly.

"No, sir," Henry said. "Ain't had a drop in over five months."

"Off the bottle, huh? Well I'll be darned."

"Yes, sir. How about that?"

The two stood, quietly looking at one another for several seconds, both seemingly waiting for the other to say something, when somewhere in the dark recesses of his mind, it suddenly dawned on Henry that Sam had given him six months pay back when he was drinking, in exchange for six months work when he sobered up. He had almost forgotten.

"I believe I owe you some time," Henry finally said, breaking the silence between the two men.

"I thought maybe you'd forgot about that," Sam smiled.

"No sir, I hadn't," Henry said flatly. "I appreciate what you did for me, Mr. Mitchell," Henry went on with all sincerity. "And I sure enough owe you."

Sam seemed happy with Henry's acknowledgment, and while he fully expected Henry to stick to his word and come and work the money off, he also knew Henry was working for someone else now. Sam knew what it was like to lose a good hand, and didn't like the idea of leaving Henry's current employer short of help, especially coming into a busy time of the year. So, as ranch folk often do when broaching what they might see as a slightly difficult subject, Sam eased the talk in a different direction until he could feel more comfortable with what he wanted to say. The two men chatted for a while longer about cattle and horses and the weather. Just before parting ways, Sam told Henry that he understood things change, and he was happy that he had a good job that suited him. He told Henry he could certainly use him, at least for the winter, but if he'd rather just pay the money back instead of coming and working it off, that'd be okay with him, too. He would leave the choice up to Henry, but also said he would like an answer soon, so he could find someone for the position if Henry wasn't going to take it. The two old-time stockmen then shook hands, Henry told him he would get back to him in a couple days, and they each returned to the needs of the day.

It was a long drive back to the ranch for Henry. About halfway there it dawned on him that some of the money Sam had given him was what ultimately got him to Jessie's ranch in the first place. It was Sam's money that had brought him to his new life, and it was a life Henry knew for certain he did not want to leave.

Henry unloaded the feed into the feed room just off the barn when he returned to the ranch, then caught Mic, saddled him up and rode off into the desert to give the situation some thought. It was the first time he'd been on a horse since the colt left over a week before, and as much as he had hoped it would help, he found he actually felt more heartsick than anything else. Between the thought of leaving the ranch and the painful loss of the gray colt, Henry could find no solace in the desert's vast and open places and ended up returning to the ranch less than an hour after he left.

He wrestled with the decision for the rest of the day, and by the time he sat down for dinner with Jessie that evening, he seemed no further ahead than when he had begun. The two of them sat quietly at the table, with the only sound between them being the ticking of the grandfather clock in the other room.

"Are you okay, Henry?" Jessie asked after long minutes of total silence. "You haven't said a word since you sat down."

Henry stopped eating and looked up. "I ran into somebody today," he said somberly.

Jessie put her fork down and wiped her mouth with her napkin. "An old friend?" .

"Well," Henry put his fork down as well. "Actually, he ain't really a friend, I guess. More like an old boss. He was someone who helped me out when I needed it." Jessie sat quietly, having never seen Henry so concerned before. "It's kind of a long story," he continued. "But I owe him six months worth of work."

"Six *months*?"

"On his place up north. It's one of the biggest cattle outfits in the country, up near Elko."

"Are you going to go?"

Suddenly, Henry couldn't seem to bring himself to look at her. "I guess I figured…I guess I wanted to talk with you about it."

"Do you *want* to go?" she asked.

"No, I don't want to go," Henry said with a deep sadness in his voice. "But I *need* to go. It's the right thing to do." He paused, and looked at her. "I owe him."

Jessie's heart sank. It seemed one of the things she found most attractive about the man—his strong sense of right and wrong—was suddenly going to be the one thing that was going to take him from her. Still, if there was one thing she knew about Henry McBride, it was that he would do the right thing. Whatever his decision, she understood in that moment, sitting at the table with him, that her heart would let her support him through it.

"Would you come back?" she asked.

"I would, if you'd have me back." His voice was so sincere that it almost hurt her to hear it.

"You have to come back," Jessie smiled. "This is your home." She paused for just a second before asking, "Isn't it?"

Henry hesitated. He hadn't really ever considered any-place except where he and Annie and Josh used to live as home, but then he hadn't really given the matter much thought lately, either. Now that Jessie asked the question of him, however, he began to realize she was actually right. This place *did* feel like home to him, and looking back over the past few months, he could even say it had felt that way for some time.

Looking into the deep blue eyes of the lovely woman sitting across from him, he smiled. "Yes," he said clearly, "it is."

"Then when will you leave?"

"I don't know yet," Henry sighed. "I guess I'll call Sam and see when he needs me. You and I can figure it out then."

"That'll be fine," she said softly.

They finished their dinner, with Henry explaining how he came to owe Sam Mitchell six months worth of work, how he'd gone there with hat in hand looking for a job, and how Sam wouldn't hire him, but how he also had enough faith in him to give him a six-month cash advance. He told her of the waitress who gave him Jessie's address, and how he ended up losing most of the money Sam gave him after a night of drinking. He then told her how he used the rest of the money he had left over to buy gas to get to her ranch.

After hearing the story, it was easy for Jessie to see why Henry was torn about his decision. While it was clear he wanted to stay with her, the bottom line was, without Sam's help it would have been next to impossible for the two of them to have had met in the first place. Without getting that six months advance, Henry wouldn't have had the money to buy breakfast at the diner in Elko. Had he not eaten at the diner, he wouldn't have met the waitress who gave him

Jessie's information, and without that he would have never gotten to the ranch. She could now see how without Sam, she may have never had Henry in her life at all, and as much as she wanted Henry to stay, she also understood that, she, too, owed Sam Mitchell a debt of thanks.

As had become their nightly ritual, Jessie washed the dishes after dinner, and Henry dried. On their way out to the porch swing to have their coffee, the phone rang. It was Mrs. Rodriguez calling to let Jessie know she was going to the market that evening and asking her if she needed anything while she was there. While Jessie talked with Mrs. R., Henry stepped outside into the cool, early evening air and took a sip from the mug he held in his hand. Looking out over the ranch, he listened to Jessie's musical laughter as she found amusement in something Mrs. R. had said. He took a deep breath, and then exhaled it all out. Yes, this place did indeed feel like home.

Then, as if something unseen was drawing him, Henry sat his cup down and walked out to the horse pasture. He stood for a minute outside the pen, then crawled through the wooden fence rails and made his way over to where the horses were grazing. The sun was setting as one by one, the horses raised their heads and made their way over to him. Two of them approached him, then two more, and three more after that. It wasn't long before the entire herd enveloped him and, smiling, he took the time to pet each horse, calling them each by name.

Jessie had finished her conversation with Mrs. Rodriguez and was now standing with her arms crossed over her chest, leaning against the corner of the open door and peacefully watching Henry and the horses. It was then, in the hazy light of the fading day, that she began to understand something about Henry that had been eluding her. Henry was a lot like those horses. The herd only went to him when it was right for them, not when it was right for him, no matter how hard he tried or how much he wanted to make it happen. For some time now, Jessie had wanted to invite Henry to stay with her, to share her life, her home and her bed, but something had always stopped her short of doing so. As she watched him there in the pen, she now understood the reason. It was because something deep inside had been telling her while the time may have been right for her, it wasn't for him. He would come to her when he was ready, and until then, she would wait.

Jessie smiled at the thought of her wanting to push the man faster than she would have thought about pushing a horse, and shaking her head in spite of herself, she turned and walked back to the porch swing, where she would practice waiting.

CHAPTER 41

Henry had parked his truck near the front porch of Jessie's house. He had packed his belongings next to him in the passenger seat, rather than placing them in the bed. The pre-dawn sky was threatening rain. His saddle, bridle, ropes, saddle pad and the old beat-up satchel that held all his clothes were packed and stacked in a three-foot area inside the cab. Henry realized as he was packing up that he had never fully unpacked the satchel when he placed it in the footlocker the day he had arrived at the ranch. It seemed ironic to him: now that he wanted to stay, his bag was packed to leave.

Henry climbed the porch steps and stopped at the front door. He knocked, but hearing no answer, he shaded his eyes and looked through the screen at the dimly lit interior of the front room. "Jessie?" he called. "Jess? Are you there?" He waited for several seconds, and hearing no answer, he called again. Again, there was no answer, and wondering if Jessie was down at the barn or perhaps doing chores, he walked toward the truck and contemplated which direction he should go to try and find her.

"Henry, wait!" he suddenly heard Jessie's voice call from in the house. She burst through the screen door carrying a small paper sack. She scampered down the steps and over to the truck where Henry was standing. "I made you some sandwiches. It's a long drive."

"You didn't have to do that."

"Well, you've got to eat." She smiled, handing him the sack, and placed her hands on her hips. "They're ham and cheese. I put some mustard in there, too. But not on the bread. It'd make them soggy. It's in those little packets at the bottom." She took a deep breath and looked up at him.

Henry set the sack on the seat, and turned back to her. "I been thinkin'…I don't know if this is such a good idea."

"You need to do this, Henry," Jessie said, trying to convince herself as much as him.

"I…"

"You go," she said, still trying to force a smile. "You know your way back. I'm not going anywhere."

Henry smiled, then reached out and took her hand. He leaned toward her, hesitated, then kissed her gently on the lips. Stepping back, he let out a sigh. "I've been worried about that all morning," he smiled.

"Me, too," They stood looking into each other's eyes until Jessie began to feel the tears welling in hers. "Go on now," she said, breaking the gaze and quickly wiping a tear. "It's a long way to Elko, and it won't get any closer with you standing here holding my hand."

"Yes, ma'am," Henry said quietly, and reluctantly let her go. He turned, climbed in the cab and started the motor. He turned back. "May."

"What?"

"May first. I'll be back on May first."

"Okay." She wiped another tear. "I'll be here."

Henry wanted to say more, but no words came. He closed the truck door, looked forward, put the truck in gear and pulled away. Jessie watched as he disappeared down the driveway, and at the last minute, she waved goodbye. In the distance, a clap of thunder rolled.

Henry traveled less than a half-mile before he stopped his truck in the middle of the road and stared into his rear-view mirror. The ranch, and Jessie, were out of sight now and he couldn't get over how badly he felt for leaving. He leaned forward, and lightly began banging his head on the steering wheel as if it might rattle something loose and help him come to a different decision other than the one he had already made. He then quickly raised his head and sat up straight. "Damn it," he grunted. He jammed the truck into reverse and quickly backed up several yards before stopping once again. He sat for several more seconds before shaking his head in disgust with himself, put the truck in gear, and drove away.

CHAPTER 42

The gray colt had known where he was even before the trailer came to a stop near the pens where he once was held. He was back at the place where he first came in contact with humans after following the herd of strange horses off the mountain and through the gate by the windmill. It was the smell of the place that gave it away long before he saw where he was. He recognized the individual odors of the first humans he had been around, one of which was Tug Caldwell, the man who came to get him out of the trailer and take him to his pen.

There were the other familiar odors as well that told the colt where he was. The smells of cattle, diesel fuel and the mules were just a few of the scents that appeared to be hanging on the afternoon breeze. But unlike the last time he was at this place, the odors didn't seem quite as overbearing to him now, and his brain had a much easier time managing and sorting them. The colt also noticed the look of the place seemed to be different as well. Before, everything was gigantic. The fences seemed to reach the sky and the out buildings appeared so tall they blocked out the sun. But now, everything was much more normal in stature and not near as colossal as they once felt to him.

The colt had quietly followed the human holding the lead rope that was attached to the halter around his head, just as Jessie and Henry had taught him. The man led him past the big catch pen and put the colt in a pen that was different than the one he had stayed in originally, the one next to the old gelding who had died during the night. This pen was smaller, closer to the barn and near another larger pen, which held four geldings.

The colt stayed there throughout the night, munching on the pile of hay that had been left for him and taking the occasional nap until morning. It was then Tug came and haltered him, took him to a hitch rail near a large tack room near the barn, groomed and saddled him and put him back in the trailer along with the four geldings from the nearby pen, who were also saddled. The horses were hauled several miles down the highway before the rig turned onto a dirt road and then traveled several more uphill miles before finally stopping in a large flat open area near a wooden catch pen darkened by age and weather. All the horses were unloaded, saddle bags and canteens were tied to the saddles, cinches were tightened, bridles were placed on their heads, lariats placed over saddle horns and a rider climbed into each one of the saddles, with Tug climbing aboard the colt.

Without any fanfare, men and horses started up a nearby hill and began what would turn out to be the first day of the two-week-long fall round up, where thousands of cattle were gathered out of the high country and brought down to the lower pastures where they would stay for the winter. The colt's first day on the job was relatively easy, and he enjoyed being out in the open country again, but he was more than a bit confused with the way he was ridden by Tug.

Unlike either Henry or Jessie, Tug sent him no pictures whatsoever and while Tug wasn't mean or overly harsh with the colt, he was stiff and hard in the way he communicated with him. If Tug wanted the colt to stop, he would pull back on the reins much harder than he needed to, which caused the normally soft and supple colt to lock the muscles in his neck as a way to protect himself from the contact. Tug would do the same thing when he turned or backed the colt up, always pulling much harder than was necessary. If he wanted the colt to go, he would often take him by surprise by jabbing him in the sides with his spurs. After the first few times of Tug doing this, the colt started to become jumpy anytime he heard the sound of Tug's spur rowels jingle. Tug noticed the effect his spurs were having on the colt and by the end of the first day had taken them off and put them in his saddlebags.

By the end of the first day, the five horses and cowboys had brought down nearly two hundred cow/calf pairs out of the high valleys and moved them to lower ground, closing gates behind them so the cattle couldn't turn and go back up. The horses were loaded in the trailer and driven back to the ranch. Once there, their saddles were removed and they were turned back into their pens without the benefit of a good brushing, the kind the colt had gotten used to getting whenever Henry or Jessie had finished working with him.

Two weeks later, and on the morning of what would turn out to be the final day of the round up, it was a very tired colt that stood in the pen when Tug came to get him. Tug had grown to not only like the young horse, but also to respect him as well. During one of the days of the round up, an old red cow decided she didn't want to come down off the mountain, and was doing everything she could to avoid capture. She had sulled up on the way down the hill numerous times, refusing to walk or try to move forward, which slowed that particular day down considerably. After finally getting to the last gate that would bring the herd to the bottom pasture, the red cow suddenly turned and, taking six others with her, bolted back up the hill.

It was at the end of a very long day, and both horses and riders were pretty well spent. Still Tug did not want to come back to that particular pasture the next day to gather those seven head again. The boys still had five more high country pastures to clear, and if they had to come back to this one, it would put them at least a half-day, and maybe a whole day, behind schedule. He couldn't afford to have that happen. He turned the colt and charged up the hill after them. He did not take the colt directly toward them, though, as that would have just caused them to run faster. Rather, he took the colt two hundred yards to the left of the little group and galloped past them, up a draw and out of their sight. The pair raced uphill for nearly a half-mile before popping out of the draw ahead of the cows. Tug slid the colt to a stop right in their path and turned the colt's body sideways to them, creating a wall for them to look at.

After having repeated the job for several days already, the colt understood how things worked. The idea was to go up on the mountain, gather the cattle, bring them down and go home. Part of the job was *not* running back up the hill a second time to turn a group of escapees back, just so they could go back down the hill again. The colt was tired, sweaty, and now mad. He and Tug had taken the responsibility of keeping the old cow moving down the hill all day in the first place, and to have her turn and bolt like that was making things hard on everybody, and he wasn't going to have it.

Standing sideways in their path, and without being asked to do so, the colt wheeled when they got close enough, and faced them head on. He pawed the ground hard with his right front foot and let out a menacing warning snort through his nose that stopped all the cows, including the old red one, who by now was just as tired as the other escapees. With every muscle in his body tight, his neck arched, nostrils flaring and his steps high and powerful, the colt moved forward. As a group, they all turned from the colt and went down the hill. Peaceably, they walked through the gate. It was now the end of the day.

After they got back to the ranch that night, the horses were unsaddled and taken back to their pens, except for the colt. On that night, and for the first time since he arrived, Tug took the time to brush him down.

Two weeks of working eight- to thirteen-hour days, along with the one run up the hill, had taken it's toll on the colt. He was physically tired and muscle-sore and when Tug slipped his halter on and began leading him from his pen, for the first time since Jessie first taught him how to lead, he hesitated. All the other horses had gotten at least one day off during the round up, some even two or three days off, and they were replaced by other, fresher horses for the cowboys to ride, but not the colt. He had worked all of them, and each morning it was getting harder and harder for him to get his mind wrapped around going up another hill. Still, each day, he somehow found a way to do it, and he did it well and never quit. It simply wasn't in his blood to do that. But on this day, all he really wanted to do was rest.

"Come on, boy," Tug said quietly. It was the first time the colt could remember Tug talking to him. "One more day, and you're done. The hard part'll be over." Tug put a little more pressure on the colt's halter and, grudgingly, the colt broke loose and followed.

There seemed to be a lightness in the men on this morning as they tacked the horses up. As much as they all loved the cowboy life, working the hills for two weeks without a break was tiring to them just as much as it was to the horses, and they all seemed excited to get the round up over with. The lightness was contagious and the colt soon found himself feeling a little better as Tug finished brushing him and threw his saddle on. Soon, the horses were all loaded, tied to the trailer in alternating nose-to-tail fashion. The first horse to go in would have his head tied to the left wall of the trailer, his hindquarters up against the right wall. The next horse would be just the opposite, with his head tied to the right and his quarters to the left, the third would again be tied to the left and so on until all the horses were loaded, and standing nose to tail.

The truck and trailer pulled out of the ranch driveway and turned right, toward the final pasture of the round up, which was seven miles to the south of the ranch. The colt, the first one loaded into the trailer, was standing with his head facing the oncoming traffic in the other lane. Just as the trailer pulled out, he received a very familiar feeling from somewhere outside the trailer.

In the opposite lane, Henry was heading north toward Elko. He had been thinking about the gray colt when he passed a truck and stock trailer pulling out of a ranch driveway. He glanced up at the trailer, as most stockmen will when passing a trailer full of cattle or horses, and thought he caught a glimpse of his old friend's gray face standing in the trailer's nose. He turned to get a second look, but by that time, they had already passed each other.

The colt, also thinking he caught a glimpse of Henry, turned his head toward the pickup and nickered. When Henry's voice didn't answer, he settled back in for the trailer ride that would take him to his next day's work.

CHAPTER 43

Henry had been a cowboy all his life, and other than taking a few years off to rodeo when he was younger, it was all he'd ever done. It was the one thing that gave him solace in those years when he could barely get out of bed without first taking a drink—in the time before Jessie. There was a certain amount of comfort in cattle. He could always depend on them. He understood their quirks, the way they thought and acted, their lowing in the evening, and bawling at feeding time. Even when his life was spinning hopelessly out of control, the cattle were always there for him.

When Jessie first hired him on, all he could think about was leaving her place so he could get back to a cattle outfit as quick as possible. Even after he stopped drinking and fell into a comfortable routine with Jessie, there were still nights when he would lay awake and think about checking on momma cows during calving season, or gathering a herd or roping a sick steer out in the open so he could doctor it.

Henry had always been a cowboy in the truest sense of the word, which is why he found it so disturbing on his first day working for Sam Mitchell on one of the biggest and most prestigious cattle outfits in the country, that all he could think about was going back to Jessie. It had been true that cattle had not only been his livelihood, they had also been his life. But as he stood next to the big sorrel gelding he'd been given for the day's work—helping to bring the last of Sam's massive herd of registered Herefords down out of the high country—he was beginning to understand that perhaps his cowboy life was now behind him.

It was his first day of the six months of days he owed to Sam, and he should have been looking forward to going up in the hills with the other hands, but he wasn't. Working cattle didn't seem to have the same draw for him it once did, and that surprised him. It was like his drinking. It seemed once it was in his past, that's where it wanted to stay. He never would have thought in a million years it could happen, that his yearning for working cattle would just wither away like the plants in the desert during the dry season, and yet that was what it was beginning to feel like.

Besides, as he watched the men he would be with that day—good hands, all of them—jerking on their horses' mouths or jabbing them with spurs because the horses wouldn't, or couldn't stand still in the crisp, early morning air, he slowly began to get a dull ache behind his right eye. It wasn't that he faulted the men for what they were doing. After all, it wasn't so very long ago he would more than likely have been one of the ones doing the very same thing. It was just that for some reason, and as of yet he hadn't figured out what that reason was, he found that sort of thing very difficult to watch.

Looking around, he realized he actually knew most of the men getting ready to move cattle out of the hills that morning, although he couldn't remember any of their names. He recognized many of them from other outfits he'd worked over the years, or from his countless nights in random saloons. But back then he never paid much attention to names. People's names weren't important and neither were the people for that matter. Back then if he needed to identify someone by name, whether in a bar or on the job, he'd just call him "Vern." It was an easy name for him to remember, and besides most cowboys actually liked it. The way they saw it, if Henry McBride, a top hand in anybody's eyes regardless of his drinking, called you Vern, then at least he thought enough of you to call you something other than, "Hey you," or "Kid." Someone like Henry calling you by name, even if it wasn't your own, was actually a bit of a compliment, and that's how most took it.

"Come on, Dave," the voice of Topher Keys boomed out over the din of hooves, spurs and laughter. Topher was easily in his sixties, slightly heavyset with thick hands and a month's worth of gray beard covering his craggy face. The five-inch brim of his worn cowboy hat shaded his eyes from sight when he held his head at just the right angle, and his voice was low and gravely from years of cigarettes and booze. He sat astride a twelve-year-old, sixteen-hand, paint mare he called Sissy, one of the only horses not dancing to and fro under their riders, and just the sound of thunderous voice commanded attention from all within earshot. "Hell, we ain't got all damn day to wait fer you to git on yer damn horse. We got work to do."

Dave was one of those men Henry had seen but never really cared to know. He was young in Henry's eyes, in his early thirties, although he did look much younger. The poor excuse for a mustache he tried to grow to make him look his age, a scraggly, light-brown, sickly little caterpillar of a thing that dusted his upper lip, actually had the opposite effect. The fact that he was also so uncoordinated that he couldn't (as Topher had put it on many occasions) seem to find his own butt with both hands, also added to his teenage-like awkwardness.

On this particular morning, every time he tried to put his foot in the stirrup, his horse, a nice little red dun gelding, kept spinning away from him. Apparently trying to discourage the horse's behavior, Dave took one of his reins and began violently slapping the horse on his neck and shoulders. The gelding turned circle after circle until, not knowing what else to do, he finally tried backing up.

"Damn you!" the kid yelled. "I'll teach you to back away from me!" He raised his hand in the air, and just as he was about to come down and strike the horse for what seemed like the fiftieth time, Henry's hand grabbed Dave's arm and stopped it from coming forward.

"That'll do," he said quietly, but firmly. "You made your point."

"Hell, Henry." The horse was still trying to back away from the seemingly mindless beating. "It's just a damn horse. You went and got all soft on us since you quit drinkin'?" The kid let out a chuckle at the weak joke he had made, and looked around to see how many of the men were joining him in the laugh. None were. They knew what the kid didn't. Henry was more serious than the kid understood and while at this point no harm had actually been done, that could change in a heartbeat if the kid pushed his luck.

"You hit this horse again, and I'll show you just how soft I am," Henry growled.

"Jesus." The kid's tone changed. Now *he* understood, too. "Okay…hell, I was just kiddin' around."

"You're pullin' his damn head around every time you put your foot in the stirrup," Henry said bluntly, turning the kid loose, turning and walking away from him. "That's why he keeps movin' away from you, you damn idiot."

Dave turned and looked at Topher, who had been sitting quietly on the big paint mare not far from the situation the entire time. "Damn," he said almost under his breath. "I think I liked him better when he was a drunk."

The horse Henry rode that day seemed to carry inside him the signature of every man who had ever ridden him. These signatures showed themselves in the way the horse responded any time Henry requested anything of him. He would jerk slightly anytime Henry asked him to move forward by putting a leg on his sides, which told Henry that someone had used spurs on him inappropriately. When asked to stop, the big gelding would jut his nose out and lean on the bit. Someone—probably a number of someones—had been hard with the bit, yanking on the reins, or holding on to his mouth unnecessarily, and for long periods of time. His neck, jaw and mouth were tight from defending himself against such acts, and while the gelding did absolutely everything Henry asked of him that day without hesitation, he was not at all soft when he did any of it. Henry thought it a shame that while the horse had the signatures of numerous riders all over him, he unfortunately didn't seem to have much of his own signature left anymore.

Still, Henry liked the big red horse, and it was him that Henry chose, along with the dun gelding Dave had been beating, to take to the line shack at the far eastern end of the ranch where Henry would be spending most of the next six months. Working the "line" on a ranch in the winter has traditionally always been a very solitary job. In the late 1800's, there had been a boom of gigantic cattle ranches that had sprung up all over the west and southwest. Millionaires from back east or overseas often owned these outfits, and the ranch held millions of cattle on hundreds of thousands of acres. Because these ranches were so vast, outposts, or line shacks, had been built at the farthest reaches of the ranch property, at sometimes anywhere from twenty- to one-hundred-mile increments and usually one, sometimes two, cowboys would be stationed in each one to keep watch on the fence lines, the ranch's livestock and also to watch for rustlers or predators. While many men thrived on the solitude living in a line shack provided, many more ended up going crazy, some even to the point of committing suicide.

The line shack on the eastern edge of Sam Mitchell's property was indeed solitary, but it also wasn't too far from the main ranch. By horseback, leading a pack string and an extra horse, which is how Henry got there, it was a nine-hour ride. By truck, it only took three hours. The shack itself had electricity—sometimes—and running water in the form of a hand pump by the sink. Filling a metal bucket and placing it on the woodstove in the middle of the one room shack would produce the hot water needed to wash either clothes or himself. Henry also had a two-way radio in which he could contact the ranch in case of an emergency, or in case they needed to contact him, as well as a weather radio—both of which ran on batteries.

The original road that led to the shack would have cut four hours off the ride to get there. Unfortunately, the hundred-year-old bridge of rough-hewn lumber that crossed the twelve-foot-wide, steep-banked creek at the half-way point between the ranch and the shack had been washed away during the massive rainstorm two summers earlier. It had yet to be replaced, and as a result, both Henry, as well as the truck that delivered the hay and grain for his horses for the winter, needed to take a five-mile detour to the south where the next closest bridge was.

Henry had packed enough supplies to last a minimum of thirty days. Someone from the ranch would head out to the shack to resupply him at the end of every month. If the weather was fair, and they had a little down time back at the home place, one of the cowboys would bring a pack string out with the supplies he needed. If the weather wasn't fair, or everyone was too busy, the supplies would be brought to him by truck. Either way, he would never go more than thirty days without fresh stocks.

Henry's duties "riding line" were much the same today as they would have been in the late 1800's. He would be checking fence and livestock, watching for rustlers, who oddly enough still operated in the west, as well as keeping an eye out for predators. Admittedly the predators these days weren't as prevalent as they had been in the 1800's and mostly came in the form of coyotes prowling around during calving season.

The area he would be keeping an eye on was much smaller then that of the line riders of the past. While one, or perhaps two men would be in charge of hundreds of square miles of range in the 1800's, Henry would only be responsible for watching about ten. Still, ten square miles of open range dotted with rolling hills, deep banked creeks and a large winding canyon, as well as three windmills and water tanks, would be enough to keep him occupied for the six-month stretch he would be putting in.

Henry was no stranger to the kind of solitude that riding line provided. For the past seventeen years he had lived a life of self-imposed solitude and felt he had gotten along just fine. When Sam Mitchell gave him his choice of jobs on the ranch, he had chosen this one. It was an easy choice, especially after two weeks of living amongst the cowboys working the ranch. He'd already had enough of them and couldn't seem to get away quickly enough.

Henry's first few days out on the line were filled with the chores needed to get the place ready for the winter. He put the supplies away, stacking the canned goods on the empty shelves near the sink, the coffee tins on the counter and leaving his clothes in the satchel and placing them on an old wooden chair near the bed. He went outside and set to repairing the corral fence that had a number of broken rails, nailed the siding back on the small hay barn where the wind had blown it loose, and made sure the windmill that kept the horses' water tank full was in good working order.

When his chores around the shack were finished, he woke one morning, mounted the big red horse, put a packsaddle on the dun with a week's worth of provisions and began his first swing through the country he would be looking after for the winter. He wanted to familiarize himself with the country, make sure the fence was in good repair, check windmills and water tanks, do a head count of the cattle that he found and check and note ear tag numbers.

Henry finished yet another dinner of canned chili he'd cooked over his campfire, realizing he had been gone from Jessie for nearly a month. The horses were hobbled and grazing peacefully nearby, both taking on the orange hue of the campfire that was keeping him warm that night. Although there was little or no wind, the night was cold, and had gotten colder since the sun went down. It was the kind of cold that made the ends of his fingers sting when exposed to the air for more than a few minutes. As Henry pulled his heavy Navajo blanket tighter around himself, he gazed up at the starry night emblazoned by a full moon. He had been thinking about Jessie non-stop since he left her, but until that very second—with the moon shining so brightly down on him that it could have been mid day—he hadn't really realized just how much he missed her, and he wondered what she was doing at that very minute.

CHAPTER 44

"Isn't it a fine full moon, tonight?" the young woman said as Jessie walked past her. The voice snapped Jessie out of the mental mist she had drifted into as she made her way back to the house. It had been a long day, the kind that had Jessie second-guessing whether or not she even wanted to continue running a guest ranch. Those kinds of thoughts didn't really enter her mind all that often, but she had to admit, they were starting to occur more frequently.

It had started that morning when she found that one of her cooks and two of her housekeepers left during the night. It seemed at some point during the past week, the cook and one of the housekeepers had decided they would go seeking fame and fortune over in Las Vegas, and the third, a somewhat naive twenty-year-old girl from the Midwest, chose to go along. As a result, Jessie spent a good part of her day helping out in the kitchen and cleaning guest cabins.

Then, there was the argument at breakfast between the newlyweds. Apparently, the bride, who had been raised in the city but had dreams of being a cowgirl, had decided to surprise her husband by using the ranch as their honeymoon destination. The bride was having the time of her life. The groom, however, would have preferred somewhere with a golf course. The discussion between them had begun some-time during the night and by the time it spilled over into morning, it wasn't really clear to anyone on the ranch just how long the new marriage was going to last. The quarrel had gotten so heated that, at one point, Jessie had to step in and separate the two, and when they refused to call a truce on the subject after thirty minutes of yelling and screaming, she finally asked them to leave the property.

Then there was the young Hollywood actor from Los Angeles who had come to the ranch because he had landed a part in an upcoming western on the pretense that he knew how to ride horses. Unfortunately, the actor was from Chi-cago and the closest he'd ever been to a live horse was look-ing out at them from his car window. Not only did he not know how to ride, but he was also scared to death of them. His agent had stayed at the ranch with his family a few years back and suggested the young man come there to learn how to ride and be around horses. In an attempt to work up his nerve just to go down to the barn, much less mount up, the actor had spent most of the day drinking in his room. By the time he was sufficiently drunk enough to make the effort, he was also too drunk to walk. He left his cabin, staggered around for five minutes, and then ended up falling into a rock garden dotted with a variety of native low-growing cactus. Not only was he covered from head to foot in cac-tus tines, but he also broke both wrists in the process. Jessie ended up driving him to the medical clinic in town and the entire way she had to listen to (between his bouts of throwing up) how he was going to sue her for putting a rock garden right where he had been trying to walk.

So now, at the end of the day, she was looking into the smiling face of this girl who had greeted her and couldn't remember her name. It was an odd feeling for Jessie, who was normally someone who never forgot anybody's name, to not be able to recall the name of a girl who had been working for her as a housekeeper for the past three weeks, and was also one of the only two that still remained after the others left during the previous night.

"Yes," Jessie smiled, not really even bothering to look up. "It is a pretty moon." She nodded to the girl with the forgotten name. "Goodnight."

"Goodnight, Miss Jessie," the girl chirped. "Have a good one."

"Thank you." She was already on her way again. "You, too." *Hillary? Hannah? Heather?*

Jessie continued across the yard, and was almost to the porch steps when she finally noticed how bright everything was. She glanced around at the ranch, and even though it was close to 10:00 p.m., she could see every building, fence, bush and rock on the place. She looked out into the desert and could see the hills where she had taken Henry to see the mustangs off in the distance. The sky was a bright, grayish blue, and so was everything in sight. It was only then she looked up at the moon the girl with the forgotten name had pointed out to her.

My God, she thought to herself. *Look at that.*

Under that most perfect, fine full moon, Jessie's thoughts turned to Henry. She missed him, she missed talking with him and she missed being with him. She hadn't realized it before, but after that long day, and now, looking up at the moon that was lighting up the desert so brightly, she suddenly felt very empty. She wondered what Henry was doing at that very moment. Wrapping her arms around herself as a cool breeze passed over her, she let out a sigh and climbed the steps.

CHAPTER 45

Topher's last cigarette butt was still smoldering in the ashtray in front of him as he lit up another. He took a long drag from the filterless Camel, its burning end glowing bright red in the dim light of the Silver Dollar Saloon, before blowing a long smooth stream of bluish smoke out his nose, the remainder pouring out his mouth as he began to talk. "Well," he tapped the cigarette's end on the edge of the ashtray, which already contained nearly an entire pack of his dead and smoldering butts. "Another year come and gone." He picked up his beer glass with the same hand in which he held his cigarette, and sucked down half of its contents. "They sure all seem to run together after a while, don't they, Lou?" He said, wiping his mouth with his sleeve, then letting out a long, low burp.

"Comes with age, I reckon, Toph." Lou, the man behind the bar nodded while he put several newly washed glasses on a shelf next to the beer taps. Lou had once been a cowboy but it all came to an end for him when he was gored and trampled by a bull while working an outfit up in Montana. From the accounts of all the men who saw the wreck, it was a wonder Lou got out of it alive. It had apparently been so traumatic, even for those who saw it, that no one would ever go into any specifics about what happened. Even Lou kept the details to himself, and over the years, people just learned to steer clear of the subject. The deep scar he carried on his face, the missing fingers on his right hand and the ever-present limp from a leg that was now an inch-and-three-quarters shorter than the other said all that anyone really needed to know about the incident.

"Aw hell," Dave said as he stepped up to the bar, pool cue in his hand. "You old-timers talk like you got one foot in the grave." He picked up his beer glass, drank down the rest of what was inside and slammed the glass to the bar. "Not me!" he yelled. "Hell, boys, I'm just gettin' started!" Dave's caterpillar moustache was now being accompanied by a scraggly light brown beard that grew in patches all over his chin, but hardly at all on his cheeks. He said he grew it to keep his face warm in the winter. Topher doubted it would keep him warm even in the summer.

He was playing pool with a local boy named Jerry who worked at the rodeo grounds part time. Jerry had wanted to get a full-time job on one of the ranches in the area, but everyone knew he was much more suited to the job he currently had. A little slow-witted, but a master of the pool table, Jerry had already taken thirteen dollars of Dave's money that night, and with his next shot would make it fourteen. As a live version of The Marshall Tucker Band's "Take the Highway" burst out of the jukebox, Jerry took an easy stroke with his stick, barely tapping the white cue ball and sending it gently across the table, where it nudged the eight ball less than three inches into the corner pocket.

"Damn." Dave stabbed the butt of his pool cue into the floor and stomped his foot. "I thought I had him that time."

Topher looked over his shoulder. "Hell, Dave," he grunted. "You still got five balls on the table."

"I know." Dave turned and motioned for Lou to fill his glass. "That was my strategy. I was gonna get all my balls lined up for good shots, then when the time was right, I was gonna run the table." Topher looked at him with an expression that said, *You're kidding, right?* "Only problem was, Jerry, there, run the table before I could."

The door swung open, causing a gust of cold February air to rush in through the bar, and a man in a large cowboy hat, heavy canvas coat and high-top boots with spurs strapped to them strolled in, closing the door behind him. He stopped briefly at the door, scanned the patrons, and seeing Topher and Dave at the bar, slowly, but deliberately sauntered over next to them.

"Bottle of Bud," he said to Lou as he pulled open his jacket and took a small wad of cash from his vest pocket. "Evenin' boys." He nodded to Dave and Topher. They nodded back.

Topher had sized the man up before he had even made it to the bar, and he didn't like him. He was going to try to pass himself off as a top hand, but Topher already knew he wasn't. His hands were the first things that gave him away. His fingers were a little too thin and clean, and his fingernails were a little too long. A man with thin, clean fingers more than likely hadn't done too much hard work in his life, and long fingernails when working around livestock just weren't smart at all. Long fingernails would always be broken and caught on things, and even when a real working cowboy was out of work, he usually kept his nails trimmed short out of habit.

Then there were the man's jeans. While this fella's jeans were well worn, they were missing one sure, telltale sign of a working stockman. Most stockmen almost always had one leg of their jeans worn a little thinner than the other. Because most people either carry hay bales off to one side, or lift bales using one leg, that particular leg of their jeans was almost always worn a little thinner than the other. This man's jeans were worn evenly.

His boots were also giving him away. Not because he was wearing high tops or because he had his jeans tucked into them in the traditional buckaroo style, but rather, because of what his boots *didn't* have. Most, if not all cowboys have a prominent scuffmark on the inside arch of their boot that comes from the arch rubbing up against the inside of a stirrup. This scuffmark, about halfway between the boot heel and the first knuckle of the cowboy's big toe, is usually black in color and looks like a large thumbprint smudge. This fella's boots were absent this mark.

"You boys workin' an outfit up here?" The man placed his money on the bar.

Dave, having seen the expression on Topher's face when he looked at the stranger, knew instinctively to be wary of the man. The previously exuberant young cowboy suddenly became quiet, turning his back slightly on the man and looking down at his beer.

"Yup," Topher said bluntly, taking another drag from his cigarette.

"The name's Chad, Chad Collins." The cowboy smiled. It was just one more thing Topher didn't like about him. Too many teeth. Very few cowboys showed all their teeth when they smiled, and even when they did, they were usually tobacco-stained, or missing. This guys teeth were neither, which made him look like he had more teeth than he should have. "You all know of any outfits up this way lookin' for help?"

"Nope," Topher grunted again.

"Naw," Dave joined in. "Not this time of year. No one hires in the winter. We even got one more hand than we need right now." He turned to Topher. "What the hell's with old Henry, anyhow? He gone and found religion or what?"

"Henry?" Chad's smile faded.

"Yeah." Dave could only stay concerned about the man for so long. "Old Henry McBride. He left the country a few years back one of the biggest drunks in four counties and come back sober as a judge. Must'a joined one of them alcoholics oblivious outfits or somethin'."

"He's workin' around here?" There was a hint of worry in the man's voice. Topher picked up on it right away, and glanced over to see the look on his face. It, too, was slightly worried.

"Yeah," Topher said, trying to get a read on the man. "He's ridin' line up in Wild Basin. I see him once a month when I take supplies up to him. You want me to tell him you said hello…Chad?"

"No, that's okay," Chad said, turning back to the bar and taking a drink from his bottle. He stayed quiet for a long time, drinking first one bottle of beer, then a second, and then a third. He thought about his last encounter with Henry McBride. It had been a dire threat Henry made that night in the parking lot of Mona's Bar and, taking Henry's threat seriously, Chad had gotten far away from Grant that night and had been looking for steady work ever since.

He had traveled east, into Colorado where he got a job on a guest ranch for the summer, but it was only for the summer and it didn't pay much. He had tried to talk his way into a management position there, but the management wasn't all that impressed with him or his skills, and sent him on his way as soon as the season was over in September. From there he traveled north to Jackson Hole, Wyoming. He took a job as a bartender at a ski resort, but was quickly fired for making improper advances toward the manager's wife. He stayed in Jackson for a time, picking up an odd job here and there, before finally deciding to make his way south. He had planned on going to Southern California to see if he could get into the movies, something he had always wanted to do, or even to Mexico where, with the little money he had set aside, he could live relatively high on the hog for a while before having to come back and get another job.

Chad thought hard about his current situation. He would never admit it to anyone, not even to himself, but he was afraid of Henry McBride. He had been afraid of him since the first day they met. Henry had seen through him right from the start, just as Topher had, and Chad knew it. In fact, Chad had been so paranoid about accidentally running into Henry on this current trip to California, he had chosen to take the northern route through Nevada, along I-80, instead of the southern, more direct one on I-15. The last thing he had expected when he stopped into the Cattlemen's Bar that night was hearing Henry was in the area, only twenty or thirty miles from where he currently stood. Had Henry not been safely riding line out in the middle of nowhere, Chad would have left his beer on the bar and been five miles down the road before the door closed behind him.

The more beer Chad drank, the more it was beginning to become clear to him that—just as Henry had warned—he may have to be looking over his shoulder for the rest of his life because that damned old man actually *could* show up anywhere. In the background, "Coal Miner's Daughter" gushed from the jukebox, and Chad knocked back the rest of his fourth beer. He stared at himself in the mirror behind the bar and motioned for Lou to bring him another. He began to seethe inside as he thought about how Henry McBride had taken his job, his woman, and now his freedom to go wherever he wanted. He was halfway through his fifth bottle before Chad convinced himself he would have no peace as long as Henry McBride was alive, and that if he were to ever get control of his life back, drastic steps were going to need to be taken.

"Okay, Dave," Topher finally said, pushing himself up from his stool. "That's it for me. I'm gonna take a piss, then I'm headin' back to the ranch. You want a ride?"

"Yeah, Toph," Dave said, taking one of the last three sips from his glass. "I'm ready too."

As soon as Topher walked away, Chad turned to Dave.

"So," he started, as cheerfully as he could make himself sound with nearly a six-pack of beer in him. "Henry is up in Wild Basin, eh?"

"Yeah." Dave took the second of three sips. "He'll be up there till after calving, then we'll go up and help him bring the pairs in for branding."

"Wild Basin…that's south of here, isn't it?" Chad was fishing for information, but Dave didn't pick up on it.

"No, you're thinking of Wind River." Dave took the last sip, then pointed at an old yellowed topographical map of the area that was framed and hung on the wall next to the back bar. "Wild Basin is to the east, see there. He's way out there by Frasier's Canyon. As the crow flies, it's only about five miles off the main road, but it's near impossible to get to it goin' that way. So we always cut through the ranch, which is longer, but a whole lot flatter and easier to travel, both horseback and with a truck."

"So he's out there by himself?"

"Yeah," Dave shrugged. "But he don't seem to mind it."

"And your buddy, there…Topper, he takes supplies out to him?"

"Topher," Dave corrected him. "Yeah, he goes out there around the fifteenth of every month. Stays for a day or two to help out with whatever Henry needs, then comes back."

"I suppose he drives the supplies out."

"Topher?" Dave chuckled. "Are you kiddin'? If Toph can't do it a horseback, he'd rather not do it at all. No, he packs everything out on mules and horses. He's only got two more trips, I think."

"Two more trips?"

"Yeah." Dave wiped his mouth with his sleeve. "He'll go out there mid March, then again mid April and then we'll all go up and bring the pairs down for branding around the first of May."

"Dave!" Topher shouted as he walked from the men's room to the front door. "Come on, goddammit. I ain't waitin' on you all night."

"I gotta go," Dave said, shaking Chad's hand. "Nice talkin' with ya." He started for the door. "I'll tell Henry I seen ya, next time I see him."

"Thanks," Chad smiled coldly. "Hopefully I'll get a chance to do that myself before long."

As Dave and Topher disappeared through the door and into the cold February night, Chad picked up his beer and walked over to the old topographical map. He stared at the Frasier Canyon area in Wild Basin and took another pull from his bottle. The jukebox belched out "Whipping Post" by The Allman Brothers Band, and Chad silently mouthed along with the words as he studied the map. When Gregg Allman came to the last line, Chad found himself quietly singing along, *Good Lord—I feel like I'm dy-in'*. He set the bottle on the bar, and smiled.

CHAPTER 46

It had been a long winter for both Henry and Jessie. Even though they had been extremely busy with the work that was in front of them, Jessie tending to her guests and the duties of the place, and Henry keeping track of the herds that passed through his area of the ranch, spring couldn't seem to come fast enough. They missed each other more than either had expected, and the longer they were apart, the lonelier each felt.

The worst of it, particularly for Henry, came in February. Up till then the weather had been relatively mild for the Wild Basin area. There had been the normal days of cold and snow, but for the most part Henry had always been able to get out and get his daily rounds done without a problem. About mid February, a band of low-pressure systems raced down from Canada, bringing with them sub-zero temperatures and two-and-a-half feet of snow. Henry was cabin-bound for nearly a week. He was only able to get out to feed his horses, check the water in the tank, which he had to break the ice off of five times a day, and go to the outhouse. He had brought several books with him, which he read sitting on a wooden chair by the woodstove, but even with that, he found it was difficult for him to get past more than a page or two before his mind began wandering back to Jessie.

By the third day of the storm, he found himself pacing the floor, stopping periodically to glance out the window, turning and heading across the room, stopping and glancing out that window, then heading back the other way. He mindlessly repeated the pattern over and over before realizing four hours had passed. While he found a certain comfort in repeating the pattern, he also understood it probably wasn't the most productive thing for him to be doing, and it was then he bundled himself up and went outside for the third time that day to break the ice off the water tank.

It was in the middle of that storm that a deep understanding began to set in for Henry. A year or so earlier, if he had been put in the same situation, he no doubt would have sat in that shack and easily drank himself to death. With nothing to live for at the time, he would have welcomed the isolation, and the ultimate end it would have brought to him. But now, things were different. Not only did the loneliness of this self-imposed remoteness overtake him, but it also gave him time to take stock of his life.

In the past, he looked at his life as a throwaway: a meaningless, despicable shell of an existence he couldn't get over with fast enough. Back then, every day he woke, he would curse himself for making it through the night, and then secretly hope that maybe *this* day would be his last.

But then he met Jessie and all that began to change. She had somehow brought him back from the brink, having done nothing more than being herself. She had been loving, kind and supportive, and had shown him that there was much more to life than climbing in and out of a bottle everyday. It was being around her that had shown Henry that his life was not a throwaway, and that in many ways, it was only just beginning. Henry could see very clearly now that the man who would have drank himself to death only a year ago no longer existed. Sitting in that shack under what seemed like a mountain of snow, a very different Henry was emerging.

One who not only *didn't* want to die but who wanted to embrace life and live it to the fullest. And he wanted to start right away.

In desperation he told himself, as he stared into the endless white that swirled and danced just outside his window, that as soon as the storm broke he was going to pack up his belongings and head back to Jessie just as fast as he could make it. But the stockman in him wouldn't let him go, and as soon as the storm did break, he was on his horse heading out to check the cattle.

A small herd of thirty heifers had passed through Henry's area and were caught out in the open when the storm hit. They had turned their backsides to the wind, put their heads down and kept walking until they came to the eastern-most fence line. There, they turned south and kept walking until they came to the corner where the eastern fence and the southern fence came together. It was there they stopped. Bunched up in the corner, and with heads low to keep out of the weather, they were soon covered under a heavy blanket of snow that the relentless northern winds pushed over them. Within hours, all thirty suffocated to death, and being held in a standing position within the drift, were frozen stiff where they stood.

It was a surreal sight that Henry came across at the far reaches of the area that was his responsibility. Bright, trackless white covered the land and reached all the way to the horizon where it abruptly ended. Above was a sky so blue it hurt his eyes. Grouped in front of him, thirty head of red-and-white heifers stood like statues in the snow, their heads low, literally frozen in time. The coyotes, foxes, magpies and crows hadn't found them yet. But they would. He pulled his heavy woolen coat up tight around him to keep the cold breeze from running down the back of his neck, then turned and rode away.

Henry had heard of cattle doing such a thing, but he had never seen it before. For a brief moment he had blamed himself for the heifers dying. If only he had been able to get out during the storm and get them out of the corner; if only he had seen them before the storm hit and pushed them to the shelter of the canyon where the rest of the herd had no doubt holed up. But then he realized the reality of the situation. Had he gone out during the storm he more than likely would have died himself, along with his horse, both likely frozen to death or just like the cattle, suffocated in the snow. Losses like these were part of the cattle business, and he knew it. But he still didn't like it.

That storm turned out to be the only one of consequence for the season. While the ranch certainly could have used the moisture the spring snows would have brought with them, Henry was happy to be dry and relatively warm during calving season, which began almost as soon as the storm passed. It was then Henry remembered why he had liked the cattle business in the first place. There was something about seeing all those red babies with white faces running and playing amongst the patches of dwindling white snow and green grass that was beginning to sprout that brought an uncontrollable smile to his face and lightness to his heart. This was what he would miss after his time with the cattle was over. Since he had another month-and-a-half left out on the line, that time would be coming to a close very soon.

As for Jessie, her winter was only slightly easier. She had her guests and employees to talk with during the day, but she missed her conversations with Henry at night. It would be years before she would realize that it had been the memory of those nightly conversations that caused her to start rethinking her priorities. But for now, it was simply something she wrestled with when she tried to get to sleep.

Not long after Henry left, Jessie began lying awake at night, going over the feeling she had gotten, and now was missing, when it had just been her, Henry and the horses on the ranch. Everything she loved or cared about had been right there, and she was now beginning to understand after all these years, that perhaps it was really all she needed. As much as she tried—and she tried a lot—she couldn't remember a time when she had been happier.

While there was no question that she was good at the guest ranch business, for the first time since she took it over she began to see it wasn't really *her* business. It was her father's. When he died, she continued in his footsteps and never gave any thought as to *why* she was doing it. But she was now. Having spent an entire summer doing what *she* wanted to do, with the person *she* wanted to do it with, had given her new eyes. Those eyes only got sharper as the guest season wore on. Dealing with the daily, and sometimes hourly issues that arose on the ranch, whether with guests, employees or both, she began to realize she was spending a lot of time doing something she really didn't want to be doing.

About midway through the season, she began looking at the idea of having this season be her last. After all, she didn't *need* to run the place as a guest ranch, because money wasn't really an issue for her. The ranch itself had been free and clear since before her father passed away. She had enough funds in the bank so that if she didn't earn another dollar for the next five years she could still live comfortably, and on top of that, the money she currently earned by training and selling horses sustained her throughout the year. The more she thought about it, the more using the ranch solely as a training and breeding facility intrigued her.

Jessie kept her thoughts to herself, and although she never spoke of the changes she was contemplating, nor had she thought she had made a decision about what she wanted to do, Mrs. Rodriguez already knew she had. Mrs. R. had known Jessie since she was a child and could often tell just by the expression on her face what she was thinking. She had been watching Jessie for months. She noticed Jessie wasn't taking reservation deposits for the following season, even though several established returning guests wanted to write her a check for their reservation before they left. She wasn't talking to the employees about coming back to work for her the next year, as she usually did, either.

Jessie had also done something else that she didn't seem to want anybody to know about. She had been calling Tom Essex at least once a week trying to buy the gray colt from him. Mrs. R. overheard Jessie talking to Tom on the phone and was surprised at the large amount of money she had offered for the horse. Still, it hadn't been enough. As often as Jessie called him, he kept turning her down.

While these signs pointed to Jessie trying to decide on making a change for the ranch, and in her life, it wasn't until the middle of April that Mrs. R. knew she had made her choice. It was then that Jessie gave Mrs. Rodriguez a ride into town to do some much-needed grocery shopping for her daughter's family. Mrs. R., always terrified when Jessie drove, tried to opt out, but in the end gave in as the family was running low on everything since her daughter had taken a second job at the local diner and been unable to get to the market.

Mrs. R. strapped herself into the passenger seat of the truck as if she were a NASCAR driver, then braced her arm against the door, hand against the seat, and both feet against the floor. She closed her eyes tightly as Jessie pulled away from the house, but was surprised when the truck didn't lurch forward. She turned to see Jessie's face calm and tranquil, as opposed to tight and tense, as it usually was when she drove. Jessie drove to town and back at the designated speed limit, or just below, and it was then Mrs. Rodriguez knew something had really changed.

At home, the emotional darkness Jessie had been experiencing during the winter since Henry had left, began to lighten. By the time she had given Mrs. R. her ride into town, there were fewer than five days till the end of the season, and seventeen until Henry was back home. Jessie had started keeping track of the days on the calendar she kept on the wall next to the refrigerator in the kitchen. Starting on April first, there was a black X through each day that had already passed. There was a red circle around the day when the season would end, and another red circle around May first, the day Henry was to return. The red circle around May first looked suspiciously like a red heart, although Jessie would deny it if anybody pressed her on it, which they didn't.

Jessie King had made her decision. Guest ranching, like cattle ranching for Henry, had become an empty place for her. It wasn't who she was anymore, and perhaps it never was. Either way, she finally knew an old chapter of her life was getting ready to close, and a new chapter was about to begin.

Mrs. Rodriguez, who had been watching her since she was a little girl, could only shake her head and wonder why it had taken her so long.

CHAPTER 47

Henry had seen the note while he was still almost one hundred yards away from the line shack. The white paper that had been stuck between the door and the age-darkened wooden doorjamb stuck out like a beacon in the night. He could only assume it was probably from Topher, or one of the other hands from the ranch. He eased the big red gelding up to the shack, dismounted and dropped the rein on the ground, a signal Henry had taught the horse during the months they had spent together to mean, "Stand still." Without moving, the gelding dropped his head and began munching on the fresh green grass that was sprouting up everywhere. Spring had finally arrived at Wild Basin, and while moisture had been hard to come by up till now, there had been just enough rain in the past week or so to brighten things up a little.

Henry stepped up on the porch and pulled the note out without having to open the door first. It was written in pencil by someone with a slightly shaky hand...Topher, he guessed. It read: *Took shortcut. Packhorse broke leg. Bring packhorse. Mile ½ into canyon.*

It was almost mid April and Topher was apparently two days early with the last of Henry's supplies. Henry had been horseback since before dawn scouting the positions of the herd in anticipation of moving them back to the ranch for branding. He was tired and had hoped to get a nap in, as had become his daily ritual when time allowed as this day had, right up until now. As Henry went to get the dun from the pen, he wondered why Topher decided to take a shortcut with his pack string, especially since he was actually two days early to begin with. But then, there was no telling why Topher did most of the things he did, and in the end, Henry retrieved the dun, gave the red gelding some grain and a long drink from the water tank, mounted up and headed for the canyon.

The canyon was little more than a ten-mile long, two-hundred-yard-wide ditch carved in gray rock to the north of Henry's line shack. It had formed when prehistoric waters receded from the area over a million years before, leaving in its wake the canyon with a box canyon in its far end. The floor of the canyon was flat and mostly sandy, and its sides rose from a height of ten feet at its mouth, to nearly seventy feet a quarter mile in. About a mile from the mouth, where Topher had apparently had his accident with the packhorse, the sides of the ravine were nearly one hundred feet tall, steep and rocky.

On a good day, getting to the mouth of the ravine from Henry's shack took him less than an hour. Getting in the mile-and-a-half to where Topher was would take another hour-and-a-half, give or take. It was a fine day for a ride, and if Henry hadn't been so tired to begin with, he probably would have enjoyed this one a little more than he was. Still, there was a bright blue, cloudless sky and a breeze from the south that warmed the normally chilly spring air, both making it difficult for him to complain too much.

The big red gelding had a lively step for having worked since before dawn. Henry had spent a lot of time with the horse since coming to the shack and was happy with how he had been coming along. Most of the tightness in the gelding's jaw and neck had all but disappeared, and his body now had suppleness to it that Henry was pleased with. The gelding's demeanor was also a far cry from the stiff, worried and mechanical horse he had gotten on that first day back in the fall. Now, whenever the gelding saw Henry coming for him, day or night, rain, snow or shine, he always nickered to him, and when he was ridden the sharp reactiveness he exhibited early on had been replaced with a willing responsiveness. That was also something that felt good to Henry.

He had gotten nearly a half-mile into the canyon when he realized that he hadn't seen any sign of horses on the canyon floor. He had seen plenty of cow sign, manure and tracks, and he had even seen the hoofprints of the big red gelding from the last time they checked the ravine a few days earlier. But no new sign, which he thought strange. Surely Topher wouldn't have walked the five-mile round trip trek from where he said the crippled horse was in the canyon to the line shack and back. Even if he did, Henry hadn't seen any human tracks either. Henry knew he was in the right canyon. It was the only one within a twenty-mile radius. But still, it seemed odd.

Henry continued deeper into the canyon, and as he closed in on the area where the note said Topher would be, he found nothing. No horse with a broken leg, no abandoned packsaddles, and more importantly, no Topher. He stood in the stirrups of his saddle to look farther down the canyon, but saw nothing. He called out twice, but received no answer. Henry came to the conclusion Topher must have meant to write *two*-and-a-half miles on his note instead of a *mile*-and-a-half, in which case he wouldn't see him, nor would Topher have heard him.

He eased the big red gelding back into a walk and had only gone a few feet when Henry noticed something shiny glinting in the sun off to his right. He rode over and found a small mirror leaning against a rock, as if someone had placed it there. It was in the perfect position to catch the eye of anybody passing by, as the angle it was at caught the sun perfectly and reflected it back toward the middle of the canyon. It was then Henry decided that Topher must have placed it there as a sign he was on the right track. Henry was just about to climb down to retrieve the mirror when without warning the big red gelding dropped like a stone out from under him. Almost simultaneously, a very loud CRACK echoed through the canyon.

All at once there was a tremendous amount of activity near Henry. The dun horse he had been holding pulled back hard in an attempt to get away from the falling red horse. Henry twisted violently in the saddle and was jerked toward the dun as he pulled back. At the same time he was going to the ground with the red gelding as he fell. Instinctively, Henry let go of the dun horse's lead rope just about the time he was slammed into the earth, knocking both the wind, and his consciousness, from his body.

Several more cracks echoed through the canyon, and as the dun gelding high-tailed it for home, dirt, dust and rocks were kicked up near where Henry and the big red horse lay. Henry came to his senses quickly, and although groggy, he tried to figure out what was happening. He was under the assumption Topher was somehow involved in what was going on, but was having a hard time quantifying that in his mind. After all, why would Topher want to harm him? They had been working friends for many years, and they had been getting along all throughout the winter. Besides, Topher wouldn't kill a perfectly good horse, which, with his leg pinned under the lifeless body of the big red gelding, someone had just done.

There was a brief pause in the action before more loud cracks sounded, and more dirt and rocks were kicked up. *Jesus*, Henry thought. *Someone's shooting at me!* He tried to free his pinned leg by putting his free foot on the seat of the saddle and his hands on the saddle horn and pushing, but it was to no avail. Another brief halt in the shooting occurred, then started up again. Bullets whizzed around Henry's head, and three more slammed into the big red horse's body. Henry was able to use the horse as a shield. He struggled once more to free his leg, and then remembered the revolver he carried in his saddlebags. He scooted his body as best he could back toward the gelding's hindquarters, and struggling due to the awkward angle at which he laid, worked feverishly to open the saddlebag and retrieve the Colt pistol.

The shooting stopped, and Henry could hear someone up in the rocks slowly making his way down to him. He kept working the saddlebag, which had its flap buckled into place, and after getting it unbuckled began to rummage around inside. The pistol was at the bottom in its holster, and it took Henry some time to locate it. He carried first aid supplies in the same pouch, and had to get past all of them before he could get to the gun. After what seemed like a lifetime, he felt the revolver's rosewood grip, and with the tips of his fingers tried to work it closer to his hand so he could get a hold of it. The heavy weapon fought him and wouldn't allow itself to be moved, and as Henry tried to reposition himself to get a better angle, and thus a little better grip, he heard a familiar voice.

"You once told me to watch my back, because the next time you saw me you were going to kill me." It was Chad, and there was an odd quiver in his voice. He was sweaty and pale, and had a glimmer in his eye that worried Henry, although Henry wasn't going to let him know it. He climbed out of the rocks and walked toward Henry, pointing a Winchester rifle at his head.

"You son of a bitch," Henry was indignant. "You shot my horse!"

"Yeah…" Chad ginned. "And I'm going to shoot more than just your horse, you old bastard!"

Henry had finally gotten a hold of the Colt, and unable to get it out of its holster, he pulled the hammer back and pointed the barrel as best he could while still in the saddle-bag at Chad, who was standing less than twenty feet away on the other side of the dead gelding. He was hoping Chad would somehow come to his senses and put the rifle down because he didn't want to have to pull the trigger on the Colt. Looking up at the poor, hopeless kid, it dawned on him that he didn't want another death on his conscience, even if it was Chad's.

"I guess maybe you should have followed your own advice," Chad smirked. "Well," there was a sinister tone in his voice, "see ya around!"

Chad took careful aim. A lone gunshot rang out, echoing up and down the canyon for what seemed a long time. Then silence.

CHAPTER 48

Jessie had finished working one of her young horses, a delicate black mare she had named Taylor. She was born on the ranch over four years before. Jessie pulled the saddle from the little mare's back and set it on the hitch rail next to where the mare was tied. She took the time to give the young horse a good brushing, something she relished doing, and then led her to the corral that the gray colt once called home. Opening the gate, she led the mare in, gently unbuckled the halter from her head and turned her loose. The mare walked calmly past her and as she did, Jessie gave her a kind pat on the rump before leaving the pen and latching the gate.

It had been a warm day, much warmer than she had expected, and although it was only two in the afternoon, Jessie could feel it was time for a break. She wandered back to the tack room, and as she pulled her saddle from the hitch rail, she thought she heard a horse whinny from a direction on the ranch where she knew none of her horses were kept. She scanned the desert, but saw nothing out of the ordinary. Shrugging it off, she took her saddle inside and placed it on her designated saddle rack. As she was leaving the tack room, she could have sworn she heard another faint but distinct whinny.

She went outside, stopping on the porch and looked in the direction from where she thought the sound had come, but saw nothing. She walked to the middle of the yard, turned a very slow three hundred and sixty degrees as she scanned the desert, but saw nothing out of the ordinary. She made her way to the house. Puffs of fine dust rose from under her feet with each step she took, and rather than tracking the dust into the front room, she decided to head for the kitchen porch where she could broom off her boots and jeans before going inside.

The broom leaned against the wall next to the back door, and as she picked it up she found a tarantula spider hiding in the shade the broom provided. She swept the spider from the porch, then the dust from her jeans and boots, and went inside. Jessie poured herself a cold glass of water from the pitcher she kept in the refrigerator, and turned to the calendar hanging on wall. She took a sip from the glass, wiped the sweat from her brow, opened the drawer she stood in front of, and pulled out a marker. The calendar had the first five days of May crossed out. Jessie crossed out the sixth. She stared at the calendar, took another sip from her glass and dejectedly tossed the marker back in the drawer.

Carrying her glass with her, she walked into the hallway. There was a small stack of mail on the hallway table that she leafed through, turning over the first three pieces before she stopped to listen. Suddenly very aware of her surroundings, and although there was no discernable sound, she found herself cocking her head as if there were. She set her glass down next to the mail, turned and looked at the front door where she felt she was being drawn. Cautiously, she made her way over and peered through the screen.

"Hello, Jess." It was Henry. He was standing at the foot of the steps, dusty and tired and holding his hat in his hands. He wanted to apologize for being late getting back to her. He wanted to tell her what happened in the canyon. How

Chad left the note for him on his door that day and how he had placed the mirror on the canyon floor, knowing Henry would see it and stop. It was the mirror that helped Chad get the drop on him, like the scenario in some B-grade western movie. He wanted to tell her how Topher, who actually *was* two days early with his supplies, had heard the shots Chad had been firing at Henry, and had come to the rim of the canyon to investigate. He wanted to explain that it had been Topher who took the final shot that day from the canyon's edge with his own Winchester and had put a stop to Chad once and for all. He wanted to tell her that a two-week investigation by the sheriff's department cleared both Henry and Topher, and that it had been the investigation that caused him to be late. But in the end, standing there with his hat in his hand, and looking up at the prettiest woman he'd ever seen, he figured maybe some other time might be better.

"I'm back." He smiled feebly.

Jessie was having a hard time believing her eyes. She had nearly given up on seeing Henry again. In her mind, she had come up with all kinds of reasons why he hadn't returned when he said he would. Perhaps he'd fallen off the wagon and was drunk in some bar somewhere, or perhaps he decided he couldn't live without the cowboy life after all, or maybe he'd found someone else that suited him better. But now, ashamed of herself for having doubted him at all, all she could do was step out on the porch and look into his tired eyes.

"You know," Henry quietly started. "It's been said that lonesome creates diseases that only friendship can cure." He paused. "Well, I guess I don't know about that. But I do know this. When I was up there bumpin' around them hills with them cows, the only thing I could think about was bein' back here, on this place, with you." He looked down at the dusty old hat in his hands, and fidgeted with it. "I know I ain't much, Jess." He looked back at her. "Truth is, I guess I never was. But I think I can be a whole lot more, if you'd be willin' to give me a chance."

Jessie, who had been holding back tears of joy, could hold them no more. She hesitated for a second, then walked down the steps and wrapped her arms around Henry's neck in a passionate embrace. Henry hugged her back with everything he had until Jessie turned and kissed him. The kiss was gently broken off and they stood happily gazing into each other's eyes. "You must be starved," Jessie said, seeing the weariness on Henry's face. She stepped away, took Henry's hand and slowly started up the steps. "Let me fix you something."

Henry stood his ground at the bottom of the steps. When she realized he wasn't coming, Jessie turned. "I brought you something," he said, nodding his head in the direction of the corner of the house. A bit perplexed, Jessie stepped down off the porch and followed as, hand in hand, Henry led her around the corner to see the gray colt standing quietly tied to the hitch rail. He was wearing an old, worn-out saddle with all of Henry's belongings tied to the back of it.

Jessie was shocked to see the colt, and quickly ran to him and hugged him around the neck. "I don't believe it!" she exclaimed. "How did you get him?" She turned and looked at Henry. "I've tried I don't know how many times to buy him from Tom, but he always said he wasn't for sale…"

Jessie turned to get a better look at the gray colt, which had grown into a fine, handsome five-year-old stallion. It was then that she noticed the saddle on the horse's back wasn't Henry's. Her smile faded. "This isn't your saddle," she said quietly, touching the beat-up and old stock saddle sitting on the horse's back. "My God…Henry! Your saddle."

Henry smiled gently. "It's all right Jess." He stepped over and patted the gray horse on the neck. "I traded it for something that meant more to me. And by God, I believe I got a bargain." He slowly reached out and took Jessie's hand, as once again her tears began to fall, leaving delicate streaks in the dust that covered her cheeks. "Besides," he ever so gently touched her face with his hands. "I didn't have enough money for a ring."

CHAPTER 49

The gray colt stood lazily under a shade tree escaping the heat of the day. His eyes were half closed and his tail lazily swished the flies from his back legs. He was tired. It had taken him and Henry three days to ride from Tom Essex's ranch, through the desert and back home to Jessie. Although, as hard as that ride had been for the colt, it didn't seem near as bad as round up had been in the fall, the riding he was subjected to by the ranch hands at the Essex place during the winter, and then branding that spring. Branding, he thought, was the worst. He had been ridden by three different men, at three different speeds, and with three different levels of harshness. Tug stopped riding him after the fall round up, and the other cowboys, all jabbing him with spurs to get him to go while at the same time using big bits to get him to stop, had ridden him instead.

He had grown to dislike the way the men on the ranch rode him, and no matter how hard he tried to do the right thing for whoever was on him, he never seemed to get any relief from the pressure they used. He found, more and more, that he needed to defend himself just to make it through the day. He had started to get a reputation as hard-mouthed and ornery. The men tried to put their signature on the colt, and over time, he had begun to refuse. Because of it, there had been talk on the ranch of having him gelded in order to get him to "calm down" and have him be more compliant. It wouldn't have helped.

And then one day, a month after branding had taken place, Henry showed up. He had come into the colt's pen and petted him on the neck as he always had. He led him to a hitch rail, put an old saddle on him with a satchel that held all his belongings tied to the back, and rode him off the ranch. For three days, the two of them headed southeast across the desert, stopping only for water, eating and sleeping. The colt had been defending himself for so long against those that had ridden him that he instinctively thought he needed to be the same way with Henry. So, when Henry first got on him, the colt continuously pushed into the bit, swished his tail in anger and shook his head defiantly. That continued throughout the first day and half of the second. But the longer the two of them rode together, the more the colt began to see that the way Henry always rode him hadn't changed. Henry was still soft in his cues to him and still dependable in the way he rode. The colt didn't have to defend himself against Henry, and eventually he began to soften up and travel for him just as he had before the Essex boys got a hold of him.

They had been in the desert for two-and-a-half days when they came across the band of wild horses Henry and Jessie had gone to watch, in a large grassy meadow a half day's ride from the ranch boundary. At first, the big bay stallion, wearing the scars of all his many battles on his body, approached defiantly, neck arched, front feet pawing at the ground, and snorting menacingly through his nose. By this time, however, the colt had scars of his own, too, and while the bay stallion knew how to fight for his herd, the gray knew how to fight for his life. Normally of relatively quiet and passive nature, the gray had had enough of defending

himself from unwarranted attacks. With Henry on his back
he spun to face the bay's challenge. Just as Henry was about
to intervene, the bay suddenly, and unexpectedly backed
down, ran back to his herd, gathered them up and pushed
them away at a gallop.

Henry and the colt traveled through the night, stopping
only for four hours to get some much needed rest, and
early the next morning they passed through the gate that
put them on Jessie's ranch. The gray became excited later
that day when he began to recognize some of the land-
marks he had seen on the ranch when Henry would take
him out for rides. There was the rocky overhang near the
creek. The tree that stood off by itself that the horses would
stand under when the weather was bad, and the narrow
game trail he and Henry had used when they ponied Mic
and other horses.

But it had been the smell of the place that caused him
to let out the two loud whinnies as they approached. They
were still nearly a mile from the main ranch when he picked
up the odor. He was able to distinguish the geldings Jessie
had put him with after taking him out of the round pen.
There were several mares he recognized, and most importantly, even a mile from the ranch, he had picked up the
faint, but sweet smell of Jessie herself. It was that odor that
made it all worth it for the gray. All the pain and suffering he had gone through when he was banished from the
herd. All the worry when he was first forced into the world
of humans, and all the confusion and defending he had to
endure with the men on the Essex ranch. All of it didn't
matter anymore when he smelled the ranch. He knew he
was returning home.

The colt, standing in the shade of the little tree, let out a
long sigh and nipped at a fly buzzing around his chest. The
ranch was quiet now, and other than the occasional horse
blowing through its nose in a paddock somewhere, there

was very little sound on the place at all. Henry and Jessie had been around to feed that morning, but the gray hadn't seen them since. He'd see them later, around feeding time, he was sure of it. They were dependable, and he liked that. It was good to be with them again, and it was good to be back at the ranch. It was his home, and he liked that, too.

CHAPTER 50

There were more trees in the cemetery than Henry remembered. More headstones, too. But then, it had been twenty
years since he'd been there last. Still, even after all those years,
it was hard on him to be there, and his heart raced as he
slowly made his way to their grave site. It seemed odd that
even after all this time, with all the extra headstones and all
the new trees, Henry was able to walk right up to where
he had last been with Annie and Josh. He removed his hat,
then stooped down and brushed leaves off of the two headstones, one that read "Loving Wife," the other "Beloved Son."
He hadn't remembered asking those words to be carved on
the stones, but then, other than being at the cemetery for
the funeral, he couldn't really remember much of anything
about that time.

He stood back up and looked down somberly at the small
piece of neatly groomed ground where Annie and Josh were
at rest. "Hi guys," he said quietly. "I'm sorry it's taken me so
long to come and see you." He paused, rolling the brim of
his hat between his fingers. "I had a few things I needed to
work out before I could…" He looked up at the blue sky
dotted with high, thin white clouds, then back to the graves.
"I guess I didn't do very well after you…after you both left."

Henry slowly, almost imperceptibly shook his head at the waste of life that on many levels, he still blamed himself for. "I can't tell you both how sorry I am...for what I...did..." was all he could get out before he began sobbing uncontrollably. He cried non-stop for several minutes, at times struggling to catch his breath. Years of sorrow and anguish and guilt poured out of him, washing down his cheeks and falling onto the grass at the foot of the graves. He was finally finding a way to forgive himself.

Henry didn't try to stop the onslaught of tears. He wouldn't have been able to anyway. He let it all empty out of him like water from a porcelain pitcher. Several minutes had passed before the wave of emotion that crashed through him began to subside, and when it did, he slowly caught his breath and wiped his face with the handkerchief he pulled from his back pocket. He forced a smile. "I'm sorry," he said breathlessly.

"I'm doing better with my life now," Henry said after another long pause. "I found someone who helped me get back on my feet and is helping me see the things in this world that I missed before." He glanced back to the road, where Jessie stood patiently by the door of the truck, her blue cotton dress blowing gently in the breeze. "You'd both like her." He turned back to the graves and forced another smile. "We even got married a couple months back." Henry held up his left hand, showing a silver wedding band he proudly wore on his finger.

He had never been comfortable wearing rings, or jewelry of any kind in the past—not that he ever had any to wear in the first place. He didn't even have a ring from when he and Annie got married. If he had, however, he doubted he would have worn it. He knew many a rancher who not only lost his wedding ring, but also the finger it was attached to when the ring got hung up in a piece of machinery or piece of tack on an unruly horse. But like so many other things in his life, that was somehow different for him now, too.

For Henry, the ring he wore was not only a symbol of his commitment to Jessie, but more importantly, it was also a symbol of a commitment to his new life. It was a life where he would try to spend more of his time looking forward and less of his time looking back. Henry was beginning to finally understand, perhaps in his own way, that life without Annie and Josh wasn't just about surviving, which is how he had been looking at it. It was about thriving. Being with Jessie helped him to see he had been given a gift not many people ever get: a second chance at life. With this second chance, he made a silent commitment to himself that he would do better. Not that he would be a saint, or otherwise be something or someone he would never be able to aspire to. But simply that he would do better. And so far, he had.

Henry stood looking down at the grass for a long time, wanting to say more but suddenly no longer feeling the need. "I guess it's time for me to go now." He placed his hat back on his head and adjusted it slightly. "I'll come again when I can." He wiped his face again with the handkerchief, and then returned it to his back pocket. "I hope wherever you are, you're both safe and warm." He smiled. "I love you both."

And with that, Henry turned and made his way back to the truck. Jessie reached up and hugged him when he got to her, then gently wiped a tear that remained on his cheek with her hand, and smiled reassuringly. "Are you okay?" she asked.

"I am now."

Jessie kissed him on his cheek, went around to the driver's side of the truck, and climbed in. Henry opened the passenger side door, then looked back toward the graves. There, standing next to one of the old trees, he could have sworn he saw Annie, her arm around Josh, and both were smiling and waving to him. He smiled back and climbed in the truck. When he looked back, they were gone.

Jessie took Henry on a drive down the main street of his old hometown. It hadn't changed much, although things in Humboldt never really did, which was one of the things Henry liked about the place. The biggest change Henry could see was the one stoplight in the middle of town where there used to only be a stop sign. It made him smile—the thought of how the sleepy little town putting in a stoplight must have been a big deal for the local population.

"Not many people in town today," Henry commented after noticing the lack of cars and pedestrian traffic. "I wonder if somethin's goin' on somewhere."

"I don't know." Jessie drove out to the end of Main and turned on Brine, the road that led to the rodeo grounds. At least a hundred cars were parked on both sides of Brine and as they got close to the entrance to the grounds, they could see countless more cars in the parking lots and around the buildings.

"Must be a rodeo, or horse sale or somethin'," Henry remarked.

"We don't really have anywhere to go right now," Jessie said, turning into the main entrance. "Why don't we go see what's going on?"

"I don't know, Jess," Henry protested weakly.

"Oh come on…it'll be fun."

"Gonna be hard-pressed to find a place to park."

"I don't know," Jessie smiled. "Maybe we'll get lucky." They took a right past the office, went past the grandstands, and then took a left at the concession stand.

"Looks like the whole damn town is here," Henry commented, looking at all the cars that were parked in every nook and cranny. Jessie drove slowly on, and found an empty parking space right next to where the event was taking place. Getting out of the truck, they followed a young couple, townsfolk by the looks of them, toward a large crowd. Stepping around the corner of Barn E, they came on a crowd of nearly two thousand people standing in front of a big white building set back from the road. There was a sign above the door on the front of the building that was covered by a large white cloth that rippled in the breeze, and a stage under it with three men and two women, all wearing jeans, white shirts and green ties symbolic of 4-H leaders, sitting on chairs behind a podium with a microphone.

"I wonder what's goin' on," Henry said leaning over to Jessie.

"Well, I bet that fellow over there could tell us." Jessie smiled, pointing to a thin cowboy walking toward them.

"My god," Henry whispered. "That's Leon Geyser. I've known him since we were kids."

Jessie turned and smiled up at Henry. "I know."

"Hello, Jessie." Leon smiled, giving her a brief and friendly hug. He then turned to Henry, and smiling broadly, first shook his hand, and then hugged him, too. "Good to see you old friend," he said, stepping back and taking a good look at the man he hadn't seen in almost twenty years. "We're glad you could make it, Henry."

"Make it?" Henry was a bit taken aback. "Make what? What's goin' on?"

"She didn't tell you?" Leon smiled.

"Tell me what?" Henry asked, turning to Jessie. Jessie smiled knowingly and shrugged.

Leon laughed. "Hell, it was all Jessie's idea." He put his hand on her shoulder. "And when I talked it over with the 4-H people and folks in town, well, they all...*we* all figured it was the right thing to do."

"I don't understand."

"You will," Leon chuckled, putting his other hand on Henry's shoulder, turning them both and leading them through the crowd and toward the stage. Leon stopped them at the stage's edge, and leaving them there, he waved to one of the men on the stage, then pointed at Henry and Jessie and nodded. The man on the stage nodded back, rose from his chair and went to the microphone.

"Could I have everyone's attention!" he called over the microphone. "Attention please!" Conversations slowly wound down until the place that was buzzing with activity only seconds before became quiet as a church. "Thank you." The man smiled. He took some notes from his shirt pocket, unfolded them, and placed them on the podium. He smiled down at Henry and Jessie, and then read from the notes. He began talking about the big white building behind him. It was a relatively new 4-H pavilion that was built from funds donated by people in town, and built exclusively by volunteer labor. Many 4-H shows had occurred in the pavilion, and countless 4-H projects had been on display there. It was where the county 4-H held their annual fundraiser dinner/dance, which allowed them to present a sizable scholarship to a deserving high school senior who wanted to go to college and study agriculture. Couples who had met while members of 4-H had used it for their wedding receptions, and it was where the potluck dinner was to be held immediately after the ceremony that day.

The man then went on to talk about the person the building had been named after. Without mentioning him by name, he talked of the boy's attributes, his smile, kindness, and willingness to help anybody at any time. He talked of all the lives he had touched, both while he was alive, and since his passing, and how the man knew the things he was saying about the boy were true, because he had been a friend and classmate of the boy twenty years before.

"When the pavilion was first built," the man said, his voice booming over the loudspeaker system, "we were unfortunately unable to get in touch with any of the boy's kin, so none of his family were here for that original dedication." He glanced down at Henry and smiled. "But today, we are fortunate enough to have his father here with us." He turned back to the crowd. "Friends and neighbors," his voice rose slightly. "It is my great honor and privilege to announce the re-dedication of the Josh McBride Memorial 4-H Pavilion."

The white cloth dropped away from the large green letters above the door that exposed Josh's name, and Henry was once again overcome. Hard as he tried, he couldn't hold back the tears, and this time, he wasn't the only one crying. As Dan Folgelberg's "Run for the Roses" began playing over the sound system, fathers and mothers, kids, couples and even grizzled old men were seen wiping tears from their eyes.

Jessie wrapped her arms around the speechless Henry as one by one, the people in the crowd came to him. Some folks simply touched him, others shook his hand or patted him gently him on the back, and still others told him how sorry they were for his loss. As the crowd moved past Henry and into the pavilion to see a display of 4-H projects from the last fifteen years, and start in on the potluck dinner, Leon Geyser stepped up. His face was leathery and his eyebrows were sprinkled with gray, but his was a welcome face in a sea of strangers.

"Jessie, here, told me a little about what you been through since you left, Henry," Leon said kindly. "I'm real glad you was able to find your way back out of the wild." He held out his hand, and Henry reached up and shook it. "Welcome back, old friend." Leon smiled, kissed Jessie on the cheek and eased past the two of them, making his way into the pavilion.

As a small group of young, smiling 4-H children gathered around Henry, Jessie stepped back.

"Yes, Henry," she said softly. "Welcome back."